AQA Biology
Third edition

GCSE

Teacher Handbook

Gemma Young
Editor: Lawrie Ryan

Oxford University Press

OXFORD
UNIVERSITY PRESS

Great Clarendon Street, Oxford, OX2 6DP, United Kingdom

Oxford University Press is a department of the University of Oxford.
It furthers the University's objective of excellence in research,
scholarship, and education by publishing worldwide. Oxford is a
registered trade mark of Oxford University Press in the UK and in
certain other countries

© Oxford University Press 2016

The moral rights of the authors have been asserted

First published in 2016

All rights reserved. No part of this publication may be reproduced,
stored in a retrieval system, or transmitted, in any form or by any
means, without the prior permission in writing of Oxford University
Press, or as expressly permitted by law, by licence or under terms agreed
with the appropriate reprographics rights organization. Enquiries
concerning reproduction outside the scope of the above should be sent
to the Rights Department, Oxford University Press,
at the address above.

You must not circulate this work in any other form and you must
impose this same condition on any acquirer

British Library Cataloguing in Publication Data
Data available

978 0 19 835943 2

10 9 8 7 6 5 4 3 2 1

Paper used in the production of this book is a natural, recyclable
product made from wood grown in sustainable forests.
The manufacturing process conforms to the environmental regulations
of the country of origin.

Printed in Great Britain by Bell and Bain Ltd. Glasgow

Lawrie would like to thank the following people for their help and
support in producing this teacher handbook. Each one has added value
to my initial efforts: Annie Hamblin, Sadie Garratt, Emma-Leigh Craig,
Amie Hewish, Andy Chandler-Grevatt.

Index compiled by INDEXING SPECIALISTS (UK) Ltd., Indexing house,
306A Portland Road, Hove, East Sussex, BN3 5LP United Kingdom.

MIX
Paper from
responsible sources
FSC FSC® C007785
www.fsc.org

Contents

This book has been written for the *AQA GCSE Biology* and *AQA GCSE Combined Science: Trilogy* courses, making them completely co-teachable. Biology only lessons are easily identifiable with their own black-bordered design, and are also formatted in italics in the below contents list for quick access.

Required practicals	v
Introduction	vi
Assessment and progress	viii
Differentiation and skills	x
Kerboodle	xii

1 Cells and organisation — 2

Chapter B1 Cell structure and transport — 4
- B1.1 The world of the microscope — 4
- B1.2 Animal and plant cells — 6
- B1.3 Eukaryotic and prokaryotic cells — 8
- B1.4 Specialisation in animal cells — 10
- B1.5 Specialisation in plant cells — 12
- B1.6 Diffusion — 14
- B1.7 Osmosis — 16
- B1.8 Osmosis in plants — 18
- B1.9 Active transport — 20
- B1.10 Exchanging materials — 22
- B1 Checkpoint — 24

Chapter B2 Cell division — 26
- B2.1 Cell division — 26
- B2.2 Growth and differentiation — 28
- B2.3 *Stem cells* — 30
- B2.4 *Stem cell dilemmas* — 32
- B2 Checkpoint — 34

Chapter B3 Organisation and the digestive system — 36
- B3.1 Tissues and organs — 36
- B3.2 The human digestive system — 38
- B3.3 The chemistry of food — 40
- B3.4 Catalysts and enzymes — 42
- B3.5 Factors affecting enzyme action — 44
- B3.6 How the digestive system works — 46
- B3.7 Making digestion efficient — 48
- B3 Checkpoint — 50

Chapter B4 Organising animals and plants — 52
- B4.1 The blood — 52
- B4.2 The blood vessels — 54
- B4.3 The heart — 56
- B4.4 Helping the heart — 58
- B4.5 Breathing and gas exchange — 60
- B4.6 Tissues and organs in plants — 62
- B4.7 Transport systems in plants — 64
- B4.8 Evaporation and transpiration — 66
- B4.9 Factors affecting transpiration — 68
- B4 Checkpoint — 70

2 Disease and bioenergetics — 72

Chapter B5 Communicable diseases — 74
- B5.1 Health and disease — 74
- B5.2 Pathogens and disease — 76
- B5.3 *Growing bacteria in the lab* — 78
- B5.4 *Preventing bacterial growth* — 80
- B5.5 Preventing infections — 82
- B5.6 Viral diseases — 84
- B5.7 Bacterial diseases — 86
- B5.8 Diseases caused by fungi and protists — 88
- B5.9 Human defence responses — 90
- B5.10 *More about plant diseases* — 92
- B5.11 *Plant defence responses* — 94
- B5 Checkpoint — 96

Chapter B6 Preventing and treating disease — 98
- B6.1 Vaccination — 98
- B6.2 Antibiotics and painkillers — 100
- B6.3 Discovering drugs — 102
- B6.4 Developing drugs — 104
- B6.5 *Making monoclonal antibodies* — 106
- B6.6 *Uses of monoclonal antibodies* — 108
- B6 Checkpoint — 110

Chapter B7 Non-communicable diseases — 112
- B7.1 Non-communicable diseases — 112
- B7.2 Cancer — 114
- B7.3 Smoking and the risk of disease — 116
- B7.4 Diet, exercise, and disease — 118
- B7.5 Alcohol and other carcinogens — 120
- B7 Checkpoint — 122

Chapter B8 Photosynthesis — 124
- B8.1 Photosynthesis — 124
- B8.2 The rate of photosynthesis — 126
- B8.3 How plants use glucose — 128
- B8.4 Making the most of photosynthesis — 130
- B8 Checkpoint — 132

Chapter B9 Respiration — 134
- B9.1 Aerobic respiration — 134
- B9.2 The response to exercise — 136
- B9.3 Anaerobic respiration — 138
- B9.4 Metabolism and the liver — 140
- B9 Checkpoint — 142

iii

3 Biological responses — 144

Chapter B10 The human nervous system — 146
- B10.1 Principles of homeostasis — 146
- B10.2 The structure and function of the nervous system — 148
- B10.3 Reflex actions — 150
- B10.4 The brain — 152
- B10.5 The eye — 154
- B10.6 Common problems of the eye — 156
- B10 Checkpoint — 158

Chapter B11 Hormonal coordination — 160
- B11.1 Principles of hormonal control — 160
- B11.2 The control of blood glucose levels — 162
- B11.3 Treating diabetes — 164
- B11.4 The role of negative feedback — 166
- B11.5 Human reproduction — 168
- B11.6 Hormones and the menstrual cycle — 170
- B11.7 The artificial control of fertility — 172
- B11.8 Infertility treatments — 174
- B11.9 Plant hormones and responses — 176
- B11.10 Using plant hormones — 178
- B11 Checkpoint — 180

Chapter B12 Homeostasis in action — 182
- B12.1 Controlling body temperature — 182
- B12.2 Removing waste products — 184
- B12.3 The human kidney — 186
- B12.4 Dialysis – an artificial kidney — 188
- B12.5 Kidney transplants — 190
- B12 Checkpoint — 192

4 Genetics and reproduction — 194

Chapter B13 Reproduction — 196
- B13.1 Types of reproduction — 196
- B13.2 Cell division in sexual reproduction — 198
- B13.3 The best of both worlds — 200
- B13.4 DNA and the genome — 202
- B13.5 DNA structure and protein synthesis — 204
- B13.6 Gene expression and mutation — 206
- B13.7 Inheritance in action — 208
- B13.8 More about genetics — 210
- B13.9 Inherited disorders — 212
- B13.10 Screening for genetic disorders — 214
- B13 Checkpoint — 216

Chapter B14 Variation and evolution — 218
- B14.1 Variation — 218
- B14.2 Evolution by natural section — 220
- B14.3 Selective breeding — 222
- B14.4 Genetic engineering — 224
- B14.5 Cloning — 226
- B14.6 Adult cell cloning — 228
- B14.7 Ethics of genetic technologies — 230
- B14 Checkpoint — 232

Chapter B15 Genetics and evolution — 234
- B15.1 The history of genetics — 234
- B15.2 Theories of evolution — 236
- B15.3 Accepting Darwin's ideas — 238
- B15.4 Evolution and speciation — 240
- B15.5 Evidence for evolution — 242
- B15.6 Fossils and extinction — 244
- B15.7 More about extinction — 246
- B15.8 Antibiotic resistant bacteria — 248
- B15.9 Classification — 250
- B15.10 New systems of classification — 252
- B15 Checkpoint — 254

5 Ecology — 256

Chapter B16 Adaptations, interdependence, and competition — 258
- B16.1 The importance of communities — 258
- B16.2 Organisms in their environment — 260
- B16.3 Distribution and abundance — 262
- B16.4 Competition in animals — 264
- B16.5 Competition in plants — 266
- B16.6 Adapt and survive — 268
- B16.7 Adaptation in animals — 270
- B16.8 Adaptations in plants — 272
- B16 Checkpoint — 274

Chapter B17 Organising an ecosystem — 276
- B17.1 Feeding relationships — 276
- B17.2 Materials cycling — 278
- B17.3 The carbon cycle — 280
- B17.4 Rates of decomposition — 282
- B17 Checkpoint — 284

Chapter B18 Biodiversity and ecosystems — 286
- B18.1 The human population explosion — 286
- B18.2 Land and water pollution — 288
- B18.3 Air pollution — 290
- B18.4 Deforestation and peat destruction — 292
- B18.5 Global warming — 294
- B18.6 The impact of change — 296
- B18.7 Maintaining biodiversity — 298
- B18.8 Trophic levels and biomass — 300
- B18.9 Biomass transfers — 302
- B18.10 Factors affecting food security — 304
- B18.11 Making food production efficient — 306
- B18.12 Sustainable food production — 308
- B18 Checkpoint — 310

Answers — 312
Index — 342

Required Practicals

Practical work is a vital part of biology, helping to support and apply your scientific knowledge, and develop your investigative and practical skills. As part of your GCSE Biology course, there are 10 required practicals you must carry out. Questions in your exams could draw on any of the knowledge and skills you have developed in carrying out these practicals.

A Required practical feature box has been included in this student book for each of your required practicals. Further support is available on Kerboodle.

	Required practical	Topic
1	**Using a light microscope.** Use a light microscope to observe, draw, and label a selection of plant and animal cells and include a scaled magnification.	B1.2
2	**Investigating the effect of antiseptics or antibiotics on bacterial growth.** Use a light microscope to observe, draw, and label a selection of plant and animal cells and include a scaled magnification.	B5.4
3	**Investigate the effect of a range of concentrations of salt or sugar solutions on the mass of plant tissue.** Investigate osmosis by measuring the how the mass of plant tissue changes in a range of concentrations of salt or sugar solutions.	B1.8
4	**Use standard food tests to identify food groups.** Detect sugars, starch, and proteins in food using Benedict's test, the iodine test, and Biuret reagent.	B3.3
5	**Investigate the effect of pH on the rate of reaction of amylase enzyme.** Students should use a continuous sampling technique to determine the time taken to completely digest a starch solution at a range of pH values.	B3.6
6	**Investigate the effect of light intensity on the rate of photosynthesis** Use an aquatic plant to observe the effect light intensity has on the rate of photosynthesis.	B8.2
7	**Investigate the effect of a factor on human reaction time.** Plan and carry out an investigation, choosing appropriate ways to measure reaction time and considering the risks and ethics of the investigation.	B10.2
8	**Investigate the effect of light or gravity on the growth of germinating seeds.** Record results both as length measurements and as accurate, labelled biological drawings to show the effects.	B11.9
9	**Measure the population size of a common species in a habitat.** Use sampling techniques to investigate the effect of a factor on the distribution of this species.	B16.3
10	**Investigate the effect of temperature on the rate of decay of fresh milk.** Measure the pH change of milk to investigate how temperature affects its rate of decay.	B17.4

Introduction

About the series

This is the third edition of the UK's number 1 course for GCSE Science. The student books have been approved by AQA, and our author teams and experts have been working closely with AQA to develop a blended suite of resources to support the new specifications.

All resources in this series have been carefully designed to support students of all abilities on their journey through GCSE Science. The demands of the new specifications are fully supported, with maths, practicals, and synoptic skills developed throughout, and all new subject content fully covered.

The series is designed to be flexible, enabling you to co-teach Foundation and Higher tiers, and Combined and Separate Sciences. Content is clearly flagged throughout the resources, helping you to identify the relevant content for your students.

Assessment is an important feature of the series, and is supported by our unique assessment framework, helping students to track and make progress.

The series is edited by Lawrie Ryan. Building on his vast experience as an author for much-loved titles such as Spotlight Science and the Chemistry for You Lawrie has become one of the best-known authors and editors of educational science books both nationally and internationally. A former Head of Science, Science Advisor, and Ofsted Inspector, he understands the demands of modern education and draws on his experience to deliver this new and innovative course that builds upon the legacy of previous editions

Your Teacher Handbook

This Teacher Handbook aims to save you time and effort by offering lesson plans, differentiation suggestions, and assessment guidance on a page-by-page basis that is a direct match to the Student Book.

With learning outcomes differentiated you can tailor the lessons and activities to suit your students and provide progression opportunities students of all abilities.

Lesson plans are written for 55-minute lessons but are flexible and fully adaptable so you can choose the activities that suit your class best.

Separate Science-only content is contained within whole topics and clearly flagged from the Combined Sciences content, enabling you co-teach using one Teacher Handbook.

Key Stage 3 and GCSE Catch-up

This table outlines Key Stage 3 knowledge that is a pre-requisite for this section. Later Section Openers will also include GCSE knowledge from earlier in the course. Quick checkpoint activities, to assess students understanding of each statement, are provided

For each statement, a suggestion for how you can help students catch up is also provided, as well as an index of which topic each statement links to.

Section opener

The Section opener provides an overview of the parts of the specification, required practicals, and maths skills covered in the section.

Specification links

This table provides an overview of the specification topics covered in the chapters of the section. It also gives an indication of which Paper each specification topic will be mainly assessed in.

Required practicals

This table indicated which required practicals are covered within this section. It also gives a list of Apparatus and techniques that could be assessed by that practical.

Maths skills

This table provides an overview of the maths skills covered in the chapters of the section.

Lesson

Specification links
This indicated the area of the *AQA GCSE Biology (9–1)* 2016 specification this lesson covers. Relevant Working scientifically and Mathematical requirements links are also provided.

Differentiated outcomes
This table summarises the possible lesson outcomes. They are ramped and divided into three ability bands. The three ability bands are explained in the Assessment and progress section. Each ability band has two to three outcomes defined, designed to cover the specification content for different ability levels

An index of questions and activities is given for each learning outcome, helping you to assess your students informally as you progress through each lesson

Practicals
These boxes provide suggestions of how Maths and Literacy skills can be developed in the lesson. Where relevant, the Maths skills are linked to the Mathematical requirements of the specification.

Maths and literacy
These boxes provide equipment lists, an outline method, and safety requirements for any practicals in the lesson. Required practicals are flagged with the Required practical icon.
Although safety requirements are given, a fully-comprehensive risk assessment should be carried out before any practical activity is undergone.

Suggested lesson plan
A suggested route through the lesson is provided, including ideas for support, extension, and homework. The right-hand column indicated where Kerboodle resources are available.

Checkpoint lesson

Overview
The Checkpoint Lesson is a suggested follow-up lesson after students have completed the automarked Checkpoint Assessment on Kerboodle. There are three routes through the lesson, with the route for each student being determined by their mark in the assessment. Each route aims to support students with progressing up an assessment band.

Checkpoint overview
This text provides a brief overview of the chapter, including the key concepts students should be confident with.

Checkpoint lesson plan
This table provides a differentiated lesson plan for the checkpoint follow-up lesson. This includes learning outcomes, starters and plenaries, supporting information for the follow-up worksheets (including any descriptions of relevant practicals), and progression suggestions to support students with progressing up a band.

Assessment and progress

Dr Andrew Chandler-Grevatt

To ensure students are fully supported to make progress through the new linear exams, AQA GCSE *Sciences Third Edition* was developed in consultation with assessment consultant, Dr Andrew Chandler-Grevatt. Andrew worked with the team to develop an assessment framework that supports students and teachers in tracking and promoting progress through Key Stage 3 and GCSE.

Andrew is has a doctorate in school assessment, and a real passion for science teaching and learning. Having worked as a science teacher for ten years, of which five were spent as an AST, Andrew has a real understanding of the pressures and joys of teaching in the classroom. His most recent projects include *Activate for KS3 Science*, for which he developed a unique assessment framework to support schools in the transition away from levels.

The new GCSE grading system (9–1)

With the new specifications and criteria comes a new grading system. The old system of grades A*–G, is being replaced with a numerical system with grades 9–1. Grade 9 is the highest, and is designed to award exceptional performance.

The new grades are not directly equivalent to the old A*–C system, although some comparisons can be drawn:

- Approximately the same proportion of students will achieve a grade 4 or above as currently achieve a grade C or above.
- Approximately the same proportion of students will achieve a grade 7 as above as currently achieve an A or above.
- The bottom of grade 1 will be aligned with the bottom of grade G.

A 'good pass' is considered to be a grade 5 or above.

Throughout the course, resources and assessments have been designed to help students working at different grades to make progress.

5-year assessment framework

Purpose

The combination of the removal of levels, new performance measures, new grading system, and more demanding GCSEs makes it more important than ever to be able to track and facilitate progress from Year 7 and all the way through secondary. Assessment plays a key role in intervention and extension, and these are both vital in helping students of all abilities achieve their potential, and add value to their projected GCSE grade.

In the absence of levels, and as we learn more about the new GCSE grades, it is important that a framework is in place in order to inform learning, teaching, and assessment from Y7-Y11.

Framework

Throughout the 5 years, it is useful to define three ability bands, which can be used to inform the design of learning outcomes, learning resources, and assessments. By defining three bands, realistic and valuable intervention and extension can be designed and implemented to help students of all abilities make progress, and improve their grade projection.

At KS3, the model is designed with the aim of encouraging every student to gain a 'secure' grasp of each concept and topic, so that they are ready to progress. These students will be on track to secure a 'good pass' (grade 5 or above) at GCSE.

In the KS3 course Activate three bands have been defined:

- **Developing**, in which students are able to know and understand a concept, and demonstrate their knowledge in simple and familiar situations.
- **Secure**, in which students are able to apply their knowledge and skills to familiar

and some unfamiliar situations, undertake analysis, and understand more complex concepts.
- **Extending**, in which students are able to evaluate and create, apply their knowledge to complex and unfamiliar situations, and demonstrate advanced use of skills.

Using the framework throughout KS3 helps you to identify which students are ready to progress, and approximately what GCSE grades they should be aiming for.

At GCSE, students can then be differentiated into three bands, aiming for different grades.

- **Aiming for 4** is for students working at the lower grades 1–3, who would have been Developing at KS3, and aspiring to a Grade 4 at GCSE. Resources and assessments for these students are supportive, and focus on developing understanding of core concepts.
- **Aiming for 6** is for students working at grades 4–6, who would have been Secure at KS3. Resources and assessments for these students help to embed core concepts, by encouraging application and analysis, and beginning to explore more complex ideas and situations.
- **Aiming for 8** provides extension for students working at grades 7–9, who are able to grasp complex concepts, and demonstrate higher order skills, such as evaluation and creation in complex and unfamiliar situations.

The framework is summarised in the table below.

Key stage 3	Band	Developing		Secure		Extending	
	Level	3	4	5	6	7	8
GCSE	Band	Aiming for 4			Aiming for 6		Aiming for 8		
	Grades	1	2	3	4	5	6	7	8	9
	Demand	Low			Standard			High		

Informing learning outcomes

The assessment framework has informed the design of the learning outcomes throughout the course. Learning outcomes are differentiated, and there is a set of learning outcomes for every lesson for each ability band.

The checkpoint assessment system

This series includes a checkpoint assessment system for intervention and extension, designed to help students of all abilities make continuous progress through the course. The system also helps you and your students to monitor achievement, and ensure all students are on-track and monitored through the new linear assessments.

Checkpoint assessments are provided in Kerboodle. These are Automarked objective tests with diagnostic feedback. Once students have completed their assessment, depending on their results, they will complete one of three follow up activities, designed for intervention and extension. Students are supported with activity sheets, and lesson plans and overviews are provided for the teacher. The three follow-up routes are:

1. **Aiming for 4** is for students who achieved low score. These resources support students by helping to develop and embed core concepts.
2. **Aiming for 6** is for students who achieved a medium score. These resources encourage students to embed and extend core concepts, and begin to apply their knowledge in more complex or unfamiliar situations.
3. **Aiming for 8** is for students who have achieved a high score. These resources encourage extensive use of more complex skills, in more complex and unfamiliar situations, helping them to reach for the top grades.

The diagram below provides an overview of how the system works.

Differentiation and Skills

Maths skills and MyMaths

With the introduction of the introduction of the new GCSE competence in maths, the support and development of maths skills in a scientific context will be vital for success.

The Student Books contain a maths skills reference section that covers all the maths required for the specification, explained in a scientific context and with a worked example for reference. Where maths skills are embedded within the scientific content, the maths is demonstrated in a Using Maths feature providing a worked example and an opportunity for students to have a go themselves.

In Kerboodle you will find maths skills interactives that are automarked and provide formative feedback. Calculation sheets provide opportunities for practice of the maths skills and links to MyMaths are shown in the Lesson Player and Teacher Handbook where additional resources exist that can be used to reinforce the maths skill. These include practice sheets and Invisi-pen worked examples.

Literacy skills

Literacy skills enable students to effectively communicate their ideas about science and access the information they need. Though the marks allocated for QWC are no longer present in the new specifications, a good degree of literacy is required to read and answer longer, structured exam questions, to access the more difficult concepts introduced in the new GCSE Programme of Study, to be able to effectively interpret and answer questions.

The student books flag opportunities to develop and practice literacy skills through the use of the pen icon. Key words are identified in the text and a glossary helps students get to grips with new scientific terms.

In Kerboodle, you will find Literacy Skills Interactives that help assess literacy skills, including the spelling of key words. Additional Literacy worksheets are available to reinforce skills learnt and provide practise opportunities.

The Teacher Handbook flags literacy suggestions and opportunities relating to the lesson. All of these features will help to develop well-rounded scientists able to access information and communicate their ideas effectively.

Working Scientifically

Working Scientifically is new to the 2016 GCSE criteria. It is divided up into four areas and is integrated into the teaching and learning of Biology, Chemistry, and Physics. The four areas are:

1. Development of scientific thinking in which students need to be able to demonstrate understanding of scientific methods and the scientific process and how these may develop over time and their associated limitations
2. Experimental skills and strategies in which students ask scientific questions based on observations, make predictions using scientific knowledge and understanding, carry out investigations to test predictions, make and record measurements and evaluate methods
3. Analysis and evaluation in which students apply mathematical concepts and calculate results, present and interpret data using tables and graphs, draw conclusions and evaluate data, are able to accuracy, precision, repeatability and reproducibility
4. Scientific vocabulary, quantities, units, symbols and nomenclature in which students calculate results and manipulate data using scientific formulae using basic analysis, SI units, and IUPAC chemical nomenclature where appropriate.

Working Scientifically is integrated throughout the Student Book with flagged Practical boxes, flagged Required Practical boxes, questions. A dedicated Working Scientifically reference chapter is also provided at the back of the Student Book to refer to during investigations, when answering Working Scientifically questions and to enable investigative skills to be developed.

In Kerboodle there are Practicals and Activities resources with their own Working Scientifically objectives, additional targeted Working Scientifically skills sheets as well as other resources such as simulations and Webquests to target specific skills areas. Questions are ramped in difficulty and opportunity to build up to and practice the practical based questions for the exam are provided.

For the required practicals the guidance provided to students acknowledges the differing degrees of support and independence required, with targeted support sheets to the key grade descriptors of Grade 4, 6, and 8, with a view to move the students over that Grade point onwards.

In the Teacher Handbook lessons will often have a working scientifically focus in mind for the activities in that lesson. Working Scientifically Learning Outcomes, where specified, are differentiated to show the expectations for the differing ability levels.

For the purpose of the practical based questions in the examination, Required practicals are flagged and practice opportunities are provided through out the Student Book in the summary questions and exam-style questions.

Differentiation
Building upon the principles of *Activate* at Key Stage 3.

Differentiation using the checkpoint system
The end of chapter Checkpoint lessons will help you to progress students of every ability, targeting the key Grade boundaries of 4, 6, and 8 to enable students to review, consolidate and extend their understanding at each of the grade lesson points.

The tasks focused at students to become secure at Grades 4 and 6 are designed to help them become more secure in their understanding and consolidate the chapter. Teacher input will help them grasp important concepts from the chapter with the opportunity for some extension for Grade 6 students.

The tasks focused at students to become secure and extend at Grade 8 are designed to develop and challenge. Students will work more independently on these tasks to free up the teacher to be able to focus on those that found the chapter more challenging.

Teacher Handbook
Lesson outcomes are differentiated and suggestions for activities throughout the lesson plans are accompanied by support and extension opportunities.

Student Book
Summary questions per lesson are ramped with a darker shading indicating a more challenging question. In the end of chapter summary questions and exam style questions, ramping occurs within the question (as would be seen in a typical exam question).

Practicals and Activities
All practicals and activities are differentiated. Where more complex areas are covered, additional support sheets may be provided to allow lower attaining students to access the activity.

For all required practicals (compulsory practicals) that may be assessed in an exam, specific support sheets are provided targeting the progression of students across the key Grades 4, 6 and 8.

Additional skills sheets may be used in conjunction with practicals to provide additional support in generic competencies such as constructing a graph etc.

Interactive Assessments
All interactive assessments are ramped in difficulty and support is provided in the feedback directing students where they can improve. In chapters with both levels of content, Higher and Foundation versions of assessment are available.

Written assessments
End of section tests and end of year tests have Foundation and Higher versions.

Kerboodle

AQA GCSE Sciences Kerboodle is packed full of guided support and ideas for running and creating effective GCSE Science lessons, and for assessing and facilitating students' progress. It is intuitive to use and customisable.

Kerboodle is online, allowing you and your students to access the course anytime, anywhere.

AQA GCSE Sciences Kerboodle consists of:
- lessons, resources, and assessment
- access to *AQA GCSE Science* Student books for both teachers and students.

Lessons, Resources, and Assessment

AQA GCSE Sciences Kerboodle offers new, engaging lesson resources, as well as a fully comprehensive assessment package, written to match the *AQA GCSE Science (9–1)* specifications.

Kerboodle offers comprehensive and flexible support for the *AQA GCSE Science (9–1)* specifications, enabling you to follow our suggested lessons and schemes of work or to create your own lessons and schemes and share them with other members of your department.

You can **adapt** many of the resources to suit your students' needs, with all non-interactive activities available as editable Word documents. You can also **upload** your own resources so that everything is accessed from one location.

Set homework and assessments through the Assessment system and **track** progress using the Markbook.

Lessons

Click on the **Lessons tab** to access the *AQA GCSE Sciences* lesson presentations and notes.

Ready-to-play lesson presentations complement every spread in the Teacher Handbook and Student Book. Each lesson presentation is easy to launch and features lesson objectives, starters, activity guidance, key diagrams, plenaries, and homework suggestions. The lesson presentations and accompanying note sections are 100% customisable. You can personalise the lessons by adding your own resources and notes, or build your own lesson plans using our resources.

Your lessons and notes can be accessed by your whole department and they are ideal for use in cover lessons.

Resources

Click on the Resources tab to access the full list of AQA GCSE Sciences resources. Use the navigation panel on the left hand side to find resources for any lesson, chapter, or topic.

Navigation panel and search bar allow for easy navigation between resources by course and chapter.

Fully customisable content to cater to all your classes. Resources can be created using the create button.

Existing resources can be uploaded on to the platform using the upload button.

Resources matching every lesson in the *AQA GCSE Biology* series are shown here.

Page navigator shows resources matching to particular pages in the student book.

Practicals and activities Fully-editable resources provided for every lesson to guide students through a practical or activity with fully integrated Working Scientifically skills. Teacher and Technician notes are provided for all practicals and activities to give further ideas on differentiation, answers, example data where appropriate, and a list of resources required by technicians.

Interactive starters or plenaries Accompany each lesson, and can be used front-of-class to maximise student participation.

Skills sheets Editable worksheets that target Maths, Literacy, and Working Scientifically skills. They provide guidance and examples to help students whenever they need to use a particular skill.

Skills interactives Auto-marked interactive activities with formative feedback that focus on key maths and literacy skills. You can use these activities in your class to help consolidate core skills relevant to the lesson, or they can be assigned as homework by accessing them through the Assessment tab.

Animations and videos Help students to visualise difficult concepts or to learn about real-life contexts, with engaging visuals and narration. They are structured to clearly address a set of learning objectives and are followed by interactive question screens to help consolidate key points and to provide formative feedback.

Simulations Allow students to control variables and look at outcomes for experiments that are difficult to carry out in the classroom or focus on tricky concepts.

Podcasts Available for every chapter to help review and consolidate key points. The podcast presents an audio summary with transcript, followed by a series of ramped questions and answers to assist students in their revision.

Targeted support sheets Available for the full ability range and are provided to help students progress as they complete their GCSE. **Bump up your Grades** target common misconceptions and difficult topics to securely move students over the key boundaries of Grades 4, 6, and 8. Extensions activities provide opportunities for higher-ability students to apply their knowledge and understanding to new contexts, whilst **Go Further** worksheets aim to inspire students to consider the subject at A Level and beyond.

WebQuests Research-based activities set in a real-life context. WebQuests are fun and engaging activities that can be carried out individually or within a group and are ideal for peer-review.

Checklists and chapter maps Self-assessment checklists for students of the key learning points from each chapter to aid consolidation and revision. For teachers there is an additional chapter-map resource that provides an overview of the chapter, specific opportunities to support and extend, and information on tackling common misconceptions.

Assessment and markbook

All of the assessment material in Kerboodle has been quality assured by our expert Assessment Advisor. Click on the **Assessment tab** to find the wide range of assessment materials to help you deliver a varied, motivating, and effective assessment programme.

Once your classes are set up in Kerboodle, you can assign them assessments to do at home or in class individually or as a group.

A **Markbook** with reporting function helps you to keep track of your students' results. This includes both auto-marked assessments and work marked by you.

Practice or test?

Many of the auto-marked assessment in the AQA GCSE Sciences Kerboodle is available in formative or summative versions.

Test versions of the assessment provide feedback on performance at the end of the test. Students are only given one attempt at each screen but can review them and see which answers they get wrong after completing the activity. Marks are reported to the markbook.

Practice versions of the assessment provide screen-by-screen feedback, focusing on misconceptions, and provide hints for the students to help them revise their answer. Students are given the opportunity to try again. Marks are reported to the Markbook.

Assessment per chapter

Through each chapter there are many opportunities for assessment and determining/monitoring progress.

▶ **Progress quizzes** Auto-marked assessments that focus on the content of the chapters. They are quick, engaging quizzes designed to be taken throughout the course to monitor progress and to focus revision.

Checkpoint assessments Auto-marked assessments designed to determine whether students have a secure grasp of concepts from the chapter. These assessments are ramped in difficulty and can be followed up by the differentiated Checkpoint Lesson activities.

▶ **On Your Marks** Improve students' exam skills by analysing questions, looking at other students' responses, interpreting mark schemes, and answering exam-style questions.

▶ **Homework activities** Auto-marked quizzes with ramped questions targeting the key Grades 4, 6, and 8 boundaries designed to help students apply and embed their knowledge and understanding from the classroom.

Formal testing

▶ **End-of-chapter tests** Provide students with the opportunity to practise answering exam-style questions in a written format. There are differentiated Foundation and Higher versions, with separate options for the combined sciences and the separate sciences. Accompanied by a fully comprehensive mark scheme, data can be entered manually into the Markbook.

▶ **Mid-point and end-of-course written tests** Provide students with the opportunity to practise answering exam-style questions in a full-length paper. There are differentiated Foundation and Higher versions, with separate options for the combined sciences and the separate sciences. Accompanied by a fully comprehensive mark scheme, data can be entered manually into the Markbook.

Kerboodle Book

The *AQA GCSE Sciences* Kerboodle Books are digital versions of the Student Books for you to use at the front of the classroom.

Access to the Kerboodle Book is automatically available as part of the Lessons, Resources, and Assessment package for both you and your students.

A set of tools is available with the Kerboodle Book so that you can personalise your book and make notes. Like all resources offered on Kerboodle, the Kerboodle Book can also be accessed using a range of devices.

1 Cells and organisation

Specification links

AQA specification section	Assessment paper
1.1 Cell structure	Paper 1
1.2 Cell division	Paper 1
1.3 Transport in cells	Paper 1
2.1 Principles of organisation	Paper 1
2.2 Animal tissues, organs and organ systems	Paper 1
2.3 Plant tissues, organs and systems	Paper 1

Required practicals

AQA required practicals	Practical skills	Topic
Use a light microscope to observe, draw and label a selection of plant and animal cells. A scale magnification must be included.	AT 1 – use appropriate apparatus to record length and area. AT 7 – use a microscope to make observations of biological specimens and produce labelled scientific drawings.	B1.2
Investigate the effect of a range of concentrations of salt or sugar solutions on the mass of plant tissue.	AT 1 – use appropriate apparatus to record mass and time. AT 3 – use appropriate apparatus and techniques to observe and measure the process of osmosis. AT 5 – measure the rate of osmosis by water uptake.	B1.8
Use qualitative reagents to test for a range of carbohydrates, lipids and proteins. To include: Benedict's test for sugars; iodine test for starch; and Biuret reagent for protein.	AT 2 – safe use of a Bunsen burner and a boiling water bath. AT 8 – use of qualitative reagents to identify biological molecules.	B3.3
Investigate the effect of pH on the rate of reaction of amylase enzyme. Students should use a continuous sampling technique to determine the time taken to completely digest a starch solution at a range of pH values. Iodine reagent is to be used to test for starch every 30 seconds. Temperature must be controlled by use of a water bath or electric heater.	AT 1 – use appropriate apparatus to record the volumes of liquids, time and pH. AT 2 – safe use of a water bath or electric heater. AT 5 – measure the rate of reaction by the colour change of iodine indicator. AT 8 – use of qualitative iodine reagent to identify starch by continuous sampling.	B3.6

Maths skills

AQA maths skills	Topic
1a Recognise and use expressions in decimal form.	B1.1, B4.2, B4.9
1b Recognise and use expressions in standard form.	B1.1, B1.2, B1.3, B4.4
1c Use ratios, fractions and percentages.	B1.6, B1.10, B3.1, B3.3, B4.1, B4.2, B4.5, B4.9
1d Make estimates of the results of simple calculations.	B1.2, B1.3, B4.2
2a Use an appropriate number of significant figures.	B1.3, B4.7, B4.9
2b Find arithmetic means	B3.6, B4.8, B4.9
2d Understand the principles of sampling as applied to scientific data.	B4.7, B4.8, B4.8, B4.9
2h Make order of magnitude calculations.	B1.1, B1.3, B1.4, B3.1
3a Understand and use the symbols: =, <, <<, >>, >, ∝, ~.	B1.2, B1.3
3d Solve simple algebraic equations.	B1.1
4a Translate information between graphical and numeric form.	B3.6, B4.9
4b Understand that $y = mx + c$ represents a linear relationship.	B3.6
4c Plot two variables from experimental or other data.	B4.9
5c Calculate areas of triangles and rectangles, surface areas, and volumes of cubes.	B1.10, B4.7, B4.9

B1 Cells and organisation

KS3 concept	GCSE topic	Checkpoint	Revision
What cells look like under a light microscope.	B1.1 The world of the microscope	Ask students to explain why we need to use a microscope to see cells.	Ask students to demonstrate how they would use a light microscope to view cells.
The similarities and differences between plant and animal cells.	B1.3 Eukaryotic and prokaryotic cells	Ask students to draw diagrams of plant and animal cells and label as many parts as they can.	Show students diagrams and images of plant and animal cells and ask them to identify them as being from a plant or animal and give reasons.
That tissues can be organised into organs with particular functions in the body.	B3.1 Tissues and organs	Ask students to identify tissues and organs that are part of the nervous system	Give students the names of a range of different tissues e.g. muscle, ligament, tendon and ask them to suggest how they are adapted to their function
Use appropriate equipment when measuring.	B1.8 Osmosis	Ask students to name which measuring instrument they would use to measure certain things e.g. the mass of a beaker.	Ask students to explain why they need to consider what size of measuring cylinder to chose when measuring different volumes of liquids.
What units to use when measuring.	B1.3 Eukaryotic and prokaryotic cells	Ask students to name the units they would use to measure a range of items, for example, the length of a leaf.	Ask students what gram and kilogram mean.
The role of diffusion in the movement of materials in and between cells.	B1.6 Diffusion	Ask students to explain why ink spreads in a glass of water.	Ask students to state what substances need to enter cells and what needs to be removed.
Reproduction in animals and plants.	B2.1 Cell division	Ask students to describe what happens during fertilisation.	Give students a 'cell' made out of modelling clay and ask them to model what happens in order for organisms to grow.
The importance of the digestive system.	B3.2 The human digestive system	Give students an outline of a person and ask them to draw in the digestive system and explain what happens to food after we eat it.	Ask students what an enzyme is.
The basic structure and function of the human gas exchange system.	B4.5 Breathing and gas exchange	Ask students to draw the respiratory system and explain its function.	Show a diagram of alveoli from a person with emphysema and ask students how this affects health.
The mechanism of breathing.	B4.5 Breathing and gas exchange	Ask students to explain why we need to breathe.	Model breathing using a bell jar model and ask students to explain what it is showing.
The role of the leaf stomata in gas exchange in plants.	B4.6 Tissues and organs in plants	Ask students to explain why plants need to exchange gases and describe the movement of gases in and out of a leaf.	Show students images of stomata and ask them to explain what they are.

B 1 Cell structure and transport
1.1 The world of the microscope

AQA spec link: 1.1.5 Students should be able to:

- understand how microscopy techniques have developed over time
- explain how electron microscopy has increased understanding of sub-cellular structures.

Limited to the differences in magnification and resolution.

An electron microscope has much higher magnification and resolving power than a light microscope. This means that it can be used to study cells in much finer detail. This has enabled biologists to see and understand many more sub-cellular structures.

Students should be able to carry out calculations involving magnification, real size, and image size using the formula:

$$\text{magnification} = \frac{\text{size of image}}{\text{size of real object}}$$

Students should be able to express answers in standard form if appropriate.

WS 1.1, 4.4
MS 1a, 1b, 2h, 3d

Aiming for	Outcome	Checkpoint	
		Question	Activity
Aiming for GRADE 4 ↓	Use a light microscope.		Main 1
	State why microscopes are useful in the study of cell biology.	1, End of chapter 1	Starter 2, Plenary 2
	Calculate total magnification.		Main 1, Homework
Aiming for GRADE 6 ↓	Describe the difference between magnification and resolution.		Main 2
	Describe the advantages and disadvantages of using a light and an electron microscope.	1	Main 2, Plenary 1
	Use the formula: magnification = size of image/size of real object.	2	Main 1, Homework
Aiming for GRADE 8 ↓	Compare and contrast the magnification and resolution obtained by using light and electron microscopes.	3	Main 2, Plenary 1
	Justify the use of an electron microscope.	3	Main 2
	Rearrange the magnification formula and measure the size of cells.	2	Main 1, Homework

Maths
Students will be introduced to units used to measure microscopic objects, such as microns (μm) and nanometres (nm) (1a, 1b). They will calculate total magnification. They will also use and rearrange the formula: magnification = size of image/size of real object (2h, 3d).

Literacy
Students follow instructions to use a light microscope and use technical vocabulary to describe its parts. They access information from the student book and use key words to describe advantages and disadvantages.

Key words
light microscope, electron microscope, resolving power

■ B1 Cell structure and transport

Practical

Title	Observation of animal cells under a microscope
Equipment	light microscope with low- and high-power objective lenses, transparent plastic ruler, calibrated micrometer eyepiece or graticule, prepared cheek cell slides
	Alternatively, students could prepare their own microscope slides: microscope slides, cover slips, methylene blue stain in a small stoppered bottle, cotton buds, mounted needle, dropping pipettes, blotting paper or filter paper in small squares, beaker of disinfectant (sodium chlorate(I) solution or 1% Virkon solution)
Overview of method	Students are provided with prepared slides of cheek cells, or they make their own. They use a light microscope to view them and draw images. They calculate magnification and specimen size.
Safety considerations	Students must take care with the glass slides because they are very fragile. Take care not to break the slide by turning the objective lens too far. Be careful with chemicals because they may stain skin and clothes. Methylene blue is harmful and maybe flammable. Sodium chlorate(I) solution is corrosive. Wear eye protection. Put any contaminated material into disinfectant. Wash hands after using chemicals.

Starter	Support/Extend	Resources
What is it? (10 min) Show students a range of magnified images of everyday objects. Students try to identify the objects and give a qualitative indication of how much bigger the image is than the actual object. **Why do we use microscopes?** (5 min) Show the class a light microscope and ask students to discuss in pairs what it is and why it is a useful scientific tool.	**Extend:** Ask students to discuss how a light microscope works. They could be given one per group to examine more closely.	

Main	Support/Extend	Resources
Observation of animal cells under a microscope (30 min) Students observe animal (cheek) cells using a light microscope and draw images. The slides can either be prepared or students can make their own. They carry out magnification calculations. **Light and electron microscopes** (10 min) Inform the class that there is a limit on what can be seen using a light microscope and introduce the electron microscope. Ask the students to use the information from the student book to describe the main advantages and disadvantages of using a light and an electron microscope. They should mention the terms magnification and resolution in their answers.	**Support:** Demonstrate the setting up of the microscope. **Support:** Show the students how to organise the information in a table. **Extend:** Ask students to extend their answer by considering the cost of an electron microscope for a biology lab.	**Practical:** Observation of animal cells under a microscope

Plenary	Support/Extend	Resources
Size order (10 min) Students arrange images of different objects in order of size. Ask students to group objects according to what can be seen by the naked eye, a light microscope, and an electron microscope. **The world of the microscope** (10 min) Students use the interactive to label a diagram of a light microscope, then summarise the difference between a light microscope and an electron microscope.	**Support:** Students could work in pairs to discuss their ideas.	**Interactive:** The world of the microscope

Homework		
Give students numerous examples to practice calculating magnification and rearranging the formula: magnification = image size/size of real object Alternatively, students can use the WebQuest to research the historical development of the microscope.	**Support:** Students only answer questions where the data is provided in tables for easy access. **Extend:** Students answer questions where data is supplied within prose.	**WebQuest:** Microscopes through the ages

kerboodle

A Kerboodle highlight for this lesson is **Calculation sheet: Magnification calculations.** Refer to the **Content map** on Kerboodle for a full list of resources and assessment.

B1.2 Animal and plant cells

AQA spec link: 1.1.2 Students should be able to explain how the main sub-cellular structures, including the nucleus, cell membranes, mitochondria, chloroplasts in plant cells, and plasmids in bacterial cells are related to their functions.

Most animal cells have the following parts:

- a nucleus
- cytoplasm
- a cell membrane
- mitochondria
- ribosomes.

In addition to the parts found in animal cells, plant cells often have:

- chloroplasts
- a permanent vacuole filled with cell sap.

Plant and algal cells also have a cell wall made of cellulose, which strengthens the cell.

Students should be able to use estimations and explain what they should be used to judge the relative size or area of sub-cellular structures.

Required practical: Use a light microscope to observe, draw, and label a selection of plant and animal cells. A scale magnification must be included.

WS 1.2
MS 1b, 1d, 3a

Aiming for	Outcome	Checkpoint	
		Question	Activity
Aiming for GRADE 4	Identify a plant and an animal cell from a diagram.		Starter 1, Plenary 1
	Name the main parts of cells.	1	Starter 1, Starter 2, Main, Homework
	Prepare a microscope slide.		Main
Aiming for GRADE 6	Describe the functions of the parts of cells.	1, 2	Main, Plenary 2
	Compare plant and animal cells.	1	Starter 1, Starter 2, Main
	Use a microscope to study plant and algal cells.		Main 1
Aiming for GRADE 8	Explain how the main structures of cells are related to their functions.		Main, Plenary 2
	Suggest reasons why some cells do not contain all cell structures.	3	Main
	Compare the sizes of cells using units of length and standard form.		Main

Maths
Students use units of length and standard form to compare the sizes of cells (1b).

Literacy
Students follow instructions to prepare microscope slides. They discuss in pairs to suggest how the school is like a model for a cell and share their ideas with the class. They use key words to label cell diagrams and describe the functions of cell structures.

Key words
nucleus, genes, chromosomes, cytoplasm, cell membrane, ions, mitochondria, ribosomes, algae, cell wall, cellulose, chloroplasts, chlorophyll, permanent vacuole

B1 Cell structure and transport

® Required practical

Title	Looking at cells
Equipment	light microscope with low- and high-power objective lenses, microscope slides, cover slips, dilute iodine solution, mounted needle, forceps, scissors, scalpel, dropping pipettes, blotting paper or filter paper in small squares, onion, *Elodea*, filamentous algae, transparent plastic ruler, calibrated micrometer eye piece or graticule
Overview of method	Students prepare slides to view plant and algal cells with a light microscope. They identify different structures within the three types of cell.
Safety considerations	Take care with sharp scalpels. Wash hands after using chemicals. Students must take care with the glass slides as they are very fragile. Take care not to break the slide by turning the objective lens too far. Iodine solution is harmful. Take care with iodine solution as it can stain skin and clothing.

Starter	Support/Extend	Resources
Label the cells (5 min) Show students unlabelled diagrams of plant and animal cells and ask them to work in small teams to name as many of the cell parts as they can. Reveal the answers. **Cell** (10 min) Students use the interactive to match the organelles of a cell with their function. Students then identify if statements on the organelles of cells are true or false.	**Support:** Just show students the animal cell.	**Interactive:** Cells

Main	Support/Extend	Resources
Looking at cells (40 min) Students make slides of plant and algal cells. They study them under a microscope and compare structures that they can see. Discuss why they cannot see all the structures in the cells and link back to work done in Topic B1.1 on magnification and resolution.	**Support:** Demonstrate how to make a slide. **Extend:** Ask students to explain why there is a difference in the cell structures that they can see in each cell (e.g., why are there no chloroplasts in onion cells?).	**Required practical:** Looking at cells

Plenary	Support/Extend	Resources
Which cell? (5 min) Show the class micrographs of cells (these can be found on the Internet) and ask them to identify them as plant or animal. **Modelling a cell** (10 min) Ask the students to work in pairs. Tell them that the school could be a model of a cell. Ask them to assign parts of the school to parts of the cell that carry out a similar role. For example, the headteacher's office is like the nucleus as they manage the school. They should justify their choices to the rest of the class.	**Support:** Use diagrams instead of micrographs.	

Homework		
Design and/or build a model cell. Students can make a physical model, for example, using food, modelling materials, or anything else they can think of.	**Extend:** Ask students to justify their use of each material.	

kerboodle

A Kerboodle highlight for this lesson is **Maths skills: Cells under a microscope.** Refer to the **Content map** on Kerboodle for a full list of resources and assessment.

B1.3 Eukaryotic and prokaryotic cells

AQA spec links: 1.1.1 Plant and animal cells (eukaryotic cells) have a cell membrane, cytoplasm, and genetic material enclosed in a nucleus.

Bacterial cells (prokaryotic cells) are much smaller in comparison. They have cytoplasm and a cell membrane surrounded by a cell wall. The genetic material is not enclosed in a nucleus. It is a single DNA loop and may have one or more small rings of DNA called plasmids.

Students should be able to demonstrate an understanding of the scale and size of cells and be able to make order of magnitude calculations, including the use of standard form.

1.1.2 Students should be able to explain how the main subcellular structures (including the nucleus, cell membranes, mitochondria, chloroplasts in plant cells and plasmids in bacterial cells) are related to their functions.

WS 1.2, 4.4
MS 1b, 1d, 2a, 2h, 3a

Aiming for	Outcome	Checkpoint	
		Question	Activity
Aiming for GRADE 4 ↓	Identify structures in prokaryotic cells.	End of chapter 2	Main 1
	State that prokaryotic cells do not contain a nucleus and eukaryotic cells do.	1	Main 1, Plenary 1
	Use orders of magnitude to correctly order objects according to size.		Main 2
Aiming for GRADE 6 ↓	Compare prokaryotic and eukaryotic cells.	3, End of chapter 2	Main 1, Plenary 1
	Describe the functions of the parts of a prokaryotic cell.	1	Main 1
	Use orders of magnitude to compare the sizes of organisms.	End of chapter 2	Main 2, Homework
Aiming for GRADE 8 ↓	Explain how the main structures of prokaryotic cells are related to their functions.		Main 1
	Perform calculations to work out orders of magnitude.	2	Main 2, Homework

Maths
Students will be introduced to orders of magnitude (2h). They will use them to order the size of objects and to compare them to say how many times bigger or smaller an object is compared with another. Students will also use units of length. Students express the size of cells using standard form (1b).

Literacy
Students will be involved in class and group discussions to put forward their ideas and opinions. They will use correct scientific terminology extracted from the student book to label cells and describe the functions of their parts.

Key words
eukaryotic cells, prokaryotic cells, bacteria

B1 Cell structure and transport

Starter	Support/Extend	Resources
Eukaryotic and prokaryotic cells (5 min) Introduce the idea that eukaryotic cells have a nucelus and organelles whilst prokaryotic cells are single-celled organisms. Show students a range of eukaryotic cells and prokaryotic cells and have them sort them accordingly. Students then sort some statements about eukaryotic cells and prokaryotic cells. **Wipe out!** (10 min) Initiate a class discussion by telling the class that you think all bacteria should be killed so no more exist on Earth. Discuss the fact that bacteria can be pathogens and cause disease but the vast majority are harmless and some are even useful (e.g., decomposers, those that make medicines and food).	**Support:** Provide the class with visual stimulus by showing images of disease, foods made by bacteria (e.g., yoghurt and cheese), a sewage treatment plant, and bottles of probiotic drinks.	**Interactive:** Eukaryotic and prokaryotic cells

Main	Support/Extend	Resources
Eukaryotic vs. prokaryotic (20 min) Show the class a diagram of a bacterial cell without labels. Introduce this as a bacterial or prokaryotic cell. Ask them how it is different to the plant and animal (eukaryotic) cells they studied in Topic B1.2. Students copy the diagram and use information from the student book to label the parts. Ask them to highlight features not found in the eukaryotic cells previously studied and write in the functions of these parts.	**Support:** Provide students with a ready-drawn diagram. Write simple functions of each part on the board for students to select. **Extend:** Ask the class what type of animal cell has flagella (sperm). Ask students to add how these structures are linked to their function.	
Scale and size (20 min) Show students a series of images of different objects and organisms of different sizes, for example, a buckyball, a grain of sand, a virus, a human hair, a child, and so on. Provide students with a range of sizes, all in metres, and have them match the image to the size. Students then answer a series of questions on orders of magnitude.	**Support:** Students can work through the Maths skills interactive to learn how to carry out order of magnitude calculations.	**Activity:** Scale and size **Maths skills:** Orders of magnitude

Plenary	Support/Extend	Resources
Cells of different organisms (10 min) Students consider sample answers to an exam question about cells from different types of organisms. Discuss their conclusions as a class.		
Euglena (5 min) Show the class a labelled diagram of *Euglena*. Ask them to discuss in pairs what type of cell they think it is and why.	**Support:** Ask them to say whether the cell is eukaryotic or prokaryotic. **Extend:** Ask them what features *Euglena* has in common with plant, animal, and bacterial cells.	

Homework		
Work out the increase in order of magnitude during the growth of a human from a fertilised egg to an adult.	**Support:** Students just find out the increase in size.	

kerboodle

A Kerboodle highlight for this lesson is **Go further: Plasmids and genetic engineering**. Refer to the **Content map** on Kerboodle for a full list of resources and assessment.

B1.4 Specialisation in animal cells

AQA spec link: 1.1.3 Students should be able to, when provided with appropriate information, explain how the structure of different types of cell relate to their function in a tissue, an organ or organ system, or the whole organism.

Cells may be specialised to carry out a particular function:

- sperm cells, nerve cells, and muscle cells in animals.

Aiming for	Outcome	Checkpoint	
		Question	Activity
Aiming for GRADE 4	Identify specialised animal cells from diagrams.		Starter 1, Main 1
	Describe the function of specialised animal cells.	1	Starter 1, Main 1, Main 2, Plenary 2
	Write a basic explanation of how animal cells are adapted.	1	Main 2
Aiming for GRADE 6	Explain why animals have specialised cells.		Main 2, Plenary 2
	Compare the structure of a specialised and a generalised animal cell.		Starter 1
	Write a coherent explanation of how animal cells are adapted.	1	Main 2
Aiming for GRADE 8	Discuss how the structure of specialised animal cells is related to their function within an organ and the whole organism.		Main 1, Main 2, Plenary 1
	Suggest the function of an unknown specialised cell based on its structure.	2, 3	Plenary 1
	Write an effectively structured explanation of how animal cells are adapted.	1	Main 2

Maths
Students consider the sizes of specialised cells(2h).

Literacy
Students write a well-structured explanation to apply their knowledge. They extract information from the student book to describe the structure and function of specialised animal cells.

Key words
specialised, synapses, sperm

■ B1 Cell structure and transport

Starter	Support/Extend	Resources
Sex cells (5 min) Show the class an image of sperm and egg cells that includes the cell sizes. Ask them to discuss in pairs how these cells differ from the generalised animal cells previously studied.	**Support:** Just focus on the sperm cell. **Extend:** Ask students why sex cells have these adaptations. **Extend:** Discuss the difference in size between the two cells and suggest a reason for this.	
Multicellular (10 min) Display an outline of a person on the board. Invite students to name a type of specialised cell that they remember from KS3 and point to where on/in the body you would find it. Discuss why you have so many different types of cell.	**Support:** Give names of cells. **Extend:** Students draw images of the specialised cells they recognise onto sticky notes and stick them to the correct area on the outline.	

Main	Support/Extend	Resources
Types of specialised cells (20 min) Students use information from the student book to label a specialised animal cell. Students then complete a table to describe the structure of specialised animal cells and explain how they are adapted to their function.	**Extend:** Students produce a model of one specialised cell.	**Activity:** Types of specialised cells
The human eye (20 min) Show students a diagram of the eye and discuss the function of the retina. Students do some research on the specialised cells found in the retina (rods and cones) and apply their understanding to write an explanation of how the structure of these cells is adapted to their function.	**Support:** Provide students with suitable sources of information. **Extend:** Students use the Internet and/or books to do their own research on the specialised photoreceptor cells in the human eye.	**Extension:** The human eye

Plenary	Support/Extend	Resources
Specialisation in animal cells (10 min) Students match specialised animal cells to their structures and functions.	**Extend:** Show students an unfamiliar specialised animal cell. Student pairs discuss what its function could be, studying its structure.	**Interactive:** Specialisation in animal cells
True or false? (10 min) Ask the students to stand up. Ask them a series of true or false questions based on the content of Topic B1.4. If they think the answer is false, they sit down.	**Extend:** Students take it in turns to ask the questions.	

Homework		
In preparation for the next lesson, ask students to find out the name of one specialised cell found in a plant and state its function.	**Extend:** Students find out how it is adapted to its function.	

B1.5 Specialisation in plant cells

AQA spec link: 1.1.3 Students should be able to, when provided with appropriate information, explain how the structure of different types of cell relate to their function in a tissue, an organ or organ system, or the whole organism.

Cells may be specialised to carry out a particular function:

- root hair cells, xylem, and phloem cells in plants.

2.3.2 Students should be able to explain how the structure of root hair cells are adapted to their functions.

Root hair cells are adapted for the efficient uptake of water by osmosis, and mineral ions by active transport.

Aiming for	Outcome	Checkpoint	
		Question	Activity
Aiming for GRADE 4 ↓	Identify specialised plant cells from diagrams.		Main 1, Plenary 1
	Describe the function of specialised plant cells.	1	Main 1, Plenary 1
	Use a light microscope to view a root hair cell.		Main 2
Aiming for GRADE 6 ↓	Compare the structure of a specialised and a generalised plant cell.		Starter 1
	Describe the adaptations of specialised plant cells.	1	Main 2, Plenary 2
	Draw a scientific drawing of a root hair cell observed using a light microscope.		Main 2
Aiming for GRADE 8 ↓	Discuss how the structure of specialised plant cells is related to their function within an organ and the whole organism.	2, 3	Main
	Design a cell, tissue, or organ to perform a certain function.		Homework
	Measure a root hair cell observed using a light microscope.		Main 2

Maths
Students work out the size of root hair cells.

Literacy
Students use information from the student book to write short verbal presentations containing key terminology. They follow instructions to use a light microscope to view root hair cells.

Key words
root hair cells, xylem, phloem

Practical

Title	Looking at root hair cells
Equipment	light microscope with low- and high-power objective lenses, prepared slides of mung bean roots, transparent plastic ruler, calibrated micrometer eyepiece or graticule
Overview of method	Students are provided with prepared slides of mung bean roots. They use a light microscope to view them and draw images. They work out the length of a root hair.
Safety considerations	Students must take care with the glass slides because they are very fragile. Take care not to break the slide by turning the objective lens too far.

■ B1 Cell structure and transport

Starter	Support/Extend	Resources
Plant cell (5 min) Show the students a diagram of a leaf cross-section and explain what it is showing. Ask them to identify a cell that is similar to the generalised plant cell previously studied (palisade cell). Discuss how other cells are different in structure and suggest why this might be. **Plant organs** (10 min) Ask students to draw a plant and label as many organs and tissues as they can. Ask students to peer assess each other's diagrams and count how many organs and tissues they have named correctly.	**Support:** Write the names of plant organs on the board for students to use (leaf, root, flower, stem). **Extend:** Discuss the functions of each organ/tissue.	

Main	Support/Extend	Resources
Specialised plant cells (20 min) Ask the students to work in groups of four. Each student researches one specialised plant cell – photosynthetic cell, root hair cell, xylem, or phloem. They use information from the student book to research their cell. Display images of the four specialised cells. Students in each group read out what they have found out (without mentioning the cell name). The other members of the class say which cell they are describing.	**Support:** Just focus on the function of the cell. **Extend:** Ask students to find out the function and adaptations of the cell.	**Practical:** Looking at root hair cells
Looking at root hair cells (20 min) Students study prepared slides showing root hair cells of mung beans using a light microscope, draw scientific drawings, and answer questions about adaptations. If you have more time, students can make their own slides. They place the roots of sprouting mung seeds on slides and dye with iodine solution.	**Support:** Show the class micrographs of root hairs so they are familiar with what they look like. This will help them to locate them on the slide. **Extend:** Students can measure the length and width of a root hair cell.	

Plenary	Support/Extend	Resources
Specialisation in plant cells (5 min) Students use the interactive to match specialised plant cells to their structures and functions. **What am I?** (10 min) Write the names of different specialised animal and plant cells on cards. Ask students to work in groups and give each student a card that they must hold in front of them without looking. Students ask questions in order to determine which cell they are.		**Interactive:** Specialisation in plant cells

Homework		
Students design cells for humans that would allow us to make our own food via photosynthesis.	**Support:** Focus on skin cells. **Extend:** Students can design new cells, tissues, and organs in different areas of the body.	

kerboodle

A Kerboodle highlight for this lesson is **Go further: How do plants know when to flower?** Refer to the **Content map** on Kerboodle for a full list of resources and assessment.

B1.6 Diffusion

AQA spec link: 1.3.1 Substances may move into and out of cells across the cell membranes via diffusion.

Diffusion is the spreading out of the particles of any substance in solution, or particles of a gas, resulting in a net movement from an area of higher concentration to an area of lower concentration.

Some of the substances transported in and out of cells by diffusion are oxygen and carbon dioxide in gas exchange, and of the waste product urea from cells into the blood plasma for excretion in the kidney.

Students should be able to explain how different factors affect the rate of diffusion.

Factors which affect the rate of diffusion are:

- the difference in concentrations (concentration gradient)
- the temperature
- the surface area of the membrane.

WS 1.2, 1.5
MS 1c

Aiming for	Outcome	Checkpoint	
		Question	Activity
Aiming for GRADE 4 ↓	State that diffusion is the spreading of the particles of any substance in solution, or particles of a gas.	1	Starter 2
	List the factors that affect the rate of diffusion.		Main 2, Plenary 1
	Write a simple hypothesis.		Main 1
Aiming for GRADE 6 ↓	Predict which way substances will move across a cell membrane.	3	Starter 2
	Explain why surface area affects the rate of diffusion.	2, End of chapter 4, 5	Main 2, Plenary 2
	Write a hypothesis using scientific knowledge.		Main 1
Aiming for GRADE 8 ↓	Explain how temperature and concentration gradient affect the rate of diffusion.	2, 3	Main 2, Plenary 1
	Write a hypothesis using detailed scientific knowledge and explain how it could be tested.		Main 1

Maths
Students carry out calculations to work out surface area and the rate of diffusion (1c).

Literacy
Students follow a method to carry out an investigation. They write well-structured hypotheses and conclusions using the correct scientific terminology.

Key words
diffusion, concentration gradient, gas exchange

Practical

Title	Diffusion demonstration/ Investigating diffusion
Equipment	100 ml beaker, potassium manganate(VII) crystals, tweezers, kettle (2 or 3 for the whole group will be sufficient), cellophane tubing in 15 cm lengths, test tube, starch solution, dropper pipette, elastic band, dilute iodine solution (dilute iodine dissolved in potassium iodide solution) in a small stoppered bottle
	For the iodine solution:
	Dissolve 6 g of potassium iodide in 200 cm^3 of water. Add 3 g of iodine crystals and make up to 1 dm^3 with distilled water. Leave for 24 hours for the iodine to dissolve. Allow 30 cm^3 per group.

B1 Cell structure and transport

	For the starch solution: Make a 1% starch solution by shaking starch powder with water and heating to boiling point. Allow 3 cm^3 per group. For the cellophane tubing: Cut 6 mm ($\frac{1}{2}$ in) tubing into 15 cm lengths and, before the experiment, soak in water and tie a knot in one end. Allow one length per group.
Overview of method	**Diffusion demonstration** Add a crystal of potassium manganate(VII) to a beaker of water at room temperature and observe for 5 minutes. Then repeat using hot water. **Investigating diffusion** Students half fill the cellophane tubing with starch solution, place inside a test tube with dilute iodine solution. After 10–15 minutes students examine the iodine and starch solutions in the test tube and cellophane tubing and record any colour changes.
Safety considerations	Make sure students are careful with the stains as they will stain skin and clothing. Iodine solution is harmful and potassium manganate(VII) is oxidising. Avoid contact with skin. Take care with hot water. Wear eye protection.

Starter	Support/Extend	Resources
Diffusion demonstration (10 min) Carry out a simple demonstration by adding a crystal of potassium permanganate(VII) to a large beaker of water at room temperature. Ask the class to make observations. Remind them that this is an example of diffusion. Then repeat using hot water. **Cell diagram** (10 min) Draw an image of an animal cell on the board. Ask students to copy it and draw arrows to show the movement of different types of substances in and out of the cell. Discuss the fact that these substances move in and out by diffusion and explain the reason for this movement in terms of differences in concentration of substances inside and outside the cell.	**Extend:** Ask students to predict what will happen and give a scientific explanation. **Extend:** Ask students to draw particle diagrams to explain what is happening. **Support:** Write the names of the substances on the board for students to use.	

Main	Support/Extend	Resources
Investigating diffusion (30 min) Students look at diffusion and one of the factors that affects the rate of diffusion – temperature. They also look at diffusion across a membrane to embed the idea that diffusion can occur across cell membranes. **Discussing factors** (10 min) Return to Starter 1 or carry it out now. Ask students to identify factors that would speed up the rate of diffusion. Examples include increasing the temperature of the water, grinding up the crystal into a powder (increasing surface area), adding more potassium permanganate crystals (increasing concentration gradient), or stirring.	**Support:** Students may need some help understanding why iodine can diffuse through the membrane but starch cannot (starch molecules are too big). **Support:** Show students how each of these changes will increase the rate of diffusion. **Extend:** Ask students to explain why these factors increase the rate of diffusion.	**Practical:** Diffusion

Plenary	Support/Extend	Resources
Diffusion (5 min) Students answer questions about diffusion. **Intestinal cell** (5 min) Show students a diagram of an intestinal cell. Ask them to discuss in pairs how it is adapted for efficient diffusion.		**Interactive:** Diffusion

Homework
Students carry out an analysis of the results from Main 1. They describe what the results show and give a scientific explanation.

kerboodle
A Kerboodle highlight for this lesson is **Literacy sheet: Brownian motion**. Refer to the **Content map** on Kerboodle for a full list of resources and assessment.

B1.7 Osmosis

AQA spec links: 1.3.2 Water may move across cell membranes via osmosis. Osmosis is the diffusion of water from a dilute solution to a concentrated solution through a partially permeable membrane.

Aiming for	Outcome	Checkpoint	
		Question	Activity
Aiming for GRADE 4 ↓	Describe what osmosis is.		Starter 1, Starter 2, Plenary 1
	State that if animal cells lose or gain too much water by osmosis they can stop working properly.	3	Starter 1, Main 2, Plenary 2, Homework
Aiming for GRADE 6 ↓	State the differences between osmosis and diffusion.	1	Plenary 1
	Use ideas about osmosis to explain why maintaining constant internal conditions in living organisms is important.	1, 2, 3	Starter 1, Main 2, Plenary 2, Homework
	Write a prediction using scientific knowledge of osmosis.	End of chapter 3	Main 1
Aiming for GRADE 8 ↓	Explain how a model shows osmosis in a cell.	End of chapter 3	Main 1
	Use the terms isotonic, hypotonic, or hypertonic to explain the movement of water across a cell membrane.	2	Main 1, Plenary 2

Maths
Students use ideas about concentration to explain osmosis.

Literacy
Students write predictions and explanations using scientific terminology. Pairs discuss ideas and feed back to the class.

Key words
osmosis, partially permeable membrane, isotonic, hypertonic, hypotonic, plasmolysis

Practical

Title	Investigating osmosis
Equipment	Visking tubing, concentrated glucose solution, water, glass tubing, disposable pipettes, rubber bands, beakers or boiling tubes
Overview of method	Soak the Visking tubing in water before the lesson. Use two pieces tied at one end and use the disposable pipettes to fill one with the glucose solution and the other with water. Attach a glass tube to each with a rubber band. Place the Visking tubing containing water into a beaker or boiling tube filled with glucose solution so the tubing is fully submerged. Repeat with the other tubing, placing this in water. Leave until the end of the lesson and observe changes to the liquid level in the tubing.

B1 Cell structure and transport

Starter	Support/Extend	Resources
Which way? (10 min) Draw a diagram of an animal cell on the board and draw dots inside to show water particles. Draw a higher concentration of dots outside the cell. Ask students to discuss in pairs what they think will happen to the movement of water. Go through their ideas and introduce osmosis as a special type of diffusion where water is moved across a partially permeable membrane.	**Support:** Remind students of the definition of diffusion. **Extend:** Use the term net movement.	
Salting meat (5 min) Show the students images of a piece of meat before and after it has been left in salt. Ask them to discuss in pairs what has happened and why. Go through their ideas and allow them to reach the conclusion that water has been lost from the meat because of a process called osmosis.	**Extend:** Ask students to consider why it is important that the salt concentration of our blood is not allowed to get too high.	

Main	Support/Extend	Resources
Investigating osmosis (20 min) Set up a demonstration as shown in the student book (Figure 1). Explain that Visking tubing is partially permeable like the cell membrane and explain what this means. Draw diagrams on the board using different coloured dots to show the concentration of solutions inside and outside the Visking tubing bags. Ask students to predict what they think will happen and why.	**Extend:** Students should use the terms isotonic, hypertonic, and hypotonic. **Extend:** Students should explain how the model represents what happens in a cell.	**Practical:** Investigating osmosis
Keeping things constant (20 min) Tell the class that the concentration of water in the blood is kept constant. Ask them to discuss in pairs why this is important and feed back to the rest of the class. Then allow the class to use information from the student book to write a full explanation using correct scientific terminology.	**Support:** Provide the start of sentences to help students produce an explanation.	

Plenary	Support/Extend	Resources
Osmosis (5 min) Students complete the interactive to match osmosis key terms with their definitions. They then sort statements into whether they describe osmosis or diffusion.		**Interactive:** Osmosis
Model cells results (10 min) Return to the model cells set up in Main 1. Show the class the results and ask them to compare these to their predictions. Ask them to state whether the outside solutions were isotonic, hypertonic, or hypotonic, and to explain what happened in terms of osmosis.	**Support:** Go through an explanation for one of the model cells and ask students to complete the other independently.	

Homework		
Students use the student book and any other available resources (such as the Internet or other textbooks) to research osmosis and its role in living things. Students use this research to produce an explanation of why osmosis is important in living organisms.	**Support:** Students only use the student book for their research. **Extend:** Supply students with more advanced resources for their research.	

kerboodle

A Kerboodle highlight for this lesson is **Bump up your grade: Osmosis**. Refer to the **Content map** on Kerboodle for a full list of resources and assessment.

B1.8 Osmosis in plants

AQA spec link: 1.3.2 Water may move across cell membranes via osmosis. Osmosis is the diffusion of water from a dilute solution to a concentrated solution through a partially permeable membrane.

Required practical: Investigate the effect of salt or sugar solutions on plant tissue.

WS 1.2

Aiming for	Outcome	Checkpoint	
		Question	Activity
Aiming for GRADE 4	State that if a plant loses too much water from its cells then they become soft.	3	Starter 1
	Write a simple method with support.		Main, Homework
	Use given data to plot a suitable graph with some support.		Main
Aiming for GRADE 6	Use osmosis to explain the effect of placing plant tissue in salt or sugar solutions.		Main
	Write a suitable plan to investigate the effect of salt or sugar solutions on plant tissue.		Main, Homework
	Calculate percentage change and use this to plot a line graph with negative numbers and draw a line of best fit.		Main
Aiming for GRADE 8	Explain the mechanisms that lead to turgid or flaccid plant cells and plasmolysis.	2, End of chapter 3	Starter 1, Main
	Write a detailed plan for an investigation independently.		Main, Homework
	Use a line graph to estimate the concentration of solution inside a plant cell.		Main

Maths
Students put raw data into a results table and calculate percentage change in length/mass. They use these results to plot a line graph that includes negative numbers. Students then use the graph to write conclusions and estimate an unknown value.

Literacy
Students research suitable methods in order to write a plan for an investigation.

Key words
turgor, plasmolysis

Required practical

Title	Investigating osmosis in plant cells
Equipment	suitable plant material (e.g., potato, sweet potato, or beetroot), range of concentrations of sugar or salt solutions, distilled water, apple corers, knives, white tiles, filter paper, tweezers, boiling tubes, measuring cylinders, rulers, balances, stopwatch
Overview of method	Students cut up their chosen plant material into regular shapes (chips or discs are commonly used). They can measure length and/or mass and then place plant material into salt or sugar solutions and leave for at least 30 minutes. They can measure the change in length/mass.
Safety considerations	Take care with sharp blades.

■ B1 Cell structure and transport

Starter	Support/Extend	Resources
Wilting plant (10 min) Show the class a wilted plant or an image of one. Ask them to discuss in pairs what has happened, why it has happened, and how they could restore the plant. **Vacuole function** (5 min) Show the class a diagram of a plant cell and ask them where the vacuole is. Ask them to write down the function of the vacuole.	**Extend:** Students should attempt to use osmosis in their answer.	

Main	Support/Extend	Resources
Investigating osmosis in plant cells (40 min) Supply students with a diagram of two plant cells showing a clear permanent vacuole. Explain that the vacuole is full of sap that contains a low concentration of sugars and minerals. Ask students to modify the diagrams to show what would happen to the cells if they were placed in a concentrated sugar solution or in water. After checking their answers, ask students to use information from the student book to add the terms turgor, turgid, and flaccid to their diagrams. Students then plan their own investigation to find out how salt or sugar solutions affect plant tissue. Allow them to do some initial research in order to find examples of suitable methods (including use of the student book). Students need to plan to collect quantitative data. They should write down their independent, dependent, and control variables before writing a simple plan. You may wish to allow time for students to do a preliminary test to check the suitability of their method. Students calculate percentage change and plot a line graph with a line of best fit. They write their conclusion and evaluate their method. Students will need another lesson to gather and analyse their results.	**Support:** Add dots to the diagram to show the difference in concentration of solution inside and outside each cell. **Extend:** Students should use the terms hypotonic and hypertonic. **Extend:** Students should draw their own diagram to show plasmolysis. **Support:** Students can work in pairs or larger groups. They may wish to use just one concentration and measure the change in length/mass of their plant material. They can plot a bar chart. **Extend:** Students should use a range of concentrations and plan to calculate percentage change of length/mass. They can draw a line graph with a line of best fit. **Extend:** Show students how they can use their graph to estimate the solute concentration in a potato cell.	**Required practical:** Investigating osmosis in plant cells

Plenary	Support/Extend	Resources
Osmosis in plants (5 min) Students use the interactive to check their understanding of this topic by completing a paragraph about osmosis in plants. **Water your plants** (5 min) Ask students to write a short explanation about why you need to water your house plants, using what they have learnt about osmosis in plant cells.	**Support:** Students can verbally explain to a partner.	**Interactive:** Osmosis in plants

Homework		
Students should complete their plan and prepare a blank results table in preparation for carrying out the investigation next lesson.		

kerboodle
A Kerboodle highlight for this lesson is **Working scientifically: Measuring mass and length**. Refer to the **Content map** on Kerboodle for a full list of resources and assessment.

B1.9 Active transport

AQA spec link: 1.3.3 Active transport moves substances from a more dilute solution to a more concentrated solution (against a concentration gradient). This requires energy from respiration.

Active transport allows mineral ions to be absorbed into plant root hairs from very dilute solutions in the soil. Plants require ions for healthy growth.

It also allows sugar molecules to be absorbed from lower concentrations in the gut into the blood which has a higher sugar concentration. Sugar molecules are used for cell respiration.

Students should be able to:

- describe how substances are transported into and out of cells by diffusion, osmosis and active transport
- explain the differences between the three processes.

Aiming for	Outcome	Checkpoint	
		Question	Activity
Aiming for GRADE 4	Define active transport as the movement of a substance against a concentration gradient using energy.	1	Starter, Plenary 1
	Identify where active transport takes place.		Starter 1, Main
	Use a representational model to show active transport.		Main
Aiming for GRADE 6	Explain why active transport is important for living organisms.	3	Main
	Explain the differences between diffusion, osmosis, and active transport.	2	Starter 1, Plenary 1
	Suggest some limitations of/improvements to a representational model that shows active transport.		Main
Aiming for GRADE 8	Describe how active transport takes place.	2	Main
	Suggest how a cell that carries out active transport is adapted to this function.		Plenary 2
	Design and evaluate a representational model to show active transport.		Main

Maths
Students can consider the difference in concentration between mineral ions in the soil and inside the root cells. They can use this to calculate the difference in orders of magnitude.

Literacy
Students use information from the student book to find out where active transport is used in humans and explain why it is important. They work in groups and follow instructions to model active transport.

Key word
active transport

B1 Cell structure and transport

Starter	Support/Extend	Resources
Absorption of mineral ions (5 min) Show the class an unlabelled diagram showing active transport in plant roots and ask them why mineral ions cannot move from the soil into the roots via diffusion. Reveal the labels and explain that mineral ions have to move from a low to a high concentration (against the concentration gradient). A process called active transport is used, which requires energy.	**Support:** Display the labels on the diagram from the start. **Extend:** Share with students the difference in concentration of mineral ions: 10 µmol/dm^3 in the soil and 100 mmol/dm^3 in the cell. Ask them to work out the difference in orders of magnitude.	
Plant roots (10 min) Ask students to write down what substances move into roots from the soil. Then ask them what process moves water into the plant roots. Explain that osmosis is used because water is travelling from a high to low concentration. Explain that mineral ions cannot move into roots via diffusion because they are very dilute in the soil. Because they have to move from a low to high concentration of mineral ions (against the concentration gradient) a process called active transport is used which requires energy.		

Main	Support/Extend	Resources
Active transport (20 min) Introduce active transport to students. Ask them to use information from the student book to find one example of where active transport is used in humans and explain why it is important. Students then work in small groups to design a model of active transport. Ask for a couple of groups to demonstrate their model, whilst the rest of the students evaluate its effectiveness and comment on possible improvements.	**Extend:** Students should explain why respiration is needed for active transport. **Extend:** Students devise their own model.	**Activity:** Active transport

Plenary	Support/Extend	Resources
Exchange of materials (10 min) Give students a series of statements on osmosis, diffusion, and active transport. Students identify which statements relate to which process. **Active transport** (10 min) Students label a diagram of active transport, then match some key words relating to active transport to their definitions.	**Extend:** Students complete the Go further activity where they look at the role of membrane ultrastructure in the exchange of materials.	**Go further:** Cell membrane adaptation for transport **Interactive:** Active transport

Homework		
Ask students to find out why increasing the amount of oxygen available to plant roots increases growth. This can be linked to use of aeration in hydroponics.		

kerboodle
A Kerboodle highlight for this lesson is **Animation: Active transport**. Refer to the **Content map** on Kerboodle for a full list of resources and assessment.

B1.10 Exchanging materials

AQA spec link: 1.3.1 A single-celled organism has a relatively large surface area to volume ratio. This allows sufficient transport of molecules into and out of the cell to meet the needs of the organism.

Students should be able to explain how the small intestine and lungs in mammals, and the roots and leaves in plants, are adapted for exchanging materials.

In multicellular organisms the smaller surface area to volume ratio means surfaces and organ systems are specialised for exchanging materials.

This is to allow sufficient molecules to be transported into and out of cells for the organism's needs. The effectiveness of an exchange surface is increased by:

- having a large surface area
- a membrane that is thin, to provide a short diffusion path
- (in animals) having an efficient blood supply
- (in animals, for gaseous exchange) being ventilated.

MS 1c, 5c

Aiming for	Outcome	Checkpoint	
		Question	Activity
Aiming for GRADE 4	State the function of exchange surfaces in plants and animals.	2	Starter 1
	State that a single-celled organism has a relatively large surface area to volume ratio.		Starter 2, Main, Plenary 2
	Calculate the surface area to volume ratio of a cube.		Main, Plenary 1
Aiming for GRADE 6	Describe how the effectiveness of exchange surfaces is increased.	End of chapter 5	Main
	Use ideas about surface area to volume ratio to describe why multicellular organisms need exchange surfaces.	End of chapter 5	Starter 2, Main
	Calculate the surface area to volume ratio of a cylinder.		Main, Plenary 1
Aiming for GRADE 8	Link ideas about diffusion to explain how the adaptations of exchange surfaces increase their effectiveness.	3, End of chapter 5	Main
	Use ideas about surface area to explain the shape of a leaf.		Plenary 1
	Calculate the surface area to volume ratio of a sphere.		Main, Plenary 1, Plenary 2

Maths
Students calculate areas and volumes of 3D shapes: cubes, cylinders, and spheres (5C). They use these to work out surface area to volume ratios (1c). Students solve a mathematical problem by calculating the area of 2D shapes (5c).

Literacy
Students use correct scientific terminology to write a scientific explanation to describe how exchange surfaces are adapted.

Key words
ventilated, alveoli, stomata

22

B1 Cell structure and transport

Starter	Support/Extend	Resources
Types of exchange surface (10 min) Ask students to match the names of some exchange surfaces in animals and plants with their functions. Discuss why these organs are important in multicellular organisms and explain that as an organism gets bigger, the distance between the surface and the centre of the organism increases – so simple diffusion is not enough to exchange materials. **Exchange of materials** (5 min) Students match up statements about surface area to volume ratio and about factors affecting the effectiveness of an exchange surface.	**Extend:** Use the term surface area to volume ratio.	**Interactive:** Exchange of materials

Main	Support/Extend	Resources
Investigating surface area to volume ratios (40 min) Students calculate surface area to volume ratios for different 3D shapes (cubes, cylinders, and spheres). Modelling clay could be provided for students to make the shapes. They decide on the best shape for a single-celled organism and explain why. Students then use the student book to explain how an exchange surface is adapted to increase its effectiveness.	**Support:** Students work in pairs to make a cube. Supply them with the surface area of a cylinder and a sphere to go through the calculations as a class. **Extend:** Students work alone to create cubes, cylinders, and spheres and perform calculations. **Support:** Students explain how roots are adapted. **Extend:** Students explain how lungs are adapted. They should apply ideas about diffusion to explain how the adaptations work.	**Activity:** Investigating surface area to volume ratios

Plenary	Support/Extend	Resources
Surface area to volume ratio (10 min) Students calculate the difference in total surface area of one 10 cm × 10 cm × 10 cm cube versus ten 1 cm × 1 cm × 1 cm cubes. **Sailors' eyeballs** (5 min) Show the class an image of *Valonia ventricosa*, also known as bubble algae or sailors' eyeballs. Tell them that they are one of the largest single-celled organisms and can grow up to 5 cm in diameter. Ask students to write down why there is a limit to how big they can grow.	**Extend:** Ask students to calculate the surface area to volume ratio of the cell.	

Homework		
Students use their surface area calculations from the lesson to explain why exchange surfaces in plants and animals have adaptations to increase surface area.		

kerboodle
A Kerboodle highlight for this lesson is **Progress quiz: Cells and organisation 2**. Refer to the **Content map** on Kerboodle for a full list of resources and assessment.

B1 Cell structure and transport

Overview of B1 Cell structure and transport

In this chapter, students have learnt about microscopy and cells, and should be able to explain how the development of microscopy techniques, particularly electron microscopy, has enabled scientists to investigate the sub-cellular structures. Students should be able to differentiate between animal and plant cells, differentiate between eukaryotic and prokaryotic cells, and identify adaptations of specialised animal and plant cells. They should also be able to use the formula $\text{magnification} = \frac{\text{size of image}}{\text{size of real object}}$.

Students should also have learnt about the transport of material into and out of cells by diffusion, osmosis, and active transport. It is important that students understand that in diffusion, material moves down a concentration gradient (from an area of high concentration to an area of low concentration); with active transport material moves against a concentration gradient (from an area of low concentration to an area of high concentration); and that osmosis is the movement of water across a partially permeable membrane to reduce a concentration gradient.

When studying the processes for transferring material, students should also be able to explain the adaptations of exchange surfaces and link these to the processes of material transport.

Required practical

All students are expected to have carried out the required practicals

Practical	Topic
Use a light microscope to observe, draw and label a selection of plant and animal cells. A scale magnification must be included.	B1.2
Investigate the effect of a range of concentrations of salt or sugar solutions on the mass of plant tissue.	B1.8

MyMaths

You can find additional support for the maths skills covered in this chapter on **MyMaths**, including understanding orders of magnitude and rearranging equations.

kerboodle

For this chapter, the following assessments are available on Kerboodle:

B1 Checkpoint quiz: Cell structure and transport
B1 Progress quiz: Cell structure and transport 1
B1 Progress quiz: Cell structure and transport 2
B1 On your marks: Cell structure and transport
B1 Exam-style questions and mark scheme: Cell structure and transport

Checkpoint follow-up lesson

A student's route through this lesson can be determined using the Checkpoint assessment. Percentage pass marks are supplied in the Checkpoint teacher notes.

For each successive route through it is assumed that the student can perform to their current route as well as previous routes. For example, students working at Aiming for 6 are assumed to be secure in Aiming for 4 knowledge and understanding and working towards achieving all the learning objectives for Aiming for 6.

	Aiming for 4	**Aiming for 6**	**Aiming for 8**
Learning outcomes	Label the sub-cellular structures of animal cells, plant cells, and bacterial cells, including their functions.	Describe the functions of the sub-cellular structures in animal cells, plant cells, and bacterial cells.	Compare the different sub-cellular structures of animal cells, plant cells, and bacterial cells, and including their functions.
	List examples of specialised plant and animal cells.	Describe examples of specialised plant and animal cells.	Describe and explain the adaptations in specialised animal and plant cells.
	State how substances are moved by diffusion, osmosis, and active transport.	Describe how substances are moved by diffusion, osmosis, and active transport.	Explain how substances are moved by diffusion, osmosis, and active transport.
		List the different factors that affect the rate of diffusion.	Describe and explain the different factors that affect the rate of diffusion.
Starter	**Cells** (5 min) Show students pictures of animal cells, plant cells, and bacterial cells, including some examples of specialised cells. Ask students to identify which type of cell each image is showing. How do we know what these cells are and what they do? How are substances moved in and out of these cells?		
Differentiated checkpoint activity	The Aiming for 4 Checkpoint follow-up sheet provides a series of highly-structured questions to support students with revising the sub-cellular structures and the processes of transporting material in to and out of cells. Students may need a teacher explanation of the functions of the sub-cellular structures and access to student books. Before students complete question 2, you may wish to demonstrate some examples of diffusion, for example, spraying air freshener or coloured liquid in water.	The Aiming for 6 checkpoint follow-up sheet provides a series of questions to support students with revising sub-cellular structures and methods of material transport in cells. Students should be able to attempt the questions without a teacher introduction, but could watch the diffusion demonstration and may need access to the student book.	Students use the Aiming for 8 Checkpoint follow-up sheet to create a visual summary of the sub-cellular structures and their functions, and specialised cells. The follow-up sheet provides some guidance on what students should include, but no specifics. Students will need A3 paper to draw their visual summary on. They also analyse some experimental data from an investigation on osmosis. They will need access to a calculator.
	Kerboodle resource C1 Checkpoint follow up: Aiming for 4, C1 Checkpoint follow up: Aiming for 6, C1 Checkpoint follow up: Aiming for 8		
Plenary	**Cells revisited** (10 min) Reshow the pictures of cells from the starter. Can students now identify all of them and say how they are specialised? Give examples of material moving into and out of cells, for example, absorption of water, mineral ions by plant roots, absorption of oxygen in the lungs. Ask students to say if the material is exchanged by diffusion, osmosis, or active transport		
Progression	To progress, give students a list of examples of specialised cells. For each cell, ask students to work in pairs to describe how the cell is adapted for its function.	To progress, encourage students to produce a visual summary using their notes from the lesson. They should then review their summary with the Aiming for 8 visual summaries produced, adding any outstanding information.	To progress, show students pictures of unfamiliar specialised cells. Ask them to identify the adaptations of the cells and make suggestions of the function of the cells, justifying their choices.

B 2 Cell division
2.1 Cell division

AQA spec links: 1.2.1 The nucleus of a cell contains chromosomes made of DNA molecules. Each chromosome carries a large number of genes.

In body cells the chromosomes are normally found in pairs.

1.2.2 Cells divide in a series of stages called the cell cycle. Students should be able to describe the stages of the cell cycle, including mitosis.

During the cell cycle the genetic material is doubled and then divided into two identical cells.

Before a cell can divide it needs to grow and increase the number of sub-cellular structures such as ribosomes and mitochondria. The DNA replicates to form two copies of each chromosome.

In mitosis one set of chromosomes is pulled to each end of the cell and the nucleus divides.

Finally the cytoplasm and cell membranes divide to form two identical cells.

Students need to understand the three overall stages of the cell cycle but do not need to know the different phases of the mitosis stage.

Cell division by mitosis is important in the growth and development of multicellular organisms.

Students should be able to recognise and describe situations in given contexts where mitosis is occurring.

WS 1.2

Aiming for	Outcome	Checkpoint	
		Question	Activity
Aiming for GRADE 4	State that human body cells have 46 chromosomes and gametes have 23.		Main 1
	State that mitosis is a stage in cell division.	2, End of chapter 2	Starter 2, Main 2, Plenary 1, Homework
	State the meaning of most of the key words – mitosis, chromosomes, gene, gametes.	1	Starter 1, Main 1, Main 2, Plenary 1
Aiming for GRADE 6	Explain why chromosomes in body cells are normally found in pairs.		Main 1
	Describe situations where mitosis is occurring.	3, 4	Main 2, Plenary 1, Homework
	Use the key words to describe the process of mitosis.	2	Main 2
Aiming for GRADE 8	Explain why genetic material must be doubled during mitosis.	3	Starter 2, Plenary 2
	Explain in detail what happens at each stage of the cell cycle.	2	Main 2
	Use the key words to write detailed explanations of why mitosis is an important process in living things and how characteristics are inherited.	3	Main 1, Main 2

■ B2 Cell division

Maths	Literacy	Key words
In Plenary 2 students consider exponential growth to calculate how long it takes for one cell to form a group of 64 cells.	Many new key words are introduced in this lesson. Students carry out activities where they consider the meanings of the words, use information from the student book to find out meanings, and use the key words in context to answer questions and write explanations.	cell cycle, mitosis

Practical

Title	Observing mitosis
Equipment	light microscopes, prepared slides showing cells carrying out mitosis
Overview of method	Students use light microscopes to observe prepared slides showing mitosis.
Safety considerations	Glass slides are fragile. Take care not to break them with the objective lens of the microscope.

Starter	Support/Extend	Resources
Cell key words (10 min) Bump up your grade sheet where students review their understanding from KS3 of the the key words nucleus, gene, DNA, and chromosome and develop their definitions. They are also introduced to the key word mitosis.	**Support:** Allow students to work in pairs or small groups and pool their ideas.	**Bump up your grade:** Cell key words
Cell division (10 min) Draw an image representing a single zygote (fertilised egg) on the board. Ask students to use what they recall from KS3 to draw images to show the stages before and after the egg is fertilised. Discuss their ideas, drawing out the process of fertilisation before and cell division after. Introduce the key word mitosis as a stage of cell division.	**Extend:** Ask students to explain why genetic material inside the zygote must be doubled during mitosis.	

Main	Support/Extend	Resources
Chromosomes (10 min) Refer students to student book section *The information in the cells*. Ask students questions about the numbers of chromosomes in body cells and gametes, and why they are found in pairs in body cells.	**Extend:** Ask students to explain why people look a bit like both of their parents.	
Observing mitosis (20 min) Show students a diagram of the cell cycle. Ask them to estimate the percentage of time involved in each of the three stages, calculate how long the interphase stage would take if the whole cycle took 24 hours, and suggest why the interphase stage is the longest.	**Extend:** Students complete an explanation of why mitosis is important in living organisms.	**Practical:** Observing mitosis
Students then complete the practical where they use light microscopes to observe prepared slides showing mitosis. Ask them to spot cells at different stages and draw examples. They can use Figure 3 from the student book to help them.		

Plenary	Support/Extend	Resources
Mitosis (10 min) Students use the interactive to match the key words from this lesson to their meanings and then carry out a cloze exercise about mitosis.	**Extend:** Tell students that the cells of some species of fly can divide every 8 minutes. Ask them to suggest why it is so much quicker than in human cells (flies have fewer chromosomes)	**Interactive:** Mitosis
Cell cycle length (5 min) Tell the class that, on average, human cells take 24 hours to divide. Ask them to calculate how long it takes for one cell to form a group of 64 cells.		

Homework		
Students produce a poster on mitosis, using an example in their explanations.	**Extend:** Encourage students to use an example such as the gecko, which can regenerate its tail.	

kerboodle
A Kerboodle highlight for this lesson is **Go further: Mitosis**. Refer to the **Content map** on Kerboodle for a full list of resources and assessment.

B2.2 Growth and differentiation

AQA spec links: 1.1.4 Students should be able to explain the importance of cell differentiation.

As an organism develops, cells differentiate to form different types of cells.

- Most types of animal cell differentiate at an early stage.
- Many types of plant cells retain the ability to differentiate throughout life.

In mature animals, cell division is mainly restricted to repair and replacement. As a cell differentiates it acquires different sub-cellular structures to enable it to carry out a certain function. It has become a specialised cell.

1.2.3 Stem cells from meristems in plants can be used to produce clones of plants quickly and economically:

- Rare species can be cloned to protect from extinction.
- Crop plants with special features such as disease resistance can be cloned to produce large numbers of identical plants for farmers.

Aiming for	Outcome	Checkpoint	
		Question	Activity
Aiming for GRADE 4 ↓	Define the terms growth and differentiation.	1	Starter 1, Plenary 1
	State why plant clones are genetically identical to each other.		Main
	Attempt to clone a plant by using apparatus correctly.		Main
Aiming for GRADE 6 ↓	Describe the importance of cell differentiation in multicellular organisms.	1	Plenary 1
	Explain how using tissue culture creates a clone of a plant.		Main
	Attempt to clone a plant by using apparatus correctly and following safety rules.		Main
Aiming for GRADE 8 ↓	Compare and contrast differentiation in plants and animals.	2	Starter 2, Plenary 2
	Explain why it is easier to clone a plant than an animal.	4	Main
	Explain and carry out a practical accurately and safely in order to successfully clone a plant.		Main

Maths
Students convert a number from standard form. Throughout the lesson they consider how an increase in the number of cells causes growth of an organism.

Literacy
Students use key words to create a flow diagram to show human growth. They use information from the student book to design a storyboard for an animation and also follow instructions to accurately carry out a practical procedure.

Key words
differentiation, stem cell, cloning

Practical

Title	Cauliflower cloning
Equipment	cauliflower florets, 100 cm³ sterile distilled water, 70% ethanol and paper towel (for wiping surfaces), 0.5% solution sodium dichloroisocyanurate (SDICN) in small glass jar with cap (for sterilising forceps), 10 ml 0.5% SDICN solution in universal bottle (28 ml glass bottle) with screw cap, test tubes containing 2–3 cm³ of plant tissue growth medium, Diluvials or small sterilised glass jars containing medium (MS, 20 g/l sucrose, 2.5 mg/l Kinetin, 0.032% SDICN), white ceramic tiles or chopping board, forceps, scalpel, Petri dish

B2 Cell division

Overview of method	Students place forceps in a jar of sterilising solution and clean the bench with ethanol. They place a small floret of cauliflower into a Petri dish and cut lengthways into small 3–5 mm^3 explants. These are placed in a jar of SDICN to sterilise for 15 minutes. The explants are placed in a test tube of agar plant growth medium and incubated for around 10 days.
Safety considerations	Wear eye protection. Sodium dichloroisocyanurate (SDICN) is toxic and a bleach that removes colour from clothing. Wear a lab coat if they are available. Wear gloves when handling bottles containing the sterilant as caps may leak. Do not inhale the chlorine vapours from the bleach. Be careful when handling sharp instruments. Ethanol is highly flammable and harmful, keep away from naked flames.

Starter	Support/Extend	Resources
Human life (10 min) Show students an image of an embryo containing a few cells and an image of a very old person. Ask them to design a flow chart to show what happens to the cells of a person as they grow older. Discuss their ideas and explain that in development from an embryo to an adult, cell division is used for growth (increase in size) as well as for repair and replacement. In adults, it is mainly just used for repair and replacement. Introduce the word growth to mean a permanent increase in size.	**Support:** Give students words to use: (e.g., mitosis, cell division, growth, repair, replacement, cell death). **Extend:** Tell students that a human adult has around 3.72×10^{12} cells. Ask them to convert this from standard form to see how many zeros this contains!	
Growth in plants and animals (5 min) Show the class an image of a tall tree and a human. Ask them to discuss in pairs how the growth of a plant and a human are the same and how they are different. Make sure students understand that in plants growth is due to cell elongation and division, whereas in humans it is just cell division.	**Support:** Draw diagrams to show the difference between cell elongation and cell division.	

Main	Support/Extend	Resources
Cauliflower cloning (40 min) Tell the class that plant cells contain undifferentiated cells in tissues called meristems. They will follow a procedure to clone a new cauliflower plant using these cells. Students work in pairs and follow the practical sheet to carry out the task. They must pay careful attention to working accurately and safely in order to ensure cloning is successful. Students then answer questions about differentiation and cloning in plants.	**Support:** Show students a video of the procedure by doing an Internet search using 'video demo - cauliflower cloning'.	**Practical:** Cauliflower cloning

Plenary	Support/Extend	Resources
Differentiation (10 min) Ask students to return to the flow chart they designed in Starter 1 and add in information about where differentiation occurs and what it is used for.		
Cell differentiation (5 min) Interactive where students select the correct word for each gap in a paragraph about cell differentiation and then sort statements into plant and animal cell groups.		**Interactive:** Cell differentiation

Homework		
Students design an animation to explain what a stem cell is, and how they differentiate to form specialised cells.		

kerboodle

A Kerboodle highlight for this lesson is **Homework: Cell division**. Refer to the **Content map** on Kerboodle for a full list of resources and assessment.

B2.3 Stem cells

AQA spec link: 1.2.3 stem cell is an undifferentiated cell of an organism which is capable of giving rise to many more cells of the same type, and from which certain other cells can arise from differentiation.

Students should be able to describe the function of stem cells in embryos, in adult animals and in the meristems in plants.

Stem cells from human embryos can be cloned and made to differentiate into most different types of human cells.

Stem cells from adult bone marrow can form many types of cells including blood cells.

Meristem tissue in plants can differentiate into any type of plant cell, throughout the life of the plant.

Knowledge and understanding of stem cell techniques are not required.

Treatment with stem cells may be able to help conditions such as diabetes and paralysis.

In therapeutic cloning an embryo is produced with the same genes as the patient. Stem cells from the embryo are not rejected by the patient's body so they may be used for medical treatment.

The use of stem cells has potential risks such as transfer of viral infection, and some people have ethical or religious objections.

Stem cells from meristems in plants can be used to produce clones of plants quickly and economically.

- Rare species can be cloned to protect from extinction.
- Crop plants with special features such as disease resistance can be cloned to produce large numbers of identical plants for farmers.

Aiming for	Outcome	Checkpoint	
		Question	Activity
Aiming for GRADE 4 ↓	State that a stem cell is a cell that is not differentiated.	1, End of chapter 3	Starter 1, Main 1
	State that plant stem cells can be used to create clones.		Starter 2, Main 1, Plenary 2
	State ways in which stem cells can be used to treat medical conditions.		Main 2, Plenary 1
Aiming for GRADE 6 ↓	Describe differences between embryonic and adult stem cells.	1	Main 1
	Explain why plant clones are produced in agriculture.	3, End of chapter 4	Starter 2, Main 1
	Describe how stem cells can be used to treat medical conditions.	2, End of chapter 5	Main 2, Plenary 1
Aiming for GRADE 8 ↓	Explain why embryonic stem cells are particularly useful for treating medical conditions.		Main, Homework
	Explain how stem cells can be used to treat medical conditions.	End of chapter 5	Main 2, Plenary 1

B2 Cell division

Maths
Students can include information in the form of data in their article on stem cells.

Literacy
Students research information from websites and write a scientific article on stem cells. They consider what makes a good article and use a checklist to plan their work.

Key words
zygote, embryonic stem cells, adult stem cells

Starter	Support/Extend	Resources
Differentiation (5 min) Ask students to write down a definition of the term differentiation. Gather ideas to come to an agreed meaning and write this on the board. Discuss why cells differentiate and remind students that undifferentiated cells are known as stem cells. **Plant copies** (10 min) Remind students of the practical they did in Topic B2.2 where they cloned a cauliflower (this is an ideal opportunity to check on how the practical is doing). Ask students to discuss in pairs reasons why people might want to clone plants. Gather together the ideas as a class.	**Extend:** Ask students to come up with examples of when cells differentiate (e.g., during embryo development or when new blood cells form in the bone marrow). **Support:** Towards the end of the discussion allow pairs to refer to information in the student book.	

Main	Support/Extend	Resources
Stem cells (15 min) Remind students about how embryonic stem cells have the potential to differentiate into any type of cell. Students then use information from the student book to help them answer questions about stem cells. **Writing scientifically with stem cells** (25 min) Provide students with example articles on stem cells. Alternatively, provide students with short examples of science articles printed from websites or cut out from magazines. Ask them to discuss in pairs what they think about the articles (Did they capture their attention and hold it? Did they explain the science well? Did they leave them wanting to know more?). Go through with the class the main points on how to write a science article. Students then research how stem cells are used to help medical conditions and use the information to write their own article on stem cells. This activity can be extended to a whole lesson.	**Support:** Provide students with a writing frame to help them organise their article. **Extend:** Students should research how stem cells could be used in the future.	**Activity:** Writing scientifically with stem cells

Plenary	Support/Extend	Resources
Peer assessment (10 min) Students use the checklist on the activity sheet to peer assess the articles written in Main 2 and give useful feedback. **Stem cells** (10 min) Interactive here students match the correct words to statements and then select words to fill in the gaps in a paragraph about stem cells.		**Interactive:** Stem cells

Homework		
In preparation for the next lesson, ask students to use the WebQuest to do some further research and find out at least one argument against using embryonic stem cells in medical research and treatments.		**WebQuest:** Embryonic stem cell research

kerboodle
A Kerboodle highlight for this lesson is **Go further: Stem cells in medical developments**. Refer to the **Content map** on Kerboodle for a full list of resources and assessment.

B2.4 Stem cell dilemmas

AQA spec link: 3.1.2 stem cell is an undifferentiated cell of an organism which is capable of giving rise to many more cells of the same type, and from which certain other cells can arise from differentiation.

Students should be able to describe the function of stem cells in embryos, in adult animals and in the meristems in plants.

Stem cells from human embryos can be cloned and made to differentiate into most different types of human cells.

Stem cells from adult bone marrow can form many types of cells including blood cells.

Meristem tissue in plants can differentiate into any type of plant cell, throughout the life of the plant.

Knowledge and understanding of stem cell techniques are not required.

Treatment with stem cells may be able to help conditions such as diabetes and paralysis.

In therapeutic cloning an embryo is produced with the same genes as the patient. Stem cells from the embryo are not rejected by the patient's body so they may be used for medical treatment.

The use of stem cells has potential risks such as transfer of viral infection, and some people have ethical or religious objections.

Stem cells from meristems in plants can be used to produce clones of plants quickly and economically.

- Rare species can be cloned to protect from extinction.
- Crop plants with special features such as disease resistance can be cloned to produce large numbers of identical plants for farmers.

Aiming for	Outcome	Checkpoint	
		Question	Activity
Aiming for GRADE 4 ↓	List some arguments for and against the use of stem cells.	2, End of chapter 5	Starter 1, Main, Plenary 1
	Verbally communicate simple ideas during a group discussion.		Starter 2, Main
Aiming for GRADE 6 ↓	Describe what therapeutic cloning can be used for.	1, End of chapter 5, 6	Main
	Explain the reasons for ethical and religious objections to use of stem cells in medicine.	2, 3, End of chapter 5	Main
	Verbally communicate well-constructed arguments.		Starter 2, Main
Aiming for GRADE 8 ↓	Explain the process of therapeutic cloning.		Main
	Evaluate the use of stem cells in medicine.	2, 3, 4, End of chapter 5	Starter 1, Main
	Clearly communicate strong, well-researched arguments in a persuasive manner.		Starter 2, Main

Maths
When reading their role-play viewpoint in the Main activity, students may be presented with evidence in the form of data and statistics that they need to interpret.

Literacy
Students summarise information to write a short 30-second presentation. They use persuasive language and communicate well to put across their viewpoint in a group discussion.

Key word
therapeutic cloning

B2 Cell division

Starter	Support/Extend	Resources
Stem cell decision (10 min) Tell students to imagine that a close friend or family member has been diagnosed with diabetes and has to inject themselves with insulin every day for the rest of their lives. There is a new treatment available using stem cells grown from embryos. Would they advise them to use the treatment? Ask the class to discuss in small groups what information they would need to find out before they could make a decision. Listen to ideas from the class and discuss that there are many possible risks to the treatment and these have to be weighed up alongside possible benefits. Also, some students may mention religious or ethical objections to using embryonic stem cells. **Ethical dilemmas** (5 min) Read out a series of statements: • Organ transplants using donated organs from people who have died. • Organ transplants from living donors. • Taking the morning-after pill. • Using contraception. • Using unwanted embryos for medical research (they will be destroyed after use). • Testing new medical treatments on healthy volunteers. • Testing new medical treatments on animals. After each statement ask students to rate out of 5 how they feel about it, with 1 being very comfortable and 5 being totally against it. Discuss individual views and elicit that different people have different viewpoints for different reasons. Before a decision can be made these have to be taken into account.	**Support:** Write the statements on cards and ask students to order them instead.	

Main	Support/Extend	Resources
Viewpoints (40 min) Assign students to the different roles shown on the activity sheet and ask them to read through their character's thoughts on the use of stem cells and prepare a 60-second speech arguing their character's viewpoint. Ask students to form groups containing all the roles and to each present their viewpoint. As a class, ask groups for the main points they found out during their discussion and record these on the board. As a class, discuss all of the points they have found, then have students individually write their own conclusions on the ethics of stem cell research.	**Extend:** Allow students to do extra research on the Internet to find further information to support their viewpoint.	**Activity:** Viewpoints

Plenary	Support/Extend	Resources
The future of stem cell research (10 min) Bump up your grade worksheet where students review the process of therapeutic cloning and the ethical difficulties involved, evaluating the potential benefits and possible drawbacks. **Stem cell dilemmas** (5 min) Interactive here students match the correct words to statements and then select words to fill in the gaps in a paragraph about stem cells.		**Bump up your grade:** The future of stem cell research **Interactive:** Stem cell dilemmas

Homework		
Students write a short report on whether they think scientists should carry on with stem cell research.	**Extend:** Students should discuss their opinion with reference to one condition for which stem cell therapy has been used as a treatment.	

kerboodle
A Kerboodle highlight for this lesson is **Literacy skills: Constructing arguments.** Refer to the **Content map** on Kerboodle for a full list of resources and assessment.

B2 Cell division

Overview of B2 Cell division

In this chapter, students have learnt about the process of cell division and should be able to describe the three overall stages of the cell cycle. Students should have an understanding of mitosis as a stage within the cell cycle, but do not need to know about the different phases of the mitosis stage. They should be able to state the genetic material in the nucleus is doubled *before* the cell divides into two.

Along with cell division, students have also studied cell differentiation, and students should be able to make connections between cell differentiation and the specialised cells and adaptations they studied in *Chapter B1 Cell structure and transport*.

Students should also have learnt about stem cells as an undifferentiated cell that has the potential to become a specialised cell within an organisms. Students should be able to describe some potential uses of stem cells, as well as the disadvantages and objections to the use of stem cells, particularly in relation to medical treatments.

MyMaths

You can find additional support for the maths skills covered in this chapter on **MyMaths**, including simple calculations.

kerboodle

For this chapter, the following assessments are available on Kerboodle:

B2 Checkpoint quiz: Cell division
B2 Progress quiz: Cell division 1
B2 Progress quiz: Cell division 2
B2 On your marks: Cell division
B2 Exam-style questions and mark scheme: Cell division

Checkpoint follow-up lesson

A student's route through this lesson can be determined using the Checkpoint assessment. Percentage pass marks are supplied in the Checkpoint teacher notes.

For each successive route through it is assumed that the student can perform to their current route as well as previous routes. For example, students working at Aiming for 6 are assumed to be secure in Aiming for 4 knowledge and understanding and working towards achieving all the learning outcomes for Aiming for 6.

	Aiming for 4	**Aiming for 6**	**Aiming for 8**
Learning outcomes	State what mitosis is needed for.	Describe cell division by mitosis.	Describe the three stages of cell division.
	State what occurs at each stage of the cell cycle.	Describe the differences between differentiation in animal cells and plant cells.	Compare the differences between differentiation in animal cells and plant cells.
	State what a stem cell is and some arguments for and against stem cell research.	State arguments for and against stem cell research.	Discuss arguments for and against stem cell research.
Starter	**Counting cells (10 min)** Ask students that if one cell takes eight hours to divide into two separate cells, how many cells would there be after three days? (256) Work as a class to come up with the answer.		
Differentiated checkpoint activity	The Aiming for 4 Checkpoint follow-up sheet provides a series of highly-structured The Aiming for 4 Checkpoint follow-up sheet provides a series of highly-structured tasks to support students with revising cell division and stem cells. Students complete a cut-and-stick activity to describe the cell cycle, sort statements according to whether they describe stem cells or differentiated cells, and review a passage on stem cell research to identify arguments for and against stemm cell research. Students may need a teacher-led discussion on what stem cells are before attempting the second activity.	The Aiming for 6 checkpoint follow-up sheet provides a series of tasks to support students with revising cell division and stem cells. Students draw a flow chart of the cell cycle, complete a cut-and-stick activity to identify features of cell differentiation in plants and animals, and to summrise the arguments for and against stem cell research. Students should be able to attempt the questions without a teacher introduction, but could work in pairs for the third activity.	Students use the Aiming for 8 Checkpoint follow-up sheet to create a flow chart to summarise the cell cycle, contrsuct a table to show the differences between differentiation in animal and plant cells, and to hold a debate on stem cell research. The follow-up sheet provides some guidance on what students should include, but no specifics.
	Kerboodle resource B2 Checkpoint follow up: Aiming for 4, B2 Checkpoint follow up: Aiming for 6, B2 Checkpoint follow up: Aiming for 8		
Plenary	**Stem cells (5 min)** Ask students to share the arguments for and against stem cells that they have identified or come up with. Students should add to their notes any that they missed.		
Progression	To progress, students should use their highlighting of the passage on stem cells to write a brief conclusion on whether they think stem cell research should be carried out or not.	To progress, students should use their discussions on stem cells to write a conclusion on whether they think stem cell research should be carried out or not.	To progress, students could be given access to the Internet to carry out further research on the uses of stem cells.

B 3 Organisation and the digestive system
3.1 Tissues and organs

AQA spec link: 2.1 Cells are the basic building blocks of all living organisms.

A tissue is a group of cells with a similar structure and function.

Organs are aggregations of tissues performing specific functions.

Organs are organised into organ systems, which work together to form organisms.

MS 1c, 2h

Aiming for	Outcome	Checkpoint	
		Question	Activity
Aiming for GRADE 4	State examples of cells, tissues, organs, and organ systems.	2	Starter 2, Main 1, Main 2, Plenary 1, Plenary 2, Homework
	Name organs found in a given organ system.		Starter 2, Main 2
	Order cells, tissues, organs, and organ systems according to their relative sizes.		Starter 1, Plenary 2
Aiming for GRADE 6	Define the terms tissue, organ, and organ system.	1, End of chapter 1	Main 1, Main 2
	Describe the function of certain organs and organ systems.		Starter 2, Main 2
	Identify tissues that make up organs.		Main 1, Plenary 2
Aiming for GRADE 8	Relate levels of organisation to familiar organ systems in order to give examples of cells, tissues, and organs.		Starter 1
	Explain why the cells of multicellular organisms are organised into tissues, organs, and organ systems.		Homework
	Suggest the function of glandular, epithelial, and muscular tissue in organs.	3, End of chapter 1	Main 1, Plenary 2

Maths
Students consider the size and scale of cells, tissues, organs, and systems (2h).

Literacy
Students use books and/or the Internet to research information about the tissues found in organs.

Key words
differentiate, tissue, organ, pancreas, organ systems

■ B3 Organisation and the digestive system

Starter	Support/Extend	Resources
Organising an organism (10 min) Ask students to rearrange the key words organ, tissue, organism, cell, and organ system into an order of their choosing. Then remind students of the hierarchy of organisation, using these key words. **Organ system** (5 min) Show the students an image of the circulatory system. Ask them to describe its function and give an example of an organ, a tissue, and a cell that it contains. Introduce how cells are arranged into tissues, and tissues into organs.	**Extend:** Ask students to write an example from the digestive system for each level.	

Main	Support/Extend	Resources
Tissue research (20 min) Ask students to work in groups of four. Each student uses books and/or the Internet to research which tissues are present in one of the following organs: heart, stomach, liver, and pancreas. They also write down the function of each tissue in the organ.	**Support:** Focus on the stomach and allow students to use the student book to find the information. **Extend:** Before they research, encourage students to suggest the functions of the different tissues in their organ based on what they know about its function.	
Happy organ systems (20 min) Supply each group of four students with a set of cards, each card showing a different organ. Students shuffle all of the cards together then deal them out evenly between the members of the group. Each student has to collect the three organ cards needed to make up an organ system. Students take it in turns to ask another student for an organ. If they have the organ in their hand, they have to give it to the asker and the asker gets to ask for another organ. If they don't have it in their hand then that student gets to ask for an organ. Once a student has collected an entire organ system, they put that group to the side. Once all the organ systems have been collected, students then play with for whole organ systems. Whichever student collects all of the organ systems wins. The organ systems to include are nervous (brain, eyes, spinal cord), digestive (stomach, pancreas, oesophagus), excretory (kidneys, bladder, liver), respiratory (lungs, trachea, bronchi), female reproductive (ovary, uterus, vagina), male reproductive (penis, testes, scrotum), and circulatory (heart, arteries, veins).	**Support:** Rather than playing the game, ask students to simply group their organ cards into organ systems. **Extend:** Include the function of the organ on the card as well, then students have to correctly identify the function when asking for an organ.	**Activity:** Happy organ systems

Plenary	Support/Extend	Resources
How organisms are made (10 min) Students use the interactive to match key words from the lesson with their definition. They then sort terms according to whether they are tissues, organs, or organ systems. **Mystery organ** (5 min) Show the students an image of the skin in cross-section. Ask them to identify different types of tissue and their functions (e.g., epithelial as a barrier, glandular to produce sweat, muscular – smooth – to raise hairs and facilitate vasoconstriction).		**Interactive:** How organisms are made

Homework		
Students choose one organ system from the lesson. They list all of the tissues and organs they know from this organ system, including their functions.	**Extend:** Ask students to suggest why organisms are organised into tissues, organs, and organ systems, using their chosen examples in their explanations.	

kerboodle

A Kerboodle highlight for this lesson is **Bump up your grade: Organising an organism**. Refer to the **Content map** on Kerboodle for a full list of resources and assessment.

B3.2 The human digestive system

AQA spec link: 2.2.1 This section assumes knowledge of the digestive system studied in Key Stage 3 science.

The digestive system is an example of an organ system in which several organs work together to digest and absorb food.

Aiming for	Outcome	Checkpoint	
		Question	Activity
Aiming for GRADE 4	Identify some of the organs of the digestive system.	End of chapter 1	Starter 1, Main, Plenary 1,
	State the function of some of the organs of the digestive system.	1	Main, Plenary 1
	State simply what happens to food during digestion.		Starter 1, Main, Plenary 1, Homework
Aiming for GRADE 6	Name all of the organs of the digestive system.		Main, Plenary 1, Homework
	Describe the functions of the organs of the digestive system.	1	Main, Plenary 1
	Summarise the process of digestion.	3	Starter 1, Main, Plenary 1, Homework
Aiming for GRADE 8	Link the process of digestion to other processes in the body in order to explain its function.		Plenary 2, Homework
	Explain in detail how the small intestine is adapted to its function.		Main
	Explain in detail what happens to food during digestion.		Main, Homework

Maths
Students use standard form and order of magnitude to calculate the length of the digestive system.

Literacy
Students interpret command words to correctly answer exam-style questions. They also produce a flow chart to summarise the process of digestion.

Key words
digestive system, pancreas, enzymes

B3 Organisation and the digestive system

Starter	Support/Extend	Resources
What happens to my food? (10 min) Ask students to draw an annotated sketch to show what they know already about what happens to food once it has been eaten. Take time to discuss prior knowledge and correct any possible misconceptions at this stage. **How long?** (5 min) Tell the students that the diameter of an average human cell is 1×10^{-6} m. The human digestive system of an adult man is around 9 million times or 6 orders of magnitude longer than this. Ask them to work out its length (9 m).	**Support:** Supply students with words they can use, such as, digestion, oesophagus, stomach, intestines, enzymes. **Extend:** Give the size of the cell as 1 μm.	

Main	Support/Extend	Resources
The digestive system (40 min) Provide students with an unlabelled diagram of the human digestive system. Students label the diagram and state the function of each organ. They can use Figure 1 in the student book to help them. Then ask the students to use the information in the student book to find one adaptation of the pancreas. Discuss that it produces enzymes that help break down the food. Ask students to further label their diagram with other adaptations of the digestive organs that help them to carry out their function. Check the answers as a class or use peer assessment.	**Extend:** Make sure students have understood the adaptations of the small intestine to its function.	**Activity:** The digestive system

Plenary	Support/Extend	Resources
Digestion (10 min) Students use the interactive to label the part of the digestive system. They then match the organs of the digestive system with their function. **Digestion's place in the body** (5 min) Read out some other processes that occur in the human body, for example, respiration or excretion. Ask students to suggest how these processes are dependent on the digestive system.	**Support:** Check that students have the correct order before moving on to the functions. **Support:** Describe what happens during each process.	**Interactive:** Digestion

Homework		
Students produce a flow chart that summarises the process of digestion.	**Extend:** Students should link their flow chart of digestion to other processes in the human body.	

kerboodle

A Kerboodle highlight for this lesson is **Homework: Animal organs**. Refer to the **Content map** on Kerboodle for a full list of resources and assessment.

B3.3 The chemistry of food

AQA spec link: 2.2.1 Carbohydrases break down carbohydrates to simple sugars. Proteases break down proteins to amino acids.

Lipases break down lipids (fats) to glycerol and fatty acids. The products of digestion are used to build new carbohydrates, lipids, and proteins. Some glucose is used in respiration.

Required practical: Use qualitative reagents to test for a range of carbohydrates, lipids, and proteins.

To include: Benedict's test for sugars; iodine test for starch; and Biuret reagent for protein.

MS 1c

Aiming for	Outcome	Checkpoint	
		Question	Activity
Aiming for GRADE 4	Recall that food contains the molecules carbohydrates, lipids (fats), and proteins.	End of chapter 2	Starter 1, Starter 2, Main
	State the function of each food molecule in the diet.	1, 2, 4, 5 End of chapter 2	Main, Plenary 1
	Carry out a food test and record results in a table.	3, End of chapter 3	Main
Aiming for GRADE 6	Describe the structure of simple sugars, starch, lipids, and proteins.	1, 2, 4, 5, End of chapter 2	Main, Homework
	Carry out multiple food tests in an organised manner.	3, End of chapter 3, 4	Main
	Design a results table to clearly record results from food tests.		Main
Aiming for GRADE 8	Explain which food molecules are polymers.		Main, Homework
	Apply knowledge of the function of food molecules in the body to give diet advice.		Plenary 2
	Suggest what a food contains using results from food tests, evaluating the observed data collected		Main

Maths
Students can calculate the percentage of each nutrient in foods using the nutritional information on the packaging (1c).

Literacy
Students use information on various websites to research information about food molecules during the Webquest. They follow instructions to carry out food tests.

Key words
carbohydrates, simple sugars, lipids, fatty acids, glycerol, proteins, amino acids, denatured

Required practical

Title	Food tests
Equipment	a range of food items, test tubes, test-tube rack, spotting tile, iodine solution, Benedict's solution, Biuret solution or dilute sodium hydroxide solution and copper sulfate solution, disposable pipettes, filter paper, water bath or beakers and a supply of hot water, sticky labels or waterproof pen
Overview of method	Test for starch: Add a few drops of iodine to the food on the spotting tile. Test for sugars: Place a food in a test tube with Benedict's solution and warm in water bath. Test for protein: Place food in test tube with 1 cm^3 of Biuret solution. Alternatively add 1 cm^3 of sodium hydroxide solution and then add a few drops of copper sulfate solution. Test for fats: Place a small amount of the food into a test tube. Add a few drops of ethanol to the solution. Shake the test tube and leave for one minute. Pour the solution into a test tube of water.

■ B3 Organisation and the digestive system

Safety considerations	Be aware of students with food allergies. Biuret solution and sodium hydroxide are corrosive. Wear chemical splash-proof eye protection. Iodine is harmful, avoid contact with skin. Ethanol is highly flammable and harmful, keep away from naked flames.

Starter	Support/Extend	Resources
Nutrient names (10 min) Ask students to write down individually a list of nutrients found in food. They then compare lists in small groups before a teacher-led group discussion on the function of each nutrient. **Foods** (5 min) Show the class some images of food or food packaging and ask them what nutrients each food is a good source of. Discuss that foods contain the nutrients carbohydrates (which are simple sugars or complex carbohydrates), proteins, and lipids (fats).	**Extend:** Ask students to study the food packaging and calculate the percentage of each nutrient in the food using the nutritional information.	

Main	Support/Extend	Resources
Food tests (40 min) Introduce students to the structure of carbohydrates, proteins, and lipids, and how each nutrient functions within the body. Students then conduct food tests on samples of food and record their results. They analyse their results to identify different nutrients present in each food source.	**Support:** Students work in pairs and carry out one test on a sample of food. Ask pairs to share their results. **Support:** Supply students with a suitable results table. **Extend:** Students complete the extension activity where they plot calibration curves to find the concentration of glucose or starch in unknown foods.	**Required practical:** Food tests **Extension:** Quantitative use of food tests

Plenary	Support/Extend	Resources
Food molecules (5 min) Students use the interactive to match the nutrient to its function. They then sort uses of nutrients into the correct categories. **Diet advice** (10 min) Ask students to work in groups. Give each group a different person who has a specific dietary need: I need to lose mass. I want to start body-building. I am running a marathon. I am pregnant. Ask groups to advise the person on how to modify their diet. Groups should feed back their advice with their reasoning.	**Extend:** Ask students to work alone and choose which person they wish to help.	**Interactive:** Food molecules

Homework		
Students complete the WebQuest to research the structure of food molecules and their function in the body. They use this information to produce a healthy eating plan for students. Alternatively, students produce a table summarising the structure and function of the nutrients they have studied this lesson.	**Extend:** Ask students to explain which of the food molecules are polymers.	**WebQuest:** Food nutrients and their functions

kerboodle

A Kerboodle highlight for this lesson is **Maths skills: Proportions and ratios of a balanced diet**. Refer to the **Content map** on Kerboodle for a full list of resources and assessment.

B3.4 Catalysts and enzymes

AQA spec links: 2.2.1 Students should be able to relate knowledge of enzymes to metabolism.

Students should be able to carry out rate calculations for chemical reactions.

Enzymes catalyse specific reactions in living organisms due to the shape of their active site.

Students should be able to use the 'lock and key theory' as a simplified model to explain enzyme action.

4.2.3 Students should be able to explain the importance of sugars, amino acids, fatty acids, and glycerol in the synthesis and breakdown of carbohydrates, proteins, and lipids.

Metabolism is the sum of all the reactions in a cell or the body.

The energy transferred by respiration in cells is used by the organism for the continual enzyme controlled processes of metabolism that synthesise new molecules.

Aiming for	Outcome	Checkpoint	
		Question	Activity
Aiming for GRADE 4	Recall that enzymes are proteins that are biological catalysts.	1, 2	Starter 2, Main, Plenary 1, Plenary 2
	State one function of enzymes inside the body.		Main, Plenary 2
	State the independent variable in a given investigation.		Main
Aiming for GRADE 6	Describe how enzymes are used in digestion.	3	Main, Plenary 2
	Use the lock and key theory to explain why the shape of an enzyme is vital for it to function.	1	Main, Plenary 2, Homework
	Identify the key variables in a given investigation.		Main
Aiming for GRADE 8	Explain how enzymes speed up reactions.	2	Main, Homework
	Explain how enzymes control metabolism.	3, End of chapter 4	Main
	Plan an experiment to investigate how different catalysts affect the rate of a reaction.		Main

Maths
Students consider rates of reactions. They plan an investigation to compare the amount of product formed over a set period of time.

Literacy
Students design an animation, including a voiceover, to explain enzyme reactions.

Key words
catalysts, active site, metabolism

Practical

Title	Breaking down hydrogen peroxide
Equipment	dilute hydrogen peroxide, pureed raw potato (acts as source of catalase – an organic catalyst), pureed boiled potato, manganese(IV) oxide (an inorganic catalyst), washing-up liquid, dropping pipette × 1 per group, spatulas × 2 per group, stopwatch, test tubes × 3 per group, test-tube rack

■ B3 Organisation and the digestive system

Overview of method	Add approximately 2 cm depth of hydrogen peroxide to three test tubes. Using the dropping pipette, add a few drops of washing-up liquid to each tube. Add a spatula of pureed potato to one test tube and start the stopwatch. When the bubbles reach the top of the test tube (or a pre-determined mark), stop the stopwatch. Add a spatula of pureed boiled potato to another test tube and start the stopwatch. When the bubbles reach the top of the test tube (or a pre-determined mark), stop the stopwatch. Add a spatula of manganese(IV) oxide to the final test tube and start the stopwatch. When the bubbles reach the top of the test tube (or a pre-determined mark), stop the stopwatch. Repeat the experiment two more times
Safety considerations	Wear eye protection. Hydrogen peroxide is an irritant. Manganese(IV) oxide is harmful.

Starter	Support/Extend	Resources
Elephant's toothpaste (5 min) Show a video of the 'Elephant's toothpaste' reaction to show the effect of a catalyst on the rate of breakdown of hydrogen peroxide. Make sure students understand that without the catalyst the breakdown still occurs, but very slowly. **Catalysts** (10 min) Ask students to write down their definition of the term catalyst. Listen to their ideas and construct a class definition. Then ask students to define the term enzymes. Take time to correct any misconceptions at this stage.	**Extend:** Students should explain how the two terms are linked.	

Main	Support/Extend	Resources
Breaking down hydrogen peroxide (40 mins) Explain to students that enzymes are biological catalysts. Explain the lock and key model of how enzymes work. Students then plan an investigation to compare how an inorganic catalyst and an enzyme (catalase) affect the rate of breakdown of dilute hydrogen peroxide in oxygen and water. They should first state their variables (independent, dependent, and control), before deciding how to measure their dependent variable. You could show the students the equipment available to help them to decide this. If there is time, allow students to carry out a trial run first.	**Support:** Write questions on the board that students should cover in their bullet points (e.g., what is a substrate?)	**Practical:** Breaking down hydrogen peroxide

Plenary	Support/Extend	Resources
Enzyme memory (10 min) Provide students with a group of cards, each card showing either a key term or definition. Students use a memory game to test their understanding of enzyme key words by matching them to their definitions. **Enzymes** (5 min) Interactive where students complete a series of paragraphs summarising the key points about enzymes. They then identify true and false statements about enzymes.	**Extend:** Students correct the false statements.	**Interactive:** Enzymes

Homework		
Students create a storyboard and voiceover script for an animation showing how enzymes work.		

kerboodle

A Kerboodle highlight for this lesson is **Animation: Enzyme action**. Refer to the **Content map** on Kerboodle for a full list of resources and assessment.

B3.5 Factors affecting enzyme action

AQA spec link: 2.2.1 Students should be able to describe the nature of enzyme molecules and relate their activity to temperature and pH changes.

Aiming for	Outcome	Checkpoint	
		Question	Activity
Aiming for GRADE 4	State that temperature and pH affect how well an enzyme works.		Main, Plenary 1, Plenary 2, Homework
	Plot a line graph.		Main, Homework
	State simply what a line graph shows about how temperature or pH affects the rate of an enzyme-catalysed reaction.	2, End of chapter 3	Main, Homework
Aiming for GRADE 6	Explain why high temperatures and changes in pH prevent enzymes from catalysing reactions.	1, 2 End of chapter 3, 4	Main, Plenary 1, Homework
	Draw a tangent to a line and calculate the rate of a reaction with guidance.		Main
	Plot a line graph and use it to draw conclusions about how temperature and pH affect the rate of an enzyme-catalysed reaction.		Main, Homework
Aiming for GRADE 8	Explain in detail how a change in temperature or pH affects the rate of an enzyme-catalysed reaction.		Main, Plenary 1, Homework
	Apply knowledge of enzymes to explain how some organisms can survive in extreme conditions.		Main
	Draw tangents in order to calculate the rate of a reaction.		Main, Homework

Maths
Students carry out mathematical analysis by drawing and using the slope of a tangent to a curve as a measure of rate of an enzyme-catalysed reaction.

Literacy
Students define key words. Higher-tier students also extract the key information from an article to create a summary tweet.

Key word
denatured

44

■ B3 Organisation and the digestive system

Required practical

Title	Factors that affect the rate of enzyme-controlled reactions
Equipment	amylase solution (0.5%), starch solution (0.5%), iodine solution, buffer solutions covering a range of pH values, plastic pipettes, measuring cylinders, test-tube rack, test tube, spotting tile, stopwatch, sticky labels or permanent pen, water baths set at different temperatures, thermometer
Overview of method	Add 2 cm³ of starch solution to a test tube. Place the tube into a water bath. Use a plastic pipette to add 2 cm³ of amylase solution to the test tube and mix. Leave the pipette in the tube. Start the stopwatch immediately after adding the amylase solution. After 10 seconds use the pipette to remove some of the mixture from the test tube and add it to iodine. Continue until the iodine stops changing colour. To investigate temperature, repeat for different temperatures of the water bath. To investigate pH, add 1 cm³ of buffer solution to the amylase solution so a range of pH values are obtained. It is recommended that this method is trialled before the lesson to check the timings are suitable for the concentration of solutions used.
Safety considerations	Use eye protection. Iodine is harmful, avoid contact with skin.

Starter	Support/Extend	Resources
Sentences (5 min) Present the class with the words enzyme, active site, substrate, and product. Ask them to create a meaningful sentence containing all these words. **Egg-speriment** (10 min) Crack an egg into a small beaker and heat it over a Bunsen burner. Ask students to describe what changes are happening to the egg. Discuss the fact that you cannot return the egg to its original state and that the proteins in the egg have changed shape or denatured due to heating.		

Main	Support/Extend	Resources
Does temperature affect the speed of an enzyme reaction? (30 min) Introduce the factors that affect enzyme reaction – temperature and pH. Students plot a line graph of enzyme activity at different temperatures. They should explain what the graph shows using ideas about collision theory, active site, and denaturation in their answer. They then draw tangents to at least three different places on the line in order to calculate the rate of the reaction at different places.	**Support:** Model to the class how to draw a tangent and calculate the rate of reaction before they do another example interdependently.	**Working scientifically:** Does temperature affect the speed of an enzyme reaction?

Plenary	Support/Extend	Resources
Reaction rate (5 min) Interactive where students study a graph to select an enzyme's optimum temperature. They then study a graph and select statements about it that are true. **Body temperature** (10 min) Ask students to write down why they think body temperature is maintained around 37 °C. Discuss their answers and explain that if it goes much lower or higher than enzymes will not work as efficiently and vital metabolic reactions would slow down.		**Interactive:** Reaction rate

Homework		
Provide students with some example data from an investigation into the effect of pH on enzyme activity. Students use the data to plot a suitable graph and draw conclusions from the data.	**Support:** Provide students with the graph for them to interpret. **Extend:** Include some anomalous results in the data.	

kerboodle

A Kerboodle highlight for this lesson is **Maths skills: Enzymes and rates**. Refer to the **Content map** on Kerboodle for a full list of resources and assessment.

B3.6 How the digestive system works

AQA spec link: 2.2.1 Students should be able to recall the sites of production and the action of amylase, proteases, and lipases. Students should be able to understand simple word equations but no chemical symbol equations are required.

Digestive enzymes convert food into small soluble molecules that can be absorbed into the bloodstream.

Carbohydrases break down carbohydrates to simple sugars. Amylase is a carbohydrase which breaks down starch. Proteases break down proteins to amino acids.

Lipases break down lipids (fats) to glycerol and fatty acids.

Required practical: Investigate the effect of a factor on the rate of an enzyme-controlled reaction.

MS 2b, 4a, 4c

Aiming for	Outcome	Checkpoint	
		Question	Activity
Aiming for GRADE 4	State that enzymes are used in digestion to break down food molecules.		Main
	Identify that carbohydrases break down carbohydrates, proteases break down proteins, and lipases break down lipids.	1	Main
	Plan a simple method to carry out an investigation.		Main
Aiming for GRADE 6	Explain why enzymes are needed for digestion.		Plenary 2
	For each food molecule, name the enzyme that acts on it, where it is produced, and which products are formed.	1	Main
	Plan and carry out an investigation in order to gather accurate results.	End of chapter 5, 6	Main
Aiming for GRADE 8	Suggest how to test for substrates and products in a model gut.		Main
	Make a prediction with a clearly structured scientific explanation.		Main
	Analyse results in order to evaluate a method and the validity of conclusions, explaining suggestions for possible improvements.	End of chapter 6	Main

Maths
Students carry out mathematical analysis by drawing and using the slope of a tangent to a curve as a measure of rate of an enzyme-catalysed reaction.

Literacy
Students use the student book to organise information into a table. They also write predictions using scientific explanations.

Key words
amylase, amino acids, fatty acids, glycerol, lipase

Required practical

Title	Factors that affect the rate of enzyme-controlled reactions
Equipment	amylase solution (0.5%), starch solution (0.5%), iodine solution, buffer solutions covering a range of pH values, plastic pipettes, measuring cylinders, test-tube rack, test tube, spotting tile, stopwatch, sticky labels or permanent pen, water baths set at different temperatures, thermometer
Overview of method	Add 2 cm³ of starch solution to a test tube. Place the tube into a water bath. Use a plastic pipette to add 2 cm³ of amylase solution to the test tube and mix. Leave the pipette in the tube. Start the stopwatch immediately after adding the amylase solution. After 10 seconds use the pipette to remove some of the mixture from the test tube and add it to iodine. Continue until the iodine stops changing colour. To investigate temperature, repeat for different temperatures of the water bath. To investigate pH, add 1 cm³ of buffer solution to the amylase solution so a range of pH values are obtained. It is recommended that this method is trialled before the lesson to check the timings are suitable for the concentration of solutions used.
Safety considerations	Use eye protection. Iodine is harmful, avoid contact with skin.

B3 Organisation and the digestive system

Starter	Support/Extend	Resources
Question creation (10 min) Present students with the terms enzyme, catalyst, active site, substrate, lock and key model, denature, digestion, carbohydrate, lipid, and protein. Ask them to write a question that has one of the key words as the answer. Ask students to read out their questions so the class can answer them. **Diffusion recap** (5 min) Draw a diagram on the board showing a cell with differing concentrations of glucose on either side of the membrane. Ask students to predict which way the glucose will move and explain why.		

Main	Support/Extend	Resources
The effect of pH on the rate of reaction of amylase (30 min) Students plan an experiment to investigate how pH affects the rate of amylase activity. Students should be guided to choose a suitable range for the independent variable and to use control variables. Students use their data to plot a line graph and answer questions in order to draw conclusions from the data and evaluate the method. Students should swap data with a group that investigated the other variable from them. More time can be devoted to this investigation next lesson.	**Support:** Students can work in pairs, with each pair investigating one pH. Pool class results. **Support:** Supply students with axes for them to plot their data on.	**Required practical:** The effect of pH on the rate of reaction of amylase

Plenary	Support/Extend	Resources
Digestive enzymes (10 min) Students use the student book spread to find out the names of enzymes, where in the digestive system they are produced, what food molecules they break down, and the name of the products. They should summarise this information as a table. **The importance of enzymes** (5 min) Students use the interactive to identify the nutrients broken down by the enzymes amylase, lipase, and protease, and the products formed. Students then identify where each of the enzymes is produced in the body.	**Support:** Provide students with an empty table with columns for: Name of enzyme, Name of substrate, Name of products. **Extend:** Students can also add where the enzyme is produced in the digestive system to their table of information. **Extend:** Encourage students to refer to what they have learnt earlier in the chapter in their explanations.	**Interactive:** How the digestive system works.

Homework		
Set the class an exam-style question to test their understanding of enzymes and their role in digestion.		

kerboodle

A Kerboodle highlight for this lesson is **On your marks: Enzymes**. Refer to the **Content map** on Kerboodle for a full list of resources and assessment.

B3.7 Making digestion efficient

AQA spec link: 2.2.1 Digestive enzymes convert food into small soluble substances that can be absorbed into the bloodstream.

Bile is made in the liver, and stored in the gall bladder. It is alkaline to neutralise hydrochloric acid from the stomach. It also emulsifies fat to form small droplets which increases the surface area. The alkaline conditions and large surface area increases the rate of fat break down by lipase.

Aiming for	Outcome	Checkpoint	
		Question	Activity
Aiming for GRADE 4 ↓	State that the stomach contains acid.		Main 1
	State that the liver produces bile.		Main 2
	Write a simple hypothesis and prediction.		Main 1, Plenary 1
Aiming for GRADE 6 ↓	Describe the functions of bile.	2	Main 2
	Calculate the mean rate of an enzyme-catalysed reaction.		Starter 1, Main 1
	Analyse data in order to determine whether a hypothesis is correct.		Main 1, Plenary 1
Aiming for GRADE 8 ↓	Explain how acid in the stomach increases the efficiency of pepsin.	1, 2	Main 1, Plenary 2
	Explain how bile increases the efficiency of fat digestion.		Main 2, Plenary 1
	Explain how the rate of an enzyme-catalysed reaction shows how efficient the reaction is.		Main 2

Maths
Students analyse data in the form of results tables and graphs. They calculate mean rates of reaction.

Literacy
Students write hypotheses for their experiments and scientific explanations of their results.

Key word
bile

Practical

Title	Breaking down protein
Equipment	test tubes × 3, test-tube rack, pepsin solution, 0.5 mol/dm^3 hydrochloric acid, three similar-sized chunks of meat
Overview of method	Set up one test tube a third full of hydrochloric acid, one test tube a third full of pepsin solution, and the final test tube a third full of a mixture of the two. Carefully add a chunk of meat to each test tube. Leave in a fume cupboard or other safe location until the next lesson.
Safety considerations	Wash hands thoroughly after handling raw meat. Clean any surfaces that have come into contact with raw meat. Hydrochloric acid is corrosive, avoid contact with skin. Wear eye protection.

Title	Functions of bile
Equipment	test tubes × 2, test-tube rack, 10 cm^3 milk, 14 cm^3 sodium carbonate solution, 10 drops phenolphthalein, washing-up liquid, 2 cm^3 lipase, stopwatch
Overview of method	Set up two test tubes, each containing 5 cm^3 milk, 7 cm^3 sodium carbonate solution, and five drops of phenolphthalein. To one tube, add a drop of washing-up liquid. Add 1 cm^3 lipase to each tube and stir, timing how long it takes for the indicator to go from pink (alkaline) to colourless (acidic).
Safety considerations	Sodium carbonate is an irritant. Wear eye protection.

■ B3 Organisation and the digestive system

Starter	Support/Extend	Resources
Rates (10 min) Give students the following situation: Two people walk to school. Sam's journey is 1 km and it takes him 20 minutes. Ruby walks 0.5 km in 15 minutes. Ask students to work out who walked at the fastest mean rate? Ask students to give their answer and explain how they worked it out. Explain that this is a mean rate as it does not tell you how their walking rate varied during the walk. Explain that the mean rate of enzyme-catalysed reactions can be worked out in a similar way – you can compare the times taken for the reaction to take place.		
The gall bladder (10 min) Show students a diagram of the gall bladder and tell them that it produces an alkaline substance called bile. Ask students to suggest why bile needs to be released into the small intestine.	**Support:** Use the Key diagram to remind students that the optimum pH for amylase is around 8.	

Main	Support/Extend	Resources
Breaking down protein (20 min) Set up the practical as detailed. Ask students to write a hypothesis for what they think will happen to the meat chunks. Then provide students with some data showing the time taken for a piece of egg white to break down in different pH solutions. Students calculate the mean rate of the reaction at each pH value. Then ask students to review their hypothesis and make any changes if necessary. The experiment will need to be revisited in a future lesson to confirm whether students' hypotheses are correct.	**Support:** A Maths skills activity is available for students to further practice calculating mean rates.	**Activity:** Breaking down protein
Functions of bile (20 min) Discuss with the class why washing-up liquid is used. Explain that it breaks large fat globules in food down into smaller droplets that are mixed (emulsified) into the water and are washed away more easily. Carry out the demonstration as outlined. Ask students to use information in the student book and the Working scientifically sheet to come up with a hypothesis for the experiment. Show them the results – the washing up liquid emulsifies the lipids, so this reaction should be quicker.		**Working scientifically:** Functions of bile

Plenary	Support/Extend	Resources
Analysing enzyme data (10 min) Students analyse rates data in the form of results tables and graphs to draw conclusions on how pH affects enzyme activity.		**Interactive:** Analysing enzyme data
Bile and enzymes (5 mins) Ask students to list all the enzymes involved in digestion and what they break down (lipase breaks down lipids, carbohydrase – amylase – break down carbohydrates, protease – pepsin – breaks down proteins). Use this as an opportunity to emphasise that bile is not an enzyme, and correct any students who list it.		

Homework
Students produce their own revision notes or podcast on the human digestive system.

kerboodle

A Kerboodle highlight for this lesson is **Extension sheet: Enzymes and digestion**. Refer to the **Content map** on Kerboodle for a full list of resources and assessment.

B3 Organisation and the digestive system

Overview of B3 Organisation and the digestive system

In this chapter, students have learnt about the principles of organisation. Building on their knowledge of differentiation and specialisation of cells, they should be able to define a tissue, an organ, and an organ system. They have studied the human digestive system as an organ system in which several organs work together to digest and absorb food, breaking down large insoluble molecules so they can be absorbed into the bloodstream. They should link this with earlier work on diffusion and exchange surfaces in B1 *Cell structure and transport*.

Students should understand the hierarchical organisation of the digestive system – for instance, the stomach is one organ, made up of muscular tissue, glandular tissue, and epithelial tissue, which digests food (especially protein).

In studying chemical digestion, students should recognise carbohydrates, proteins, and lipids as large molecules that need to be digested, and be able to name the molecules they are broken down into. They should be familiar with the enzymes that digest carbohydrates, proteins, and lipids, along with the sites of production of these enzymes in the digestive system.

Students should be familiar with enzyme action and understand that enzymes are proteins with a specific shape including the active site. They should recall the lock and key model in which the substrate has a specific shape complementary to the active site, allowing it to bind to the active site where the reaction takes place, releasing products. They should be able to define enzymes as biological catalysts that are reused after each reaction. Students have studied the effect of high temperature and extremes of pH on enzymes in changing the active site, which denatures the enzyme. They should be aware of how each part of the digestive system is adapted to provide an optimum pH for each enzyme, including the role of bile in the small intestine.

Required practical

All students are expected to have carried out the required practicals:

Practical	Topic
Use standard food tests to identify food groups. Detect sugars, starch, and proteins in food using Benedict's test, the iodine test, and Biuret reagent.	B3.3
Investigate the effect of pH on the rate of reaction of amylase enzyme. Students should use a continuous sampling technique to determine the time taken to completely digest a starch solution at a range of pH values.	B3.6

MyMaths

You can find additional support for the maths skills covered in this chapter on **MyMaths**, including considering size and scale, using standard form and order of magnitude, and working with percentages, means, and line graphs.

kerboodle

For this chapter, the following assessments are available on Kerboodle:

B3 Checkpoint quiz: Organisation and the digestive system
B3 Progress quiz: Organisation and the digestive system 1
B3 Progress quiz: Organisation and the digestive system 2
B3 On your marks: Organisation and the digestive system
B3 Exam-style questions and mark scheme: Organisation and the digestive system

Checkpoint follow-up lesson

A student's route through this lesson can be determined using the Checkpoint assessment. Percentage pass marks are supplied in the Checkpoint teacher notes.

For each successive route through it is assumed that the student can perform to their current route as well as previous routes. For example, students working at Aiming for 6 are assumed to be secure in Aiming for 4 knowledge and understanding and working towards achieving all the learning outcomes for Aiming for 6.

	Aiming for 4	**Aiming for 6**	**Aiming for 8**
Learning outcomes	Name the parts of the digestive system.	Describe the function of the different parts of the digestive system.	Explain the function of the different parts of the digestive system.
	Give the function of the different parts of the digestive system.	Describe the effects of temperature on enzyme activity.	Explain how the digestive system is adapted for its function.
	State the effect of temperature on enzyme activity.		Explain the effect of temperature on enzyme activity.
Starter	**Name the parts (5 min)** Students work in pairs to write down as many parts of the digestive system as they can remember in two minutes. Aiming for 4 and Aiming for 6 students may need a review of the parts and functions from the teacher. Aiming for 8 students can test each other to see if they can remember the functions of each part.		
Differentiated checkpoint activity	Aiming for 4 students work through the follow-up sheet to revise the parts of the digestive system and the effect of temperature on enzyme activity. The questions are highly-structured and students could work in pairs.	Aiming for 6 students work through the follow-up sheet to revise the parts of the digestive system and the effect of temperature on enzyme activity. The questions provide some prompts and students could work in pairs if they require further support.	Aiming for 8 students work through the follow-up sheet to describe the journey of food through the digestive system, then analyse results from an experiment on the effect of temperature on enzyme activity. The questions provide minimal support, and students should be aiming to work independently.
	Kerboodle resource B3 Checkpoint follow-up: Aiming for 4, B3 Checkpoint follow-up: Aiming for 6, B3 Checkpoint follow-up: Aiming for 8		
Plenary	**Enzyme activity (5 minutes)** Pairs of students will need mini-whiteboards and pens. Ask pairs to draw enzyme activity graphs on their mini-whiteboards, one showing the effect of changes in temperature and one for pH. Check understanding by asking them to explain their graphs. Aiming for 8 students could also draw graphs to show the effect of changing substrate concentration. Briefly revisit the lists from the starter. Can students add any more parts and functions of the digestive system?		
Progression	For extra support, the axes could be already drawn on graph paper. To progress, give students an unlabelled diagram of the human digestive system and ask them to label and annotate it without their notes from the lesson. They should compare their diagram with their notes, adding anything they missed.	To progress, ask students to give one adaptation of each part of the human digestive system. Students could add a third column to the table they created as part of the checkpoint activity.	To progress, students could calculate rates of reaction in different conditions, and plot graphs. They could design an experiment to investigate the effect of pH on enzyme activity, including a prediction of their results.

B4 Organising animals and plants

4.1 The blood

AQA spec link: 2.2.3 Blood is a tissue consisting of plasma, in which the red blood cells, white blood cells, and platelets are suspended.

Students should know the functions of each of these blood components.

Students should be able to recognise different types of blood cells in a photograph or diagram, and explain how they are adapted to their functions.

WS 1.4, 1.5
MS 1c

Aiming for	Outcome	Checkpoint Question	Checkpoint Activity
Aiming for GRADE 4	State the main components in blood.	2	Starter 2, Main, Plenary 1, Homework
	Recognise the components of blood from photomicrographs.		Starter 2, Main, Plenary 2
	Describe the function of each component in blood.	1, 2, 3	Main, Plenary 1
Aiming for GRADE 6	Summarise the process of blood clotting.	3	Main, Plenary 2
	View blood under a light microscope and recognise components.		Main, Plenary 2
	Explain how red blood cells are adapted to their function.		Main, Plenary 2
Aiming for GRADE 8	Suggest how white blood cells are adapted to their function.	3	Main, Plenary 2,
	Estimate the diameter of a red blood cell and comment on its uncertainty.		Main
	Evaluate in detail a model of the blood.		Plenary 1, Homework

Maths
Students use percentages to show the composition of blood (1c). Some students may draw pie charts and estimate the diameter of a red blood cell.

Literacy
Students evaluate a model of the blood.

Key words
plasma, red blood cells, white blood cells, platelets, urea, urine, haemoglobin

B4 Organising animals and plants

Practical

Title	Blood components
Equipment	light microscope, prepared slides of blood smears, calibrated micrometer eyepiece or graticule, transparent plastic ruler
Overview of method	Students work in pairs to view blood under a light microscope. Higher-tier students can estimate the diameter of a red blood cell.
Safety considerations	You can buy blood smear slides from school suppliers. Do not prepare them at school from animal or human blood. Students must take care with the glass slides as they are very fragile.

Starter	Support/Extend	Resources
Why do we have blood? (10 min) Ask students why we have blood. Students discuss the answer with a partner. Ask for feedback from the class and use it to create a list of ideas on the board. **Blood cells** (5 min) Show students a photomicrograph of a sample of blood. Ask them if they can name any of the structures.	**Extension:** Ask students if they can state any functions of these structures.	

Main	Support/Extend	Resources
Blood components (4 min) Allow students to work in pairs to study prepared microscope slides of blood smears under a light microscope. Students should be able to use Figure 4 in the student book to identify and name red blood cells, white blood cells, and platelets. Students then use the student book to complete a table showing the components of blood, their functions, adaptations, and percentage compositions.	**Support:** Set up the microscopes in advance and focus the slides on a high magnification. **Extend:** Ask students to estimate the diameter of a red blood cell and comment on uncertainty. As red blood cells are small, students will have to measure the length of a group of cells and then divide by how many there are. **Extend:** Ask students to draw a pie chart to show the percentage composition of blood.	**Practical:** Blood components

Plenary	Support/Extend	Resources
Blood model (10 min) Build a model of blood by adding sunflower oil (plasma), small red counters (red blood cells), white marshmallows (white blood cells), and lentils (platelets) to a large beaker. Ask the students what each part represents, what its function is, and how much of each you should put in to make an accurate representation of the composition of blood. **Blood and blood cells** (5 min) Interactive where students summarise how different components of the blood are adapted for their function. They then decide whether statements are true or false.	**Extend:** Ask students to evaluate the model.	**Interactive:** Blood and blood cells

Homework		
Students design their own model of blood.	**Extend:** Students should evaluate their model.	

kerboodle

A Kerboodle highlight for this lesson is **Bump up your grade: What's in our blood?** Refer to the **Content map** on Kerboodle for a full list of resources and assessment.

B4.2 The blood vessels

AQA spec link: 2.2.2 The heart is an organ that pumps blood around the body in a double circulatory system.

The body contains three different types of blood vessel:

- arteries
- veins
- capillaries.

Students should be able to explain how the structure of these vessels relates to their functions.

Students should be able to use simple compound measures such as rate and carry out rate calculations for blood flow.

WS 1.5
MS 1a, 1c, 1d

Aiming for	Outcome	Checkpoint	
		Question	Activity
Aiming for GRADE 4 ↓	State the three main types of blood vessel and recognise them from diagrams.		Main, Plenary 1, Homework
	Estimate heart rate.		Starter 1, Main
Aiming for GRADE 6 ↓	Explain how the structure of blood vessels relates to their function.	1, 2	Main, Plenary 1, Homework
	Comment on how accurate estimations are.		Main
Aiming for GRADE 8 ↓	Explain in detail the importance of a double circulatory system.	3	Main, Plenary 2
	Explain how to make estimates more accurate in terms of precision of data.		Main

Maths
Students measure their pulse rate and use estimation (1d). They consider how to make estimates more accurate.

Literacy
Students summarise information from the student book to describe the structure and function of blood vessels.

Key words
valves, double circulatory system, arteries, veins, capillaries

B4 Organising animals and plants

Starter	Support/Extend	Resources
Heartbeat estimation (5 min) Ask students to estimate how many times they think their heart beats in a minute and write this value down. Ask a few students for their estimates. **The circulatory system** (10 min) Show students a diagram of the circulatory system. Point out the main structures (heart and blood vessels). Ask them to trace the path of blood through the system and discuss with a partner what happens at each capillary bed.	**Support:** Go through how to estimate with students. **Extend:** Ask the students to predict how this would change if they started moving around.	

Main	Support/Extend	Resources
Blood flow (40 min) Using a diagram of the circulatory system, discuss with students the path the blood takes through the body. Explain that humans have a dual circulatory system and explain what this means and why it is important. Point out the locations of arteries, veins, and capillaries on the diagram. Ask students to use information from the student book to draw sketches and make notes on their structure and function. Students then work in pairs to measure each other's pulse. First counting how many beats they can feel in 5 seconds, then 10 seconds, 30 seconds, and finally 60 seconds. Students then use their measurements for each timeframe to estimate beats per minute. Compare their results with their estimates from Starter 1, if used. Discuss why estimating is useful, but not as accurate as measuring.	**Support:** If students struggle to understand the path taken by blood through the body, show them a suitable animation. **Extend:** Project photomicrographs of sections through arteries and veins to show differences in the structures of the walls. **Extend:** Discuss whether repeating measurements would make the estimates more accurate, and why. **Extend:** Students suggest reasons for any differences between the values obtained in Starter 1 and Main 2.	**Activity:** Blood flow.

Plenary	Support/Extend	Resources
Which vessel? (10 min) Interactive where students match the blood vessel to the correct diagram. They then match the descriptions to the correct blood vessel. **Fish circulation** (5 min) Show the class an image showing a fish's single circulatory system. Ask them to say how it is different from human circulation.	**Extend:** Ask students to suggest disadvantages of a single circulatory system.	**Interactive:** Which vessel?

Homework		
Ask students to find out about how blood is circulated in fish (single circulatory system). They can draw a diagram to show it and describe how it works.	**Extend:** Students can compare and contrast single and double circulatory systems.	

kerboodle

A Kerboodle highlight for this lesson is **Extension sheet: Blood vessels**. Refer to the **Content map** on Kerboodle for a full list of resources and assessment.

B4.3 The heart

AQA spec links: 2.2.2 Students should know the structure and functioning of the human heart.

The heart is an organ that pumps blood around the body in a double circulatory system. The right ventricle pumps blood to the lungs where gas exchange takes place. The left ventricle pumps blood around the rest of the body.

Knowledge of the blood vessels associated with the heart is limited to the aorta, vena cava, pulmonary artery, pulmonary vein, and coronary arteries. Knowledge of the names of the heart valves is not required.

2.2.4 In coronary heart disease layers of fatty material build up inside the coronary arteries, narrowing them. This reduces the flow of blood through the coronary arteries, resulting in a lack of oxygen for the heart muscle. Stents are used to keep the coronary arteries open. Statins are widely used to reduce blood cholesterol levels which slows down the rate of fatty material deposit.

WS 1.3, 1.4

Aiming for	Outcome	Checkpoint	
		Question	Activity
Aiming for GRADE 4	Describe the function of the heart.	1	Starter 2, Main
	State the main structures of the human heart.		Starter 1, Main
	List examples of problems that can develop in blood vessels in the human heart.		Starter 1, Main
Aiming for GRADE 6	Describe the function of the main structures of the human heart.		Starter 1, Main, Plenary 2
	Describe the problems that can develop in blood vessels in the human heart, and their treatments.	3, 4 End of chapter 3	Main
	Suggest advantages and disadvantages of using stents and statins.		Main
Aiming for GRADE 8	Explain in detail how the structure of the different parts of the human heart is related to their function.	1, 2, End of chapter 1	Main, Plenary 1
	Recognise the main structures of the heart when carrying out a heart dissection.		Main
	Evaluate the use of stents and statins in treating problems with blood vessels.	4, End of chapter 3	Main, Plenary 2

Maths
Students interpret data and statistics to help them evaluate the use of stents

Literacy
Students use a range of new terminology to name structures in the heart and describe the cardiac cycle.

Key words
coronary arteries, atria, vena cava, deoxygenated blood, pulmonary vein, ventricles, pulmonary artery, aorta, coronary heart disease, stents, statins

Practical

Title	Sheep heart dissection
Equipment	one heart per small group, scissors, mounted needle, dissecting board, gloves, eye protection
Overview of method	Identify the coronary arteries and the main blood vessels. Cut into the heart to show the four chambers. Discuss the difference in thickness of ventricles between the two sides. Point out the valves and discuss their function to keep blood flowing in the correct direction.
Safety considerations	Wash hands after handling the heart. Take care with sharp instruments, allowing one person at a time to do the cutting. Wear gloves and eye protection.

■ B4 Organising animals and plants

Starter	Support/Extend	Resources
The structure of the heart (10 min) Introduce the structure of the human heart using a diagram. Ask students to suggest some ways in which the function of the heart could be disrupted. **Circulation review** (5 min) Starting with a unit of blood in the right side of the heart, pick students to state where the blood will go next until it has done a complete circuit.	**Support:** Display an image of the human circulatory system.	

Main	Support/Extend	Resources
Sheep heart dissection (40 min) This can be done as a demonstration or grouped practical. Students should draw a simplified and labelled diagram of the heart based on the dissection. Students who do not wish to be involved with the practical due to religious or moral objections can complete the questions in the student book, then complete the Bump up your grade worksheet to understand the role of valves in controlling direction of blood flow in the heart. Ask students to predict what the effect of a blockage in one of the coronary arteries would be. After initial discussion in pairs, allow them to use information from the student book to write a short answer. Discuss the effects of fatty buildups as a class. Ask students to write advice to an imaginary patient who has been told they need to have a stent fitted and then take statins for the rest of their life. Students should explain the function of the stent and statins, and also what the operation will involve.		**Practical:** Sheep heart dissection **Bump up your grade:** Valves and blood flow

Plenary	Support/Extend	Resources
Heart misconceptions (5 min) Present the class with a series of incorrect statements about the heart based on common misconceptions and ask students to correct them, for example, the blood goes into one side of the heart and then the other (in fact both sides are full of blood at the same time). **Describing the heart** (10 min) Interactive where students label a diagram of the heart to show the different structures. They then summarise the flow of blood through the heart.	**Extend:** Ask students to create their own statements and test a partner.	**Interactive:** Describing the heart

Homework		
To revise this section on the heart, students write and record their own revision podcast. They should discuss the circulatory system and the role of the heart, blood vessels, and blood.	**Support:** Provide students with a series of simple questions that they can answer to structure their notes.	

kerboodle
A Kerboodle highlight for this lesson is **Homework: The heart**. Refer to the **Content map** on Kerboodle for a full list of resources and assessment.

B4.4 Helping the heart

AQA spec links: 2.2.2 The natural resting heart rate is controlled by a group of cells located in the right atrium that act as a pacemaker. Artificial pacemakers are electrical devices used to correct irregularities in the heart rate.

2.2.4 Students should be able to evaluate the advantages and disadvantages of treating cardiovascular diseases by drugs, mechanical devices, or transplant.

In some people heart valves may become faulty, preventing the valve from opening fully, or the heart valve might develop a leak. Students should understand the consequences of faulty valves. Faulty heart valves can be replaced using biological or mechanical valves.

In the case of heart failure a donor heart, or heart and lungs can be transplanted. Artificial hearts are occasionally used to keep patients alive whilst waiting for a heart transplant, or to allow the heart to rest as an aid to recovery.

WS 1.3, 1.4
MS 1b

Aiming for	Outcome	Checkpoint	
		Question	Activity
Aiming for GRADE 4 ↓	State that the heartbeat is maintained by a group of cells that acts as a pacemaker.	1	Main 1, Homework
	give some ways in which the heart can stop functioning efficiently.		Starter 1
	Describe why a person may need an artificial pacemaker or an artificial heart.	2	Starter 1, Main 1, Main 2, Plenary 1
Aiming for GRADE 6 ↓	Explain why an irregular heartbeat is detrimental to health.		Main 1
	Describe why people may have objections to heart transplants.	4	Main 2, Plenary 1
	Summarise the advantages and disadvantages of different treatments for heart problems.	3	Main 2, Plenary 2
Aiming for GRADE 8 ↓	Explain how a natural pacemaker maintains the heartbeat.	1	Main 1
	Suggest how an artificial pacemaker regulates an irregular heartbeat.	2	Main 1
	Evaluate in detail the different methods used in the treatment of heart problems.	4	Main 2, Plenary 1

Maths
Students calculate how many times the heart beats in a year or a lifetime. Students can also estimate the number of heartbeats in 85 years, using standard form to express this number (1b).

Literacy
Students use supplied advantages and disadvantages of different treatments for heart conditions to identify the correct treatment for a series of patients.

■ B4 Organising animals and plants

Starter	Support/Extend	Resources
Heart problems (10 min) Show the students a diagram of the outside of the heart. Ask them to discuss in small groups what can go wrong with the heart. Listen to their ideas as a class. **Heartbeat** (10 min) Tell the class that the heart rate of the average person is 70 beats per minute. Ask them to calculate how many times the average human heartbeats in a year.	**Support:** Before the discussion, describe the function of the coronary arteries. **Extend:** Students should estimate how many beats this is in a lifetime of 85 years (ignoring leap years) and express this to 3 s.f and in standard form (3.13×10^9)	

Main	Support/Extend	Resources
Controlling the heartbeat (15 min) Ask students to consider what causes the heart to pump. Reveal that it works from an electric current that your body produces. Fill a water balloon with water. Use a pen to draw the four heart chambers. Explain that an electrical current produced by a group of cells called the pacemaker in the right atrium causes the top of the heart to contract. Squeeze the balloon at the top so all the water goes to the bottom. Explain that the electrical current then moves down the heart. Squeeze the balloon at the bottom, so all the water goes back up to the top. Link this movement to the cardiac cycle studied in Topic B4.3. Then use this model to show an irregular heartbeat where the top and bottom do not pump in a coordinated manner. **Which one should I have?** (25 min) Students look at the advantages and disadvantages of artificial pacemakers, biological valves, artificial valves, artificial hearts, and heart transplants, including ethical issues. They help patients to come to a decision about which they should choose.		**Working scientifically:** Which one should I have?

Plenary	Support/Extend	Resources
Benefits and drawbacks of treatments (10 min) Play the role of a person who needs a heart transplant. Ask the students questions about why you may need an artificial heart, how it works, and any concerns you have about a heart transplant, including ethical issues. **How does it work?** (5 min) Use the interactive, which lists many different treatments for cardiovascular disease. Students link each treatment to the explanation of how it works.		**Interactive:** How does it work?

Homework		
Students use the WebQuest to guide them through researching more about heart transplants.		**WebQuest:** Heart transplants

kerboodle

A Kerboodle highlight for this lesson is **Bump up your grade: Benefits and drawbacks of pacemakers and artificial hearts**. Refer to the **Content map** on Kerboodle for a full list of resources and assessment.

B4.5 Breathing and gas exchange

AQA spec link: 2.2.2 Students should know the structure and functioning of the human lungs, including how lungs are adapted for gaseous exchange.

MS 1c

Aiming for	Outcome	Checkpoint	
		Question	Activity
Aiming for GRADE 4	List the main structures of the gas exchange system.		Main 2, Plenary 2
	State that gas exchange happens in the alveoli.	2	Main 2
	Use data in the form of percentages to describe the differences between the composition of inhaled and exhaled air.	3	Starter 1
Aiming for GRADE 6	Describe the function of the main structures of the gas exchange system.		Main 2
	Describe how alveoli are adapted for gas exchange.	3	Main 2
	Describe the processes of ventilation and gas exchange.	1, 2, End of chapter 4	Main 2
Aiming for GRADE 8	Evaluate in detail a model of the lungs.		Plenary 1
	Explain in detail how the adaptations of alveoli result in efficient gas exchange.	3, End of chapter 4	Main 2
	Explain the differences between the composition of inhaled and exhaled air.	3	Main 2

Maths
Students use percentages to analyse the composition of gases in inhaled and exhaled air (1c).

Literacy
Students use correct terminology to label parts of the gas exchange system and describe their functions. Students can also evaluate a model of the lungs.

Key word
capillaries

■ B4 Organising animals and plants

Starter	Support/Extend	Resources
Inhaled and exhaled air (10 min) Use the interactive to assess students' understanding of how the composition of different gases differs between inhaled and exhaled air. Students sort percentages of gases to describe inhaled and exhaled air. Discuss why the composition changes and introduce the concept of gas exchange in the lungs. **How do you breathe?** (5 min) Ask students to write down a short paragraph that explains how you breathe in and out. Ask them to exchange ideas with a partner and choose some pairs to present their explanation to the rest of the class.	**Support:** Provide useful keywords, such as mouth, nose, trachea (windpipe), and lungs. **Extend:** Students should refer to the diaphragm in their paragraphs.	**Interactive:** Inhaled and exhaled air

Main	Support/Extend	Resources
Lung model (15 min) Present to the class the bell jar model of the lungs. You may have a large model or can make one easily using a plastic bottle and balloons. Ask the students how they would use this to show inhalation and exhalation. Many will think that you blow air into the neck of the bottle. Demonstrate how it is in fact the contraction and relaxation of the diaphragm that changes the volume and hence pressure of the inside of the chest cavity and this results in inflation and deflation of the lungs. Use this to address any misconceptions. **Ventilation** (25 min) Explain to students the mechanisms of ventilation and the exchange of gases in the alveoli. Then, ask students to label a diagram of parts of the gas exchange system, describe their function, any adaptations of each structure, and explain what happens during gaseous exchange.	**Support:** Show students a pluck (heart and lungs of an animal) to make the links between the model and real-life more apparent. **Extend:** Students should include an explanation that links the gas exchange that occurs in the lungs to the differences between inhaled and exhaled air.	**Activity:** Ventilation

Plenary	Support/Extend	Resources
How we breathe in and out (10 min) Bump up your grade worksheet where students use a model of the lungs to understand how volume changes result in pressure changes and cause inhalation and exhalation. **Labelling the system** (5 min) Display a diagram of the gas exchange system and invite students to name the parts.	**Extend:** Students evaluate the model by writing down ways in which it is similar to and differs from real human lungs **Extend:** Ask students to also describe the function of each part.	**Bump up your grade:** How we breathe in and out

Homework		
Ask students to write down 10 short interesting facts about the lungs and gas exchange.	**Extend:** Encourage students to research interesting facts.	

kerboodle

A Kerboodle highlight for this lesson is **Calculation sheet: Pie charts of gases**. Refer to the **Content map** on Kerboodle for a full list of resources and assessment.

B4.6 Tissues and organs in plants

AQA spec links: 2.3.1 Students should be able to explain how the structures of plant tissues are related to their functions.

Plant tissues include:
- epidermal tissues, which cover the plant
- palisade mesophyll
- spongy mesophyll
- xylem and phloem
- meristem tissue found at the growing tips of shoots and roots.

The leaf is a plant organ. Knowledge limited to epidermis, palisade and spongy mesophyll, xylem and phloem, and guard cells surrounding stomata.

2.3.2 The roots, stem, and leaves form a plant organ system for transport of substances around the plant.

Aiming for	Outcome	Checkpoint	
		Question	Activity
Aiming for GRADE 4	Recognise examples of plant organs and state their functions.	End of chapter 5	Starter 1, Plenary 1
	Use a light microscope to view a cross-section of a leaf.		Main
	State the functions of different plant tissues.	1, End of chapter 5	Main, Homework
Aiming for GRADE 6	Describe how plant organs are involved in the transport system.	2	Starter 1, Main, Plenary 1
	Use a microscope to identify the different tissues in a cross-section of a leaf.		Main
	Explain how the structures of tissues in the leaf are related to their functions.	2, End of chapter 5	Main, Plenary 2
Aiming for GRADE 8	Suggest what type of plant organs unfamiliar structures are.		Main, Plenary 1
	Use a light microscope to draw a cross-section of a leaf and calculate scale.		Starter 2, Main
	Suggest functions for unknown plant tissues.		Main, Homework

Maths
Students perform a calculation involving the conversion of units.

Literacy
Students use scientific terminology to label a diagram and explain the functions of plant tissues and organs.

Key words
epidermal, palisade mesophyll, spongy mesophyll, xylem, phloem

B4 Organising animals and plants

Starter	Support/Extend	Resources
Plant organs (10 min) Interactive where students match plant organs with their functions and then label a diagram to show the main structures of a plant stem and root cross-section.	**Extend:** Encourage students to add the names of as many tissues and cells as they can. Discuss how plant organs can be grouped into systems.	**Interactive:** Plant organs
A sense of scale (5 min) Tell the class that the giant redwood tree can have a trunk that is 40 metres tall. Ask them to calculate how many plant cells of length 100 μm can fit end-to-end up the trunk.	**Support:** Guide students through how to carry out the calculation. Explain how to convert μm into m.	

Main	Support/Extend	Resources
Looking at leaves (40 min) Supply groups of students with named diagrams of the plant tissues xylem, phloem, meristem, and epidermal. Ask them to discuss the organs where each tissue is found, their functions, and how each is adapted for its function. Students then use light microscopes to study prepared slides of leaf cross-sections. They use a labelled diagram to identify the cells and tissues they can see and describe their functions. Ask students to explain how their functions are related to their structure.	**Support:** Refer groups to the student book. **Support:** Some students may have difficulty in conceptualising what a cross-section is. Explain that it is like slicing a cake to see the layers. **Extend:** Students should draw what they see and attempt to identify different tissues. **Extend:** Students use the Go further sheet to apply their knowledge to tissues that are used for plant defences, and suggest the functions of the unknown tissues.	**Practical:** Looking at leaves **Go further:** Plant defences

Plenary	Support/Extend	Resources
Name the organ (5 min) Display a range of plant organs from different plants (roots, stems, leaves, and flowers) and ask students to name what type of organ it is. Discuss similarities between organs from different plants and recap their functions. **Tissue adaptations** (10 min) List the different tissues in the leaf and ask students to state one adaptation of each. This could be done using mini-whiteboards.	**Support:** Use mainly familiar examples, for example, carrots. **Extend:** Use mainly unfamiliar organs, for example, flowers from exotic plants.	

Homework		
Students choose a plant organ other than the leaf and carry out research using books and/or the Internet to find out the names and functions of tissues in this organ. They can draw labelled diagrams of the organ.	**Support:** Give students a list of suitable plant organs to study, for example, root or flower. **Extend:** Students can choose the organ they wish to study.	

B4.7 Transport systems in plants

AQA spec link: 2.3.2 Students should be able to explain how the structure of xylem and phloem are adapted to their function.

Xylem tissue transports water and mineral ions from the roots to the stems and leaves. It is composed of hollow tubes strengthened by lignin adapted for the transport of water in the transpiration stream.

Phloem tissue transports dissolved sugars from the leaves to the rest of the plant for immediate use or storage. The movement of food through phloem is called translocation.

Phloem is composed of tubes of elongated cells. Cell sap can move from one phloem cell to the next through pores in the end walls.

Detailed structure of phloem tissue or the mechanism of transport is not required.

MS 2a, 2d, 5c

Aiming for	Outcome	Checkpoint	
		Question	Activity
Aiming for GRADE 4 ↓	Describe the function of xylem and phloem tissue.	1, 2	Starter 2, Main, Plenary 2, Homework
	Describe evidence for movement of water through xylem.		Main
Aiming for GRADE 6 ↓	Describe why transport in plants is important.	1, 3	Starter 1, Starter 2, Main, Homework
	Explain how the structure of xylem and phloem is adapted to their functions.	2	Main, Plenary 1
Aiming for GRADE 8 ↓	Explain in detail how the rate of transport through a plant can be measured.		Main

Maths
Students explain how to measure the rate of water transport through the xylem.

Literacy
Students use information from the student book to describe the functions of xylem and phloem. Students explain how systemic pesticides work and evaluate their use.

Key word
translocation

Practical

Title	Movement through the xylem
Equipment	stalks of celery, small beakers, water coloured with Eosin or ink, knives (for cutting sections), tweezers (for removing xylem vessels), cutting tiles, paper towels
Overview of method	Leave celery in the coloured water for a few hours or overnight. Students cut cross-sections of the stalks to see the xylem tissue, which has been stained. They can also cut longitudinal sections and remove the xylem vessels.
Safety considerations	Take care when handling knives.

■ B4 Organising animals and plants

Starter	Support/Extend	Resources
Substance journeys (10 min) State the names of some substances that are transported in plants (water, mineral ions, sugars) and ask students to describe their journey — where did they start, where are they going, and how will they get there? **Aphid attack** (5 min) Show the class images of aphids attacking a plant and a magnified image of an aphid feeding on a plant that shows its sharp mouthparts. Question students about what the aphid is feeding on and why this damages the plant.	**Support:** Show the different journeys and ask students to choose the one that best describes each substance, for example, soil → roots → stem → leaf would be water. **Extend:** Students should explain what will happen to the substance once it has reached its destination.	

Main	Support/Extend	Resources
Xylem and phloem (20 min) Supply students with celery sticks that have been left overnight in ink. They cut the sticks to see how the dye has stained the xylem walls. Students then look back at Topic B1.5 in the student book and explain how the structure and function of xylem cells are adapted for their function. Then introduce how sap is tapped from trees in order to make maple syrup. If possible, show photos of a video from the Internet. Discuss with the class where the sugars in the tree trunk (stem) come from and how they are transported, or translocated, in the phloem. Ask students to look back at Topic B1.5 in the student book and explain how phloem cells are adapted for their function.	**Extend:** Students should suggest how celery left in ink could be used to measure the rate of flow of water up a stem, for example, by measuring how far up the ink has reached in four hours.	**Practical:** Xylem and phloem

Plenary	Support/Extend	Resources
Label the diagram (5 min) Provide groups of students with two sticky notes that say xylem and phloem. Display a series of images showing transverse and cross-sections of roots, stems, and leaves to show the vascular systems. Ask them to stick their labels on the diagrams to explain how their structures are linked to their functions. **Xylem and phloem** (10 min) Interactive where students complete sentences about xylem and phloem. They then choose whether statements describe xylem or phloem.	**Support:** Use longitudinal sections only, which have key features labelled. **Extend:** Use a range of diagrams, some of which are not labelled.	**Interactive:** Xylem and phloem

Homework		
Students design an infographic that explains the transport system of a plant. This is a graphic poster that contains very little text. It can be done on the computer or by hand.	**Support:** Show students examples of infographics and discuss how they show complex information simply.	

kerboodle
A Kerboodle highlight for this lesson is **Calculation sheet: Transpiration data**. Refer to the **Content map** on Kerboodle for a full list of resources and assessment.

65

B4.8 Evaporation and transpiration

AQA spec link: 2.3.2 Xylem tissue transports water and mineral ions from the roots to the stems and leaves. It is composed of hollow tubes strengthened by lignin adapted for the transport of water in the transpiration stream.

The role of stomata and guard cells is to control gas exchange and water loss.

MS 2b, 2d

Aiming for	Outcome	Checkpoint	
		Question	Activity
Aiming for GRADE 4	State that transpiration is the evaporation of water vapour from the leaves.	End of chapter 6	Main, Plenary 1
	State the function of stomata.	1	Starter 1, Main, Plenary 1
	Calculate the mean number of stomata on a given area of leaf.	4	Main
Aiming for GRADE 6	Describe how transpiration maintains the movement of water from roots to leaves.	2, 3	Main, Homework
	Describe how the opening and closing of stomata is controlled by guard cells.		Main
	Use sampling to estimate the number of stomata on a leaf.		Main
Aiming for GRADE 8	Evaluate drinking from a straw as a model for transpiration.		Plenary
	Explain in detail how stomata control transpiration.	1	Main
	Suggest reasons for differences in the number and distribution of stomata, as well as their adaptations.		Main, Plenary 2

Maths
Students estimate the number of stomata on a leaf. They carry out sampling and calculate means to increase the repeatability of their results (2b, 2d).

Literacy
Students define the key words transpiration, transpiration stream, stomata, and guard cells. They write a conclusion based on scientific understanding. They also write creatively to explain the journey of a water molecule.

Key words
guard cells, transpiration, transpiration stream

Practical

Title	Investigating stomata
Equipment	a plant (spider plants, red hot pokers, and geranium work well), microscope with eyepiece graticule (calibrated for different magnifications) or stage graticules on microscope slides, nail varnish, sticky tape, glass slides
Overview of method	Students carry out several epidermal peels using nail varnish and study these under a light microscope. They count the number or density of stomata in several fields of view.
Safety considerations	Students must take care with the glass slides as they are very fragile. Students may have allergic reactions to nail varnish or plant sap. They should wear gloves.

66

B4 Organising animals and plants

Starter	Support/Extend	Resources
Stomata (5 min) Show the class a magnified image of a stoma and ask them to discuss what it could be and its function. **In and out** (10 min) Draw or project an image of a leaf on the board. Ask students to copy this and add arrows to show the movement of gases into and out of the leaf. Review their ideas and explain that gas exchange happens in the leaf – carbon dioxide enters and oxygen leaves. This happens through tiny holes on the leaf called stomata.	**Support:** Ask students to show the movement of oxygen and carbon dioxide.	

Main	Support/Extend	Resources
Investigating stomata (10 min) Explain that water vapour can also move out of the leaf through the stomata. Introduce this as transpiration. Ask students to define the words transpiration, transpiration stream, stomata, and guard cells. Demonstrate how you can carry out a epidermal peel to view stomata under the microscope. Ask students to discuss in small groups what you could investigate about the stomata using this method and how you would go about doing so. Examples include comparing the number of stomata on different types of plant, on different leaves on one plant, and in different areas of a leaf. Discuss the use of sampling to study different leaves and different areas on a leaf. Students then carry out the practical in small groups. They count the number of stomata in several fields of view before calculating a mean and writing a conclusion.	**Support:** Model how guard cells are involved with the opening of stomata by using a long balloon. **Extend:** Extend this model by looking at how water entering and leaving the guard cells affects the opening of stomata. **Support:** Students can just count the number of stomata they can see in the field of view. **Support:** Model how to calculate a mean by using the Maths skills interactive. Students can practice the skill by completing the Calculation sheet. **Extend:** Students can calculate the area of the field of view to estimate the number of stomata on the whole leaf.	**Practical:** Investigating stomata **Maths skills:** Calculating the mean **Calculation sheet:** Mean

Plenary	Support/Extend	Resources
Transpiration terms (10 min) Interactive where students match up key words with their definitions then explain how water moves through a plant. **Plant adaptations** (10 min) Show students images of the leaves of marram grass and cacti. Ask them to suggest how their stomata may be specially adapted, and why.	**Extend:** Students make predictions about the distribution of stomata in floating and submerged water plants.	**Interactive:** Transpiration terms

Homework		
Students write a description of the journey of a water molecule as it travels from the soil, through the plant, and into the air via transpiration. They can describe the route the molecule takes, the form it is in at each point, and if it meets any other substances on its journey.	**Support:** Provide students with a writing frame that contains questions they must answer to help them structure their work.	

kerboodle

A Kerboodle highlight for this lesson is **Working scientifically: Sampling**. Refer to the **Content map** on Kerboodle for a full list of resources and assessment.

B4.9 Factors affecting transpiration

AQA spec link: 2.3.2 Students should be able to explain the effect of changing temperature, humidity, air movement, and light intensity on the rate of transpiration.

Students should be able to understand and use simple compound measures such as the rate of transpiration.

Students should be able to:

- translate information between graphical and numerical form
- plot and draw appropriate graphs, selecting appropriate scales for axes
- extract and interpret information from graphs, charts and tables.

MS 1a, 1c, 2a, 2d, 4a, 4c, 5c

Aiming for	Outcome	Checkpoint	
		Question	Activity
Aiming for GRADE 4	Recognise the factors that affect transpiration.		Starter 1, Main, Plenary 1, Homework
	Describe how a potometer can be used to estimate the volume of water lost by a plant.	1	Main
	Identify control variables when investigating rate of transpiration.		Main
Aiming for GRADE 6	Explain why temperature, humidity, light intensity, and amount of air flow affect the rate of transpiration.	1, 2, End of chapter 6	Starter 1, Main
	Describe the differences between a moving bubble potometer and a mass potometer.		Main
	Make a prediction using scientific knowledge when investigating rate of transpiration.	2, End of chapter 6	Main
Aiming for GRADE 8	Apply particle model to explain in detail why temperature, humidity, light intensity, and amount of air flow affect the rate of transpiration.		Starter 1, Main
	Summarise plant adaptations to control water loss, and explain how they work.	1, 2, 3	Plenary 2
	Evaluate in detail the use of a potometer to measure the rate of transpiration.	1, End of chapter 6	Main

Maths
Students see how a potometer can be used to measure the rate of water uptake in cm/s.

Literacy
Students describe how potometers work and write predictions using correct scientific terminology.

B4 Organising animals and plants

Starter	Support/Extend	Resources
Drying clothes (10 min) Display an image of clothes drying outside on a washing line. Use the interactive, where students select what factors would affect how quickly washing dries and then sort whether descriptions would increase or decrease the rate of drying. Then discuss the fact that clothes dry because of evaporation, the rate of which is increased by high temperature, low humidity, and degree of air flow (wind).	**Extend:** Ask students to explain why each of these conditions increase the rate of evaporation using particle theory.	**Interactive:** Drying clothes
Observing water loss (5 min) The day before the lesson, set up a potted plant so its aerial parts are enclosed in a plastic bag. Show the class the plant and ask them to explain why there is condensation inside the bag.	**Support:** Provide students with key words transpiration, evaporation, and stomata to use in their explanation.	

Main	Support/Extend	Resources
Factors affecting transpiration (40 min) Explain to students that the rate of evaporation increases as temperature increases, humidity decreases, and air flow increases. Demonstrate how a mass potometer and a moving bubble potometer can be used to measure the uptake of water by a plant. Discuss how leaving the equipment in different conditions would affect the rate of water uptake, and why. Mention why light intensity increases rate of transpiration (it does not affect evaporation). Ask students to draw diagrams of the equipment and describe briefly how it works. Students then make a prediction and plan a fair test to investigate one of the factors that affect the movement of water through a plant by transpiration.	**Extend:** Students discuss the limitations of potometers as a means of measuring the amount of water lost by transpiration. **Extend:** Students should include a scientific explanation in their prediction (e.g., explain how the variable affects the rate of transpiration in terms of energy and particles).	**Activity:** Factors affecting transpiration

Plenary	Support/Extend	Resources
Factors that affect transpiration (5 min) Read out a series of conditions and for each one ask students to stand up if they think it will increase the rate of transpiration or sit down if they think it will decrease the rate of transpiration.		
Wilting (10 min) Show an image of a plant that has wilted. Ask students to explain why this has happened, and how it helps prevent further water loss.	**Extend:** Ask students to suggest why leaves have shiny cuticles.	

Homework
Ask students to find one adaptation that some plants have to reduce water loss by transpiration. They should explain how it works, and why it is important for the plant's survival.

kerboodle

A Kerboodle highlight for this lesson is **Extension sheet: Water uptake in plants**. Refer to the **Content map** on Kerboodle for a full list of resources and assessment.

B4 Organising animals and plants

Overview of B4 Organising animals and plants

In this chapter, students have learnt about the organisation of animals and plants. They should be able to recognise the components of blood, describe their functions, and summarise the process of blood clotting. They should recognise the three main types of blood vessel, link their structures with their functions, and understand the importance of a double circulatory system.

In studying the heart, students should be able to describe the main structures of the human heart and their functions. They should be aware of problems that can develop in the blood vessels and their treatments. They should know how the heartbeat is maintained by the pacemaker, and why some people may have problems with their heart and may need an artificial pacemaker or artificial heart. Students should be able to compare different treatments of heart problems.

Students have studied breathing and gas exchange, and should recognise the main structures of the gas exchange system along with their functions. They should know that gas exchange happens in the alveoli and describe adaptations of alveoli. They should be able to describe the processes of ventilation and gas exchange and the differences in composition of inhaled and exhaled air.

In studying plant tissues and organs, students should be familiar with the different plant tissues and their functions. They should recognise plant organs such as a leaf. They should understand that the roots, stem, and leaves form a plant organ system for transport of substances around the plant. They should be able to state the functions of xylem and phloem tissue. In studying transpiration, they should understand the function of stomata and recognise factors that affect transpiration rate.

MyMaths

You can find additional support for the maths skills covered in this chapter on **MyMaths**, including, working with percentages, estimation, means, and interpreting data.

kerboodle

For this chapter, the following assessments are available on Kerboodle:

B4 Checkpoint quiz: Organising animals and plants
B4 Progress quiz: Organising animals and plants 1
B4 Progress quiz: Organising animals and plants 2
B4 On your marks: Organising animals and plants
B4 Exam-style questions and mark scheme: Organising animals and plants

Checkpoint follow-up lesson

A student's route through this lesson can be determined using the Checkpoint assessment. Percentage pass marks are supplied in the Checkpoint teacher notes.

For each successive route through it is assumed that the student can perform to their current route as well as previous routes. For example, students working at Aiming for 6 are assumed to be secure in Aiming for 4 knowledge and understanding and working towards achieving all the learning outcomes for Aiming for 6.

	Aiming for 4	**Aiming for 6**	**Aiming for 8**
Learning outcomes	State simply the structure of the heart.	Describe the structure of the heart.	Describe the functions of parts of the heart.
	Describe the structure of the blood vessels.	Describe the function of the blood vessels.	Explain how the structure of the blood vessels is related to their functions.
	State the factors that affect transpiration.	Describe the factors that affect transpiration.	Explain the factors that affect transpiration.
	State how light intensity affects transpiration.	Describe how light intensity affects transpiration.	Explain how light intensity affects transpiration.
Starter	**Heart dissection (10 min)** Demonstrate the dissection of a heart. You will need a sheep heart and dissection instruments. Ask targeted questions to review the names and functions of parts of the heart and associated blood vessels.		
Differentiated checkpoint activity	Students use the Aiming for 4 follow-up sheet to label a diagram of the heart, complete a table on the structure of the blood vessels, and plan an experiment on the factors that affect transpiration, plotting a graph of the effect of light intensity on rate of transpiration. The follow-up sheet is highly-structured and provides students with guidance in planning their experiment. Students will need graph paper, rulers, and pencils and should work in pairs or small groups.	Students use the Aiming for 6 follow-up sheet to label a diagram of the heart, create a table on the structure of the blood vessels, and plan an experiment on the factors that affect transpiration. The follow-up sheet provides prompts to complete the activities and and guidance in planning their experiment. Students will need A3 paper and should work in pairs or small groups.	Students use the Aiming for 8 follow-up sheet to describe the pathway that blood takes through the heart. They then plan an investigation into the factors that affect transpiration, swapping their plans with another group to evaluate them. The follow-up sheet provides minimal support, but students should work in pairs to plan their investigation. Students will need A3 paper.
	Kerboodle resource B4 Checkpoint follow-up: Aiming for 4, B4 Checkpoint follow-up: Aiming for 6, B4 Checkpoint follow-up: Aiming for 8		
Plenary	**Review (5 min)** Show pictures of blood vessels on screen and ask students to name them. Then give each student two different coloured cards. Say a range of different environmental stimuli, such as increasing the temperature. Ask students to show one coloured card if the factor will increase transpiration, and another colour if it will decrease it.		
Progression	For support, the axes could be already drawn on graph paper. To progress, students should state how each factor they list will affect transpiration.	To progress, students should explain how each factor they list will affect transpiration.	To progress, students should plan their investigation independently.

2 Disease and bioenergetics

Specification links

AQA specification section	Assessment paper
3.1 Communicable disease	Paper 1
3.2 Monoclonal antibodies	Paper 1
3.3 Plant disease	Paper 1
4.1 Photosynthesis	Paper 1
4.2 Respiration	Paper 1

Required practicals

AQA required practicals	Practical skills	Topic
Investigate the effect of antiseptics or antibiotics on bacterial growth using agar plates and measuring zones of inhibition.	AT 1 – use appropriate apparatus to record length and area. AT 3 – use appropriate apparatus and techniques to observe and measure the process of bacterial growth. AT 4 – safe and ethical use of bacteria to measure physiological function and response to antibiotics and antiseptics in the environment. AT 8 – the use of appropriate techniques and qualitative reagents in problem-solving contexts to find the best antibiotic to use or the best concentration of antiseptic to use.	B3.1
Investigate the effect of light intensity on the rate of photosynthesis using an aquatic organism such as pondweed.	AT 1 – use appropriate apparatus to record the rate of production of oxygen gas produced; and to measure and control the temperature of water in a large beaker that acts as a 'heat shield'. AT 2 – use a thermometer to measure and control temperature of water bath. AT 3 – use appropriate apparatus and techniques to observe and measure the process of oxygen gas production. AT 4 – safe and ethical use and disposal of living pondweed to measure physiological functions and responses to light. AT 5 – measuring rate of reaction by oxygen gas production.	B4.1

Maths skills

AQA maths skills	Topic
1a Recognise and use expressions in decimal form.	B5.4, B8.2
1b Recognise and use expressions in standard form.	B5.4
1c Use ratios, fractions and percentages.	B6.5, B8.2, B9.2
1d Make estimates of the results of simple calculations.	B5.4
2a Use an appropriate number of significant figures.	B5.4
2b Find arithmetic means.	B6.4
2c Construct and interpret frequency tables and diagrams, bar charts, and histograms.	B5.1, B7.1, B7.3, B7.4, B7.5, B8.2
2d Understand the principles of sampling as applied to scientific data.	B5.1, B7.1, B7.3, B7.4, B7.5
2g Use a scatter diagram to identify a correlation between two variables.	B5.1, B7.1, B7.3, B7.4, B7.5
2h Make order of magnitude calculations.	B5.2, B5.4
3a Understand and use the symbols: $=, <, \ll, \gg, >, \propto, \sim$.	B8.2
3d Solve simple algebraic equations.	B8.2
4a Translate information between graphical and numeric form.	B5.1, B7.1, B7.3, B7.4, B7.5, B8.2, B9.2
4c Plot two variables from experimental or other data.	B8.2
5c Calculate areas of triangles and rectangles, surface areas, and volumes of cubes.	B5.4

B2 Disease and bioenergetics

KS3 concept	GCSE topic	Checkpoint	Revision
The consequences of imbalances in the diet.	B7.4 Diet, exercise, and disease	Ask students to evaluate examples of different diets to describe how healthy they think they are and what they would change.	Ask students the effects of certain imbalances in the diet, for example, too much sugar, not enough iron.
The importance of bacteria in the human digestive system.	B5.2 Pathogens and disease	Ask students if they agree with the statement 'we would be healthier with no bacteria in our bodies'.	Ask students to explain the function of bacteria in the human digestive system.
The impact of exercise and smoking on the human gas exchange system.	B7.3 Smoking and the risk of disease	Ask students to predict what happens to heart and breathing rate as they exercise and explain why.	Ask students to state three ways that smoking can harm health.
The effects of recreational drugs on behaviour, health, and life processes.	B7.1 Non-communicable diseases	Ask students to state three ways that alcohol can harm a person, to include effects on behaviour.	Ask students to state three arguments for and against a ban on smoking.
The use of drugs to treat diseases.	B6.3 Discovering drugs	Ask students to name as many medicinal drugs as they can.	Ask students to suggest why we do not have a drug that can cure a cold.
The basic principles of photosynthesis.	B8.1 Photosynthesis	Ask students to write down the word equation for photosynthesis.	Ask students to suggest how to increase the growth of a plant.
The differences between aerobic and anaerobic respiration.	B9.1 Aerobic respiration	Ask students to write down the word equation for aerobic respiration.	Ask students to write down how people use anaerobic respiration in yeast.
Presenting data using tables and graphs.	B5.1 Health and disease	Ask students to write down simple instructions for someone on how to design a results table to draw a line graph.	Give students some simple data to plot as a line graph.
Why scientists publish their results.	B6.4 Developing drugs	Ask students to explain what a journal and peer review is.	Ask students to predict what would happen if scientists never published their results.
State examples of everyday applications of science and technology.	B6.1 Vaccination	Ask students to list the things they have used in their day so far that have been developed by scientists.	Ask students to form arguments against the statement 'scientific research has never benefited anyone'.

B 5 Communicable diseases

5.1 Health and disease

AQA spec link: 2.2.5 Students should be able to describe the relationship between health and disease and the interactions between different types of disease.

Health is the state of physical and mental wellbeing.

Diseases, both communicable and non-communicable, are major causes of ill health. Other factors including diet, stress, and life situations may have a profound effect on both physical and mental health.

Different types of disease may interact.
- Defects in the immune system mean that an individual is more likely to suffer from infectious diseases.
- Viruses living in cells can be the trigger for cancers.
- Immune reactions initially caused by a pathogen can trigger allergies such as skin rashes and asthma.
- Severe physical ill health can lead to depression and other mental illness.

Students should be able to translate disease incidence information between graphical and numerical forms, construct and interpret frequency tables and diagrams, bar charts and histograms, and use a scatter diagram to identify a correlation between two variables.

Students should understand the principles of sampling as applied to scientific data, including epidemiological data.

MS 2c, 2d, 2g, 4a

Aiming for	Outcome	Checkpoint	
		Question	Activity
Aiming for GRADE 4	Describe health as a state of physical and mental wellbeing.	1	Starter 1, Main 1
	State some causes of ill health.	2	Starter 2, Plenary 2, Homework
	Draw a simple conclusion from data on health.	3, End of chapter 3	Main 2, Plenary 1
Aiming for GRADE 6	Describe the difference between communicable and non-communicable diseases.	2	Starter 2
	Use a scatter diagram to identify a correlation between two variables.		Main 1, Plenary 1
	Construct and interpret bar charts, frequency tables, frequency diagrams, and histograms.	3, End of chapter 4	Main 2
Aiming for GRADE 8	Suggest how communicable diseases are spread.		Starter 2
	Suggest links between lifestyle and health.	4	Starter 1, Plenary 2, Homework
	Discuss the validity of a statement based on evidence in the form of data.		Main 2, Homework

B5 Communicable diseases

Maths
Students interpret data in the form of frequency tables, histograms, and scatter graphs (2g, 4a). They construct their own frequency diagrams (2c).

Literacy
Students use group and paired discussion to talk through their ideas about health.

Key words
communicable (infectious) diseases, pathogens, non-communicable diseases

Starter	Support/Extend	Resources
Healthy and unhealthy (10 min) Divide the class in half. Ask students in each half to work in small groups to draw a labelled image of a healthy person or an unhealthy person. Discuss their ideas and define what is meant by health. **Illnesses** (5 min) Ask the class to work in groups. Give each group an illness or condition, for example, measles, asthma, depression, or lung cancer. Ask them to discuss what causes their allocated illness. Discuss what is meant by health, and the different factors that affect it.	**Extend:** Ask students to classify the illnesses as communicable or non-communicable and, if communicable, describe how they are spread.	

Main	Support/Extend	Resources
Interpreting health data (40 min) Show the class a recent headline from a newspaper that shows a link between an activity/food and health. Ask them how you can be sure that it is true. Explain that these stories are usually based on data from research but that sometimes the data is interpreted incorrectly. Demonstrate how to interpret a scatter graph to work out the correlation. Students are then presented with statements about health along with evidence in the form of data. They analyse the data and decide whether it backs up the statements. Discuss the need to back up a correlation with a plausible cause before it can be validated and accepted as meaningful. A correlation might be just an association between factors, if no causal link can be established.	**Extend:** Supply students with data from the research for them to study. **Support:** During the activity students will need to construct and interpret frequency tables, frequency diagrams, and histograms. Take time to go through these methods first.	**Activity:** Interpreting health data

Plenary	Support/Extend	Resources
What does it show? (5 min) Students use the interactive to study a graph that shows the interaction between different factors and health. Students answer questions about what the graph is showing **Test the claim** (10 min) Give students the controversial statement: people on low incomes get ill more often. Ask them to discuss in pairs whether they think this is likely, and back up their conclusion using their scientific knowledge.	**Support:** Give students a range of possible answers for them to choose from. **Extend:** Ask pairs to also discuss how they could investigate this possible link.	**Interactive:** What does it show?

Homework
Nodding disease is an illness that occurs in parts of Africa. Scientists do not know what causes it. Ask students to carry out research into possible hypotheses, and the evidence that supports them.

B5.2 Pathogens and disease

AQA spec link: 3.1.1 Students should be able to explain how diseases caused by viruses, bacteria, protists, and fungi are spread in animals and plants.

Pathogens are microorganisms that cause infectious disease. Pathogens may be viruses, bacteria, protists, or fungi. They may infect animals and can be spread by direct contact, by water, or by air.

Bacteria and viruses may reproduce rapidly inside the body.

Bacteria may produce poisons (toxins) that damage tissues and make us feel ill.

Viruses live and reproduce inside cells, causing cell damage.

WS 1.4
MS 2h

Aiming for	Outcome	Checkpoint	
		Question	Activity
Aiming for GRADE 4 ↓	State that pathogens are microorganisms that cause disease.	1	Main
	Describe ways in which pathogens can be spread.	2, End of chapter 1	Main
Aiming for GRADE 6 ↓	Describe how bacteria and viruses cause disease.	1	Main, Plenary 1
	Explain why communicable diseases spread rapidly following a natural disaster.		Main
Aiming for GRADE 8 ↓	Explain why viruses are always pathogens, but not all bacteria are.		Starter 2, Plenary 2
	Explain how pathogens are passed from one organism to another, and use this to suggest ways of preventing the spread.	2, 3, End of chapter 1	Main

Maths
Students discuss the sizes of viruses and bacteria using SI units of length (2h).

Literacy
Students summarise key concepts as spider or concept diagrams. They also produce an animation, including a voiceover script.

Key words
communicable diseases, microorganisms, viruses

B5 Communicable diseases

Starter	Support/Extend	Resources
Communicable diseases (5 min) Ask the class to list any communicable (infectious) diseases they have had. Discuss which are the most common.	**Extend:** Students should write down what they think causes each disease, for example, a cold is caused by a virus.	
Bacteria discussion (10 min) Present the class with the statement: all bacteria are harmful. Ask students to discuss in groups whether they agree with this, and why.	**Support:** Provide the class with visual stimulus by showing images of for example, foods made by bacteria (e.g., yoghurt and cheese), infected cuts and antibiotics.	

Main	Support/Extend	Resources
Pathogens and the spread of diseases (40 min) Introduce the term pathogen as a microorganism that causes infectious diseases in living things, including plants. Students then use the student book to design an animation about how pathogens, including viruses, protists, and bacteria, cause disease. They can design them as a drawn storyboard or, if you have longer, use an application on a tablet or computer to make an animation. The animations should include a voiceover script.	**Support:** Provide students with a storyboard template to help them plan their animation. **Extend:** Students should do extra research on how viruses infect cells.	**Activity:** Pathogens and the spread of diseases
Students then create a spider diagram to summarise the ways in which pathogens are spread. Ask them to use their diagram to explain why diseases spread more quickly following a natural disaster like an earthquake.	**Extend:** Students can create a concept diagram by explaining the links. Ask them to add ideas on how to prevent the spread of pathogens by each method.	

Plenary	Support/Extend	Resources
Bacteria or virus? (5 min) Interactive where students select the correct definition of a pathogen. They then choose whether statements are describing bacteria or viruses.	**Support:** Remind students that bacteria are cells, whereas viruses invade cells.	**Interactive:** Bacteria or virus?
Pathogen (10 min) Ask students to write down why bacteria are sometimes pathogens, but viruses are always pathogens.	**Extend:** Students should use examples of bacteria that are not pathogens in their explanation.	

Homework		
Students design a social network profile page for a pathogen of their choice. They can include the scientific name of the pathogen, an image, what type of pathogen it is, and what disease it causes in the information section. In the timeline they could include posts about how the pathogen has spread, what hosts it has infected, and what symptoms it has caused. Students can be as imaginative as they like, as long as they use accurate scientific information.		

GCSE Biology only

B5.3 Growing bacteria in the lab

AQA spec link: 1.1.6 Bacteria multiply by simple cell division (binary fission) as often as once every 20 minutes if they have enough nutrients and a suitable temperature.

Bacteria can be grown in a nutrient broth solution or as colonies on an agar gel plate.

Uncontaminated cultures of microorganisms are required for investigating the action of disinfectants and antibiotics.

Students should be able to describe how to prepare an uncontaminated culture using aseptic technique.

They should be able to explain why:

- Petri dishes and culture media must be sterilised before use to kill unwanted microorganisms
- inoculating loops used to transfer microorganisms to the media must be sterilised by passing them through a flame
- the lid of the Petri dish should be secured with adhesive tape to prevent microorganisms from the air contaminating the culture, and stored upside down
- in school and college laboratories, cultures should be incubated at a maximum temperature of 25 °C.

Required practical: Investigate the effect of antiseptics or antibiotics on bacterial growth.

WS 2.2, 2.4

Aiming for	Outcome	Checkpoint	
		Question	Activity
Aiming for GRADE 4	State that bacteria reproduce by cell division and this is called binary fission.		Starter 1
	Prepare a bacterial culture on agar gel.		Main, Plenary 2
	Follow the rules needed to prepare an uncontaminated culture.		Main
Aiming for GRADE 6	Explain why numbers of bacteria on an agar plate will eventually stop growing.	3	Homework
	Explain why it is important to use an uncontaminated culture to investigate bacterial growth.		Main
	Describe and explain why each safety rule is needed in order to safely prepare, incubate, and dispose of a culture.	2	Main
Aiming for GRADE 8	Explain what is meant by exponential growth and analyse a graph showing it.		Starter 1, Homework
	Suggest how to measure the growth of bacteria and discuss uncertainty.		Main
	Plan a detailed investigation to find out how a variable affects the growth of bacteria.		Main

Maths
Students consider exponential growth and why bacteria numbers increase so rapidly.

Literacy
Students follow a method with several steps to complete the practical successfully. They create their own list of rules.

Key words
binary fission, culture medium, agar gel, inoculate

78

■ B5 Communicable diseases

Required practical

Title	Growing useful organisms
Equipment	sterile Petri dish containing nutrient agar, inoculating loop, adhesive tape, marker pen or chinagraph pencil, culture of a bacterium (such as *Bacillus subtilis*) in a small capped bottle, disinfectant solution, Bunsen burner, examples of antiseptics (e.g., Lysol, antibacterial liquid soap, mouthwash, liquid toothpaste), distilled water, small beakers, tweezers, small pieces of filter paper (use a hole punch to cut circles)
Overview of method	Students use prepared sterile Petri dishes containing nutrient agar. They use aseptic technique to inoculate the plate with a bacterial culture. They then divide the plate into quarters and place a piece of filter paper soaked in an antiseptic plus a control soaked in water into each quarter. The plates are incubated until the next lesson.
Safety considerations	Bench tops need to be prepared with disinfectant or alcohol well before the experiment, and cleaned with disinfectant after the epxeriment. No naked flames during this procedure.

Starter	Support/Extend	Resources
Bacterial reproduction (5 min) Ask students to draw the outline of one bacterium and then draw a series of diagrams to show how they think bacteria reproduce. Go through their ideas and show them how bacteria reproduce by dividing in half (binary fission). **KWL analysis** (10 min) Show the class an image of bacterial colonies grown on an agar plate. Ask them what they know, about the plate, and what they want to know.	**Support:** Show students an animation of binary fission. **Extend:** Discuss what is meant by exponential growth.	

Main	Support/Extend	Resources
Growing useful organisms (40 min) Students investigate the effect of antiseptics or antibiotics on bacterial growth. Students prepare an uncontaminated culture of bacteria. Discuss why it is important to use sterile conditions and produce an uncontaminated culture. Supply students with small circles of filter paper and a range of different antiseptics. They use tweezers to soak the paper and place on different labelled sections of their dish. Leave the dishes to incubate until the next lesson. Students then create a list of rules for preparing uncontaminated cultures in the lab.	**Support:** Demonstrate the procedure and answer any questions before students carry out the practical. **Extend:** Ask students to plan how they could investigate a variable that affects bacteria growth and discuss uncertainty in measurements. **Extend:** Students should explain why each rule is needed.	**Required practical:** Growing useful organisms

Plenary	Support/Extend	Resources
What have I learnt? (5 min) Show students the image of bacterial colonies grown on an agar plate again. Ask them to list three things they have learnt this lesson. **How to grow bacteria** (10 min) Interactive where students put the steps of the method used to prepare a culture of bacteria in the correct order.	**Extend:** Students should write down five things.	**Interactive:** How to grow bacteria

Homework		
Ask students to write down whether they think bacteria grown on an agar plate will keep growing forever, and suggest why they think this.	**Extend:** Students should find a graph that shows exponential bacterial growth, describe what the shape of the graph shows them, and use it to explain their answer.	

GCSE Biology only

B5.4 Preventing bacterial growth

AQA spec link: 1.1.6 Bacteria multiply by simple cell division (binary fission) as often as once every 20 minutes if they have enough nutrients and a suitable temperature.

Students should be able to calculate cross-sectional areas of colonies or clear areas around colonies using πr².

Students should be able to calculate the number of bacteria in a population after a certain time if given the mean division time.

(H) Students should be able to express the answer in standard form.

Required practical: Investigate the effect of antiseptics or antibiotics on bacterial growth.

WS 2.2, 2.4
MS 1a, 1b, 1d, 2a, 2h, 5c

Aiming for	Outcome	Checkpoint	
		Question	Activity
Aiming for GRADE 4 ↓	Describe the difference between antiseptics, disinfectants, and antibiotics.	1	Starter 2, Plenary 2
	Write a prediction.		Main 2
	Measure the diameter of clear areas around colonies.		Main 3
Aiming for GRADE 6 ↓	Explain when an antiseptic, a disinfectant, and an antibiotic would be used.		Starter 2
	Calculate the number of bacteria in a population after a certain time if given the mean division time.	End of chapter 2	Starter 1, Main 1, Plenary 1
	Calculate the area of the clear areas around colonies using πr².	3, End of chapter 2	Main 3
Aiming for GRADE 8 ↓	Write a prediction using detailed scientific knowledge.		Main 2
	Calculate the number of bacteria in a sample when using a counting chamber.		Main 2
	Apply knowledge of sampling techniques to ensure samples are representative.		Main 3

Maths
Students calculate the number of bacteria in a population after a certain time, with higher-tier students expressing this number in standard form (1b). They also measure the diameter of a circle and calculate area using πr² (5c).

Literacy
Students write detailed predictions, conclusions, and evaluations using scientific terminology.

Required practical

Title	Analysing bacterial growth
Equipment	culture plates from last lesson, transparent plastic ruler
Overview of method	Students measure the clear area around each circle and calculate the area using πr².
Safety considerations	Do not allow students to open the plates. Used cultures should be disposed of according to safety regulations.

■ B5 Communicable diseases

Starter	Support/Extend	Resources
Binary fission (5 min) Remind students that bacteria reproduce by dividing in two. Ask students to calculate how many bacteria are present after four hours if a bacterium divides once every hour. **Bacteria killers** (10 min) Show students images of bottles of antibiotics, disinfectants, and antiseptics. Ask them what the difference is between them, and when each example would be used.	**Support:** Guide students through the example. **Extend:** Set the calculation with the bacterium dividing once every 20 minutes.	

Main	Support/Extend	Resources
Analysing bacterial growth (40 min) Work through the Using maths box in the student book to show students how to calculate the number of bacteria in a population. Give students further examples of calculations for them to solve. Then discuss examples of when the students have made hypotheses and predictions in their everyday lives. Remind them of the plates they set up last lesson and ask them to use their knowledge of the uses of different antiseptics and information from the student book to predict what they will see on their plates. Allow students to study their plates from Topic B5.3, but remind them not to open them. They should measure the clear area around each circle and calculate the area using πr^2. They then write a conclusion explaining whether their prediction was correct, and evaluating their investigation.	**Extend:** Show students a graph showing the growth curve of a bacterial population. Ask them to explain the shape. **Extend:** Students should explain the reasoning behind their prediction. **Support:** Students just measure the diameter of the clear area. **Extend:** Students should pool results, applying sampling techniques to choose clear areas that are representative and calculating the mean area.	**Required practical:** Analysing bacterial growth

Plenary	Support/Extend	Resources
Antiseptic, antibiotic, or disinfectant? (10 min) Interactive where students match the biological term with its correct meaning. Students then decide what would be best to use in different scenarios. **Antibiotic plate** (5 min) Show the class an image of an agar plate with clear areas used to test the effectiveness of antibiotics. Ask them to write down what it shows.	**Support:** Explain that antibiotics are drugs that inhibit the growth of bacteria.	**Interactive:** Antiseptic, antibiotic, or disinfectant?

Homework		
Provide students with results from an investigation to evaluate the effectiveness of different concentrations of disinfectant.		

kerboodle

A Kerboodle highlight for this lesson is **Maths skills: Area of bacterial colonies**. Refer to the **Content map** on Kerboodle for a full list of resources and assessment.

B5.5 Preventing infections

AQA spec link: 3.1.1 Students should be able to explain how the spread of diseases can be reduced or prevented.

Aiming for	Outcome	Checkpoint	
		Question	Activity
Aiming for GRADE 4 ↓	List some ways in which communicable diseases are spread.	End of chapter 1	Starter 1, Starter 2, Main
	Take a role in designing a form of communication to inform the public about how to prevent the spread of a disease.		Main
Aiming for GRADE 6 ↓	Describe how the spread of diseases can be reduced or prevented.	1, End of chapter 1	Starter 1, Starter 2, Main, Plenary 1
	Communicate to the public about how to stop the spread of a disease.		Main
Aiming for GRADE 8 ↓	Use scientific knowledge to explain in detail how different methods reduce or prevent the spread of disease.	2	Starter 1, Starter 2, Main, Plenary 1
	Use an example to explain how scientific method has been applied to help prevent the spread of disease.	2	Plenary 2, Homework

Literacy
Students create a public health campaign in the form of posters, leaflets, and advertisements.

Key word
vaccines

B5 Communicable diseases

Starter	Support/Extend	Resources
Hand washing (5 min) Show students an image of a doctor or nurse washing their hands. Ask them to write down why this is important. **The plague** (10 min) Tell the class that the Great Plague was spread by fleas. Tell them some methods that people in the past used to try to stop the spread of the plague (isolating infected families, carrying sweet-smelling flowers, covering the face, praying). Ask them to discuss how useful they think each method was, and what they would recommend instead.	**Extend:** Discuss this in light of antibiotic-resistant bacteria. **Support:** Show students images and/or video for stimulus.	

Main	Support/Extend	Resources
Public health campaign (40 min) Ask students to read the information in the student book on preventing the spread of communicable diseases. Then divide the class into groups and give details about recent epidemics, for example, swine flu in the UK, Ebola in Africa, MERS in South Korea, cholera in Haiti, and so on. Groups research a disease and how it is spread. They then create a campaign to educate people about how to keep healthy and reduce the spread of the disease. This could include a poster, leaflet, or advertisement, or all three if you have more time. Ask groups to present their campaigns and ask students to peer assess their work based on scientific accuracy and how useful it would be.	**Support:** Explain what is meant by an epidemic. **Extend:** Students should consider the campaign in light of where the epidemic is taking place and the circumstances surrounding it, for example, the earthquake in Haiti.	**Activity:** Public health campaign

Plenary	Support/Extend	Resources
How would you control the spread? (10 min) Supply students with the name of a communicable disease and how it is spread. Ask them to suggest which control methods would work. **The work of Semmelweis** (5 min) Students look at the work of Semmelweis. They match the stages of the scientific method (observe, hypothesise, predict, test, conclude) to what he did.	**Support:** Display the different methods for students to choose from. Do this as a class discussion. **Extend:** Students should give reasons for their choices.	**Interactive:** The work of Semmelweis

Homework		
Students produce a flow chart to describe how they would respond to a mysterious disease outbreak if they were part of the Government. Students use their scientific knowledge to justify each action.	**Extend:** Encourage students to refer to knowledge from previous topics and include how they would investigate the cause and treatment of the disease.	

kerboodle

A Kerboodle highlight for this lesson is **Literacy sheet: Lister, Pasteur, Nightingale, and Semmelweis**. Refer to the **Content map** on Kerboodle for a full list of resources and assessment.

B5.6 Viral diseases

AQA spec link: 3.1.2 Measles is a viral disease showing symptoms of fever and a red skin rash. Measles is a serious illness that can be fatal if complications arise. For this reason most young children are vaccinated against measles. The measles virus is spread by inhalation of droplets from sneezes and coughs.

HIV initially causes a flu-like illness. Unless successfully controlled with antiretroviral drugs the virus attacks the body's immune cells. Late stage HIV infection, or AIDS, occurs when the body's immune system becomes so badly damaged it can no longer deal with other infections or cancers. HIV is spread by sexual contact or exchange of body fluids such as blood which occurs when drug users share needles.

Tobacco mosaic virus (TMV) is a widespread plant pathogen affecting many species of plants including tomatoes. It gives a distinctive 'mosaic' pattern of discolouration on the leaves which affects the growth of the plant due to lack of photosynthesis.

Aiming for	Outcome	Checkpoint	
		Question	Activity
Aiming for GRADE 4	Name some diseases that are caused by viruses.		Starter 1, Main 1, Plenary 2
	Describe how measles and HIV are spread.	End of chapter 5	Main 1, Plenary 2
	Summarise information in a table.		Main 1
Aiming for GRADE 6	Describe how measles, HIV, and tobacco mosaic virus affect the infected organism.	1, 2, 4	Main 1, Plenary
	Interpret data to describe how the number of people infected with measles in the UK has changed over time.	1, 3	Main 2
	Design a table and use it to summarise information.		Main 1
Aiming for GRADE 8	Explain how measles, HIV, and tobacco mosaic virus affect the infected organism.	1, 2, 4	Main 1, Plenary 2
	Explain why viral infections are often more difficult to prevent and treat than bacterial infections.	End of chapter 3	Plenary 1
	Write a persuasive letter to parents urging them to vaccinate their children against measles.		Main 2

Maths
Students interpret a line graph that shows how the number of cases of measles has changed in the UK.

Literacy
Students organise information from the student book into a table. They also write a persuasive letter to parents on why they should vaccinate their children against measles.

B5 Communicable diseases

Starter	Support/Extend	Resources
What is the pathogen? (10 min) Interactive where students select true or false for a series of statements about viral disease. They then match the statements to the correct disease. **Killer viruses** (5 min) Ask students to summarise how viruses cause damage in a tweet (less than 140 characters).		**Interactive:** What is the pathogen?

Main	Support/Extend	Resources
Viral infections (20 min) Ask students to read through the information on measles, HIV, and the tobacco mosaic virus in the student book. They should then summarise the information in a table showing disease, pathogen, ways to reduce spread, symptoms, and treatment. **Measles vaccination** (20 min) Show students a graph that shows the number of cases of measles in the UK since the start of the 20th century. Ask pairs to discuss what it shows and possible explanations for this. Discuss their thoughts. Tell them that in the early 2000s many parents stopped giving their children the MMR vaccine because of claims that it caused autism. Tell them that, even though these claims were later shown to be false, many children are still not being vaccinated. Ask students to write an open letter telling parents why they should vaccinate their children against measles.	**Extend:** Ask students to design their own table–do not give them the headings of columns. **Support:** Inform students of the year that the measles vaccination was introduced (1968).	**Activity:** Measles vaccination

Plenary	Support/Extend	Resources
Treatment (10 min) Ask students to write down reasons why viral infections are often more difficult to prevent and treat than bacterial infections. **Viral statements** (5 min) Name a viral disease and choose a student to give one piece of information on this disease. They then choose another student to add some more information, and so on.		

Homework		
Ask students to do their own research into another viral disease and write another section similar to those in the student book on this disease. Alternatively, students can complete the WebQuest, which asks them to research pathogens and choose which one they think is the world's worst pathogen.	**Support:** Provide a framework with sentence starters.	**WebQuest:** The World's worst pathogen

kerboodle
A Kerboodle highlight for this lesson is **Go further: HIV**. Refer to the **Content map** on Kerboodle for a full list of resources and assessment.

B5.7 Bacterial diseases

AQA spec link: 3.1.3 *Salmonella* food poisoning is spread by bacteria ingested in food, or on food prepared in unhygienic conditions. In the UK, poultry are vaccinated against *Salmonella* to control the spread. Fever, abdominal cramps, vomiting, and diarrhoea are caused by the bacteria and the toxins they secrete.

Gonorrhoea is a sexually transmitted disease (STD) with symptoms of a thick yellow or green discharge from the vagina or penis and pain on urinating. It is caused by a bacterium and was easily treated with the antibiotic penicillin until many resistant strains appeared. Gonorrhoea is spread by sexual contact. The spread can be controlled by treatment with antibiotics or the use of a barrier method of contraception such as a condom.

Aiming for	Outcome	Checkpoint	
		Question	Activity
Aiming for GRADE 4 ↓	Name some diseases that are caused by bacteria.		Main, Plenary
	Describe how *salmonella* and gonorrhoea are spread.	2, 3	Main
Aiming for GRADE 6 ↓	Describe similarities and differences between *salmonella* and gonorrhoea.		Main
	Describe how the spread of *salmonella* and gonorrhoea is controlled.	2, 3, 4	Main
Aiming for GRADE 8 ↓	Suggest why more people die from viral diseases than from bacterial diseases.	1	Starter 1
	Explain in detail how methods to control the spread of *salmonella* and gonorrhoea work.		Main

Maths
Students could include figures and statistics in their information poster/leaflet.

Literacy
Students organise information to describe the similarities and differences between *Salmonella* and gonorrhoea. They also create an information poster or leaflet suitable for the general public on bacterial diseases.

Key word
sexually transmitted disease (STD)

B5 Communicable diseases

Starter	Support/Extend	Resources
Why do more people die from viral infections? (10 min) Present some examples of viral and bacterial infections. Ask students to discuss the question in pairs and list their ideas. Discuss their ideas as a class and use this opportunity to review understanding of how bacteria and viruses differ in the way they infect and harm an organism, the use of antibiotics, and how the mutation of viruses makes it difficult to develop vaccines. **Antibiotic resistance** (5 min) Share with the class a headline or news video about antibiotic resistance. Discuss why this is a problem, and what scientists are trying to do about it.	**Support:** Focus on one reason, for example, bacterial infections can be treated using antibiotics.	

Main	Support/Extend	Resources
***Salmonella* and gonorrhoea** (40 min) Introduce these as bacterial infections. Discuss the similarities and differences between them. Students produce a table in summary. Students then write advice on *salmonella* or gonorrhoea suitable for patients at a doctor's surgery. This can be a poster warning people how to avoid getting *salmonella* from a summer barbeque, or a leaflet on how to tell if you have gonorrhoea and the treatments available. Share with the class a news story on the fact that gonorrhea may soon be untreatable due to antibiotic resistance. Ask students to work in small groups to summarise the story in one sentence. After listening to these, discuss as a class why antibiotic resistance is a problem.	**Support:** Provide students with a table containing suitable column headings, for example, type of pathogen, how it spreads. **Extend:** Students could write a leaflet as this will enable them to use more scientific explanations.	**Activity:** *Salmonella* and gonorrhoea

Plenary	Support/Extend	Resources
Bacteria true or false (10 min) Students use the interactive to identify if a series of statements on bacterial infections are true or false. They then match the statements to the correct disease. **Bacterial disease in plants** (5 min) Show the class an image of a crown gall, which is caused by a bacterial infection. Ask them to write down how it would cause ill health in the plant.	**Extend:** Ask students to make up their own quiz for a partner.	**Interactive:** Bacteria true or false

Homework		
Ask students to find out about the work of Dr. John Snow in the 19th century. They should write out a report or bullet points outlining what he found out about the infectious disease cholera.		

B5.8 Diseases caused by fungi and protists

AQA spec links: 3.1.4 Rose black spot is a fungal disease where purple or black spots develop on leaves, which often turn yellow and drop early. It affects the growth of the plant as photosynthesis is reduced. It is spread in the environment by water or wind. Rose black spot can be treated by using fungicides and/or removing and destroying the affected leaves.

3.1.5 The pathogens that cause malaria are protists.

The malarial protist has a life cycle that includes the mosquito. Malaria causes recurrent episodes of fever and can be fatal. The spread of malaria is controlled by preventing the vectors, mosquitos, from breeding and by using mosquito nets to avoid being bitten.

Aiming for	Outcome	Checkpoint	
		Question	Activity
Aiming for GRADE 4 ↓	State that rose black spot is caused by fungi and malaria is caused by protists.		Main 1, Main 2, Plenary 2
	Use a diagram to describe the life cycle of the malaria protist.	2	Main 2
	State some ways in which malaria is controlled.	End of chapter 1	Main 2
Aiming for GRADE 6 ↓	Describe how rose black spot affects the plant and how it is treated.	1	Main 1
	Link ways of controlling the spread of malaria to specific parts of the protist's life cycle.	2, 3	Main 2
Aiming for GRADE 8 ↓	Explain how rose black spot affects the growth of a plant.	1	Main 1
	Explain why it is so expensive to stop the spread of malaria.		Main 2, Plenary 1

Maths
Students study a graphic that shows how many people are killed by different animals each year.

Literacy
Students use information from the student book to advise a rose grower on rose black spot and annotate the life cycle of the malaria protist. Students also write a short persuasive speech.

B5 Communicable diseases

Starter	Support/Extend	Resources
Fungal infections (5 min) Show images of a range of fungal infections, for example, athlete's foot, rose black spot, potato blight, and ringworm. Ask students what they think they have in common, and reveal that they are all fungal infections. **World's deadliest animal** (10 min) Ask the class which animal they think kills the most people worldwide each year. After hearing a few suggestions show them a graphic from the Internet showing the world's deadliest animals, which shows that the answer is mosquitoes. Ask them to write down why they think this is the case.	**Extend:** Discuss that some fungal infections can be fatal to humans if the fungi colonises inside the body. **Extend:** Students can use the numbers in the graphic to calculate how many times more deadly mosquitoes are than sharks. It is up to them to decide how to do this.	

Main	Support/Extend	Resources
Rose black spot (15 min) Show images of rose black spot. Tell the class that a rose grower has sent these in and asked for advice on what it is, whether it is harmful, and how to stop it. Students use the student book to research the disease and reply to the grower. **Stop malaria** (25 min) Introduce malaria to students, including how it kills, how many people it affects, and where this happens in the world. Explain that malaria is caused by a protist, and discuss the life cycle of the malaria protist. Ask students to produce a plan to eradicate malaria. They should refer to the life cycle of the protist that causes the disease, and annotate each stage with methods that can be used to prevent the spread.	**Support:** Supply a writing frame so students can structure their replies. **Extend:** Students should explain how each method works.	**Activity:** Stop malaria

Plenary	Support/Extend	Resources
Malaria charity (10 min) Ask students to act as fundraisers for a malaria charity and write one short speech that can be used to persuade people to donate money. **Fungi and protist** (5 min) Students decide whether diseases are cause by fungi or protists. They then type in answers to complete a passage about the spread and control of malaria.	**Extend:** Students should explain why a lot of money is needed if you want to eradicate malaria.	**Interactive:** Fungi and protists

Homework		
Students create an A4 page for a revision guide that summarises everything they have learnt so far about pathogens, including bacteria, viruses, fungi, and protists. They should include an example of a disease caused by each pathogen.	**Extend:** Students should add information on symptoms, treatments, and ways of preventing the spread of the disease.	

B5.9 Human defence responses

AQA spec link: Students should be able to describe the non-specific defence systems of the human body against pathogens, including the:

- skin
- nose
- trachea and bronchi
- stomach.

Students should be able to explain the role of the immune system in the defence against disease. If a pathogen enters the body the immune system tries to destroy the pathogen.

White blood cells help to defend against pathogens by:

- phagocytosis
- antibody production
- antitoxin production.

Aiming for	Outcome	Checkpoint	
		Question	Activity
Aiming for GRADE 4 ↓	Describe some ways in which the human body defends itself against the entry of pathogens.	End of chapter 3	Starter 1, Main 1, Plenary 2
	State that white blood cells help defend the body against pathogens.		Starter 2, Main 2, Plenary 2
	Show how one part of a model is similar to real life.		Plenary 1
Aiming for GRADE 6 ↓	Describe how human body defence mechanisms stop the entry of pathogens.	End of chapter 3	Starter 1, Main 1, Plenary 2
	Describe the role of white blood cells in the defence against disease.	3, End of chapter 3	Starter 2, Main 2, Plenary 2
	Use a model to explain how the body defends itself against disease.		Plenary 1
Aiming for GRADE 8 ↓	Explain how a reduced or overactive immune system can cause illness.	2	Main 2
	Explain in detail how antibody production fights pathogens.		Main 2
	Evaluate an analogy of the human defence systems against disease.		Plenary 1

Maths
Students can analyse data on white blood cell counts or interpret a graph that shows antibody production following an infection.

Literacy
Students use information from the student book and other secondary sources to research defence mechanisms.

■ B5 Communicable diseases

Starter	Support/Extend	Resources
What's the link? (10 min) Present students with the following list: organs skin, blood, and stomach. Ask them what they think they all have in common (the objectives of the lesson should be a big clue—they are organs in humans that help defend against infection). Then ask students for their answer, and reasons why they think this. **Phagocytosis** (5 min) Show the class an animation or video of white blood cells ingesting pathogens. Question students on what it is showing and why it is important for our health.	**Extend:** Ask students to create another list of three things that are involved in defending the body against pathogens. **Support:** Supply students with the key words white blood cell, pathogen, and immune system.	

Main	Support/Extend	Resources
Human defence systems (20 min) Discuss that humans have many mechanisms to stop pathogens from entering the body. Supply groups of students with a long piece of paper (you can use a roll of cheap wallpaper). Ask one volunteer to lie down on the paper so someone else can draw round them. Then ask students to add drawings and labels to illustrate parts of the defence system. After recording their initial thoughts, allow groups to use information from the student book to add further information. Students should either copy the diagram or take a photo, print it out, and attach to their notes. Then students explain the role of white blood cells in defending our bodies against invading pathogens. For example: • Why are your white blood cells known as the second line of defence? • State and describe the three main ways in which white blood cells can destroy pathogens. • Suggest why it takes a while for you to start to get better following an infection. • Explain why you can't get chickenpox twice.	**Extend:** Students should explain how each method works. They can use extra resources for research.	**Activity:** Human defence systems

Plenary	Support/Extend	Resources
Model defences (5 min) Ask students to explain how different parts of a castle are analogous to the human body's defence mechanisms (e.g., the walls of the castle are like the skin because they both keep invaders out). **Where is it found?** (5 min) Interactive activity where students select the correct defence mechanisms in the human body. They then match the defence mechanism to where it is found in the human body.	**Extend:** Ask students to evaluate this analogy.	**Interactive:** Where is it found?

Homework		
Ask students to design their own model or analogy to explain one, or a number of, defence mechanisms.		

kerboodle

A Kerboodle highlight for this lesson is **Bump up your grade: Human defence responses**. Refer to the **Content map** on Kerboodle for a full list of resources and assessment.

GCSE Biology only

B5.10 More about plant diseases

AQA spec link: 3.3.1 **H** Plant diseases can be detected by:
- stunted growth
- spots on leaves
- areas of decay (rot)
- growths
- malformed stems or leaves
- discolouration
- the presence of pests.

Identification can be made by:
- reference to a gardening manual
- taking infected plants to a laboratory to identify the pathogen
- using testing kits that contain monoclonal antibodies.

Plants can be infected by a range of viral, bacterial, and fungal pathogens as well as by insects.

Knowledge of plant diseases is restricted to tobacco mosaic virus as a viral disease, black spot as a fungal disease, and aphids as insects.

Plants can be damaged by a range of ion deficiency conditions:
- stunted growth caused by nitrate deficiency
- chlorosis caused by magnesium deficiency.

Knowledge of ions is limited to nitrate ions needed for protein synthesis and therefore growth and magnesium ions needed to make chlorophyll.

WS 1.4

Aiming for	Outcome	Checkpoint	
		Question	Activity
Aiming for GRADE 4	Describe some signs of plant disease.		Starter 2, Main
	Name organisms that can cause disease in plants.	End of chapter 4	Starter 2, Main, Plenary 1
	State that plants can be damaged by ion deficiency.		Main
Aiming for GRADE 6	Describe how a plant disease is detected, and the methods used to identify the cause.		Main
	Explain how disease damages a plant.	3	Main
	Match signs of plant disease to ion deficiency.	1	Main, Plenary 1
Aiming for GRADE 8	Analyse data on plant growth to write conclusions using scientific knowledge.		Main
	Suggest how plant diseases affect food security.		Plenary 2
	Explain in detail how and why ion deficiencies affect plant growth.	1	Main

■ B5 Communicable diseases

Maths	Literacy	Key words
Students analyse data from an experiment about the effects of mineral deficiencies on plant growth.	Students use information from the student book to describe what causes disease in plants.	aphids, chlorosis, monoclonal antibodies

Starter	Support/Extend	Resources
True or false? (5 min) Tell the class that only animals get ill. Ask them to discuss this in pairs. Listen to the feedback and make a list of all the ways in which plants can be unhealthy. **Plant doctors** (10 min) Either collect a variety of unhealthy plant specimens, or show images of unhealthy plants. Ask the students to study the plants and describe their symptoms.	**Extend:** You might also like to discuss that bacteria can also get ill. Bacteriophages are viruses that infect bacterial cells. **Extend:** Students can suggest possible reasons for the ill health.	

Main	Support/Extend	Resources
Plant diseases (40 min) Ask students to suggest what causes ill health in plants. They then use the student book to make a list of the causes of plant disease, and how each damages a plant. They then analyse the results of an experiment about the effects of mineral deficiencies on plant growth, commenting on changes in the appearance of the plants, differences in the height of the seedlings, and changes in dry mass.	**Extend:** Students should write a page for a gardening book about the different methods used to diagnose plant diseases. **Extend:** Students should comment on how the effects of each mineral deficiency affect plant growth.	**Activity:** Plant diseases

Plenary	Support/Extend	Resources
What' the disease? (10 min) Show the class a series of images showing plant diseases, and ask them to name the problem. **Food security** (5 min) Tell the class that plant diseases are a huge problem for food security. Ask them to discuss in groups what they think this means.	**Support:** Focus on the effects of tobacco mosaic virus, black spot, and aphids. **Support:** Explain that having food security means that everyone on Earth has enough food to be healthy.	**Interactive:** What's the disease?

Homework		
Students choose one example of a plant disease they have learnt about this lesson. They produce a small leaflet explaining how to diagnose and treat the disease.		

GCSE Biology only

B5.11 Plant defence responses

AQA spec link: 3.3.2 Students should be able to describe physical and chemical plant defence responses.

Physical defence responses to resist invasion of microorganisms:

- Cellulose cell walls.
- Tough waxy cuticle on leaves.
- Layers of dead cells around stems (bark on trees) which fall off.

Chemical plant defence responses:

- Antibacterial chemicals.
- Poisons to deter herbivores.

Mechanical adaptations:

- Thorns and hairs deter animals.
- Leaves which droop or curl when touched.
- Mimicry to trick animals.

Aiming for	Outcome	Checkpoint	
		Question	Activity
Aiming for GRADE 4 ↓	State examples of plant defence responses.	1	Starter, Main, Plenary 1
	Describe why plants need to defend themselves.		Main
Aiming for GRADE 6 ↓	Classify plant defences as physical, chemical, or mechanical.		Main, Plenary 1
	Carry out research using secondary resources of own choice to present examples of plant defence responses.		Main
Aiming for GRADE 8 ↓	Explain in detail how plant defence responses work.	2	Main
	Interpret information from a scientific article to explain how plant-to-plant communication can be used as a form of defence.		Main

Maths
Challenge students to describe what tests they would run and how they would analyse the data.

Literacy
Students use information from the student book to label and classify plant defence responses. Students also interpret a scientific article. Students research how disease-resistant plants have been developed.

■ B5 Communicable diseases

Starter	Support/Extend	Resources
Tea tree oil (10 min) Show students a bottle of tea tree oil or a product that contains it. Explain that it is used because it has antibacterial properties. Ask them why plants would produce a chemical like this, and what the advantage is for them. **Mystery image** (5 min) Show students a magnified image of a nettle leaf. Ask them to suggest what it is. After revealing the answer, discuss why nettles sting.	**Extend:** Ask students to name any other plant-based antibacterial chemicals that they have come across.	
Main	**Support/Extend**	**Resources**
Plant defences (40 min) Discuss why plants need to defend themselves, and from what. Ask students to draw a picture of a plant and use information from the student book to label all the methods plants use to defend themselves. They can use a key to classify them as physical, mechanical, and chemical methods. Provide students with some unusual and interesting methods of plant defences. They identify whether they are mechanical, physical, or chemical. Introduce the concept of disease-resistant plants and ask students to suggest what these are, and why farmers may choose to grow them.	**Extend:** Students should explain how each method works. **Extend:** Provide students with a scientific article about how acacia plants communicate with each other as a form of defence. They should then explain what the article is about. **Extend:** Ask students to research how disease-resistant plants have been developed.	**Activity:** Plant defences
Plenary	**Support/Extend**	**Resources**
Physical, mechanical, or chemical? (5 min) Interactive activity where students select true or false in a series of statements about plant defence responses. They then sort defence mechanisms into whether they are physical barriers, chemical barriers, or mechanical adaptations. **New antibiotics** (10 min) Remind students about the problems surrounding antibiotic-resistant bacteria and tell them that new antibiotics could be developed from plants. Ask them how they would go about testing plant chemicals for their suitability as a new antibiotic.	**Support:** Remind students that the chemicals need to inhibit bacterial growth and be non-toxic to humans. **Extend:** Ask students to describe what tests they would run, and how they would analyse the data.	**Interactive:** Physical, mechanical, or chemical?
Homework		
Challenge students to design a super-plant that uses many of the different types of defence they have learnt about. Ask them to consider why, in reality, plants only use a few.		

B5 Communicable diseases

Overview of B5 Communicable diseases

In this chapter, students have seen how the concept of health (as a state of physical and mental well-being) is affected by communicable (infectious) diseases.

They have looked at the different pathogens that can cause communicable disease, including bacteria, viruses, and protists, and how these can be spread between organisms – both animals and plants. As part of this, they have looked at the development of simple hygiene methods to prevent the spread of pathogens as well as the isolation of individuals who are infected, the destruction of or control of vectors, and the use of vaccination.

Students should be able describe the different pathogens, the symptoms and treatments of a range of different animal and plant diseases, and the different defence mechanisms of the human body and plants.

They should also complete the required practical to grow bacteria in the laboratory to investigate the effect of disinfectants and antibiotics.

Practical skills

All students are expected to have carried out the required practical:

Practical	Topic
Investigate the effect of antiseptics or antibiotics on bacterial growth using agar plates and measuring zones of inhibition.	B5.4

MyMaths

You can find additional support for the maths skills covered in this chapter on **MyMaths**, including calculating the area of a circle.

kerboodle

For this chapter, the following assessments are available on Kerboodle:

B5 Checkpoint quiz: Communicable diseases
B5 Progress quiz: Communicable diseases 1
B5 Progress quiz: Communicable diseases 2
B5 On your marks: Communicable diseases
B5 Exam-style questions and mark scheme: Communicable diseases

Checkpoint follow-up lesson

A student's route through this lesson can be determined using the Checkpoint assessment. Percentage pass marks are supplied in the Checkpoint teacher notes.

For each successive route through it is assumed that the student can perform to their current route as well as previous routes. For example, students working at Aiming for 6 are assumed to be secure in Aiming for 4 knowledge and understanding and working towards achieving all the learning objectives for Aiming for 6.

	Aiming for 4	**Aiming for 6**	**Aiming for 8**
Learning outcomes	State some examples of communicable diseases in humans and plants.	Describe the symptoms and treatments of some communicable diseases in humans and plants.	Explain how a particular pathogen causes a communicable disease.
	State simply some methods for preventing the spread of communicable diseases.	Describe the way that some communicable diseases are spread from person to person.	Explain how different methods for preventing the spread of communicable diseases disrupt the lifecycle of a pathogen.
	State the defence mechanisms of the body against disease.	Describe the defence mechanisms of the body against disease.	Explain how the defence mechanisms of the body prevent or treat infection.
Starter	**Listing diseases (10 min)** Students work in pairs to write down as many diseases as they can in two minutes. Then show students a list on the board of the diseases they have covered in this chapter, including measles, HIV, gonorrhoea, flu, athletes foot, malaria, tobacco mosaic virus, rose black spot, cancer, type 1 and type 2 diabetes. Did they miss any? Add any relevant diseases to the list on the board.		
Differentiated checkpoint activity	Students use the Aiming for 4 follow-up sheet to complete a table to describe the causes of the communicable diseases studied in this chapter, and how they are spread. They then list the human defence mechanisms, stating simply how they help defence against disease. The follow-up sheet provides structured support. Students will need A3 paper.	Students use the Aiming for 6 follow-up sheet to complete a table to describe the causes of the communicable diseases studied in this chapter, and how they are spread. They then list the human defence mechanisms, stating simply how they help defend against disease. The follow-up sheet contains more diseases for students to describe and provides limited support. Students should attempt the activity without their student books. Students will need A3 paper.	Aiming for 8 students create a visual summary on the content studied in this chapter. The follow-up sheet provides simple prompts and students should would independently. If available, students could be given access to the Internet and other textbooks to research unfamiliar diseases as part of this activity.
	Kerboodle resource B5 Checkpoint follow up: Aiming for 4, B5 Checkpoint follow up: Aiming for 6, B5 Checkpoint follow up: Aiming for 8		
Plenary	**Sorting diseases (10 min)** Revisit the list of diseases from the Starter. Ask students to sort them. Aiming for 4 students should sort them into communicable and non-communicable diseases; Aiming for 6 students should sort them according to whether they are caused by bacteria, viruses, or protists; and Aiming for 8 students should sort them according to whether they are caused by bacteria, viruses, and protists, and whether they are plant or animal diseases (so there are six piles).		
Progression	To progress, students swap notes with an Aiming for 6 student, and add any extra information included in the Aiming for 6 follow-up sheet to their Aiming for 4 follow-up sheet.	To progress, students should review Aiming for 8 visual summaries, identifying any errors or missing content. They could use the visual summaries to add further detail to their notes from the lesson.	To progress, students initially create their visual summary without access to their notes from the chapter. They then review their visual summary against their notes, correcting any errors and adding in any extra information.

B 6 Preventing and treating disease
6.1 Vaccination

AQA spec link: 3.1.7 Students should be able to explain how vaccination will prevent illness in an individual, and how the spread of pathogens can be reduced by immunising a large proportion of the population.

Vaccination involves introducing small quantities of dead or inactive forms of a pathogen into the body to stimulate the white blood cells to produce antibodies. If the same pathogen re-enters the body the white blood cells respond quickly to produce the correct antibodies, preventing infection.

Students do not need to know details of vaccination schedules and side effects associated with specific vaccines.

WS 1.4

Aiming for	Outcome	Checkpoint	
		Question	Activity
Aiming for GRADE 4 ↓	Describe why people are vaccinated.	1	Starter 1
	State that vaccines contain dead or inactive forms of a pathogen.		Main 1
Aiming for GRADE 6 ↓	Explain how vaccination works.	2, 3, End of chapter 1	Starter 2, Main 1
	Describe what an antibody and an antigen are.	1	Starter 2, Main 1, Plenary 1
Aiming for GRADE 8 ↓	Explain why, if a large proportion of the population is vaccinated, the spread of the pathogen is reduced.	End of chapter 3	Main 2, Plenary 2
	Apply ideas about specificity of antibodies.		Main 1

Maths
Students consider what we mean by size of risk.

Literacy
Students use information from the student book to explain how vaccination works in the form of a storyboard. They also use websites to research risks of vaccination and write an informed conclusion.

Key word
vaccine

B6 Preventing and treating disease

Starter	Support/Extend	Resources
Vaccination (5 min) Show the class an image of someone having a vaccination. Ask them what is happening, and ask why people have vaccinations. Ask students to name any vaccinations they have had. **Antigens and antibodies** (10 min) Draw a diagram of a pathogen surrounded by antibodies attached to antigens and ask students to copy it, or provide them with the unlabelled diagram. Then ask them to label and annotate as many key features as they can.	**Extend:** Explain that vaccinations are also called immunisations. Ask students to suggest why. **Support:** Draw lines to the pathogen, antigens, and antibodies and provide a word bank. **Extend:** Discuss why antibodies are specific.	

Main	Support/Extend	Resources
How do vaccinations work? (30 min) Students use information in the student book to create a storyboard to explain how vaccinations work. Students' storyboards should include the following stages in the process of vaccination: • Vaccine contains dead or inactive forms of pathogen. • Vaccine injected into body. • White blood cells produce antibody against pathogen. • (Several years later) live pathogen infects body. • White blood cells make antibody quickly, pathogen is destroyed. Higher-tier students should include information on the specificity of antibodies. **Vaccination** (10 min) Bump up your grade worksheet where students analyse the ethics of vaccination, why people may choose not to have a vaccination, and potential impacts this could have on the wider population in terms of herd immunity.	**Support:** Supply students with a template for the storyboard that contains the stages. They draw pictures to explain what is happening at each stage.	**Activity:** How do vaccinations work? **Bump up your grade:** Vaccination

Plenary	Support/Extend	Resources
Vaccination (5 min) Use the interactive in which students match key words on the subject of vaccination to their definitions. **Smallpox** (10 min) Tell the class that smallpox is a viral disease that has been eradicated. This was achieved by means of a worldwide vaccination programme. Ask students to read the information on herd immunity in the student book and then write down how this works.	**Extend:** Students should consider whether children should still be offered the smallpox vaccine and, if so, justify why they think this.	**Interactive:** Vaccination

Homework		
Explain to students that in some countries, such as the USA, children are given the chickenpox vaccine. Students research the risks involved in having the chickenpox vaccine versus not having it, and come to their own conclusion. Students use their findings to create a presentation that persuades parents that they should lobby their local MP for the vaccine. Alternatively, students use their knowledge of vaccinations to explain why you can't get chickenpox twice.	**Support:** Discuss with students what is meant by size of risk. Discuss the risks involved in familiar activities (e.g., being in a car or being struck by lightning).	

kerboodle

A Kerboodle highlight for this lesson is **Maths skills: Calculating risk**. Refer to the **Content map** on Kerboodle for a full list of resources and assessment.

B6.2 Antibiotics and painkillers

AQA spec link: 3.1.8 Students should be able to explain the use of antibiotics and other medicines in treating disease.

Antibiotics, such as penicillin, are medicines that help to cure bacterial disease by killing infective bacteria inside the body. It is important that specific bacteria should be treated by specific antibiotics.

The use of antibiotics has greatly reduced deaths from infectious bacterial diseases. However, the emergence of strains resistant to antibiotics is of great concern.

Antibiotics cannot kill viral pathogens.

Painkillers and other medicines are used to treat the symptoms of disease but do not kill pathogens.

It is difficult to develop drugs that kill viruses without also damaging the body's tissues.

WS 1.4

Aiming for	Outcome	Checkpoint	
		Question	Activity
Aiming for GRADE 4 ↓	Describe what an antibiotic is.		Starter 2, Main 1
	State that viral infections cannot be treated with antibiotics.		Main 1, Plenary 1
	Decide when a painkiller or antibiotic should be used to treat an illness.	1	Main 2, Plenary 1
Aiming for GRADE 6 ↓	Describe how antibiotics work.		Main 1
	Describe what is meant by antibiotic-resistant bacteria.	End of chapter 5	Main 1, Plenary 2
	Explain why it is difficult to develop drugs to treat viral infections.	2	Main 1
Aiming for GRADE 8 ↓	Suggest a reasoned explanation for a pattern in data.	3	Starter 1
	Explain in detail how antibiotic-resistant bacteria arise.	End of chapter 5	Main 1, Plenary 2
	Explain why scientists are constantly developing new antibiotics.		Main 1

Maths
Students compare graphs and suggest what they show.

Literacy
Students use information from the student book to answer a series of questions on antibiotics.

Key word
drugs

■ B6 Preventing and treating disease

Starter	Support/Extend	Resources
Deaths from maternal septicaemia (10 min) Show students Figure 2 in the student book. Reveal how the graph shows the impact of the introduction of antibiotics on deaths from maternal septicaemia. **Key words** (5 min) Write the words antibiotics, antiseptics, antibodies, analgesics, and disinfectant onto the board. Ask students to suggest what these key words for the lesson mean.	**Extend:** Students should suggest reasoned explanations for the trend in the graph.	
Main	**Support/Extend**	**Resources**
How do antibiotics work? (20 min) Explain that antibiotics are drugs used to treat bacterial infections. Ask students to answer a series of questions to find out more: • How do antibiotics work? • Why won't your doctor give you antibiotics for 'flu? • Why is it difficult to treat viral infections? • Why are antibiotics becoming less useful? Students can use the student book to find the answers. **Doctor, doctor** (20 min) Ask students why we use painkillers, and ask them to name some examples. Discuss that painkillers are used to treat the symptoms of a disease, for example, to stop a headache if you have a cold, but they cannot cure the disease. Ask the class to work in groups. Provide each group with patient cards that contain symptoms. Students take part in a role-play exercise where a doctor must prescribe various patients with either antibiotics or paracetamol depending on their symptoms.	**Extend:** Students should think about why scientists are constantly developing new antibiotics, and why you must finish a course of antibiotics even if you begin to feel better.	**Activity:** Doctor, doctor
Plenary	**Support/Extend**	**Resources**
Antibiotic or painkiller? (5 min) State a list of illnesses, for example, cold, salmonella, measles, gonorrhoea, and migraine. Ask students if they would treat each illness with painkillers or antibiotics. **Antibiotic resistance** (10 min) Interactive where students complete a paragraph on antibiotic resistance by choosing the correct words to fill in the gaps.	**Extend:** Ask students for reasons.	**Interactive:** Antibiotic resistance
Homework		
Students produce a poster to explain the difference between antiseptics, antigens, antibiotics, and antibodies.		

kerboodle

A Kerboodle highlight for this lesson is **Literacy skills: Key words**. Refer to the **Content map** on Kerboodle for a full list of resources and assessment.

B6.3 Discovering drugs

AQA spec link: 3.1.9 Students should be able to describe the process of discovery and development of potential new medicines, including preclinical and clinical testing.

Traditionally drugs were extracted from plants and microorganisms.

- The heart drug digitalis originates from foxgloves.
- The painkiller aspirin originates from willow.
- Penicillin was discovered by Alexander Fleming from the *Penicillium* mould.

Most new drugs are synthesised by chemists in the pharmaceutical industry. However, the starting point may still be a chemical extracted from a plant.

Aiming for	Outcome	Checkpoint	
		Question	Activity
Aiming for GRADE 4	Name some drugs based on extracts from plants or microorganisms.		Starter 1, Plenary 1
	Order the events that led to the development of penicillin.	1	Main 1
	Draw a simple conclusion using data.		Main 2
Aiming for GRADE 6	Describe how new antibiotics are tested for effectiveness.		Main 2
	Discuss the advantages and disadvantages of looking for new drugs from living organisms.	3	Main 2
	Analyse data to draw conclusions on the effectiveness of new antibiotics.		Main 2
Aiming for GRADE 8	Suggest why mould naturally produces antibiotics.		Main 1
	Discuss how effective herbal remedies are.		Plenary 2
	Analyse data to evaluate the effectiveness of new antibiotics and make a reasoned decision on which one to develop further.		Main 2

Maths
Students analyse data on the effectiveness of plant and microorganism extracts on the growth of bacteria.

Literacy
Students order key events in the development of penicillin. They carry out group discussions to share their ideas and opinions.

102

■ B6 Preventing and treating disease

Starter	Support/Extend	Resources
Making connections (10 min) Show the class images of a willow tree, a foxglove, mould, and a beaver tail. Ask students what these have in common. After a quick discussion, ask them to read the first page of this topic in the student book, then ask for their ideas again. Discuss that the images all represent sources of substances that modern drugs are based on. **Rainforest problem** (5 min) Show the class an image or video that shows part of a rainforest being destroyed. Ask students to discuss in pairs why this could hinder the search for cures for diseases.	**Extend:** Give examples of drugs that are based on plants found in rainforests (e.g., quinine, an antimalarial medication from the cinchona tree).	

Main	Support/Extend	Resources
The discovery of penicillin (20 min) Provide pairs of students with cards showing the events/stages in how penicillin was discovered and developed into a useful drug. Students put them into the correct order. Present students with the statement: If Fleming was a tidier scientist we would not have any antibiotics. Ask pairs to write down one argument that supports this statement, and one that refutes it. **Drug development** (20 min) Students analyse data on the effectiveness of plant and microorganism extracts on the growth of bacteria. They use the data to decide which extract is the best option to go on to the next stage of drug development.	**Extend:** Ask students why they think mould produces an antibiotic.	**Activity:** The discovery of penicillin **Working scientifically:** Drug development

Plenary	Support/Extend	Resources
Matching drugs (5 min) Call out plants or microorganisms for students to the name of the drug that was developed from it. **Discovering drugs** (10 min) Interactive activity where students match the drug to the plant it was originally extracted from. Students then answer a multiple choice question about the discovery and development of penicillin.		**Interactive:** Discovering drugs

Homework		
Students complete the WebQuest where they research different medicines that are produced from plants. Alternatively, ask students to find a recent news story on the development of a new drug from plants. They should summarise the findings in their own words.	**Support:** Supply a suitable story.	**WebQuest:** Medicines from plants

kerboodle

A Kerboodle highlight for this lesson is **Bump up your grade: The past, present, and future of drugs**. Refer to the **Content map** on Kerboodle for a full list of resources and assessment.

B6.4 Developing drugs

AQA spec link: 3.1.9 Students should be able to describe the process of discovery and development of potential new medicines, including preclinical and clinical testing.

New medical drugs have to be tested and trialled before being used to check that they are safe and effective.

New drugs are extensively tested for toxicity, efficacy, and dose.

Preclinical testing is done in laboratory using cells, tissues, and live animals.

Clinical trials use healthy volunteers and patients:

- Very low doses of the drug are given at the start of the clinical trial.
- If the drug is found to be safe, further clinical trials are carried out to find the optimum dose for the drug.
- In double blind trials, some patients are given a placebo.

WS 1.6
MS 2b

Aiming for	Outcome	Checkpoint	
		Question	Activity
Aiming for GRADE 4 ↓	State that new medical drugs have to be tested to check that they are safe and effective.	End of chapter 4	Starter 1, Main, Plenary 1
	Give the procedures used to trial a new drug in the correct order.	2, End of chapter 4	Main
	Describe what is meant by a placebo.		Main, Plenary 1
Aiming for GRADE 6 ↓	Explain why each procedure in drugs testing and trialling is used.	3, End of chapter 4	Main, Plenary 1
	Describe how a double blind trial is carried out.		Main, Plenary 1
	Explain why a placebo is used during drug trialling.	2	Main, Plenary 1
Aiming for GRADE 8 ↓	Describe in some detail how new medical drugs are tested and trialled for safety, effectiveness, toxicity, efficacy, and dose.	1, End of chapter 4	Main
	Critically analyse the results from a double blind trial.		Main
	Explain why the results of drug trials are published in journals.		Main

Maths
Students consider the time and cost associated with drug trialling. They also analyse results.

Literacy
Students use information from the student book to create a flow chart to summarise the stages of drug trialling.

Key words
preclinical testing, clinical trial, placebo

■ B6 Preventing and treating disease

Starter	Support/Extend	Resources
Would you volunteer? (5 min) Ask students who would volunteer to have a new drug tested on them. Discuss why new drugs need to be tested on humans. **Costs of drug development** (10 min) Tell the class that it costs around £1700 million to bring a new medicine from first tests to readiness to be prescribed. Ask students to work in pairs to list as many of the costs that they can think of associated with this process.	**Extension:** Ask students whether they would think differently if they got paid, or if the drug was a possible new treatment for an illness they had (e.g., hay fever). **Support:** Refer students to Figure 2 in the student book.	

Main	Support/Extend	Resources
Carrying out a double blind test (40 min) Discuss that before a new drug is given to the public, it is necessary to ensure that it is safe and effective. Students use information from the student book to create a flow chart that outlines the stages involved in a drug trial, what happens at each stage, and the time and money spent on each stage. Students then work in pairs and carry out a double blind trial to test if a type of exercise can improve memory. Collate the results as a class and discuss what they show. Use the results to talk about what is meant by a double blind test, what placebos are, and where/why these are used in drug trials.	**Support:** Provide an outline flow chart with the main stages named. Students describe what happens at each stage. **Extension:** Students should mention where in the trial drugs are tested for toxicity, efficacy, and dose. **Extend:** Students should use the student book and the Internet to research how drug trials are published.	**Activity:** Carrying out a double blind test

Plenary	Support/Extend	Resources
Check your understanding (10 min) Students complete the questions at the end of this topic in the student book (not Question 2a). **What happens during a drug trial?** (5 min) Interactive where students decide the correct order for the stages in developing a new drug. They then suggest the words to fill the gaps to complete a paragraph outlining what happens during a double blind trial.	**Support:** Supply Provide the missing words and ask the students to say which goes into which gap. **Extend:** Ask students to write their own cloze activity to test a partner.	**Interactive:** What happens during a drug trial?

Homework		
Students either write their own podcast or make revision notes on the chapter so far.		

GCSE Biology only — Higher tier

B6.5 Making monoclonal antibodies

AQA spec links: 3.2.1 Students should be able to describe how monoclonal antibodies are produced.

Monoclonal antibodies are produced from a single clone of cells. The antibodies are specific to one binding site on one protein antigen and so are able to target a specific chemical or specific cells in the body.

They are produced by stimulating mouse lymphocytes to make a particular antibody. The lymphocytes are combined with a particular kind of tumour cell to make a cell called a hybridoma cell. The hybridoma cell can both divide and make the antibody. Single hybridoma cells are cloned to produce many identical cells that all produce the same antibody. A large amount of the antibody can be collected and purified.

3.2.2 Students should be able to describe some of the ways in which monoclonal antibodies can be used.

Some examples include:

- For diagnosis such as in pregnancy tests.
- In laboratories to measure the levels of hormones and other chemicals in blood, or to detect pathogens.
- In research to locate or identify specific molecules in a cell or tissue by binding to them with a fluorescent dye.

Students are not expected to recall any specific tests or treatments but given appropriate information they should be able to explain how they work.

WS 1.3
MS 1c

Aiming for	Outcome	Checkpoint	
		Question	Activity
Aiming for GRADE 6	Describe what a monoclonal antibody is.	1, End of chapter 6	Starter 2, Main
	Outline the procedure used to produce monoclonal antibodies.		Main, Plenary 2, Homework
	Give some uses of monoclonal antibodies.	3, End of chapter 6	Starter 1, Main, Plenary 1
Aiming for GRADE 8	Explain why hybridoma cells are used to produce monoclonal antibodies.	2	Main, Homework
	Explain in detail how pregnancy tests work.		Starter 1, Main
	Describe how monoclonal antibodies are used to produce ELISA tests and outline how they are used.	End of chapter 6	Plenary 1

Maths
Tell students that most home pregnancy tests are 99% accurate. Ask them to explain what this means (1c).

Literacy
Students interpret information from the student book to create their own diagrams to explain how monoclonal antibodies are produced.

Key word
hybridomas

106

■ B6 Preventing and treating disease

Starter	Support/Extend	Resources
Pregnancy test (5 min) Tell students that a fetus produces a hormone (HCG), which enters the mother's urine. Ask them to use this information to speculate as to how a pregnancy test could work. (You may also wish to show students an advertisement for a pregnancy testing kit.). Reveal that this will be answered in more detail later.	**Support:** Show the class an example of a pregnancy testing kit for them to study in more detail.	
Types of antibodies (10 min) Show the class an image of lots of different antibodies with different antigen-binding sites. Label this 'polyclonal antibodies'. Ask them to discuss in pairs what they think monoclonal antibodies are.	**Support:** Remind students how antibodies bind to antigens through specific antigen-binding sites.	

Main	Support/Extend	Resources
Monoclonal antibodies (40 min) Discuss with the class what monoclonal antibodies are, and explain how they are made. Ask students to use information in the student book to summarise this in writing. Then explain to students how pregnancy tests use monoclonal antibodies. Students create a leaflet found in a pregnancy test, explaining how it works using simple diagrams. Students could use the Internet to further research the use of monoclonal antibodies for their leaflets.	**Extend:** Students should consider ethical issues associated with producing monoclonal antibodies. **Support:** Provide important key words or steps for students to include.	**Activity:** Monoclonal antibodies

Plenary	Support/Extend	Resources
ELISA tests (10 min) Supply students with information about ELISA tests, including how they work, and their applications. Students then write down three key bullet points about them.		**Interactive:** Order the stages
Order the stages (5 min) Interactive activity where students select the correct description of a monoclonal antibody. They then order the five stages of making monoclonal antibodies.		

Homework		
Students create a flow chart summarising how monoclonal antibodies are produced. Their flow chart should include diagrams of each stage.		

GCSE Biology only — Higher tier

B6.6 Uses of monoclonal antibodies

AQA spec link: 3.2.2 Students should be able to describe some of the ways in which monoclonal antibodies can be used.

- To treat some diseases: for cancer the monoclonal antibody can be bound to a radioactive substance, a toxic drug or a chemical which stops cells growing and dividing. It delivers the substance to the cancer cells without harming other cells in the body.

Students are not expected to recall any specific tests or treatments but given appropriate information they should be able to explain how they work.

Monoclonal antibodies create more side effects than expected. They are not yet as widely used as everyone hoped when they were first developed.

WS 1.3

Aiming for	Outcome	Checkpoint	
		Question	Activity
Aiming for GRADE 6 ↓	Describe the ways in which monoclonal antibodies can be used to treat cancer.	1	Main
	Outline the advantages and disadvantages of using monoclonal antibodies.	2, End of chapter 6	Main, Plenary 1
Aiming for GRADE 8 ↓	Explain in detail how the methods of using monoclonal antibodies to treat cancer work.	1	Main
	Evaluate the use of monoclonal antibodies in treating cancer compared to other treatments.	2	Main

Maths
Students study success rates of different cancer treatments.

Literacy
Students create an engaging presentation on how monoclonal antibodies can be used to treat cancer.

B6 Preventing and treating disease

Starter	Support/Extend	Resources
Magic bullet (5 min) Tell students that when they were first developed, monoclonal antibodies were described as a 'magic bullet' for disease. Ask groups of students to discuss what they think was meant by this. **Monoclonal antibodies** (10 min) Ask students to write down bullet points showing what they remember about monoclonal antibodies from B6.5. They can group them under the headings what, why, and how.	**Support:** Students can work in small groups and pool ideas.	

Main	Support/Extend	Resources
Treating cancer (40 min) Explain that cancer cells and normal cells have different surface antigens. Use a diagram or image to reinforce your explanation. Ask students to explain why monoclonal antibodies could be used to target cancer cells, and how they would be made. Then divide the class into groups and assign each group one of the three methods by which monoclonal antibodies are used to treat cancer, as outlined in the student book. Ask each group to produce an engaging presentation to explain how their treatment works. Their presentation should include an advantage and disadvantage of their treatment method.	**Extend:** Allow groups access to the Internet to search for further information such as useful animations.	**Activity:** Treating cancer

Plenary	Support/Extend	Resources
The end for monoclonal antibodies? (10 min) Ask the class if they think scientists should keep on spending time and money researching and developing monoclonal antibodies, or if they think they should start to concentrate on other drug treatments. Students can vote by a show of hands. **Uses of monoclonal antibodies** (5 min) Students use the interactive to answer a multiple choice question and then select true or false in a series of statements about monoclonal antibodies.	**Extend:** Students should explain their decision.	**Interactive:** Uses of monoclonal antibodies

Homework		
Students research other cancer treatments such as chemotherapy and radiotherapy and compare these to treatments using monoclonal antibodies.		

kerboodle

A Kerboodle highlight for this lesson is **Maths skills: Calculating percentage change**. Refer to the **Content map** on Kerboodle for a full list of resources and assessment.

B6 Preventing and treating disease

Overview of B6 Preventing and treating disease

In this chapter, students have studied the prevention of disease by vaccination. They should know how the immune system works and what is meant by an antigen. They should appreciate that the shapes of antigens and antibodies are complementary. They should understand what a vaccine contains and how it works, giving examples, and the concept of herd immunity. They should understand that memory cells remain in the body to provide long-term immunity.

Students have studied the treatment of disease by drugs including painkillers and antibiotics. They should understand that painkillers such as aspirin and paracetamol treat the symptoms and not the cause of disease. They should be aware that antibiotics are drugs used to cure bacterial infections. They should know how they work and be aware of the current crisis of antibiotic-resistant strains of bacteria, linking with work in B14.8 *Antibiotic resistant bacteria*.

Students have studied the discovery of drugs in plants and microbes, including the discovery of penicillin. They should be aware of how drugs are made today to be effective and safe, and be able to outline the processes of clinical trials including double blind trials and using placebos.

This chapter includes the higher-tier GCSE Biology only topic of the production and uses of monoclonal antibodies. Higher-tier GCSE Biology students should be able to name lymphocytes as the white blood cells responsible for producing antibodies. They should recall the stages in stimulating the correct lymphocyte to be made and then fused with a tumour cell to form a hybridoma cell. They should link this work with B2 *Cell division* and B5.9 *Human defence responses*. They should be able to give examples of how monoclonal antibodies are used, as well as their disadvantages.

MyMaths

You can find additional support for the maths skills covered in this chapter on **MyMaths**, including working with graphs, data analysis, and calculating means.

kerboodle

For this chapter, the following assessments are available on Kerboodle:

B6 Checkpoint quiz: Preventing and treating disease
B6 Progress quiz: Preventing and treating disease 1
B6 Progress quiz: Preventing and treating disease 2
B6 On your marks: Preventing and treating disease
B6 Exam-style questions and mark scheme: Preventing and treating disease

Checkpoint follow-up lesson

A student's route through this lesson can be determined using the Checkpoint assessment. Percentage pass marks are supplied in the Checkpoint teacher notes.

For each successive route through it is assumed that the student can perform to their current route as well as previous routes. For example, students working at Aiming for 6 are assumed to be secure in Aiming for 4 knowledge and understanding and working towards achieving all the learning outcomes for Aiming for 6.

	Aiming for 4	Aiming for 6	Aiming for 8
Learning outcomes	State the differences between vaccination, antibiotics, and painkillers.	Describe the differences between vaccination, antibiotics, and painkillers.	Explain the differences between vaccination, antibiotics, and painkillers.
	State simply the stages in the process of vaccination.	Describe how vaccination protects against disease.	Explain how vaccination protects against disease.
	State the stages of drug development.	Describe the stages of drug development.	Discuss the advantages and disadvantages of the development of monoclonal antibodies.
Starter	**Pass the ball (10 min)** Each group will require a ball, such as a tennis ball. Students work in small groups to revise their work on vaccination, antibiotics, and painkillers for 5 minutes. Each group has a ball. When the ball is passed to a student, they give a fact on vaccination, antibiotics, and painkillers before passing the ball to the next person. If they can't think of a fact they sit out. The teacher can review the difference between vaccination, antibiotics, and painkillers.		
Differentiated checkpoint activity	Aiming for 4 students use the follow-up sheet to create a comic strip to describe the process of vaccination. They then answer some highly-structured questions to summarise how new drugs are developed. Students should be provided with a template or guidance on what each panel should include. They can work in pairs.	Aiming for 6 students use the follow-up sheet to produce a comic strip to describe the process of vaccination. They then produce a timeline to describe how drugs are developed. The follow-up sheet provides simple statements to describe what should be included in the comic strip, that students can choose to use. They should work independently for the comic strip but in pairs for the timeline.	Aiming for 8 students use the follow-up sheet to produce a comic strip to explain the process of vaccination. They then briefly summarise the process to develop new drugs. Students studying *AQA GCSE Biology* should then go on to discuss the advantages and disadvantages of using monoclonal antibodies in treatment.
	Kerboodle resource B6 Checkpoint follow-up: Aiming for 4, B6 Checkpoint follow-up: Aiming for 6, B6 Checkpoint follow-up: Aiming for 8		
Plenary	**Drug development review (5 min)** Review the stages of drug development. Start with the first stage on the board and ask students to provide the next step until all the stages are present.		
Progression	To progress, Aiming for 4 students should peer-review comic strips produced by Aiming for 6 students.	To progress, Aiming for 6 students should peer-review comic strips produced by Aiming for 8 students.	To progress, students should evaluate the use of monoclonal antibodies, and write a conclusion on their opinion on using monoclonal antibodies in treatments.

B 7 Non-communicable diseases

7.1 Non-communicable diseases

AQA spec link: 2.2.6 Students should be able to:

- discuss the human and financial cost of these noncommunicable diseases to an individual, a local community, a nation, or globally
- explain the effect of lifestyle factors including diet, alcohol, and smoking on the incidence of non-communicable diseases at local, national, and global levels.

Risk factors are linked to an increased rate of a disease.

They can be:

- aspects of a person's lifestyle
- substances in the person's body or environment.

A causal mechanism has been proven for some risk factors, but not in others.

Students should be able to understand the principles of sampling as applied to scientific data in terms of risk factors.

Students should be able to translate information between graphical and numerical forms; and extract and interpret information from charts, graphs and tables in terms of risk factors.

Students should be able to use a scatter diagram to identify a correlation between two variables in terms of risk factors.

WS 1.4, 1.5
MS 2c, 2d, 2g, 4a

Aiming for	Outcome	Checkpoint	
		Question	Activity
Aiming for GRADE 4	Name some non-communicable diseases.	1, End of chapter 1	Starter 2
	List some risk factors that are linked to an increased rate of a disease.	End of chapter 1	Main, Homework
	Identify correlations in data.	End of chapter 1	Main, Plenary 2
Aiming for GRADE 6	Classify diseases as communicable or non-communicable.		Starter 2
	Draw conclusions from data on risk factors.	End of chapter 5	Main
	Decide whether a link is causal.	3, End of chapter 1	Main, Plenary 2
Aiming for GRADE 8	Describe some impacts of non-communicable diseases.		Homework
	Identify risk factors from data.	3, End of chapter 3	Main
	Explain why a correlation does not prove a causal mechanism.	End of chapter 1	Main, Plenary 2

Maths
Students interpret data on risk factors in the form of tables, charts, and graphs (4a). They look for correlations and explain relationships between factors and the increase in risk of disease (2g).

Literacy
Students take part in group and class discussions. Students write down their tips to minimise the risk of developing a non-communicable disease.

Key words
carcinogens, ionising radiation, correlation, causal mechanism

112

■ B7 Non-communicable diseases

Starter	Support/Extend	Resources
Top killer diseases (10 min) Tell students that in 2012 some examples of the top 10 diseases that caused death were lung cancer, HIV/AIDS, stroke, heart disease, diabetes, and lung infections. Ask them to order the examples with the biggest killer first, before revealing the answers.	**Extend:** Students should suggest risk factors for some of the diseases.	**Interactive:** Top killer diseases
Communicable or non-communicable? (5 min) Read out a list of diseases and ask the class to state whether they are communicable or non-communicable.	**Support:** Remind students what is meant by communicable and non-communicable diseases.	

Main	Support/Extend	Resources
How big is the risk? (40 min) Supply students with a range of risk factors that are lifestyle choices, for example, eating lots of sugary foods, smoking cigarettes, and not carrying out regular exercise. Ask students to place each risk factor on a continuum line showing effect on health, and to explain their choice.	**Extend:** Students should suggest ways in which each risk factor is linked to disease.	**Working scientifically:** How big is the risk?
Then provide groups of students with a range of data showing links between risk factors and different diseases. Ask students to interpret the data and look for correlations and causal links.	**Support:** Go through how to interpret data on risk factors by analysing one piece of data as a class.	

Plenary	Support/Extend	Resources
Tips for healthy living (5 min) Ask students to write down their top five tips to minimise the risk of developing a non-communicable disease.	**Extend:** Students should explain the science behind each of their tips.	
Correlation and causation (10 min) Bump up your grade worksheet where students answer questions to define the terms correlation and causation, and explain how they are applied.		**Bump up your grade:** Correlation and causation

Homework		
Research published in 2012 suggested that each lung cancer patient costs the NHS over £9000 a year. Also in 2012, the Department of Health launched a two-month-long anti-smoking campaign that cost £2.7 million. Ask students to consider whether they think the Department of Health is justified in spending £2.7 million on a campaign to encourage people to quit smoking.	**Extend:** Encourage students to find data on other financial and social costs of lung cancer and include these in their justifications.	

kerboodle

A Kerboodle highlight for this lesson is **Calculation sheet: Risk factor calculations**. Refer to the **Content map** on Kerboodle for a full list of resources and assessment.

B7.2 Cancer

AQA spec link: 2.2.7 Students should be able to describe cancer as the result of changes in cells that lead to uncontrolled growth and division.

Benign tumours are growths of abnormal cells which are contained in one area, usually within a membrane. They do not invade other parts of the body.

Malignant tumour cells are cancers. They invade neighbouring tissues and spread to different parts of the body in the blood where they form secondary tumours.

Scientists have identified lifestyle risk factors for various types of cancer. There are also genetic risk factors for some cancers.

Aiming for	Outcome	Checkpoint	
		Question	Activity
Aiming for GRADE 4	Define a tumour as a mass of abnormally growing cells.	1	Starter 1, Main, Plenary 1
	State some causes of cancer.		Main, Plenary 2
	List some of the benefits and risks of chemotherapy.	2, 3	Main, Plenary 1
Aiming for GRADE 6	Describe the difference between benign and malignant tumours.	1	Main, Plenary 1
	Describe why carcinogens and ionising radiation increase the risk of tumours forming.		Main
	Analyse data to assess the risks and benefits of chemotherapy.		Homework
Aiming for GRADE 8	Explain how benign and malignant tumours can be life-threatening.	1	Main, Plenary 1
	Link a lack of control in the cell cycle to tumour formation.		Starter 2
	Evaluate the risks of chemotherapy in relation to data, drug testing, and consequences in order to come to an informed decision.		Homework

Maths
Students access data and statistics to analyse the risks and benefits of a new chemotherapy drug.

Literacy
Students use information from the student book to answer questions about tumours. They also complete a Webquest using information from the Internet to evaluate risks and come to a decision on the use of chemotherapy.

Key words
tumour, benign tumours, malignant tumour cells, cancer

B7 Non-communicable diseases

Starter	Support/Extend	Resources
What do I already know? (5 min) Ask students to write down what they already know about cancer. Discuss whether there is anything they would like to find out. Sensitivity is needed during this activity and the rest of the lesson as students may have been affected by some of the issues covered. **Cell cycle order** (10 min) 🄷 Provide students with the stages of the cell cycle from Topic B2.1. Students put the stages in the correct order. Discuss how cells may sometimes stop responding to the normal mechanisms that control the cell cycle and divide rapidly.	**Support:** Allow students to work in pairs or small groups before nominating one person to feed back their ideas.	**Interactive:** Cell cycle order

Main	Support/Extend	Resources
Cancer (40 min) Introduce the term tumour as a mass of abnormally dividing cells. Explain the difference between benign and malignant tumours, and suggest how they cause health problems. Students then create a leaflet or a poster to educate the public about the causes of cancer (e.g., carcinogens, ionising radiation, some viruses), and some of the risks and benefits of cancer treatments (e.g., radiotherapy, chemotherapy). They can use information from books and the Internet.	**Support:** Supply Provide students with a planning framework that outlines what information they need to include. **Extend:** Students should include information on how to reduce the risk of developing cancer. They should include data and statistics.	**Activity:** Cancer

Plenary	Support/Extend	Resources
What have I learnt? (5 min) Ask students to write down three new things they have learnt in the lesson. Ask a few students for feedback and record this. **Cancer risk factors** (10 min) Read out some lifestyle choices, for example, smoking, a stressful job, a diet high in fat, having the HPV vaccination, using sunbeds. Ask students to raise two hands if they think a lifestyle choice greatly increases the risk of cancer, one hand if they think there is a link, and no hands if they think there is no link. Ask students to justify their choice.		

Homework		
Students complete the WebQuest to analyse information, statistics, and data to advise a person on whether to take a new chemotherapy drug.		**WebQuest:** Judging the risk of disease

kerboodle

AKerboodle highlight for this lesson is **Go further: Epidemiology of lung cancer**. Refer to the **Content map** on Kerboodle for a full list of resources and assessment.

B7.3 Smoking and the risk of disease

AQA spec link: 2.2.6 A causal mechanism has been proven for some risk factors, but not in others.

- The effects of smoking on cardiovascular disease.
- The effect of smoking on lung disease and lung cancer.
- The effects of smoking on unborn babies.
- Carcinogens as risk factors in cancer.

Many diseases are caused by the interaction of a number of factors.

Students should be able to understand the principles of sampling as applied to scientific data in terms of risk factors.

Students should be able to translate information between graphical and numerical forms; and extract and interpret information from charts, graphs and tables in terms of risk factors.

Students should be able to use a scatter diagram to identify a correlation between two variables in terms of risk factors.

WS 1.5
MS 2c, 2d, 2g, 4a

Aiming for	Outcome	Checkpoint	
		Question	Activity
Aiming for GRADE 4 ↓	Name the harmful substances found in tobacco smoke.	1	Main, Plenary 1
	State that smoking increases your risk of developing lung diseases.	End of chapter 2	Starter 1
Aiming for GRADE 6 ↓	Describe the effects of the harmful substances found in tobacco smoke.	1, 4, End of chapter 2	Starter 1, Main, Plenary 1, Homework
	Analyse data to describe evidence for the link between smoking and lung disease.	2, 3	Starter 2, Main
Aiming for GRADE 8 ↓	Explain in detail the effects of the harmful substances found in tobacco smoke.	End of chapter 2	Starter 1, Main
	Suggest possible causal mechanisms to explain trends shown in data, and explain how the causal link between smoking and lung cancer was identified.	2, 3	Starter 2, Main, Plenary 2

Maths
Students study data in the form of tables, charts, and graphs (4a) to identify links between smoking and non-communicable diseases (2g).

Literacy
Students use information from the student book to create a spider diagram to show the effects of the harmful substances found in tobacco smoke. They also carry out research to outline arguments that support and confute a statement.

Practical

Title	The effects of smoking
Equipment	cigarette, filter pump or hand-operated vacuum pump, clamp stand, boss and clamp, matches, dishes to collect ash from cigarettes, 250 cm³ conical flask, two-holed rubber bung, two delivery tubes, glass tube with two one-holed bungs, mineral wool for aquarist filters, universal indicator solution, distilled water, plastic pipette

B7 Non-communicable diseases

Overview of method	Half fill the conical flask with water and add a few drops of universal indicator solution. Put the bung with the two delivery tubes into the conical flask, so that one delivery tube is in the water and the other is attached to the filter pump. Put the mineral wool into the middle of the glass tube, put a bung in both ends of the glass tube, and attach the glass tube to the delivery tube that has the other end in the water. Insert the cigarette holder and cigarette into the other bung. Run air through the unlit cigarettes for 10 minutes to show there is no change to the cotton wool or indicator. Then, start the filter pump and light the cigarette. Run until the cigarette is nearly smoked. Note the changes to the cotton wool and the indicator. Using gloves, you can remove the cotton wool and place into a beaker. This can be passed round the class for students to smell.
Safety considerations	Carry out the procedure in a fume cupboard. It is essential to avoid skin contact with the tars collected.

Starter	Support/Extend	Resources
Standardised packaging (10 min) Show students an image of the plans for new standardised cigarette packaging in the UK from 2016. Ask them to vote on whether they think this is a good idea, and explain their reasoning. **Smoking links** (5 min) Show students a graph that indicates the link between smoking and lung cancer for them to interpret.	**Extend:** Students should work in groups to design their own packaging. **Support:** Provide students with a list of possible conclusions for them to choose from. **Extend:** Students should use their knowledge about the causes of cancer to suggest a causal mechanism.	

Main	Support/Extend	Resources
The effects of smoking (40 min) Carry out the demonstration to show some of the products of smoking cigarettes. Ask students to write down what the experiment showed. Students then create a spider diagram to show the substances in cigarette smoke and their effect on health. Students then analyse data on smoking and risk factors, and describe how they provide evidence for causal links between smoking and various non-communicable diseases.	**Support:** Provide a partially completed spider diagram for students to complete.	**Practical:** The effects of smoking

Plenary	Support/Extend	Resources
Tobacco smoke (10 min) Call out the name of substances in tobacco smoke. Students have to identify the associated health problems. **Trends in smoking** (5 min) Students use the interactive to analyse a graph and answer questions about how the number of people smoking in the UK has changed over the last 50 years.	**Support:** Provide the substance and health problem for students to match up. **Extend:** Ask students to predict the trend before showing it to them.	**Interactive:** Trends in smoking

Homework		
Provide the class with the statement: E-cigarettes are less harmful than normal cigarettes. Ask students to carry out some research and write down at least one argument for and one argument against this statement.	**Extend:** Students should explain the arguments using detailed scientific knowledge.	

kerboodle

A Kerboodle highlight for this lesson is **Extension sheet: Carbon monoxide and blood**. Refer to the **Content map** on Kerboodle for a full list of resources and assessment.

B7.4 Diet, exercise, and disease

AQA spec link: 2.2.6 Students should be able to:

- discuss the human and financial cost of these noncommunicable diseases to an individual, a local community, a nation, or globally
- explain the effect of lifestyle factors including diet, alcohol, and smoking on the incidence of non-communicable diseases at local, national, and global levels.

Risk factors are linked to an increased rate of a disease.

They can be:

- aspects of a person's lifestyle
- substances in the person's body or environment.

A causal mechanism has been proven for some risk factors, but not in others.

- The effects of diet and exercise on cardiovascular disease.
- Obesity as a risk factor for Type 2 diabetes.

Many diseases are caused by the interaction of a number of factors.

Students should be able to understand the principles of sampling as applied to scientific data in terms of risk factors.

Students should be able to translate information between graphical and numerical forms; and extract and interpret information from charts, graphs and tables in terms of risk factors.

Students should be able to use a scatter diagram to identify a correlation between two variables in terms of risk factors.

MS 2c, 2d, 2g, 4a

Aiming for	Outcome	Checkpoint	
		Question	Activity
Aiming for GRADE 4 ↓	Describe some health problems caused by a poor diet and lack of exercise.		Starter 2, Main, Plenary 1
	List some ways in which people can avoid becoming overweight.	End of chapter 5	Starter 2, Main, Homework
Aiming for GRADE 6 ↓	Describe causal mechanisms for the link between exercise and health.	1, 2	Starter 1, Main
	Suggest measures to prevent a further rise in the number of people with type 2 diabetes.	4	Main
Aiming for GRADE 8 ↓	Suggest reasons for the correlation between exercise and health, and decide which are causal.	2	Starter 1, Plenary 2
	Explain in detail why eating a poor diet can lead to health problems.		Main 1, Plenary 1

B7 Non-communicable diseases

Maths
Students interpret graphs and charts to describe patterns and suggest possible relationships (2g).

Literacy
Students use information from the student book to create flow charts that show how eating too much food can lead to health problems. They discuss in groups measures to prevent young people in the UK developing type 2 diabetes.

Key word
obesity

Starter	Support/Extend	Resources
Exercise and health (10 min) Tell the class that people who exercise are healthier (less likely to develop non-communicable diseases) than those who don't exercise. Ask students to list possible reasons why. **Energy in, energy out** (5 min) Show the students the trailer for the documentary film *Super Size Me*. Ask pairs to discuss why you could become obese if you eat too much.	**Extend:** Show Students Figure 1 in the student book, which shows evidence for a correlation between exercise and health. Ask students to suggest non-causal and causal mechanisms. **Support:** Tell students that fat acts as a store of energy.	

Main	Support/Extend	Resources
Preventing the diabetes epidemic (40 min) Provide groups of students with some sticky notes. Ask them to write down information from the student book about the effects on the body of eating too much unhealthy food and not taking enough exercise. Students should stick the notes down on the desk to create flow charts. These should contain several paths describing how eating unhealthily leads to the problems outlined in the student book, such as type 2 diabetes and heart disease Then tell the class that the number of people their age being diagnosed with type 2 diabetes is rising. Students should explain why, using what they have learnt. Ask groups to work as a Government advisory group and come up with suggestions to stop this epidemic.	**Support:** Supply Provide the notes with information written on them and ask the groups to use these to create their flow diagram. **Extend:** Students should explain why preventing young people developing type 2 diabetes is important. They can consider the social and economic impacts.	**Activity:** Preventing the diabetes epidemic

Plenary	Support/Extend	Resources
Health problems (10 min) Students use the interactive to choose which health problems are associated with a poor diet and lack of exercise. **Obesity data** (5 mins) Show students a piece of data that that shows a correlation between a factor and obesity, for example, country of residence, age, sex, ethnicity, or income. They then describe the pattern.	**Extend:** Students also explain the causal mechanisms. **Support:** For each piece of data supply two descriptions of the pattern, one true and one false. Students must decide which is correct. **Extend:** Ask students to suggest a causal mechanism for the correlation.	**Interactive:** Health problems

Homework		
Students give advice to an overweight person on how to lose weight and not gain it back.	**Extend:** Students should justify each point they make with scientific knowledge.	

B7.5 Alcohol and other carcinogens

AQA spec link: 2.2.6 A causal mechanism has been proven for some risk factors, but not in others.

- The effect of alcohol on the liver and brain function.
- The effects of alcohol on unborn babies.
- Carcinogens, including ionising radiation, as risk factors in cancer.

Many diseases are caused by the interaction of a number of factors.

Students should be able to understand the principles of sampling as applied to scientific data in terms of risk factors.

Students should be able to translate information between graphical and numerical forms; and extract and interpret information from charts, graphs and tables in terms of risk factors.

Students should be able to use a scatter diagram to identify a correlation between two variables in terms of risk factors.

WS 1.4
MS 2c, 2d, 2g, 4a

Aiming for	Outcome	Checkpoint	
		Question	Activity
Aiming for GRADE 4	State that drinking too much alcohol can affect liver and brain function.	End of chapter 4	Starter 2, Main 1, Plenary 1
	State that alcohol can affect unborn babies.		Main 1
	Define the term carcinogen.	1	Main 2
Aiming for GRADE 6	Describe the short- and long-term effects of drinking alcohol.	2, End of chapter 4	Starter 2, Main 1, Plenary 1
	Describe the effects of alcohol on unborn babies.		Main 1
	Describe the link between ionising radiation and cancer.		Main 2, Homework
Aiming for GRADE 8	Explain in detail how drinking alcohol affects the nervous system.		Main 1
	Evaluate evidence on the effects of alcohol on a developing baby.	End of chapter 4	Main 1
	Explain the link between ionising radiation and cancer.		Main 2, Homework

Maths
Students study data and use it to support or refute the claim that pregnant women should not drink alcohol (2g).

Literacy
Students practice answering an extended answer exam-style question.

Starter	Support/Extend	Resources
Which drug is the most harmful? (10 min) Provide students with a piece of paper or a mini-whiteboard. Ask them to write down which recreational drug they think is the most harmful and reveal their answers. Show them data that claims that alcohol is the most harmful. Discuss why this is by considering the effects of alcohol on the individual and society. **Alcohol effects** (5 min) Students list examples of how drinking alcohol affects the body.	**Support:** Write a list of different drugs on the board for students to choose from. **Extend:** Students should state whether each effect is short – or long-term.	

Main	Support/Extend	Resources
The effects of alcohol (30 min) Students look at the effects of alcohol on the body and on baby development. They analyse the given evidence and use it to come to their own conclusion on the risks of alcohol, and to support or refute the claim that pregnant women should not drink alcohol. **Ionising radiation** (10 min) Explain that ionising radiation is a carcinogen. Ask students for suggestions of sources of ionising radiation that they may come into contact with. After hearing their ideas, allow students to use the student book to list them. Discuss the fact that coming into contact with ionising radiation increases the risk of developing cancer. Ask students to list lifestyle choices that will increase this risk, for example, using tanning beds or having x-rays.	**Extend:** Students complete the Go further activity. **Extend:** Show students an online radon map and study how high the risk of radon is in your local area.	**Working scientifically:** The effects of alcohol **Go further:** Alcohol – a depressing story

Plenary	Support/Extend	Resources
Effects of alcohol (10 min) Bump up your grade worksheet where students analyse data on the effects of alcohol and determine cause-and-effect relationships. **Alcohol statements** (5 min) Use the interactive, which asks students to type in answers to complete sentences about the effects of alcohol on the body.	**Support:** Outline the steps needed to answer an extended answer exam-style question. **Support:** Use the simple Interactive that supplies a choice of endings.	**Bump up your grade:** Effects of alcohol **Interactive:** Alcohol statements

Homework		
Ask students to suggest why there is concern that people living near Fukushima in Japan are at an increased risk of developing cancer.	**Extend:** Students should use scientific knowledge to explain their ideas.	

kerboodle

A Kerboodle highlight for this lesson is **Calculation sheet: Measuring risk**. Refer to the **Content map** on Kerboodle for a full list of resources and assessment.

B7 Non-communicable diseases

Overview of B7 Non-communicable diseases

In this chapter, students have studied non-communicable diseases and should understand what is meant by risk factors for a disease. They should have analysed the impact of disease at several different levels. Students should recognise correlations between data sets and the need for evidence to secure a causal mechanism. They should understand the difference between correlated data and causal mechanisms, and be able to read graphs and quote data to support correlations and causations.

Students have studied cancer and the different types of tumour, along with the general causes and treatment of cancer. They should link this to mitosis and the cell cycle in B2 *Cell division*.

Students should be aware of the risks of diseases from smoking, linked to work on the heart and blood vessels in B4 *Organising animals and plants*. They should recall the roles of nicotine, carbon monoxide, and tar, and understand how each specifically affects health, as well as recalling the dangers of smoking whilst pregnant. They should have applied the concept of a causal mechanism to data on smoking and developing lung cancer. Students should understand the impact of smoking on the heart.

In considering the effect of diet and exercise on disease, students should appreciate the connection between obesity and other diseases such as type 2 diabetes.

Students have studied alcohol and health, and should understand the effect of alcohol on the brain and liver, and of drinking alcohol during pregnancy. Finally students should be aware of the sources and carcinogenic effects of ionising radiation.

MyMaths

You can find additional support for the maths skills covered in this chapter on **MyMaths**, including data interpretation.

kerboodle

For this chapter, the following assessments are available on Kerboodle:

B7 Checkpoint quiz: Non-communicable diseases
B7 Progress quiz: Non-communicable diseases 1
B7 Progress quiz: Non-communicable diseases 2
B7 On your marks: Non-communicable diseases
B7 Exam-style questions and mark scheme: Non-communicable diseases

Checkpoint follow-up lesson

A student's route through this lesson can be determined using the Checkpoint assessment. Percentage pass marks are supplied in the Checkpoint teacher notes.

For each successive route through it is assumed that the student can perform to their current route as well as previous routes. For example, students working at Aiming for 6 are assumed to be secure in Aiming for 4 knowledge and understanding and working towards achieving all the learning outcomes for Aiming for 6.

	Aiming for 4	**Aiming for 6**	**Aiming for 8**
Learning outcomes	State some examples of non-communicable disease.	Describe some examples of non-communicable disease.	Describe some examples of non-communicable disease and their effects.
	State some of the risk factors for some non-communicable diseases.	Describe some of the risk factors for some non-communicable diseases.	Explain some of the risk factors for some non-communicable diseases.
	State some methods of prevention of some non-communicable diseases.	Describe some methods of prevention of some non-communicable diseases.	Explain some methods of prevention of some non-communicable diseases.
Starter	**Non-communicable diseases (5 min)** Have a prepared list of non-communicable diseases covered up on the board. Remind the class of the difference between a communicable and a non-communicable disease. Ask student pairs to write down as many non-communicable diseases as they can in 2 minutes. Show students the list on the board. Did they miss any? Add any relevant diseases to the list.		
Differentiated checkpoint activity	Students work in pairs or small groups to visit four of the six stations previously set up with a profile of a different person as detailed in the teacher's notes. Students all follow the same method, taking the role of a GP to give advice to each person, using the differentiated worksheets. They spend 10 minutes at each station before moving on. The teacher should keep a check on time and move students on as appropriate. It may be useful to have a few student books at each station.		
	The Aiming for 4 sheet is highly structured, with detailed prompts for each student.	The Aiming for 6 sheet is fairly structured, providing prompts for each patient.	The Aiming for 8 sheet has little structure, with generic prompts rather than individual patients.
	Kerboodle resource B7 Checkpoint follow-up: Aiming for 4, B7 Checkpoint follow-up: Aiming for 6, B7 Checkpoint follow-up: Aiming for 8		
Plenary	**Profile review (10 min)** Review the profiles of each of the six people. Ask – what diseases are they at risk from? What advice would you give them?		
Progression	To progress, once students have reviewed two patients with the Aiming for 4 follow-up sheet, give students the Aiming for 6 follow-up sheet to review their final two patients.	To progress, once students have reviewed two patients with the Aiming for 6 follow-up sheet, give students the Aiming for 8 follow-up sheet to review their final two patients.	To progress, once students have reviewed two patients with the Aiming for 8 follow-up sheet, encourage students to review their final two patients without any prompt information.

B 8 Photosynthesis
8.1 Photosynthesis

AQA spec link: 4.1.1 Photosynthesis is represented by the equations:

carbon dioxide + water $\xrightarrow{\text{light}}$ glucose + oxygen

Students should recognise the chemical symbols: CO_2, H_2O, O_2, and $C_6H_{12}O_6$.

Students should be able to describe photosynthesis as an endothermic reaction in which energy is transferred from the environment to the chloroplasts by light.

Aiming for	Outcome	Checkpoint	
		Question	Activity
Aiming for GRADE 4 ↓	Describe how plants get the materials they need for growth.		Starter 2, Main 1
	State the word equation for photosynthesis.	4, End of chapter 1	Main 1, Plenary 1
	Describe why plants need light to carry out photosynthesis.		Main 1
Aiming for GRADE 6 ↓	Describe how the leaf is adapted for photosynthesis.	1, End of chapter 1	Main 2
	Write the balanced symbol equation for photosynthesis.	4	Main 1, Plenary 1
	Describe an experiment to prove that plants carry out photosynthesis when exposed to light.	3	Starter 1
Aiming for GRADE 8 ↓	Explain how adaptations of the leaf make photosynthesis efficient.		Main 2
	Explain why photosynthesis is an endothermic reaction.	4	Main 1
	Explain why chlorophyll is needed for photosynthesis.		

Maths
Students consider why symbol equations need to be balanced, and what this means.

Literacy
Through group and paired discussion students develop ideas about how plants increase mass and how leaves are adapted.

Key words
glucose, endothermic reaction

Practical

Title	Producing oxygen
Equipment	*Elodea canadensis* (Canadian pondweed), glass funnel, beaker of water, test tube full of water, lamp
Overview of method	The pondweed can be collected from a pond or bought from a garden centre. Place a few stems of the plant in a beaker of water and place the glass funnel on top. Invert the test tube of water over the end of the funnel. Leave with the light from the lamp shining on the equipment for a few hours, so that enough gas collects in the test tube to carry out the test for oxygen.
Safety considerations	Wash hands after contact with pond water.

B8 Photosynthesis

Starter	Support/Extend	Resources
Producing oxygen (10 min) Show the class the equipment and ask students to name the gas in the bubbles forming on the plant. Test the gas collected in the test tube by placing a glowing splint inside. Show that it relights – proving that oxygen is formed. **How do trees grow?** (5 min) Tell students that trees grow by turning substances from the soil into new tissues. Ask them to discuss the statement in pairs. Listen to ideas from the class and discuss what is true and what is false about the statement.	**Extend:** Students should explain what the experiment shows.	

Main	Support/Extend	Resources
Photosynthesis equations (20 min) Discuss photosynthesis as a reaction that plants and algae use to produce glucose from carbon dioxide and water. Oxygen is also a product. Students complete the Calculation sheet, which guides them through how to represent photosynthesis as a word equation and balanced symbol equation, and explains why light is required. **Leaf structure** (20 min) Introduce the leaf as the site of photosynthesis. Sort students into groups and assign each student within the group one feature of a leaf, for example, thin, green, flat, shiny, has veins. Give each student a diagram of a leaf and ask students to annotate their diagram with the reasons why leaves have this feature. Students then copy each other's annotations to create a fully labelled diagram of the adaptations of leaves.	**Extend:** Students should use the Internet to research why chlorophyll is important for photosynthesis. **Support:** Provide groups with different examples of leaves that they can handle.	**Activity:** Leaf structure

Plenary	Support/Extend	Resources
The photosynthesis equations (10 min) Bump up your grade worksheet where students learn the word equation and balanced symbol equation for photosynthesis. **Photosynthesis** (5 min) Interactive where students are given graphs showing the rate of photosynthesis and answer multiple choice questions about them.		**Bump up your grade:** The photosynthesis equations **Interactive:** Photosynthesis

Homework		
Tell students that one idea to combat global warming is to increase the amount of algae in the sea by adding iron, which acts as a fertiliser. Ask them to describe how this could result in reducing carbon dioxide levels in the air.	**Support:** Remind students that rising carbon dioxide levels are linked to global warming.	

kerboodle
A Kerboodle highlight for this lesson is **Go further: An oxygen detective story**. Refer to the **Content map** on Kerboodle for a full list of resources and assessment.

B8.2 The rate of photosynthesis

AQA spec link: 4.1.2 Students should be able to explain the effects of temperature, light intensity, carbon dioxide concentration, and the amount of chlorophyll on the rate of photosynthesis.

Students should be able to:

- measure and calculate rates of photosynthesis
- extract and interpret graphs of photosynthesis rate involving one limiting factor
- plot and draw appropriate graphs selecting appropriate scale for axes
- translate information between graphical and numeric form.

H These factors interact and any one of them may be the factor that limits photosynthesis.

Students should be able to explain graphs of photosynthesis rate involving two or three factors and decide which the limiting factor is.

Students should understand and use inverse proportion – the inverse square law and light intensity in the context of photosynthesis.

WS 1.4
MS 1a, 1c, 2c, 3a, 3d, 4a, 4c

Aiming for	Outcome	Checkpoint	
		Question	Activity
Aiming for GRADE 4	List the factors that affect the rate of photosynthesis (temperature, carbon dioxide concentration, light intensity, amount of chlorophyll).	1	Starter 2, Main, Plenary 2, Homework
	State simply the relationship between these factors and the rate of photosynthesis.	End of chapter 1	Starter 2, Main, Homework
	Plot a line graph and write a simple conclusion.	End of chapter 2	Main, Homework
Aiming for GRADE 6	Describe why low temperature, shortage of carbon dioxide, shortage of light and shortage of chlorophyll limit the rate of photosynthesis.	End of chapter 2	Main
	Suggest which factor limits the rate of photosynthesis in a given situation.	1, End of chapter 1	Plenary 2
	Interpret and explain graphs of photosynthesis rate involving one limiting factor.	2	Starter 1, Main, Homework
Aiming for GRADE 8	Apply knowledge of enzymes to explain why a high temperature affects the rate of photosynthesis.		Main
	Predict how the rate of photosynthesis will be affected with more than one limiting factor.	3	Plenary 1
	Understand and use the inverse square law and light intensity in the context of photosynthesis.		Main

Maths
Students draw line graphs using lines of best fit (4a). They analyse line graphs and explain the relationships between variables (2g). Higher-tier students use the inverse square law (3a).

Literacy
Students write an analysis of their line graph including a scientific explanation for their results.

Key word
limiting factors

B8 Photosynthesis

Practical

Title	Light intensity and rate of photosynthesis
Equipment	*Elodea canadensis* (Canadian pondweed), glass funnel, beaker of water, test tube or small measuring cylinder full of water, lamp, metre rule, stopwatch, thermometer.
Overview of method	Place a few stems of the plant in a beaker of water and place the glass funnel on top. Invert the test tube or small measuring cylinder of water over the end of the funnel. Students gradually move the lamp away from the plant and measure how much oxygen is produced at each point over a period of time. They can do this by counting the number of bubbles or by using a measuring cylinder and measuring the volume produced. They should use the thermometer to make sure that temperature remains constant.
Safety considerations	Wash hands after contact with pond water. Lamp may get hot. Do not handle electrical equipment with wet hands.

Starter	Support/Extend	Resources
Graph shapes (10 min) Draw several axes on the board (labelled *x* and *y*). Then add a variety of different-shaped line graphs on the axes and ask students to describe the relationship between the variables on each. **Plant growth** (5 min) Ask students how the growth of plants differs in the summer and winter. Question them as to why this is and draw out the ideas that in the summer it is warmer and there are more hours of sunlight.	**Extend:** Ask students to suggest a real-life relationship that each graph could be representing.	

Main	Support/Extend	Resources
Light intensity and rate of photosynthesis (40 min) Students use *Elodea* in water with a lamp shining on it to investigate the effect of light intensity of the rate of photosynthesis. Students measure the volume of oxygen produced when the lamp is placed at varying distances away from the plant. They collect results. Discuss how and why it is difficult to control temperature. Students draw line graphs of their results. Ask them to write an analysis of what their results show. On the board draw line graphs showing how other limiting factors affect the rate of photosynthesis. Students then use information from the student book plus the simulation to explain the shape of each graph. The practical element may be time-consuming. Either complete over two lessons or do this as a demonstration.	**Support:** Provide students with a given method to follow. **Extend:** Students should plan a suitable method and choose range and intervals. **Extend:** Students should use the inverse square law (where light intensity is proportional to 1 over the distance squared from the source) and plot these points on a graph. **Extend:** Draw graphs with more than one limiting factor.	**Practical:** Light intensity and rate of photosynthesis

Plenary	Support/Extend	Resources
Data handling skills (10 min) Interactive where students are given graphs showing the rate of photosynthesis and answer multiple choice questions about them. **What is the limiting factor?** (5 min) Read out a variety of scenarios, for example, tomato plants growing in a greenhouse, and ask students to suggest the factor limiting the rate of photosynthesis.		**Interactive:** Data handling skills

Homework		
Students complete a data analysis exercise using an experiment looking at the effect of changing carbon dioxide concentration on the rate of photosynthesis.		

kerboodle

A Kerboodle highlight for this lesson is **Calculation sheet: Calculating the equation of a straight line**. Refer to the **Content map** on Kerboodle for a full list of resources and assessment.

B8.3 How plants use glucose

AQA spec link: 4.1.3 The glucose produced in photosynthesis may be:

- used for respiration
- converted into insoluble starch for storage
- used to produce fat or oil for storage
- used to produce cellulose, which strengthens the cell wall
- used to produce amino acids for protein synthesis.

To produce proteins, plants also use nitrate ions that are absorbed from the soil.

Aiming for	Outcome	Checkpoint	
		Question	Activity
Aiming for GRADE 4 ↓	List some ways in which plants use glucose.	1, End of chapter 1	Starter 1, Main, Plenary
	Test a leaf for starch and state some safety rules.	2, 3, End of chapter 3	Starter 2, Main
Aiming for GRADE 6 ↓	Describe all the ways in which plants use glucose, including how they make proteins.	1, 2, End of chapter 1, 4	Main, Plenary 1, Plenary 2
	Evaluate risks involved in the starch test.		Main
Aiming for GRADE 8 ↓	Explain how carnivorous plants are adapted to their environment.	4	Main, Homework
	Explain how and why plants convert glucose to starch for storage.	2	Main

Maths
Students can discuss how food tests could be used quantitatively. They can consider how the concentration of molecules is related to the intensity of the resulting colour, and how this could be measured using a spectrometer.

Literacy
Students use information from the student book to list uses of glucose in plants. They also follow instructions and write down potential hazards.

Key words
nitrate ions, mineral ions

Practical

Title	Testing for starch
Equipment	destarched and illuminated plants, beakers, Bunsen burners, tripods, gauzes, ethanol, boiling tubes, dilute iodine solution in dropping bottles, white tiles, tongs, tweezers, eye protection
Overview of method	Use the Bunsen burner to boil a beaker half full of water. Remove the leaf to be tested and use tongs to place it into the boiling water for 10 minutes. Turn off the Bunsen burner. Place a boiling tube of ethanol into the hot water and place the leaf inside. Leave for 5 minutes until the ethanol has gone dark green. Wash the leaf in the water and spread onto a white tile. Add drops of iodine over the leaf and note the areas that go blue-black.
Safety considerations	Wear eye protection. Ethanol is highly flammable and harmful, keep away from naked flames. Iodine is harmful, avoid contact with skin.

B8 Photosynthesis

Starter	Support/Extend	Resources
Plant products (5 min) Show the class a variety of products made from plant materials, for example, cotton fabric, wooden object, dried fruit, and olive oil. Question them about the function of the product, and what part of the plant it was made from. **Food test reminder** (10 min) Remind students about the food tests carried out in Topic B3.3. With help from the class demonstrate the tests for glucose, starch, and protein on a range of plant substances, for example, potato, peas, nuts, and banana.	**Extend:** Discuss with the class how these tests could be used quantitatively	

Main	Support/Extend	Resources
Testing for starch (40 min) Ask students to list what plants use glucose for. Allow them to use information from the student book to complete their lists. Describe starch as a long molecule made up of many repeating units of glucose. Demonstrate that glucose is soluble in water but starch isn't by adding both to water and stirring. Ask students to write down why plants store glucose in their cells as starch. Students then carry out the starch test on leaves that have been kept in the light and leaves that have been kept in the dark. Before they start, ask them to read through the method, write down any potential hazards, and state how they will minimise risk.	**Extend:** Students should explain how plants make proteins. **Extend:** Students should be able to use osmosis in their explanation. **Support:** Go through each stage of the experiment with the students before they start.	**Practical:** Testing for starch

Plenary	Support/Extend	Resources
Match the uses (5 min) Interactive where students match the name of a product made from glucose with its use in the plant. **The fate of glucose** (10 min) Bump up your grade worksheet where students answer questions to link the formation of glucose in respiration with its use in the production of proteins, lipids, starch, and cellulose.		**Interactive:** Match the uses **Bump up your grade:** The fate of glucose

Homework		
Ask students to find out about carnivorous plants such as the Venus fly trap. They should describe the places where they live and explain how and why they eat insects, linking this to how they make proteins.	**Extend:** Students should describe how carnivorous plants are adapted to their environment.	

kerboodle
A Kerboodle highlight for this lesson is **Go further: Balancing supply and demand of glucose**. Refer to the **Content map** on Kerboodle for a full list of resources and assessment.

Higher tier

B8.4 Making the most of photosynthesis

AQA spec link: 4.1.2 Limiting factors are important in the economics of enhancing the conditions in greenhouses to gain the maximum rate of photosynthesis whilst still maintaining profit.

WS 1.4

Aiming for	Outcome	Checkpoint	
		Question	Activity
Aiming for GRADE 6	Describe why greenhouses increase plant growth.	1	Starter 2, Main 1, Homework
	Comment on the cost-effectiveness of adding heat, light, or carbon dioxide to greenhouses.	3	Main 1
	Discuss the benefits of using greenhouses and hydroponics.	1	Main 1, Main 2, Plenary 1
Aiming for GRADE 8	Explain in detail how using greenhouses can help control limiting factors and increase the rate of photosynthesis.	3	Starter 2, Main 1, Homework
	Use data to comment on the cost-effectiveness of greenhouses.	3	Main 1
	Evaluate the use of greenhouses and hydroponics in terms of economics.	1	Main 1, Main 2, Plenary 1

Maths
Students consider the economics of using greenhouses. They analyse costs and profits to calculate the cost-effectiveness of adding extra heat, light, and carbon dioxide.

Literacy
Students use the Internet to research greenhouses and hydroponics. They write a sales pitch to persuade people to buy a greenhouse of their own design.

■ B8 Photosynthesis

Starter	Support/Extend	Resources
Multiple factors (10 min) Students select the correct limiting factors for graphs showing rate of photosynthesis when more than one limiting factor is acting. **What does it show?** (5 min) Show students a bar chart showing the yield of tomato plants grown inside and outside a greenhouse (Figure 1 in the student book). Ask them to interpret the chart.	**Extend:** Students should give a scientific explanation for the data.	**Interactive:** Multiple factors

Main	Support/Extend	Resources
Greenhouse economics (20 min) Introduce students to the use of greenhouses to increase the growth of plants and therefore increase profits for growers. Link each feature of a greenhouse to the limiting factors of photosynthesis. Students are then presented with data looking at the costs of running a greenhouse, and potential profits. They use the data to decide on the cost-effectiveness of adding extra carbon dioxide, heat, and light to the greenhouse. **Hydroponics** (20 mins) Introduce students to the use of hydroponics to increase the growth of plants and therefore increase profits for growers. Students then complete the Literacy worksheet to analyse given text on hydroponics.		**Activity:** Greenhouse economics **Literacy sheet:** Hydroponics

Plenary	Support/Extend	Resources
Evaluating greenhouses (10 min) Tell the class that a smallholder is considering buying a greenhouse to expand the range of fruit and vegetables they can grow and sell. Ask students to write down advice, to include the benefits of using a greenhouse but also the potential issues. **Plants on Mars** (5 min) Introduce the fact that if people are to live on Mars they will need to grow plants for food. Supply groups of students with a list of problems affecting growth of plants on Mars (e.g., low temperature, lack of soil minerals, no liquid water) and ask them to discuss possible ways to overcome them.	**Extend:** Students should evaluate the economics (potential profit versus costs).	

Homework		
Students research further the use of greenhouses and hydroponics to increase the growth of plants and therefore increase profits for growers. They use this information to design their own greenhouse and write a sales pitch. Alternatively, provide students with an image of a greenhouse (or have them draw their own) and ask them to annotate it to show how it affects the limiting factors of photosynthesis. Students should include graphs in their annotations.	**Support:** Provide students with a diagram of an outline of a greenhouse which they can use as a template for their design.	

kerboodle

A Kerboodle highlight for this lesson is **Calculation sheet: Cost-effectiveness**. Refer to the **Content map** on Kerboodle for a full list of resources and assessment.

B8 Photosynthesis

Overview of B8 Photosynthesis

In this chapter, students have studied photosynthesis in both plants and algae. They should be familiar with the word equation for photosynthesis, and also the symbol equation in the case of higher-tier students. They should be aware that photosynthesis is an endothermic reaction.

Students have studied the adaptations of leaves to achieve maximum efficiency in photosynthesis. They should link this work with B1.2 *Animal and plant cells*, B1.5 *Specialisation in plant cells*, and B4.6 *Tissues and organs in plants*.

Students have studied factors that affect the rate of photosynthesis. They should understand the concept of limiting factors. They should have carried out data interpretation exercises and be able to explain the results. Higher-tier students should understand that that any one factor could become limiting as the factors interact. These students should be confident in analysing two or three factors displayed on a graph and deciding which factor is limiting. They should be confident describing the inverse square law as applied to light intensity.

All students should be aware of the fate of glucose – its use in respiration, and also how it can be assimilated into starch and cellulose. They should link this with B1.2 *Animal and plant cells*, B1.7 *Osmosis*, and B9 *Respiration*. Students should also consider the need for nitrate ions as well as glucose to make proteins, and how glucose can be used to make lipids. They should link this with B3.3 *The chemistry of food* where they carried out food tests.

Finally students have considered the use of greenhouses and studied how the conditions can be monitored and manipulated to achieve the highest rate of photosynthesis. Higher-tier students should have an appreciation of the economics of increasing the rate of photosynthesis – they should be aware that using a greenhouse is expensive, and weigh it up against the profit gained in increased biomass.

Required practical

All students are expected to have carried out the required practical:

Practical	Topic
Investigate the effect of light intensity on the rate of photosynthesis. Use an aquatic plant to observe the effect light intensity has on the rate of photosynthesis.	B8.2

MyMaths

You can find additional support for the maths skills covered in this chapter on **MyMaths**, including working with ratios and balancing symbol equations, working with graphs, analysing costs and profits, and, for higher-tier students, the inverse square law.

kerboodle

For this chapter, the following assessments are available on Kerboodle:

B8 Checkpoint quiz: Photosynthesis
B8 Progress quiz: Photosynthesis 1
B8 Progress quiz: Photosynthesis 2
B8 On your marks: Photosynthesis
B8 Exam-style questions and mark scheme: Photosynthesis

Checkpoint follow-up lesson

A student's route through this lesson can be determined using the Checkpoint assessment. Percentage pass marks are supplied in the Checkpoint teacher notes.

For each successive route through it is assumed that the student can perform to their current route as well as previous routes. For example, students working at Aiming for 6 are assumed to be secure in Aiming for 4 knowledge and understanding and working towards achieving all the learning outcomes for Aiming for 6.

	Aiming for 4	Aiming for 6	Aiming for 8
Learning outcomes	Complete the word equation for photosynthesis.	State the word equation for photosynthesis.	State the symbol equation for photosynthesis.
	State how a leaf is adapted for photosynthesis.	Describe how a leaf is adapted for photosynthesis.	Explain how a leaf is adapted for photosynthesis.
	State and describe the factors that affect photosynthesis.	Describe the factors that affect photosynthesis.	Explain the factors that affect photosynthesis.
Starter	**Sticky note plant (10 min)** Each small mixed-ability group will need a photocopied picture of a plant including the roots and the soil, and arrow sticky notes. In their groups, students attach sticky notes onto the picture to show what is needed and what is produced during photosynthesis. Go through each group's results to build up word and symbol equations on the board.		
Differentiated checkpoint activity	Students work in small groups to observe a cross-section of a leaf under a microscope.		
	Aiming for 4 students label a diagram of a leaf using labels provided, then match the tissues with their adaptations for photosynthesis.		
	Aiming for 6 students draw their cross-section of a leaf, labelling it with the labels provided and giving simple descriptions of the adaptations of each tissue.		
	Aiming for 8 students draw and label their cross-section of a leaf. Their labels should include information on how the tissue is adapted for photosynthesis.		
	All students then apply their understanding of photosynthesis to explain how the yield of plants can be increased in a greenhouse. The Aiming for 4 follow-up sheet provides highly-structured prompt questions to direct students' understanding. The Aiming for 6 follow-up sheet provides prompt questions to direct students' understanding. The Aiming for 8 follow-up sheet provides simple headings for students to cover when creating their explanations.		
	Kerboodle resource B8 Checkpoint follow-up: Aiming for 4, B8 Checkpoint follow-up: Aiming for 6, B8 Checkpoint follow-up: Aiming for 8		
Plenary	**True or false? (5 min)** Each student will need two cards of different colours. Read some statements out about photosynthesis to check students' understanding. Students show one coloured card for true, and the other one for false. Examples of statements could include – oxygen is a product of photosynthesis (true). Most photosynthesis happens in the cuticle (false). Increasing light intensity increases the rate of photosynthesis (true).		
Progression	Students can work towards sketching graphs to show the effects of temperature and carbon dioxide on the rate of photosynthesis.	Students can work towards including magnifications on their micrographs and writing the symbol equation for photosynthesis.	Show students examples of variegated leaves or other types of leaves. Ask them to suggest how these differences from a typical green leaf may affect the rate of photosynthesis of the plant.

B 9 Respiration
9.1 Aerobic respiration

AQA spec link: 4.2.1 Students should be able to describe cellular respiration as an exothermic reaction which is continuously occurring in living cells.

The energy transferred supplies all the energy needed for living processes.

Respiration in cells can take place aerobically (using oxygen) or anaerobically (without oxygen), to transfer energy.

Students should be able to compare the processes of aerobic and anaerobic respiration with regard to the need for oxygen, the differing products, and the relative amounts of energy transferred.

Organisms need energy for:

- chemical reactions to build larger molecules
- movement
- keeping warm.

Aerobic respiration is represented by the equations:

glucose + oxygen → carbon dioxide + water

Students should recognise the chemical symbols:
$C_6H_{12}O_6$, O_2, CO_2, and H_2O.

Aiming for	Outcome	Checkpoint	
		Question	Activity
Aiming for GRADE 4	State the word equation for aerobic respiration.	1, End of chapter 3	Main 2, Plenary 2
	List ways in which living organisms use energy.	2	Starter 1, Main 1, Plenary 1, Homework
	Identify a control.	End of chapter 1	Main 2
Aiming for GRADE 6	Write the balanced symbol equation for respiration.	1	Main 1
	Describe respiration as an exothermic reaction.		Main 1, Plenary 2
	Plan an investigation to include a control.	3	Main 2
Aiming for GRADE 8	Apply understanding of respiration in new contexts.	1, 2, End of chapter 3, 4	Starter 1, Plenary 1, Homework
	Explain why respiration is an exothermic reaction.		Main 1
	Explain why a control is necessary in some scientific investigations.	End of chapter 1	Main 2

Maths
Students plan an investigation to measure carbon dioxide production and temperature.

Literacy
Students use information from the student book to answer questions about respiration. They also write an article for a scientific magazine.

Key words
aerobic respiration, exothermic reaction

B9 Respiration

Starter	Support/Extend	Resources
Energy gels (10 min) Show the class some examples of energy gels. Ask them to discuss in pairs why cyclists in events such as the Tour de France use them. Draw out the idea that they are high in glucose, which is the source of energy for the body. **What do you already know?** (5 min) Ask students to write down three key points about respiration that they already know. Share these as a class.	**Extend:** Ask students to explain why the cyclists will have a breakfast high in starch, such as porridge.	

Main	Support/Extend	Resources
Hunt the answers (15 min) Give students a number of questions about respiration and ask them to use the student book to find the answers. Questions can include: What are the reactants/products in aerobic respiration? Where does respiration take place in the cell? Respiration is exothermic – what does this mean? Why is respiration an exothermic reaction? Why do living things need to carry out respiration? **Investigating respiration** (25 min) Remind students of the word equation for aerobic respiration. Students then plan an investigation to prove that living organisms carry out respiration. They will need to use controls in their plan. If you have time, you can allow students to carry out the investigation in the next lesson.	**Support:** Ask students to work in groups, within which each person is responsible for finding the answer to one question. **Extend:** Students can complete the Go Further activity. **Support:** Focus on measuring thermal energy. **Extend:** Students should plan two investigations, one to measure thermal energy and one to measure production of carbon dioxide, including an explanation of controls set up.	**Practical:** Investigating respiration

Plenary	Support/Extend	Resources
Sperm cells (10 min) Show students a diagram of a sperm cell to show the large number of mitochondria in the middle section. Ask students to write down an explanation for why sperm cells contain so many mitochondria. **Aerobic respiration** (5 min) Students complete the interactive to review and assess understanding about aerobic respiration.	**Support:** Discuss the role of the sperm cell before students write their explanation.	**Interactive:** Aerobic respiration

Homework		
Students write an article for a general science magazine on the deadly poison cyanide that inhibits respiration. The article needs to be scientifically accurate and interesting. You may wish to discuss how to write a scientific article before students leave the lesson.		

kerboodle

A Kerboodle highlight for this lesson is **WebQuest: Did dinosaurs have warm blood?** Refer to the **Content map** on Kerboodle for a full list of resources and assessment.

B9.2 The response to exercise

AQA spec link: 4.2.2 During exercise the human body reacts to the increased demand for energy.

The heart rate, breathing rate, and breath volume increase during exercise to supply the muscles with more oxygenated blood.

MS 1c, 4a

Aiming for	Outcome	Checkpoint	
		Question	Activity
Aiming for GRADE 4 ↓	Describe how heart rate, breathing rate, and breath volume change with exercise.	1, End of chapter 2	Starter 1, Main, Plenary 1
	Draw a suitable chart/graph to display data with some support.	1, End of chapter 2	Main
Aiming for GRADE 6 ↓	Explain why heart rate, breathing rate, and breath volume change with exercise.	3	Main
	Choose the best way to display data and calculate percentage changes.	1	Main
Aiming for GRADE 8 ↓	Explain why stores of glycogen change with exercise.	2	Main
	Justify the choice of chart/graph used to display data.		Main

Maths
Students calculate percentage changes (1c). They choose how to display categoric and continuous data (4a).

Literacy
Students write a scientific explanation for change in heart rate during and after exercise

Key word
glycogen

Practical

Title	The effects of exercise
Equipment	mat or step, stopwatch, data loggers
Overview of method	Students work in pairs to carry out an investigation where they measure each other's pulse rate before, during, and after exercise. They can choose the exercise, dependent on the equipment available.
Safety considerations	Be aware of any underlying medical conditions that may prevent students from taking part. Students should be discouraged from competing with each other during the physical exercises.

B9 Respiration

Starter	Support/Extend	Resources
Changes during exercise (10 min) Show the class a short video of people carrying out exercise, for example, a rowing race, marathon, or group exercise class. Ask the class what changes they think were happening to the participants' bodies during the exercise. **Why exercise?** (5 min) Discuss with the class what exercise they enjoy, and why it is important for health that people do some physical activity.	**Extend:** Tell the class that there is evidence that people who take regular exercise are healthier than those who don't. Ask them to list possible reasons why.	

Main	Support/Extend	Resources
The effects of exercise (40 min) Discuss with students how they think heart rate, breathing rate, and breath volume change with exercise. Demonstrate how to measure the pulse at the wrist or neck. Students work in pairs to carry out an investigation where they measure each other's pulse rate before, during, and after exercise. They record results in a table. Students then analyse the data by: • Calculating the percentage change in resting heart rate after exercise. • Drawing suitable charts to display their data (Higher-tier students should be able to justify their choice). Ask students to use the information in the student book to write a scientific explanation for the change in heart rate.	**Extend:** Students should also investigate how exercise affects breathing rate. **Support:** Demonstrate how to calculate percentage changes. **Extend:** Students should also explain the changes in breathing rate, breath volume, and amount of stored glycogen.	**Practical:** The effects of exercise

Plenary	Support/Extend	Resources
Exercise data (5 min) Show the class a series of graphs that show changes to the body during exercise. Ask them to describe what each shows. **Exercise effects** (10 mins) Students complete a series of questions and activities on how exercise affects the body.	**Support:** Use bar charts and simple line graphs. **Extend:** Use line graphs that show more than one change.	**Interactive:** Exercise effects

Homework		
Tell the class that before a period of sustained exercise you should eat some starchy food. Ask students to explain why, using a flow chart of events that includes an explanation of the role of glycogen.		

kerboodle

A Kerboodle highlight for this lesson is **Calculation sheet: Calculating percentage changes**. Refer to the **Content map** on Kerboodle for a full list of resources and assessment.

B9.3 Anaerobic respiration

AQA spec links: 4.2.1 Respiration in cells can take place aerobically (using oxygen) or anaerobically (without oxygen), to transfer energy.

Students should be able to compare the processes of aerobic and anaerobic respiration with regard to the need for oxygen, the differing products, and the relative amounts of energy transferred.

Anaerobic respiration in muscles is represented by the equation:

glucose → lactic acid

As the oxidation of glucose is incomplete in anaerobic respiration much less energy is transferred than in aerobic respiration.

Anaerobic respiration in plant and yeast cells is represented by the equation:

glucose → ethanol + carbon dioxide

Anaerobic respiration in yeast cells is called fermentation and has economic importance in the manufacture of bread and alcoholic drinks.

4.2.2 If insufficient oxygen is supplied anaerobic respiration takes place in muscles. The incomplete oxidation of glucose causes a build up of lactic acid and creates an oxygen debt. During long periods of vigorous activity muscles become fatigued and stop contracting efficiently.

H Blood flowing through the muscles transports the lactic acid to the liver where it is converted back into glucose. Oxygen debt is the amount of extra oxygen the body needs after exercise to react with the accumulated lactic acid and remove it from the cells.

Aiming for	Outcome (Level)	Checkpoint Question	Activity
Aiming for GRADE 4	State the word equation for anaerobic respiration in animals, plants, and microorganisms.	2, End of chapter 3	Main 2
	Describe the reason why cells respire anaerobically.		Main 1
	Give some uses of fermentation.		Main 2
Aiming for GRADE 6	Write the balanced symbol equation for anaerobic respiration in plants and microorganisms.	2	Main 2
	Compare and contrast aerobic and anaerobic respiration.		Main 2, Plenary 1
	Explain why muscles get tired during exercise.	1, End of chapter 4	Starter 2, Main 1
Aiming for GRADE 8	Compare and contrast anaerobic respiration in animals, plants, and microorganisms.		Main 2, Plenary 1
	Explain in detail why heart and breathing rate continue to be high for a period of time after exercise.	3, End of chapter 3	Main 1
	Write a prediction based on scientific knowledge.		Main 1

■ B9 Respiration

Maths
Students use the formula speed = distance/time to calculate the average speed of runners. This can also be extended to convert units.

Literacy
Students use information from the student book to explain why muscles get tired and start to burn after a period of intense exercise.

Key words
anaerobic respiration, lactic acid, fermentation

Practical

Title	Making lactic acid
Equipment	stopwatch
Overview of method	Students repeatedly clench and relax their fist. They compare how long they can do this with their arm at different positions.

Starter	Support/Extend	Resources
Speedy calculations (10 min) Provide the class with data so they can calculate and compare the average speed of a 100 m sprinter and a marathon runner. Ask the students why the marathon runner has to run a lot slower, and what would happen if they tried to run a marathon at sprint pace. **Muscle contraction** (5 min) Ask the class to stand up on tiptoes. Whilst they are doing so, talk about their calf muscles having to contract to keep them in this position. Question them on how their muscles feel and why they could not do this for very long.	**Support:** Remind students how to calculate speed. **Extend:** Use a mixture of units so students have to convert them to find speed in metres/second.	

Main	Support/Extend	Resources
Making lactic acid (20 min) Discuss that muscles start to feel tired and burn after a period of intense exercise. Ask students to describe why by referring to information about anaerobic respiration in the student book, and then show the video. Students then repeatedly clench and relax their fist. They compare how long they can do this for with their arm at different positions, for example, down by their side, held horizontally in front of them, and held up in the air. They should find that they tire most quickly with their arm in the air, because blood cannot travel so quickly to the arm muscles. **Anaerobic respiration** (20 min) Show students images of useful products of fermentation (bread, wine, soy sauce, etc.) and ask them what these have in common. Introduce the word equation for anaerobic respiration in plants and microorganisms and the balanced symbol equation for higher-tier students. Students then complete the Bump up your grade worksheet to compare and contrast anaerobic respiration in animals, plants, and microorganisms.	**Extend:** Ask students to complete their scientific explanation from the practical carried out last lesson by explaining why heart and breathing rate remain high after exercise. **Extend:** Students write a prediction using scientific knowledge. **Extend:** Show students an image of wine brewing in a demijohn with an airlock. Ask them to apply the symbol equation for fermentation to explain the function of the airlock.	**Practical:** Making lactic acid **Bump up your grade:** Anaerobic respiration

Plenary	Support/Extend	Resources
Testing fitness (10 min) Ask students to measure their resting heart rate and breathing rate. Explain that the fitter they are, the lower the resting heart and breathing rate will be. Then ask students to exercise for one minutes, measure the increase in heart and breathing rate, and measure how long it takes for them to return to normal. Explain how all three of these measurements can be used to determine how fit they are. **Energy from respiration** (5 min) Interactive where students match key terms around respiration with their definition. They then complete a paragraph to explain why anaerobic respiration occurs.		**Interactive:** Energy from respiration

Homework
Ask students to use information in the student book to create a series of revision cards that a student could use when revising respiration.

kerboodle
A Kerboodle highlight for this lesson is **Extension sheet: Alcoholic yeasts**. Refer to the **Content map** on Kerboodle for a full list of resources and assessment.

B9.4 Metabolism and the liver

AQA spec links: 4.2.2 Ⓗ Blood flowing through the muscles transports the lactic acid to the liver where it is converted back into glucose. Oxygen debt is the amount of extra oxygen the body needs after exercise to react with the accumulated lactic acid and remove it from the cells.

4.2.3 Students should be able to explain the importance of sugars, amino acids, fatty acids and glycerol in the synthesis and breakdown of carbohydrates, proteins, and lipids.

Metabolism is the sum of all the reactions in a cell or the body.

The energy transferred by respiration in cells is used by the organism for the continual enzyme controlled processes of metabolism that synthesise new molecules.

Metabolism includes:

- conversion of glucose to starch, glycogen, and cellulose
- the formation of lipid molecules from a molecule of glycerol and three molecules of fatty acids
- the use of glucose and nitrate ions to form amino acids which in turn are used to synthesise proteins
- respiration
- breakdown of excess proteins to form urea for excretion.

All of these aspects are covered in more detail in the relevant specification section but are linked together here.

Aiming for	Outcome	Checkpoint	
		Question	Activity
Aiming for GRADE 4 ↓	Define metabolism as the sum of all reactions in a cell or the body.	1	Main
	List some metabolic reactions.	1	Starter 2, Main, Plenary 2
Aiming for GRADE 6 ↓	Ⓗ Describe the role of the liver in repaying the oxygen debt.	3	Main
	Discuss whether it is possible to increase metabolism.		Homework
Aiming for GRADE 8 ↓	Explain the link between protein consumption and concentration of urea in urine.		Main
	Evaluate information to assess credibility.		Homework

Maths
Students consider what is meant by basal metabolic rate (BMR) and perform calculations on energy input and output.

Literacy
Students use information from books and the Internet to find information and evaluate information.

Key word
metabolism

140

B9 Respiration

Starter	Support/Extend	Resources
The liver and alcohol (5 min) Remind students that drinking too much alcohol can lead to liver disease. Ask them to discuss in pairs why they think this is. Discuss the fact that one role of the liver is to detoxify poisonous substances such as ethanol. **Reactions in living organisms** (10 min) Ask students to work in groups to write down a list of reactions that occur inside living organisms. Collate these on the board.	**Extend:** Students should state which reactions they think require the transfer of energy from respiration to take place.	

Main	Support/Extend	Resources
Metabolic reactions (40 min) Introduce the term metabolism as a sum of all the reactions that happen in a cell or the body. Ask students if they have heard the term before, for example, someone saying that they have a fast metabolism. Discuss what metabolism means when used in this sense. Ask students to refer to the student book to write down a list of some of these reactions. Assign pairs of students one reaction each and ask them to use other pages from the student book or other books to find out more details about the reactants and products. Students should then design an animation showing the reaction, which they can show to the rest of the class.	**Extend:** Students should include information on the function of their reaction.	**Activity:** Metabolic reactions

Plenary	Support/Extend	Resources
Metabolism (10 min) Provide students with a list of adaptations of the liver, for example, cells have a lot of mitochondria and that cells grow and regenerate rapidly. Ask students to suggest why the liver has these adaptations. **Which reaction?** (5 min) Interactive where students review a list of reactions to identify the ones that take place in the human body.	**Extend:** Some reactions are shown as symbol equations.	**Interactive:** Which reaction?

Homework		
Students carry out Internet research to find out whether it is possible to increase metabolism.	**Extend:** Students should evaluate claims that some foods can increase metabolism.	

kerboodle

A Kerboodle highlight for this lesson is **Literacy sheet: The liver**. Refer to the **Content map** on Kerboodle for a full list of resources and assessment.

B9 Respiration

Overview of B9 Respiration

In this chapter students have studied respiration, and should recall that this is one of the most important processes in living cells. They should be able to describe the process of respiration and write the word equation, and higher-tier students should also be able to write the balanced symbol equation. Students should have looked at mitochondria as the site of respiration, linking this with B1.2 *Animal and plant cells* and cell specialisation in B1.4 and B1.5. Students should be able to list examples of living processes that need the energy released from respiration. They should link this with work in B1.9 *Active transport*, in particular the transport of mineral ions into the root hair cell.

Students have studied the response of humans to exercise, including changes in heart rate, breathing rate, and breakdown of glycogen, all to increase the rate of respiration in muscle cells. They should link this with work on the heart and blood vessels in B4 *Organising animals and plants*.

In studying anaerobic respiration, students should be aware of this process in mammalian muscles, and be able to write the word equation. Students should be aware that anaerobic respiration occurs in yeast cells and some plant cells. They should know that fermentation is an economically important reaction and be able to write the word equation, with higher-tier students knowing the balanced symbol equation for fermentation. Higher-tier students should also be able to link aerobic respiration in mammalian muscles to the oxygen debt.

Students have studied metabolism, and should be able to list common metabolic reactions. They should ink these with B8.1 *Photosynthesis* and B8.3 *How plants use glucose*. Finally higher-tier students should recall the roles of lactic acid, urea formation, and the liver.

MyMaths

You can find additional support for the maths skills covered in this chapter on **MyMaths**, including working with percentages, displaying data, using equations, and performing calculations.

kerboodle

For this chapter, the following assessments are available on Kerboodle:

B9 Checkpoint quiz: Respiration
B9 Progress quiz: Respiration 1
B9 Progress quiz: Respiration 2
B9 On your marks: Respiration
B9 Exam-style questions and mark scheme: Respiration

Checkpoint follow-up lesson

A student's route through this lesson can be determined using the Checkpoint assessment. Percentage pass marks are supplied in the Checkpoint teacher notes.

For each successive route through it is assumed that the student can perform to their current route as well as previous routes. For example, students working at Aiming for 6 are assumed to be secure in Aiming for 4 knowledge and understanding and working towards achieving all the learning outcomes for Aiming for 6.

	Aiming for 4	**Aiming for 6**	**Aiming for 8**
Learning outcomes	State the word equation for aerobic respiration.	State the word equations for aerobic and anaerobic respiration.	State the word and symbol equations for aerobic and anaerobic respiration.
	State the effects of exercise on respiration.	Describe the effects of exercise on respiration.	Explain the effects exercise has on respiration.
	State the uses of energy released from respiration.	Describe the uses of energy released from respiration.	Compare anaerobic respiration and aerobic respiration.
Starter	**Exercise (5 min)** Ask one or more students to run on the spot for 1 minute. Ask targeted questions such as – what happened to your heart and breathing rate? Can you explain why? What does respiration have to do with it?		
Differentiated checkpoint activity	Students work in small groups moving around the five stationsand spending a few minutes at each station. Aiming for 4 and Aiming for 6 students will require an introduction and may need access to the Student Book or teacher prompts. You will need: • station 1 – mirrors that have been kept in fridge • station 2 – boiling tubes, limewater, a straw, and goggles • station 3 – two conical flasks with cress seeds on cotton wool suspended from a bung, one of the flasks containing pyrogallol solution • station 4 – two thermos flasks with thermometers, one containing germinating peas, and one containing boiled peas • station 5 – a beaker with containing respiring yeast or bread dough. Aiming for 4 and Aiming for 6 students then create a revision sheet on respiration. The Aiming for 4 follow-up sheet provides a template with detailed prompts of what to include in their revision sheet. The Aiming for 6 follow-up sheet provides a template with simple prompts to guide students with what to include in their revision sheets. Aiming for 8 students work in pairs to write an exam-style question.		
	Kerboodle resource B9 Checkpoint follow-up: Aiming for 4, B9 Checkpoint follow-up: Aiming for 6, B9 Checkpoint follow-up: Aiming for 8		
Plenary	**True or false? (5 min)** Read some statements out about respiration to check students' understanding. Students indicate whether each statement is true or false.		
Progression	Students can work towards writing word equations for aerobic and anaerobic respiration.	To progress, students should work towards comparing aerobic and anaerobic respiration in their revision sheet.	To progress, students should write an extended-answer exam-style question, and try to imitate the mark scheme style of these types of questions.

3 Biological responses

Specification links

AQA specification section	Assessment paper
5.1 Homeostasis	Paper 2
5.2 The human nervous system	Paper 2
5.3 Hormonal coordination in humans	Paper 2
5.4 Plant hormones	Paper 2

Required practicals

AQA required practicals	Practical skills	Topic
Plan and carry out an investigation into the effect of a factor on human reaction time.	AT 1 – use appropriate apparatus to record time. AT 3 – selecting appropriate apparatus and techniques to measure the process of reaction time. AT 4 – safe and ethical use of humans to measure physiological function of reaction time and responses to a chosen factor.	B10.2
Investigate the effect of light or gravity on the growth of germinating seeds. Record results both as length measurements and as accurate, labelled biological drawings to show the effects.	AT 1 – use appropriate apparatus to record length and time. AT 3 – selecting appropriate apparatus and techniques to measure the growth of shoots or roots. AT 4 – safe and ethical use of plants to measure physiological function of growth in response to light or gravity. AT 7 – observations of biological specimens to produce labelled scientific drawings.	B11.9

Maths skills

AQA maths skills	Topic
1c Use ratios, fractions and percentages.	10.5, 12.2
1d Make estimates of the results of simple calculations.	11.1, 11.5, 12.3, 12.4, 12.5
2b Find arithmetic means.	10.2
2c Construct and interpret frequency tables and diagrams, bar charts, and histograms.	10.2, 10.3, 10.4, 11.2, 11.3, 11.4, 11.6
4a Translate information between graphical and numeric form.	10.2, 10.3, 10.4, 11.2, 11.8, 11.10

B3 Biological responses

KS3 concept	GCSE topic	Checkpoint	Revision
The basic structure of neurones.	B10.2 The structure and function of the human nervous system	Ask students to draw a diagram of a neurone (nerve cell).	Ask students how neurons are adapted and why these features are important for their function.
The importance of light to plants for photosynthesis.	B11.9 Plant hormones and responses	Ask students to explain why plants need light to grow.	Show students an image of a plant growing towards the light and ask them what is happening and why.
The basic processes of human reproduction.	B11.5 Human reproduction	Ask students to name hormones that control puberty.	Ask students to draw a diagram to show the menstrual cycle.
How the rate of enzyme action is affected by temperature changes.	B12.1 Controlling body temperature	Ask students what human body temperature is.	Ask students to describe what happens when enzymes get too hot.
Urea is produced as a waste product from the breakdown of excess protein in the liver.	B12.3 The human kidney	Ask students to describe the function of the kidneys.	Ask students to describe what happens to urine when a person drinks a lot, or a little.
Plan an investigation by changing one variable.	B10.2 The structure and function of the human nervous system	Ask students to define the terms independent, dependent and control variables.	Give students simple questions e.g. does the temperature of tea affect how quickly sugar dissolves and ask them to state the independent and dependent variables they would use to investigate it.
Use information from tables and graphs to answer simple questions.	B11.3 Treating diabetes	Give students examples of simple tables and graphs and ask them to state what they show.	Tell students a story and ask them to plot a line graph to show it e.g. the amount of light falling on a plant during a day.
Describe the advantages and disadvantages of applications of science.	B11.8 Infertility treatments	Ask students to list advantages and disadvantages of a familiar application of science, for example, cars.	Ask students to discuss in groups whether cars should be banned.

B 10 The human nervous system
10.1 Principles of homeostasis

AQA spec link: 5.1 Students should be able to explain that homeostasis is the regulation of the internal conditions of a cell or organism to maintain optimum conditions for function in response to internal and external changes.

Homeostasis maintains optimal conditions for enzyme action and all cell functions.

In the human body, these include control of:
- blood glucose concentration
- body temperature
- water levels.

These automatic control systems may involve nervous responses or chemical responses.

All control systems include:
- cells called receptors, which detect stimuli (changes in the environment)
- coordination centres (such as the brain, spinal cord, and pancreas) that receive and process information from receptors
- effectors, muscles or glands, which bring about responses which restore optimum levels.

Aiming for	Outcome	Checkpoint Question	Checkpoint Activity
Aiming for GRADE 4	Name some human internal conditions that are controlled.	3	Starter 1, Main, Homework
	Show the pathway of a control system as receptor, coordination centre, effector.	2	Starter 2, Main, Plenary 2
Aiming for GRADE 6	Define homeostasis.	1, End of chapter 1	Main, Plenary 1
	Explain why internal conditions need to be maintained.	3, End of chapter 1	Starter 1, Main
	Identify stimuli, receptors, coordination centres, and effectors in examples of nervous and chemical responses.	2, 3	Main, Plenary 2
Aiming for GRADE 8	Apply knowledge of enzymes and osmosis to explain in detail why internal conditions need to be maintained.	3, End of chapter 1	Main
	Explain how drugs affect homeostasis.		Main
	Explain how nervous and chemical responses differ.		Main, Plenary 2

Maths
Students use ideas about concentration to apply the concept of osmosis to explain why internal conditions need to be kept constant.

Literacy
Students use information from the student book to explain why conditions need to be kept constant. Students have the opportunity to write a summary tweet of homeostasis. They also write a page in a desert survival manual.

Key words
homeostasis, receptors, stimuli, coordination centres, effectors

■ B10 The human nervous system

Starter	Support/Extend	Resources
Lost in the desert (10 min) Tell students to imagine that they are lost in the middle of a desert. Ask them to discuss with a partner what problems they are likely to face. Discuss their ideas, which might include lack of water, high temperature in the day, low temperature at night, and lack of food. **Stimulus and response** (5 min) Name a stimulus, for example, a loud sound, the smell of food, or an escaped lion entering the classroom. Ask the class to suggest responses that their bodies would make.	**Extend:** Pairs can also discuss what mechanisms their bodies have to combat these problems.	

Main	Support/Extend	Resources
Controlling internal conditions (40 min) Ask students to list examples of conditions inside the body that are kept constant. Introduce the term homeostasis and explain what it means. Students use information from the student book to explain why these conditions need to be kept constant. Then use one example of an internal condition that needs to be kept constant to guide students through the pathway of a control system (receptor, coordination centre, effector). Students then repeat this for different examples.	**Support:** Give one example, for example, body temperature. **Extend:** Students should use ideas about osmosis and enzymes to explain the importance of homeostasis. **Extend:** Students should complete examples of both chemical and nervous pathways and explain the differences between them. **Extend:** Students complete the Extension sheet that looks at how drugs affect homeostasis.	**Activity:** Controlling internal conditions **Extension:** Drugs and homeostasis

Plenary	Support/Extend	Resources
Homeostasis tweet (5 min) Ask students to write a tweet (less than 140 characters) to explain what homeostasis means. **Chemical and nervous responses** (10 min) Use the interactive to provide students with a series of stimuli, receptors, coordination centres, and effectors involved in examples of nervous and chemical responses for students to sort accordingly.	**Extend:** Students should use the names read out to build examples of control pathways.	**Interactive:** Chemical and nervous responses

Homework		
Students write a page in a desert survival manual that explains the dangers of being in a desert in terms of homeostasis, and suggests some survival tips.	**Support:** Provide students with a writing frame.	

kerboodle

A Kerboodle highlight for this lesson is **Bump up your grade: The demands of a control system**. Refer to the **Content map** on Kerboodle for a full list of resources and assessment.

B10.2 The structure and function of the human nervous system

AQA spec link: 5.2.1 Students should be able to explain how the structure of the nervous system is adapted to its functions.

The nervous system enables humans to react to their surroundings and to coordinate their behaviour.

Information from receptors passes along cells (neurones) as electrical impulses to the central nervous system (CNS). The CNS is the brain or the spinal cord. The CNS coordinates the response of effectors which may be muscles contracting or glands secreting hormones.

stimulus → receptor → coordinator → effector → response

Students should be able to extract and interpret data from graphs, charts and tables, about the functioning of the nervous system.

Students should be able to translate information about reaction times between numerical and graphical forms.

Required practical: Plan and carry out an investigation into the effect of a factor on human reaction time.

MS 2b, 2c, 4a

Aiming for	Outcome	Checkpoint	
		Question	Activity
Aiming for GRADE 4 ↓	Identify the stimuli that sense organs detect.	2, End of chapter 3	Starter 1
	Describe what a neurone and a nerve are.	1, End of chapter 2	Main, Homework
	Measure reactions times using repeats to increase accuracy.		Main
Aiming for GRADE 6 ↓	Describe the pathway of impulses from receptor to effector.		Plenary 1
	Describe how information is passed along neurones.	1	Starter 2, Main, Plenary 1
	Evaluate a method and describe how accuracy could be increased.	1	Starter 2, Main, Plenary 2
Aiming for GRADE 8 ↓	Explain in detail how the nervous system coordinates a response.	3, End of chapter 3	Starter 2, Homework
	Evaluate results in detail in order to discuss precision and accuracy.		Main
	<insert another learning outcome>		

Maths
Students investigate how changing the number of repeated measurements increases accuracy. They measure and record reaction times, calculate means (2b), identify anomalous results, and draw suitable graphs (4a). They use these to analyse results.

Literacy
Students create their own glossary of key words.

Key words
sense organs, neurones, nerves, central nervous system, sensory neurones, motor neurones, effectors

148

B10 The human nervous system

Required practical

Title	Measuring reaction times
Equipment	metre rule, music via mobile device/laptop and headphones, cola drink, cups, access to Internet
Overview of method	Students work in pairs. They should choose one factor to investigate. Suitable examples include the consumption of cola (which contains caffeine), listening to music, gender, or talking to someone. Students can also choose a suitable method of measuring reaction times, such as dropping a metre ruler.
Safety considerations	Do not consume drinks in the laboratory. If students choose to investigate consuming caffeine, the experiment should be conducted in a non-laboratory environment.

Starter	Support/Extend	Resources
Sense organs (5 min) Students use the interactive to identify the external stimulus that a range of sense organs detect. **What happens?** (10 min) Ask students to write down the sequence of events that happens when they see a tennis ball coming towards them and prepare to hit it.	**Support:** Provide the class with some useful key words, such as light, eyes, receptors, neurones, impulses, brain, and muscles.	**Interactive:** Sense organs

Main	Support/Extend	Resources
Measuring reaction times (40 min) Introduce students to the nervous system, including the different parts of the nervous system. Students then work in pairs, choosing one factor to investigate. Suitable examples include the consumption of cola (which contains caffeine), listening to music, gender, or talking to someone. Students can also choose a suitable method of measuring reaction times. This can be dropping a metre rule or using an online reaction tester. Their plan should also include a results table. Discuss the importance of repetition. Ask students to write their plan to include independent, dependent, and control variables, prediction, and method. Check methods and, in the next lesson, allow students to carry out their investigation. They should analyse results, and write a conclusion and evaluation.	**Support:** Supply Provide students with a suitable method for measuring reaction times. **Extend:** Students should evaluate their results in greater detail and discuss how accurate their measurements were (showing the range of repeat sets of readings on their graph). They should include how they could change their method to make the results more accurate.	**Required practical:** Measuring reaction times

Plenary	Support/Extend	Resources
Nervous system ordering (5 min) Write on the board the different parts of the nervous system – stimulus, receptor, sensory neurone, coordinator, motor neurone, effector. Ask students to put them into the correct order. **What happens now?** (10 min) Ask students to use what they have learnt in the lesson to improve the sequence written down in Starter 2.	**Extend:** Students should use this to write an example of an event that uses the pathway, for example, picking up a book. **Support:** Allow students to work in pairs so they can peer assess each other's work and recommend improvements.	

Homework		
Provide students with the list of key words for the lesson. Students write a glossary of the key words. They can include diagrams as well.	**Support:** Supply students with a sheet that includes the key words and cloze sentences from the student book that describe them.	

kerboodle

A Kerboodle highlight for this lesson is **Calculation sheet: How many repeats?** Refer to the **Content map** on Kerboodle for a full list of resources and assessment.

B10.3 Reflex actions

AQA spec link: 5.2.1 Students should be able to explain how the various structures in a reflex arc – including the sensory neurone, synapse, relay neurone, and motor neurone – relate to their function. Students should understand why reflex actions are important.

Reflex actions are automatic and rapid; they do not involve the conscious part of the brain.

Students should be able to extract and interpret data from graphs, charts and tables, about the functioning of the nervous system.

Students should be able to translate information about reaction times between numerical and graphical forms.

MS 2c, 4a

Aiming for	Outcome	Checkpoint	
		Question	Activity
Aiming for GRADE 4	Identify reflex actions.		Starter 1, Main 1, Plenary 2
	Describe why reflex actions are important.	1	Starter 2, Main 1
	Order the events involved in a reflex action.	3	Main 2, Plenary 1, Homework
Aiming for GRADE 6	Describe how reflex actions are fast and automatic.	2	Main 2
	Describe the events involved in a reflex action.	3, End of chapter 3, 4	Main 2, Plenary 1, Homework
	Describe the function of synapses.	End of chapter 4	Main 2
Aiming for GRADE 8	Explain in detail how impulses travel across a synapse.	3, End of chapter 4	Main 2, Homework
	Apply knowledge of synapses to explain the effects of drugs.		Main 2

Maths
Discuss with students how fast reflex actions are – an impulse travels around a reflex arc in around a millisecond. Use this as an opportunity to discuss what the prefix 'milli' means.

Literacy
Students use a range of information, from animations to text in the student book, to convey what happens during a reflex action.

Key words
reflexes, reflex arc, relay neurone, synapses

B10 The human nervous system

Starter	Support/Extend	Resources
Voluntary or involuntary? (10 min) Explain to students what is meant by voluntary and involuntary (reflex) actions. Then, read out a list of examples that is a mixture of each, for example, picking up a ringing phone, moving hand away from a hot pan, talking, sneezing, blinking, shivering, swallowing. Ask them to put their hand up if the action is involuntary. **Importance of reflex actions** (5 min) Give the class a few examples of reflex actions. Ask them to write down a few bullet points on what might happen to them if they did not experience reflex actions. Listen to their ideas and discuss the role of reflexes in protecting the body.	**Extend:** After using a few of your own, invite students to think of their own examples for the class. **Support:** Rather than writing bullet points, allow students to discuss their ideas in small groups.	

Main	Support/Extend	Resources
Reflexes (20 min) Provide students with instructions on how to carry out a range of reflex tests, for example, the knee jerk, blink, pupil, and ankle reflex tests. Students carry out the tests and write down the stimulus and response. They then explain why each reflex might be useful. **The reflex arc** (20 min) Use a diagram of the reflex arc to go through the pathway from stimulus to response. Students often get confused about where in the body the parts are. It may be helpful to use a model skeleton if you have one, and show the pathway with a piece of coloured string. Ask students to write down what happens during a reflex action and describe why it is fast and automatic.	**Extend:** Students should carry out some research and write down more examples of reflexes and why they are useful. This can include responses that only babies have. **Support:** Provide students with the events in the incorrect order and ask them to sequence them correctly. **Extend:** Students should explain in detail what happens at a synapse and why synapses are needed. They can then apply their knowledge by explaining how drugs can affect the synapses.	**Practical:** Reflexes **Literacy sheet:** The reflex arc

Plenary	Support/Extend	Resources
Reflex key words (10 min) Students use the interactive to match each part of the reflex arc with its definition. They then arrange the parts of the reflex arc so they are in the correct order. **Controlling reflex actions** (5 min) Discuss with students whether there are any examples of when you can override your reflexes, for example, not dropping a hot plate until you find a safe place to put it, or continuing with a race even though you have been injured. Are there any that you can never have any control over (e.g., blinking, iris reflex). Build up lists of examples of each.	**Support:** Have the words on the board so students can choose which you are describing.	**Interactive:** Reflex keywords

Homework		
Ask students to create a storyboard or time-lapse animation to explain what happens at a synapse.	**Support:** Students can do this for what happens during a reflex arc instead.	

kerboodle

A Kerboodle highlight for this lesson is **Go further: Drugs and synapses**. Refer to the **Content map** on Kerboodle for a full list of resources and assessment.

GCSE Biology only

B10.4 The brain

AQA spec link: 5.2.2 The brain controls complex behaviour. It is made of billions of interconnected neurones and has different regions that carry out different functions.

Students should be able to identify the cerebral cortex, cerebellum, and medulla on a diagram of the brain, and describe their functions.

(H) Students should be able to explain some of the difficulties of investigating brain function and treating brain damage and disease.

Neuroscientists have been able to map the regions of the brain to particular functions by studying patients with brain damage, electrically stimulating different parts of the brain, and using MRI scanning techniques. The complexity and delicacy of the brain makes investigating and treating brain disorders very difficult.

WS 1.5
MS 2c, 4a

Aiming for	Outcome	Checkpoint	
		Question	Activity
Aiming for GRADE 4	Identify the main structures of the brain.		Main
↓	Display data as a suitable graph or chart.		Main
Aiming for GRADE 6	Describe the function of brain structures.	1, 2, End of chapter 5	Starter 1, Main, Plenary 2
	(H) Describe how regions of the brain have been mapped to particular functions.	3, End of chapter 6	Starter 2, Main
↓	Choose the correct way to display data.		Main
Aiming for GRADE 8	**(H)** Evaluate in detail the benefits and risks of investigating and treating brain disorders.	3, End of chapter 6	Main
	(H) Consider ethical dilemmas surrounding brain research.	3	Main, Plenary 1
↓	Independently plan a method to test a hypothesis.		Main

Maths
Students record results (2c) and draw a suitable graph or chart to display them (4a).

Literacy
Students take part in paired, group, and class discussions. They use the Internet to research myths about the brain.

Key words
cerebral cortex, cerebellum, medulla

Practical

Title	The structure and function of the brain
Equipment	two clamp stands, clamps, and boss, 30×30 cm sheet of hardboard, 15×15 cm mirror, A4 sheet of paper with 5-pointed star, A4 sheet of acetate, sticky tack, fine-nib pen, cloth, stopwatch

■ B10 The human nervous system

Overview of method	Use the sticky tack to attach the paper to the acetate. Use one clamp to hold the hardboard above the paper and acetate and the other clamp to hold the mirror perpendicular to the hardboard.
	Students work in pairs. The subject should be able to see both the star and the position of the pen on the acetate in the mirror.
	The other student starts a timer and the subject draws around the star shape, keeping in between the two lines, as quickly as possible.
	The time taken is recorded as well as the number of errors where the subject has crossed the lines.
	The acetate is removed and the cloth used to remove the pen lines. It is then placed back in the same place and the test is repeated at least a further 14 times.
	Students then plot graphs of the time taken and the number of errors against the number of the trial.

Starter	Support/Extend	Resources
Brain function (5 min) Ask students to discuss in pairs the function of the brain and make a list of their thoughts. Discuss these as a class. **Brain scanning** (10 min) Show the class a video about brain scanning. Do an internet search for 'Steve gets a brain scan'. This is a suitable video from the Wellcome Trust. Afterwards, discuss why we use brain scans.	**Support:** Allow students to use the information in the student book to supplement their ideas.	

Main	Support/Extend	Resources
The structure and function of the brain (40 min) Provide students with an unlabelled diagram of the brain. Students use the student book to to colour in the different regions and create a key that includes the names of the regions and their functions. Students then complete a practical where they carry out a co-ordination task several times to see if they improve by learning. They then analyse their results by drawing a suitable graph or chart. **H** Higher-tier students then complete the Bump up your grade worksheet to investigate studies of the brain and new techniques for imaging the brain.	**Extend:** Supply a diagram of the brain so students have to apply knowledge in order to label it. **Support:** Provide students with a results table and discuss with them which type of graph to draw. **Extend:** Students should plan another method to test a hypothesis.	**Practical:** The structure and function of the brain **Bump up your grade:** The structure and function of the brain

Plenary	Support/Extend	Resources
An ethical dilemma (10 min) Tell students that a researcher has invited a friend to get their brain scanned as part of her research. In conducting the scan the researcher notices an abnormality. Should she tell her friend what she saw? Ask students to discuss this dilemma. **Areas of the brain** (5 min) Students match the area of the brain to its function. Higher-tier students should then complete a summary of the difficulties with treating brain injuries and disease.	**Extend:** Include meninges, which are membranes that encase the brain.	**Interactive:** Areas of the brain

Homework		
Students complete the WebQuest where they research methods of studying the brain, including CAT scans and MRI. Alternatively, give students a list of brain myths for them to research. For example, we only use 10% of our brains, exercise makes us smarter, a bigger brain is a cleverer brain, we are born with all the brain cells we will ever have, different sides of the brain do different things.	**Support:** Students should just find out whether the myths are true or false. **Extend:** Students should find evidence that backs up the myths or refutes them.	**WebQuest:** Investigating brain function

kerboodle

A Kerboodle highlight for this lesson is **Literacy skills: Matching parts to function in the brain**. Refer to the **Content map** on Kerboodle for a full list of resources and assessment.

GCSE Biology only

B10.5 The eye

AQA spec link: 5.2.3 Students should be able to relate the structures of the eye to their functions. This includes:

- adaptation to dim light.

The eye is a sense organ containing receptors sensitive to light intensity and colour.

Students should be able to identify the following structures on a diagram of the eye and explain how their structure is related to their function:

- retina
- optic nerve
- sclera
- cornea
- iris
- ciliary muscles
- suspensory ligaments.

WS 1.2
MS 1c

Aiming for	Outcome	Checkpoint	
		Question	Activity
Aiming for GRADE 4 ↓	Identify the main structures of the eye.		Main 1
	Describe what happens to the eye in bright light.		Starter 2, Main 2
Aiming for GRADE 6 ↓	Relate the structures of the eye to their functions.	1, End of chapter 7	Main 1
	Describe how the eye focuses light.	3	Main 2
Aiming for GRADE 8 ↓	Draw an accurate ray diagram to show how the eye focuses light.	3	Main 2
	Explain in detail the changes to the eye in response to changes in light intensity.	2	Plenary 1

Maths
There is an opportunity for students to calculate percentages as part of Starter 1(c).

Literacy
Students write down their observations about the iris reflex. They use information from the student book to label a diagram of the eye and answer a series of questions.

Key words
retina, sclera, cornea, iris, pupil, lens, suspensory ligaments, ciliary muscles

■ B10 The human nervous system

Starter	Support/Extend	Resources
Can you believe your eyes? (10 min) Show the class a series of optical illusions or the infamous blue/black dress that sparked discussion in February 2015. Ask students what they can see. For each optical illusion, students should calculate the percentage of students who can see it. **How do we see?** (5 min) Ask class to write a short sentence to explain how they think we see objects.	**Extend:** Use this as an opportunity to link what was learnt last lesson about the brain to explain vision. **Support:** Rather than write, students can draw simple ray diagrams with arrows. **Extend:** Students should also write an example of a stimulus-to-response pathway where light is the stimulus.	

Main	Support/Extend	Resources
Structure of the eye (25 min) If you wish, you can carry out an eye dissection as a demonstration, or show a video of one. Alternatively, if you have a 3D model of the eye you can use this. Provide students with a diagram of the eye to label with the different parts and their functions using information from the student book. Students then build a 2D model of the eye. **Finding the blind spot** (15 min) Discuss how the light that enters the eye is focused on the retina, and how this initiates an impulse. Students can also try and find their blind spot (using the student book) and explain why you have one.	**Extend:** Students should be able to explain in detail how each structure is related to its function. **Support:** You could use cloze sentences and provide students with a diagram for them to add rays of light to. **Extend:** Students should be able to draw an accurate ray diagram to show how light is focused in the eye.	**Activity:** Structure of the eye

Plenary	Support/Extend	Resources
Explaining the pupil reflex (5 min) Students may have carried out the pupil reflex in Topic B10.3. Ask them to use what they have learnt in this lesson to explain why we have the pupil reflex. **What does it do?** (10 min) Students use the interactive to label a diagram of the eye. They then match each part of the eye with its function.	**Support:** Refer students to information in the student book.	**Interactive:** What does it do?

Homework		
In preparation for next lesson, ask students to find out what myopia and hyperopia are.	**Support:** Direct students to a suitable website such as NHS Choices.	

kerboodle

A Kerboodle highlight for this lesson is **Extension sheet: Investigating visual acuity in humans**. Refer to the **Content map** on Kerboodle for a full list of resources and assessment.

GCSE Biology only

B10.6 Common problems of the eye

AQA spec link: 5.2.3 Students should be able to relate the structures of the eye to their functions. This includes:

- accommodation to focus on near or distant objects

Accommodation is the process of changing the shape of the lens to focus on near or distant objects.

To focus on a near object:

- the ciliary muscles contract
- the suspensory ligaments loosen
- the lens is then thicker and refracts light rays strongly.

To focus on a distant object:

- the ciliary muscles relax
- the suspensory ligaments are pulled tight
- the lens is then pulled thin and only slightly refracts light rays.

Two common defects of the eyes are myopia (short sightedness) and hyperopia (long sightedness) in which rays of light do not focus on the retina.

- Generally these defects are treated with spectacle lenses which refract the light rays so that they do focus on the retina.
- New technologies now include hard and soft contact lenses, laser surgery to change the shape of the cornea, and a replacement lens in the eye.

Students should be able to interpret ray diagrams, showing these two common defects of the eye and demonstrate how spectacle lenses correct them.

WS 1.2, 1.4

Aiming for	Outcome	Checkpoint	
		Question	Activity
Aiming for GRADE 4 ↓	State that the lens changes shape to focus on near or distant objects.		Starter 2, Main, Plenary 1
	Describe what causes long and short sightedness.	3, End of chapter 7	Starter 2, Main, Homework
Aiming for GRADE 6 ↓	Describe how the lens changes shape to focus on near or distant objects.	1, 2	Main, Plenary 1
	Describe how lenses and surgery can help with long and short sightedness.		Homework
Aiming for GRADE 8 ↓	Draw accurate ray diagrams to explain what happens during accommodation and what causes long and short sightedness.	3	Main
	Evaluate the risks and benefits of surgery to treat long and short sightedness.	3	Homework

Maths
Students will measure their range of accommodation and use the formula: range = 1/near distance − 1/far point distance. They will be introduced to the unit dioptres, which is the reciprocal of metres (m^{-1}), used to measure the optical power of lenses.

Literacy
Students use the student book and/or the Internet to research myopia and hyperopia. They create a leaflet or webpage from a company that offers laser eye surgery and replacement lenses, explaining how the treatments work.

■ B10 The human nervous system

Starter	Support/Extend	Resources
Vision problems (5 min) Ask whether any students are short- or long-sighted and invite them to tell the rest of the class how it affects their vision and how they correct it. **Near and far** (10 min) Ask students to hold out their finger at arm's length and focus on it. Then, focus on an object a long way away (out of a window if possible) and then back to their finger. Discuss why their finger went out of focus when they looked at the distant object, and vice versa.	**Extend:** Encourage students to use what they know about how the eye focuses light.	

Main	Support/Extend	Resources
Accommodation and eye defects (40 min) Introduce accommodation as the ability of the eye to see both at distance and close-up. Provide students with diagrams of the eye focusing on near and distant objects. Ask them to annotate the diagram to show what changes in the eye, and why these changes are needed in order to form an image on the retina. They can use the information in the student book. Students then measure their range of accommodation. They look out through an open window. If they can see things that are far away very sharply, you say that their eyes see things as far as 'infinity'. Students with glasses may wish to take them off. If they find they cannot see things very far away, they should find the farthest distance at which they can see an object comfortably and clearly by looking at objects at various distances. Students then look at a book held at arm's length, and bring it closer and closer until the print can no longer be seen comfortably and clearly. They should measure how far this is. The range is in dioptres (1/distance in m) and is calculated as $$\frac{1}{\text{near distance}} - \frac{1}{\text{far point distance}}$$ For many the far point distance will be infinity, so their range will simply be $$\frac{1}{\text{near distance}}$$ Students then analyse a graph that shows how the range of accommodation changes with age. Introduce myopia and hyperopia and relate these conditions to the process of accommodation.	**Support:** Provide diagrams with rays of light drawn on them. **Extend:** Provide diagrams without rays drawn and ask students to add them. **Support:** Students can use the Maths skills interactive for help with the calculation. **Extend:** Students should explain why the range changes with age.	**Activity:** Accommodation and eye defects **Maths skills:** Reciprocals

Plenary	Support/Extend	Resources
Eyes cloze activity (10 min) Students use the interactive or to choose the correct words to explain what happens when you focus on near and then far objects. **Summary** (5 min) Ask students to write down three summary points about what they learnt in the lesson.		**Interactive:** Eyes cloze activity

Homework		
Students carry out research into myopia and hyperopia to find out what causes these conditions and how contact lenses or glasses, laser eye surgery, and replacement lenses can help correct them. Students use their research to create a leaflet or webpage for a company that offers laser eye surgery and replacement lenses, explaining how the treatments work.	**Extend:** Students should also evaluate these treatments by looking at risks and benefits.	

kerboodle
A Kerboodle highlight for this lesson is **Calculation sheet: Calculating lens strength**. Refer to the **Content map** on Kerboodle for a full list of resources and assessment.

B10 The human nervous system

Overview of B10 The human nervous system

In this chapter students have studied the principles of homeostasis, and should be able to give some examples and outline the control system involved. They should link this work with studies on enzyme action in B3.2 *The human digestive system* and B3.4 *Catalysts and enzymes*.

Students should recall details of the human nervous system and its structure and function. They should link this with work on nerve cells in B1.4 *Specialisation in animal cells*. They should be able to describe a reflex arc, with detail of synaptic transmission. Students should appreciate that receptors detect a change in a stimulus and not the stimulus itself. They should be able to describe an electrical impulse accurately.

Students studying *AQA GCSE Biology* have studied the brain, linking each area with its function. There is a higher-tier topic of investigating the brain and the treatment of brain damage. Students should link this with the role of the brain in controlling body temperature, the role of the pituitary gland in the brain, and the role of ADH release in maintaining water and nitrogen balance in the body, studied in *B12 Homeostasis in action*.

Students studying *AQA GCSE Biology* have also studied the structure and function of the human eye and the process of accommodation. They should understand that the ciliary muscles contract in accommodation. These students should be able to describe common defects of the eye including myopia, hyperopia, and the role of new technology in the treatment of these conditions.

Required practical

All students are expected to have carried out the required practical:

Practical	Topic
Investigate the effect of a factor on human reaction time.	B10.2
Plan and carry out an investigation, choosing appropriate ways to measure reaction time and considering the risks and ethics of the investigation.	

MyMaths

You can find additional support for the maths skills covered in this chapter on **MyMaths**, including the effect of repeated measurements on accuracy, measuring and recording reaction times, calculating means, working with graphs, using percentages, and applying equations in calculating range of vision.

kerboodle

For this chapter, the following assessments are available on Kerboodle:

B10 Checkpoint quiz: The human nervous system
B10 Progress quiz: The human nervous system 1
B10 Progress quiz: The human nervous system 2
B10 On your marks: The human nervous system
B10 Exam-style questions and mark scheme: The human nervous system

Checkpoint follow-up lesson

A student's route through this lesson can be determined using the Checkpoint assessment. Percentage pass marks are supplied in the Checkpoint teacher notes.

For each successive route through it is assumed that the student can perform to their current route as well as previous routes. For example, students working at Aiming for 6 are assumed to be secure in Aiming for 4 knowledge and understanding and working towards achieving all the learning outcomes for Aiming for 6.

	Aiming for 4	**Aiming for 6**	**Aiming for 8**
Learning outcomes	State how a reflex action is coordinated.	Describe how a reflex action is coordinated.	Explain how a reflex action is coordinated.
	State the structure of the brain.	Describe the structure of the brain.	Describe the function of parts of the brain.
	State the structure of the eye.	Describe the structure of the eye.	Describe function of the parts of the eye.
	Describe how the eye focuses on near and distant objects.	Describe how the eye focuses on near and distant objects.	Explain the changes to the eye when focusing on near and distant objects.
			Explain some causes and treatment for myopia and hyperopia.
Starter	**Pass it on (10 minutes)** Ask the class to hold hands in a big circle. One person squeezes the hand of their neighbour, who then quickly passes the squeeze along. The teacher times the 'impulse' passing using a stopwatch. Then make an unexpected loud sound such as ringing a bell or shouting. If any students jump, explain this is a reflex action. Student pairs then write down as many reflex actions as they can think of. Pairs could compare their list with a neighbouring pair.		
Differentiated checkpoint activity	Students use the Aiming for 4 follow-up sheet to carry out one of three activities. Students can either describe a reflex arc, label a diagram of the brain and match the different parts to their functions, or label a diagram of the eye and match their different parts to their functions.	Students use the Aiming for 6 follow-up sheet to carry out one of three activities. Students can either describe a reflex arc, label a diagram of the brain and describe the function of the different parts, or label a diagram of the eye and describe the function of the different parts.	Students use the Aiming for 8 follow-up sheet to carry out one of three activities. Students can either create a flow chart to describe a reflex arc, label a diagram of the brain and create a table to summarise the functions of the different parts, or label a diagram of the eye and summarise ways problems with the eye can be treated.
	Students studying *AQA GCSE Combined science: Trilogy* should carry out the first activity. Students studying *AQA GCSE Biology* should choose which activity to carry out, based on their perceived weakest subject area.	Students studying *AQA GCSE Combined science: Trilogy* should carry out the first activity. Students studying *AQA GCSE Biology* should choose which activity to carry out, based on their perceived weakest subject area.	Students studying *AQA GCSE Combined science: Trilogy* should carry out the first activity. Students studying *AQA GCSE Biology* should choose which activity to carry out, based on their perceived weakest subject area.
	All the activities are highly-structured, with lots of prompts and key words provided to support students revision.	All the activities provide simple prompts to support students.	The follow-up sheet provides minimal support for students.
	Kerboodle resource B10 Checkpoint follow-up: Aiming for 4, B10 Checkpoint follow-up: Aiming for 6, B10 Checkpoint follow-up: Aiming for 8		
Plenary	**True or false? (5 minutes)** Each student will need two cards of different colours. Read some statements out about the human nervous system to check students' understanding. Students show one coloured card for true, and the other one for false.		
Progression	Students may need a brief introduction from the teacher. Teachers will need to check student's answers or provide them with answers to check each other's work.	To progress, provide students with a copy of a flow chart created with the Aiming for 8 follow-up sheet. Give students some example scenarios and ask them to write a brief explanation of the reflex arc using the flow chart.	Students could be given access to the Internet to further research problems with the eye.

B 11 Hormonal coordination
11.1 Principles of hormonal control

AQA spec link: 5.3.1 Students should be able to describe the principles of hormonal coordination and control by the human endocrine system.

The endocrine system is composed of glands which secrete chemicals called hormones directly into the blood stream. The blood carries the hormone to a target organ where it produces an effect. Compared to the nervous system the effects are slower but act for longer.

The pituitary gland in the brain is a 'master gland' which secretes several hormones into the blood in response to body conditions. These hormones in turn act on other glands to stimulate other hormones to be released to bring about effects.

Students should be able to identify the position of the following on a diagram of the human body:

- pituitary gland
- pancreas
- thyroid
- adrenal gland
- ovary
- testes.

MS 1d

Aiming for	Outcome	Checkpoint	
		Question	Activity
Aiming for GRADE 4 ↓	Match the pituitary gland, pancreas, thyroid, adrenal gland, ovary, and testes to their position on a diagram of the human body.		Main 1, Plenary 2
	Describe how hormones are chemicals secreted into the bloodstream by glands, and have an effect on a target organ.	1	Starter 2, Main 1, Plenary 1
Aiming for GRADE 6 ↓	Explain why the pituitary gland is known as a 'master gland'.	3	Main 1, Plenary 1
	Describe the role of hormones released by endocrine glands.		Starter 1, Main 1, Plenary 2
Aiming for GRADE 8 ↓	Compare and contrast nervous and hormonal action.	2	Main 1
	Apply knowledge to suggest and explain how changes in hormone production could affect the body.	4	Main 1

Maths
Students estimate the time taken for a nervous message to travel through the body from brain to foot compared with a hormonal one. The fastest nervous impulses travel at around 100 m/s. Blood flowing through an artery can reach 0.5 m/s. Discuss how accurate students' estimations would be based on the fact that there is a wide range of speeds, and how accurate these measurements are (1d).

Literacy
Students discuss hormones and their functions in pairs. They use information from the student book to label a diagram and answer a series of questions.

Key words
endocrine system, hormones, insulin, adrenaline, pituitary gland, ADH, follicle stimulating hormone (FSH)

■ B11 Hormonal coordination

Starter	Support/Extend	Resources
Hormones (10 min) Ask students to work alone and write down any hormones they have heard of. Then ask them to share their lists in pairs and discuss whether they know any extra information about them, for example, where in the body they are produced, or what they do. Ask pairs to share what they know with the rest of the class to build up a list on the board. **Getting nervous** (5 min) Ask students to share with the class what kinds of situations make them feel nervous, and how this affects their body. Discuss that these feelings of 'butterflies' – increased heart rate and sweaty palms – are brought about by the hormone adrenaline.	**Support:** Write a list of hormones on the board that students may have heard of, for example, oestrogen, testosterone, insulin, and adrenaline, for pairs to discuss.	

Main	Support/Extend	Resources
Endocrine glands (40 min) Supply students with an outline of the human body for them to draw on the endocrine glands, which they can label with the name and function. They can use information from the student book to do this. Then, set a series of questions looking at the hormones that these glands produce, how hormones travel to their target organs, and the differences between hormonal and nervous control.	**Extend:** Students should suggest the effects on the body if glands make too much or too little of the hormones named in the student book. Students complete the Go further sheet on hormones and cell signalling.	**Activity:** Endocrine glands **Go further:** How do hormones talk to cells?

Plenary	Support/Extend	Resources
Modelling hormones (10 min) Split the class up into groups of around five students and assign each student as either the endocrine glands, blood, or organs. The gland and organ groups should sit together at desks in separate locations. Assign each organ group a name (heart, lungs, kidneys, etc.), which should be displayed on the desk. The blood groups stand up in between the gland and organ groups. Provide the gland groups with blank cards. The 'gland' students should write simple instructions on the cards, for example, stand up, or wave your hands around. Then, they give them one at a time to a 'blood' student and tell them the name of the organ they wish to target. The blood student passes the card on and the 'organ' students carry out the instruction. Instructions should be continuously and concurrently passed from the glands to target organs. After a few minutes, stop the game and discuss how this models what happens in the body. **Glands and hormones** (5 min) Use the interactive to test understanding of the endocrine hormones and their functions.	**Extend:** Question the students on how they could change the model to show the function of the pituitary gland, which produces hormones that trigger the action of other glands.	**Interactive:** Glands and hormones

Homework		
Ask students to find out what the difference is between endocrine glands and exocrine glands.	**Extend:** Students should list some examples of exocrine glands and their functions.	

kerboodle

A Kerboodle highlight for this lesson is **Bump up your grade: The endocrine system**. Refer to the **Content map** on Kerboodle for a full list of resources and assessment.

B11.2 The control of blood glucose levels

AQA spec link: 5.3.2 Blood glucose concentration is monitored and controlled by the pancreas.

If the blood glucose concentration is too high, the pancreas produces the hormone insulin that causes glucose to move from the blood into the cells. In liver and muscle cells excess glucose is converted to glycogen for storage.

Students should be able to explain how insulin controls blood glucose (sugar) levels in the body.

Type 1 diabetes is a disorder in which the pancreas fails to produce sufficient insulin. It is characterised by uncontrolled high blood glucose levels.

In Type 2 diabetes the body cells no longer respond to insulin produced by the pancreas.

Students should be able to compare Type 1 and Type 2 diabetes and explain how they can be treated.

Students should be able to extract information and interpret data from graphs that show the effect of insulin in blood glucose levels in both people with diabetes and people without diabetes.

H If the blood glucose concentration is too low, the pancreas produces the hormone glucagon that causes glycogen to be converted into glucose and released into the blood.

Students should be able to explain how glucagon interacts with insulin in a negative feedback cycle to control blood glucose (sugar) levels in the body.

WS 1.3
MS 2c, 4a

Aiming for	Outcome	Checkpoint	
		Question	Activity
Aiming for GRADE 4 ↓	State that blood glucose concentration is controlled by the pancreas.		Main
	State that there are two types of diabetes.		Main, Homework
Aiming for GRADE 6 ↓	Describe what happens when blood glucose levels become too high or too low.	2	Starter 1, Main, Plenary 2
	Describe the difference in the causes of Type 1 and Type 2 diabetes.	3	Main, Homework
Aiming for GRADE 8 ↓	Explain how glucagon interacts with insulin to control blood glucose levels.	4, End of chapter 1	Main, Plenary 2
	Explain why it is important to control the level of glucose in the blood.	2	Main

Maths
Students plot and analyse line graphs of how blood glucose concentration changes after a meal (4a).

Literacy
Students watch a simulation and use it to describe how blood glucose levels are controlled. They explain the difference between glucose, glycogen, and glucagon.

Key words
insulin, obese, glucagon, Type 1 diabetes, Type 2 diabetes

B11 Hormonal coordination

Starter	Support/Extend	Resources
Digesting sugar (10 min) Ask students to use what they have learnt about digestion to write down what happens in their body after eating a slice of sugary cake. **'Urine' testing** (5 min) Model a 'urine' test (use two samples of diluted tea). To one sample add glucose. Use Clinistix to test the samples. Discuss that the sample with no glucose is normal. The other is from a person with diabetes.	**Support:** Provide the start of sentences to help scaffold the answer. **Extend:** Discuss why blood glucose levels will increase after eating cake. **Extend:** Students should explain why there shouldn't be any glucose in the urine.	

Main	Support/Extend	Resources
Control of blood glucose levels (40 min) Explain to students how the body controls blood glucose levels. Explain that diabetes is a condition where a person cannot control their blood glucose levels. Measuring blood glucose levels after a sugary meal is a way of diagnosing diabetes. Supply data of the concentration of glucose in the blood following a meal for a person without diabetes and a person with Type 1 diabetes. Ask students to plot the data as graphs and analyse what they show. Students then use information in the student book to describe what causes Type 1 and Type 2 diabetes.	**Support:** Students only need to know what happens when blood glucose levels get too high. **Extend:** Students should explain why it is important to control the level of glucose in the blood. **Extend:** Students should show on their graph when insulin would be released in a healthy person. **Extend:** Students complete the Extension sheet where they present and interpret data on blood glucose at different activity levels.	**Activity:** Control of blood glucose levels **Extension sheet:** Control of blood glucose

Plenary	Support/Extend	Resources
Glucose, glycogen, and glucagon (10 min) Ask students to write down definitions for each of these words to make sure they understand the difference. **Order the events** (5 min) Students use the interactive to put statements in the correct order to describe what happens when blood glucose levels become too high or low.	**Support:** Students only need to know about glycogen and glucose. **Support:** Supply students with complete statements for them to order.	**Interactive:** Order the events

Homework		
Students produce a table to compare Type 1 and Type 2 diabetes.		

kerboodle

A Kerboodle highlight for this lesson is **Literacy skills: Glucose, glycogen, and glucagon**. Refer to the **Content map** on Kerboodle for a full list of resources and assessment.

B11.3 Treating diabetes

AQA spec link: 5.3.2 Type 1 diabetes is normally treated with insulin injections.

In Type 2 diabetes a carbohydrate controlled diet and an exercise regime are common treatments. Obesity is a risk factor for Type 2 diabetes.

Students should be able to compare Type 1 and Type 2 diabetes and explain how they can be treated.

Students should be able to extract information and interpret data from graphs that show the effect of insulin in blood glucose levels in both people with diabetes and people without diabetes.

MS 2c

Target	Outcome	Checkpoint	
		Question	Activity
Aiming for GRADE 4	State that Type 1 diabetes is normally treated with insulin injections.	1, 3	Starter 2, Main, Plenary 1
	State that Type 2 diabetes can be treated by changes to diet and exercise.	1, 4	Main
	Describe data that shows a link between obesity and Type 2 diabetes.		Homework
Aiming for GRADE 6	Explain why Type 1 diabetes is treated with insulin injections.	3, End of chapter 1	Starter 2, Main, Plenary 1
	Explain how Type 2 diabetes can be treated by changes to diet and exercise.	1, 4	Main
	Describe how the production of insulin for people with diabetes has developed over time.	2	Main
Aiming for GRADE 8	Evaluate different treatments for Type 1 diabetes.	2	Main
	Explain in detail how lifestyle choices affect the risk of developing Type 2 diabetes.		Main, Plenary 2, Homework
	Summarise how scientists are working to find a cure for diabetes.	4	Main

Maths
Students analyse data that shows the link between Type 2 diabetes and obesity.

Literacy
Students write content for a webpage explaining treatments to people with diabetes. They then use information from secondary sources to create a timeline to show how treatments have developed over time. They also answer a 6-mark exam-style question and use a model answer for assessment.

Key word
overweight

■ B11 Hormonal coordination

Starter	Support/Extend	Resources
Diabetes thought shower (10 min) Ask students to work in small groups and give each group an A3 piece of paper. Students should write down everything they know about diabetes. **Insulin injection** (5 min) Show the class an image of a person injecting themselves with insulin. Ask them to say what it has to do with diabetes.	**Support:** Write some key words on the board for students to refer to. **Extend:** Students should explain why people with Type 1 diabetes need to inject themselves with insulin.	

Main	Support/Extend	Resources
Diabetes webpage (40 min) Supply students with a template for a webpage, based on NHS Choices. They should write treatment information for people with Type 1 and Type 2 diabetes. Discuss the need to keep it simple but still informative. Their webpage should include a timeline to show how treatments for diabetes have changed over time. Students should add a date, the discovery, and how this changed the lives of people with diabetes. They can use information from the student book and other resources if available.	**Support:** Show students an example of a real page from NHS Choices that explains the treatment of an illness. **Support:** Provide a template with the dates added onto a timeline. **Extend:** Students should include information on recent attempts to find a cure for diabetes. **Extend:** Students should also evaluate different treatments for Type 1 diabetes.	**Activity:** Diabetes webpage

Plenary	Support/Extend	Resources
Exam question (10 min) Set the class the following 6-mark practice question: Describe how insulin controls blood glucose levels and explain why a person with diabetes may need to change their insulin levels at certain times. Go through a model answer with the class. **Lifestyle factors** (5 min) Students use the interactive to assess a series of lifestyle choices (eating lots of sugary food, taking plenty of exercise, smoking, etc.) to decide if they will increase the risk of developing Type 2 diabetes.	**Extend:** Students should explain why certain lifestyle choices increase the risk.	**Interactive:** Lifestyle factors

Homework		
Supply the class with data that shows the link between Type 2 diabetes and obesity. Ask students to describe what it shows.	**Extend:** Students should research and explain the science behind this correlation.	

kerboodle

A Kerboodle highlight for this lesson is **Progress quiz: Hormonal coordination 1**. Refer to the **Content map** on Kerboodle for a full list of resources and assessment.

Higher tier

B11.4 The role of negative feedback

AQA spec link: 5.3.7 Students should be able to explain the roles of thyroxine and adrenaline in the body.

Adrenaline is produced by the adrenal glands in times of fear or stress. It increases the heart rate and boosts the delivery of oxygen and glucose to the brain and muscles, preparing the body for 'flight or fight'.

Thyroxine from the thyroid gland stimulates the basal metabolic rate. It plays an important role in growth and development.

Thyroxine levels are controlled by negative feedback.

WS 1.2
MS 2c

Aiming for	Outcome	Checkpoint	
		Question	Activity
Aiming for GRADE 6 ↓	Describe the function of adrenaline and thyroxine.	2, End of chapter 5	Starter 1, Main, Plenary 2
	Interpret and explain diagrams of negative feedback control.	2	Starter 2, Main, Plenary 1
Aiming for GRADE 8 ↓	Explain in detail how adrenaline prepares the body for 'fight or flight'.	End of chapter 5	Starter 1, Main, Plenary 2
	Design labelled flow diagrams of negative feedback control.		Main 2, Plenary 1

Maths
Students interpret and explain diagrams of negative feedback control, and also design their own (2c).

Literacy
Students use information from the student book to describe the effects of adrenaline on the body and research goitres.

Key words
thyroxine, thyroid stimulating hormone (TSH)

B11 Hormonal coordination

Starter	Support/Extend	Resources
Start the lesson with a bang! (5 min) During the usual start to the lesson, suddenly make a loud noise, for example, by slamming a book on a desk or turning on loud music. Invite students to comment on how they felt and write a list of the effects of a shock like this on the body. **Thermostat** (10 min) Explain to students that a thermostat works in a similar way to a negative feedback system. Students then use the interactive to complete a paragraph explaining how a thermostat is similar to a negative feedback system. They then complete sentences to describe what a negative feedback system is.	**Extend:** Students should suggest what hormone was released to bring about these changes, and why they are useful.	**Interactive:** Thermostat

Main	Support/Extend	Resources
Effects of hormones (40 min) Tell the class that adrenaline is often called the 'fight or flight' hormone. Ask them to use the information in the student book to research adrenaline and thyroxine. They should include information on the glands that produce each hormone, when the hormone is released, how the hormone is transported in the body to target organs, what the target organs are, and the effect the hormone has on them. Use Starter 2 here if not already used. Then ask the students to design their own negative feedback diagram to show how the level of thyroxine is controlled. Ask students to discuss in pairs what the possible effects of an underactive or overactive thyroid gland might be. Show them the answers by searching on the NHS Choices website for the conditions.	**Support:** Focus on the gland where adrenaline is released, and its target organs. **Support:** Provide a blank diagram for students to fill in. **Extend:** Students should also design a diagram to show how adrenaline levels are controlled.	**Activity:** Effects of hormones

Plenary	Support/Extend	Resources
Controlling blood glucose levels (10 min) Students consolidate their understanding from the last two lessons to explain how the control of blood glucose levels is another example of negative feedback. **Fight and flight** (5 min) Ask students to suggest situations where the level of adrenaline in their bodies would increase. For each example they should be able to explain how the changes it causes would help them in that situation.	**Extend:** Students should draw a diagram to explain this. **Support:** Supply Provide the class with a suitable example.	

Homework		
Ask students to write a passage in a book or action film script describing a situation where a character has a flight or fight response. They should include the situation they are in, what happens to their body, and how this helps them.		

kerboodle

A Kerboodle highlight for this lesson is **Literacy sheet: Adrenaline and thyroxine**. Refer to the **Content map** on Kerboodle for a full list of resources and assessment.

B11.5 Human reproduction

AQA spec link: 5.3.4 Students should be able to describe the roles of hormones in human reproduction, including the menstrual cycle.

During puberty reproductive hormones cause secondary sex characteristics to develop.

Oestrogen is the main female reproductive hormone produced in the ovary. At puberty eggs begin to mature and one is released approximately every 28 days. This is called ovulation.

Testosterone is the main male reproductive hormone produced by the testes and it stimulates sperm production.

Several hormones are involved in the menstrual cycle of a woman.

- Follicle stimulating hormone (FSH) causes maturation of an egg in the ovary.
- Luteinising hormone (LH) stimulates the release of the egg.
- Oestrogen and progesterone are involved in maintaining the uterus lining.

MS 1d

Aiming for	Outcome	Checkpoint	
		Question	Activity
Aiming for GRADE 4 ↓	Identify oestrogen and testosterone as reproductive hormones in women and men respectively.	1, 2, End of chapter 2, 3	Starter, Main 1, Plenary 1
	Describe what happens during the menstrual cycle.	3, End of chapter 2	Main 2
Aiming for GRADE 6 ↓	Compare and contrast the changes to boys and girls during puberty.	2, End of chapter 3	Main 1
	Name the hormones involved in the menstrual cycle.	3	Main 2, Plenary 1
Aiming for GRADE 8 ↓	Explain why fertility changes with age in men and women.	3	Plenary 2, Homework
	Explain the role of each hormone in the menstrual cycle.	3, End of chapter 2	Main 2, Plenary 1

Maths
Students interpret diagrams of the menstrual cycle. You could also ask them to estimate the number of eggs that are present in a girl's ovaries when she is born (if she releases one a month from puberty until the menopause) (1d).

Literacy
Students unscramble anagrams to name reproductive hormones. Students use a range of sources of information to describe what happens in the menstrual cycle. They also write an informed opinion.

Key words
oestrogen, ovaries, ovulation, testosterone

168

B11 Hormonal coordination

Starter	Support/Extend	Resources
Changes during puberty (10 min) Ask students to write a list of changes that happen to boys and girls during puberty. **Scrambled hormones** (5 min) Write anagrams of oestrogen and testosterone on the board. Tell the class that they are examples of the hormones they will be learning about today, and ask them to unscramble them.	**Support:** Divide the class in two and ask students to just list changes for boys or girls. **Support:** Write the first letter of each hormone as a clue. **Extend:** Students should suggest one action of each hormone on the body.	

Main	Support/Extend	Resources
Secondary sexual characteristics (15 min) Describe primary sexual characteristics as the ones you are born with, and secondary sexual characteristics as ones that develop during puberty. If they haven't already done so, students should make a list of the changes that occur in boys and girls during puberty. Ask students to write down the secondary sexual characteristics that they all agree are correct into their notes. Then allow students to use the information in the student book to add any others that they did not originally think of, and state the hormones involved in their development.	**Support:** If groups either did changes to boys or girls in Starter 1 then at this point they can join another group and look at both genders. **Extend:** Students should highlight secondary sexual characteristics that both genders share.	
The menstrual cycle (25 min) Supply students with an unlabelled diagram of the female human reproductive system and ask them to label it. Go though the events of the menstrual cycle with the class using diagrams and information from the student book. Supply students with a diagram of the cycle for them to label key events.	**Support:** Use a diagram that shows the events in the whole of the female reproductive organs, rather than just changes to the uterus lining.	**Activity:** The menstrual cycle

Plenary	Support/Extend	Resources
Menstrual cycle hormones (10 min) Students use the interactive to match the key terms from the lesson to a question that could have the key term as an answer.		**Interactive:** Menstrual cycle hormones
Fertility changes (5 min) Tell the class that women stop being able to have children naturally when they are around 50 years of age, but men can continue to father children well into old age. Ask students to discuss why this is.	**Extend:** Students should also suggest why the risk of birth defects increases as men and women get older.	

Homework		
Tell the class about the world's oldest mother, Omkari Singh, who had twins at the age of 70 using donor eggs (and IVF). Ask students to write their opinion on whether they think this is a good idea, and to explain why.		

Higher tier

B11.6 Hormones and the menstrual cycle

AQA spec link: 5.3.4 Students should be able to explain the interactions of FSH, oestrogen, LH and progesterone, in the control of the menstrual cycle.

Students should be able to extract and interpret data from graphs showing hormone levels during the menstrual cycle.

MS 2c

Aiming for	Outcome	Checkpoint	
		Question	Activity
Aiming for GRADE 6 ↓	Name the glands that produce the hormones oestrogen, progesterone, LH, and FSH.		Main 1, Plenary 2
	Describe the function of the hormones that control the menstrual cycle.	1, End of chapter 2	Starter, Main, Plenary 2, Homework
Aiming for GRADE 8 ↓	Explain the interactions of hormones in the control of the menstrual cycle.	3, End of chapter 2	Main 1, Plenary 1
	Interpret in detail a graph showing how levels of hormones change during the menstrual cycle.	2	Main 2

Maths
Students interpret a diagram of the menstrual cycle that shows how the levels of hormones change (2c).

Literacy
Students organise information from the student book into a table.

■ B11 Hormonal coordination

Starter	Support/Extend	Resources
Menstrual cycle review (10 min) Display a diagram of the menstrual cycle from Topic B5.5 and students use the interactive to answer a series of questions to check their understanding. **Follicles** (5 min) Show the class an image of eggs developing in follicles in the ovary. Ask them what they think the image is showing.	**Extend:** Students should make up their own questions and pose them to each other. **Support:** Give students a choice of what the image could be (e.g., sperm inside testes, eggs in the oviduct).	**Interactive:** Menstrual cycle review

Main	Support/Extend	Resources
Hormones and the menstrual cycle (40 min) Ask students to use information from the student book to create a table to show information on each of the hormones involved in the menstrual cycle (FSH, LH, oestrogen, and progesterone). They should include the name of the gland it is secreted from, and its action on the body. Then provide students with copies of Figure 3 from the student book, which shows the changing levels of the female sex hormones throughout the menstrual cycle. Ask students to work in pairs and write questions for each other on what the diagram shows (e.g., On which day does ovulation occur? What happens to the uterus lining as levels of oestrogen increase?).	**Support:** Go through one hormone together as a class as an example. **Extend:** Students should identify examples of negative feedback in the menstrual cycle. **Support:** Provide students with suitable questions.	**Activity:** Hormones and the menstrual cycle

Plenary	Support/Extend	Resources
Design a diagram (10 min) Ask students to design a diagram to help them remember how the hormones involved in the menstrual cycle interact with each other. This can be in the form of boxes containing the name of the hormone with connecting arrows to show how they interact. **Which hormone?** (5 min) Provide students with cards showing the names of hormones. Ask a series of questions and ask students to hold up the hormone (or hormones) you are describing.	**Support:** Supply the Provide students with a partially finished diagram for them to complete. **Extend:** Ask questions where more than one hormone could be the answer (e.g., Which hormone is secreted by the pituitary gland?).	

Homework		
Students can write down why women who struggle to become pregnant may be given injections of FSH.	**Extend:** Students should do some extra research on the drawbacks of fertility drugs.	

kerboodle

A Kerboodle highlight for this lesson is **Calculation sheet: Interpreting a menstrual cycle diagram**. Refer to the **Content map** on Kerboodle for a full list of resources and assessment.

B11.7 The artificial control of fertility

AQA spec link: 5.3.5 Students should be able to evaluate the different hormonal and non-hormonal methods of contraception.

Fertility can be controlled by a variety of hormonal and non-hormonal methods of contraception.

These include:

- oral contraceptives that contain hormones to inhibit FSH production so that no eggs mature
- injection, implant, or skin patch of slow release progesterone to inhibit the maturation and release of eggs for a number of months or years
- barrier methods such as condoms and diaphragms which prevent the sperm reaching an egg
- intrauterine devices which prevent the implantation of an embryo or release a hormone
- spermicidal agents which kill or disable sperm
- abstaining from intercourse when an egg may be in the oviduct
- surgical methods of male and female sterilisation.

WS 1.3, 1.4

Aiming for	Outcome	Checkpoint	
		Question	Activity
Aiming for GRADE 4 ↓	Describe what contraception is and list examples.	1	Starter 1, Main
	Categorise contraceptives as hormonal and non-hormonal.		Main
Aiming for GRADE 6 ↓	Explain how contraceptives work.	2	Main, Plenary 1
	List the advantages and disadvantages of different contraceptives.	2, 3	Main
Aiming for GRADE 8 ↓	Apply knowledge of hormones in the menstrual cycle to suggest how hormonal contraceptives work.	End of chapter 4	Starter 2
	Evaluate different methods of contraception in detail.		Main

Maths
Students study statistics on the effectiveness of different types of contraception.

Literacy
Students design a leaflet, poster, or webpage on methods of contraception. Some may also tailor the content for different audiences.

Key word
contraception

B11 Hormonal coordination

Starter	Support/Extend	Resources
What is contraception? (5 min) Ask students to write down their answer to this question. Ask them to share their ideas in order to come up with an agreed class definition. **The contraceptive pill** (10 min) **H** Introduce the contraceptive pill as a contraceptive. Tell the class that one type contains oestrogen. Ask them to use what they have learnt about the function of oestrogen to suggest why.	**Support:** Use images of examples of contraceptives to initiate ideas.	

Main	Support/Extend	Resources
Contraceptive advice (15 min) Discuss the fact that contraception is a way of preventing pregnancy. Ask students to work in small groups to list examples of different contraceptives that they have heard about. Then, after hearing their ideas and making a class list, allow students to use the student book to add any extras that were not mentioned. Students then categorise the contraceptives as hormonal or non-hormonal, and explain what the difference is.	**Support:** Provide the groups with images of different contraceptives to help them write their list.	**Activity:** Contraceptive advice
Discuss the fact that there are many different forms of contraception. Ask students to design a leaflet, poster, or webpage on the methods of contraception listed in Main 1. This should be written for people who want general advice on contraception and the options available to them. Students should list the advantages and disadvantages of each method of contraception.	**Support:** Focus on just one or two different methods. **Extend:** Students could each write for a different audience, for example, young people not in serious relationships, young couples who may have children in a few years, older couples who do not wish to have any more children.	

Plenary	Support/Extend	Resources
Advantages and disadvantages (5 min) Students match advantages and disadvantages to different forms of contraception. **The male pill?** (10 min) Carry out a class discussion on the male pill which may be a possibility in the future. Talk about how it could work and if the students think it is a good idea.		**Interactive:** Advantages and disadvantages

Homework		
Students create a summary table of the different forms on contraception covered this lesson. The table should include a brief description of how the method works, advantages, and disadvantages.		

Higher tier

B11.8 Infertility treatments

AQA spec link: 5.3.6 Students should be able to explain the use of hormones in modern reproductive technologies to treat infertility.

This includes giving FSH and LH in a 'fertility drug' to a woman. She may then become pregnant in the normal way.

In Vitro Fertilisation (IVF) treatment:

- IVF involves giving a mother FSH and LH to stimulate the maturation of several eggs.
- The eggs are collected from the mother and fertilised by sperm from the father in the laboratory.
- The fertilised eggs develop into embryos.
- At the stage when they are tiny balls of cells, one or two embryos are inserted into the mother's uterus (womb).

Although fertility treatment gives a woman the chance to have a baby of her own:

- it is very emotionally and physically stressful
- the success rates are not high
- it can lead to multiple births which are a risk to both the babies and the mother.

WS 1.1, 1.3, 1.4
MS 4a

Aiming for	Outcome	Checkpoint	
		Question	Activity
Aiming for GRADE 6 ↓	Describe what is meant by infertility and suggest reasons for it.		Starter 1, Starter 2, Main
	Describe the steps used in IVF.	1, End of chapter 4	Main
	Outline the issues surrounding IVF.	4	Main, Plenary 1, Homework
Aiming for GRADE 8 ↓	Describe how FSH and IVF can be used to help treat infertility.	2, End of chapter 4	Main, Plenary 2
	Evaluate the advantages and disadvantages of IVF.	3	Plenary 1
	Use different viewpoints to make an informed decision on unused IVF embryos.		Main

Maths
Students draw a chart to show how the success rate of IVF changes as the mother gets older (4a).

Literacy
Students use information from a variety of sources including the student book, news articles, data, and websites to discuss the issues surrounding IVF.

■ B11 Hormonal coordination

Starter	Support/Extend	Resources
What is infertility? (5 min) Ask pairs to discuss this question and come up with a definition that they can share with the class.	**Support:** Provide the definition plus two incorrect definitions and ask pairs to discuss which they think is correct.	
Causes of infertility (10 min) Provide small groups with diagrams of the male and female reproductive systems. Ask them to discuss possible reasons why a man or a woman may be infertile. Ask groups to share their ideas and list them on the board.	**Support:** Explain first what is meant by infertile.	

Main	Support/Extend	Resources
Solving fertility problems (40 min) Introduce the ways in which men and women can have fertility difficulties. Ask groups to continue the discussion to come up with ways of helping couples with each of the fertility problems identified. For example, one suggestion might be that the woman does not regularly release an egg from her ovaries. One solution would be to give her FSH injections to stimulate the eggs in the ovaries to mature. Listen to the ideas of the class on solving fertility problems and introduce IVF as one method. Describe the process of IVF. Ask students to use information from the student book to write a description of what happens. They can include diagrams to help them. Ask students to display the data shown in Table 1 of the student book as a graph, and explain what it shows.	**Extend:** Groups could also discuss what kinds of medical tests could be used to understand the nature of the problem, for example, blood tests to check hormone levels. **Support:** Supply Provide students with the stages of IVF in the wrong order. They can cut these out and arrange them into the correct order. **Extend:** Students should also discuss the ethical dilemma of what to do with the embryos not selected during IVF.	**Activity:** Solving fertility problems

Plenary	Support/Extend	Resources
IVF: advantages and disadvantages (10 min) Ask students to work in small groups to list the benefits and drawbacks of IVF.	**Support:** Supply Provide statements and ask groups to categorise them as benefits or drawbacks.	
Fertility (5 min) Students use the interactive to answer a series of true or false questions on fertility treatments.		**Interactive:** Fertility

Homework		
Students complete the WebQuest to research the debate surrounding IVF treatment, including the advantages and disadvantages. Alternatively, introduce the concept of saviour siblings and ask students to write down their opinion on this use of IVF.		**WebQuest:** The IVF debate

kerboodle

A Kerboodle highlight for this lesson is **Bump up your grade: Artificial control of fertility**. Refer to the **Content map** on Kerboodle for a full list of resources and assessment.

GCSE Biology only

B11.9 Plant hormones and plant responses

AQA spec link: 5.4.1 Plants produce hormones to coordinate and control growth and responses: to light, phototropism; and gravity, gravitropism (geotropism). Unequal distributions of auxin cause unequal growth rates in plant roots and shoots.

Required practical: Investigate the effect of light or gravity on the growth of newly germinated seedlings.

Record results as both length measurements and as careful, labelled biological drawings to show the effects.

Aiming for	Outcome	Checkpoint	
		Question	Activity
Aiming for GRADE 4	Describe that plant shoots grow towards the light and away from the force of gravity, and roots grow in the direction of the force of gravity.		Starter 2, Main, Plenary 2
	Identify plant responses as phototropism or gravitropism.		Main, Plenary 1
	Plan and carry out an investigation into the effect of light on plant growth, given support.		Main, Homework
Aiming for GRADE 6	Explain why plants need tropisms.	1	Starter 1, Main
	Use diagrams and descriptions to explain how plant shoots and roots respond to light and gravity.	2	Main, Plenary 2
	Plan and carry out an investigation into the effect of light on plant growth, with limited guidance.		Main, Homework
Aiming for GRADE 8	Explain in detail how the production and diffusion of auxin affects the growth of shoots and roots.		Main, Plenary 2
	Independently plan and carry out an investigation into the effect of light on plant growth.		Main, Homework
	Predict the results of an investigation of tropisms, with detailed scientific reasons.	3	Main

Maths
Students may plan a way of collecting quantitative results.

Literacy
Students use a range of information to write descriptions of how plant shoots and roots respond to light and gravity.

Key words
tropism, phototropism, gravitropism, auxin

Required practical

Title	Investigating newly germinated shoots
Equipment	range of newly germinated seeds (e.g., cress, rapid-cycling *Brassica rapa* (fast plants), *Sinapis alba* (white mustard), *Raphanus sativus* (radish) – choose seedlings with straight shoots (hypocotyls) if possible), Petri dishes, cotton wool, compost, small containers (e.g., plastic cups/yoghurt pots), photographic filters (e.g., red, green and blue), a range of transparent and translucent materials, small cardboard boxes, (e.g., shoeboxes), scissors and adhesive tape, lamps or a light bank, light meter,

B11 Hormonal coordination

Overview of method	Students work in small groups to write a hypothesis on the effect of light on the growth of seedlings, and then plan a method to allow them to investigate it.
	Suitable ideas include investigating the effect of no light, light from one direction, different coloured light, and intensity of light.
Safety considerations	Wash hands after handling compost. Be aware of any students with relevant allergies.

Starter	Support/Extend	Resources
What do plants need? (10 min) Ask students to write a list of everything plants need in order to grow healthily. As a class, discuss how plants get each of these things.	**Extend:** Students should be able to link this to photosynthesis.	
Phototropism (5 min) Show the class an image of plant stems bending towards the light (or set up a plant in advance so it displays this growth). Ask students why the plant has grown like this.		

Main	Support/Extend	Resources
Investigating newly germinated shoots (40 min plus time another lesson) Introduce to students the concepts of photostropism and gravitropism. Build on the Starter activities to discuss why it is important for plant growth that plant shoots to grow upwards and towards light, and that roots grow downwards. Provide students with unlabelled diagrams of the seedlings and ask them to annotate the diagrams and write captions in their own words to explain what is happening.	**Support:** Supply Provide students with a range of key words that they must include (phototropism, light, gravitropism, gravity).	**Required practical:** Investigating newly germinated shoots
Students then work in small groups to write a hypothesis on the effect of light on the growth of seedlings, and then plan a method to allow them to investigate it. They may need reminding to set one or more controls so they can accurately describe the effect of the independent variable. After checking their method, allow students to set up their investigation, and leave it for at least five days for the seedlings to grow.	**Support:** Students can simply set up an experiment using germinated cress seeds in a box with a hole cut in the side to investigate the effect of light from one direction.	
	Extend: They Students should also write a scientific prediction.	

Plenary	Support/Extend	Resources
Call my bluff (10 min) Give pairs a key word from the lesson. They come up with the correct definition and two incorrect definitions. They share these with another group, who have to spot the right answer.	**Extend:** Supply Provide students with words and definitions associated with the topic that they have not come across, for example, ethylene, geotropism, micropropagation.	
Which way? (5 min) Students use the interactive to look at a diagram of an investigation into the effect of light on newly germinated shoots and complete sentences about what is happening.	**Extend:** Invite students to draw where the concentration of auxin would be highest.	**Interactive:** Which way?

Homework		
Ask students to write down how they are going to gather results for the investigation in order to answer their hypothesis. Students may wish to simply observe and compare the seedlings in the test and control conditions.	**Extend:** Students should plan a way of collecting quantitative data.	

kerboodle

A Kerboodle highlight for this lesson is **Working scientifically: Does light affect the germination of seedlings?** Refer to the **Content map** on Kerboodle for a full list of resources and assessment.

GCSE Biology only — Higher tier

B11.10 Using plant hormones

AQA spec links: 5.4.1 Gibberellins are important in initiating seed germination.

Ethene controls cell division and ripening of fruits.

The mechanisms of how gibberellins and ethene work are not required.

5.4.2 Students should be able to describe the effects of some plant hormones and the different ways people use them to control plant growth.

Plant growth hormones are used in agriculture and horticulture.

Auxins are used as:

- as weed killers
- as rooting powders
- for promoting growth in tissue culture.

Ethene is used in the food industry to control ripening of fruit during storage and transport.

Gibberellins can be used to:

- end seed dormancy
- promote flowering
- increase fruit size.

WS 1.3, 1.4
MS 4a

Aiming for	Outcome	Checkpoint	
		Question	Activity
Aiming for GRADE 6 ↓	Describe some uses of plant hormones (giberellins, ethene, and auxins) in agriculture, horticulture, and the food industry.	1, 3	Starter 1, Starter 2, Main, Plenary 2, Homework
	Observe the effects of plant hormones.		Main
Aiming for GRADE 8 ↓	Explain how the effects of plant hormones are useful in agriculture, horticulture, and the food industry.	2	Starter 1, Starter 2, Main, Plenary 2, Homework
	Evaluate the use of synthetic plant hormones.		Main, Homework

Maths
Students collect quantitative data and display it using graphs (4a).

Literacy
Groups write an advert for herbicides and present it to the rest of the class.

Key words
gibberellins, horticulture, agriculture

Practical

Title	Plant growth hormones
Equipment	**Weed killer** frame quadrat (50 cm × 50 cm), measuring tape, string and four pegs to mark out an area, weed killer, identification sheet of common weeds **Rooting powder** two 9 cm plant pots, potting compost, hormone rooting powder, small beaker, water, two cuttings of a suitable plant, scalpel, labels, eight small canes, two polythene bags, two elastic bands

B11 Hormonal coordination

Overview of method	**Weed killer**
	Students select a suitable grassy area of the school playing field and mark out an area of 1 metre × 1 metre with string and pegs. They use the quadrat to count and record the number of each of the different weed species before applying the weed killer. Once a week for a fortnight they repeat the observations.
	Rooting powder
	Students take two sets of cuttings. They use hormone rooting powder on one set but not the other. After around two weeks of growth they can study the roots.
Safety considerations	Take care when handling powders, sprays, or liquids. Wear eye protection when applying weed killers. Instructions given by the manufacturers for making up solutions or for the application of the compounds should be followed carefully. Wash hands after using or handling any of the compounds. Take care when using scalpels.

Starter	Support/Extend	Resources
Spraying crops (5 min) Ask students to work in pairs. Show the class an image of a farmer spraying their crops with chemicals. Ask the pairs to list possible reasons why they are doing this. Discuss their ideas.	**Support:** Introduce the term 'herbicide' as a name for a selective weed killer.	
What's the problem? (10 min) Ask the class a series of questions. For example, what's the problem with: • picking ripe fruit to transport to the supermarket? • weeds growing in crop fields? • trees that produce small fruit? Gather responses and introduce synthetic plant hormones as a solution to these problems.	**Support:** Ask students to work in groups and supply each with one question to discuss.	

Main	Support/Extend	Resources
Plant growth hormones (40 min plus an additional lesson to assess results) Ask students to work in small groups. They carry out two experiments where they observe and evaluate the effects of plant hormones. In the first they take two sets of cuttings and use hormone rooting power on one set. They can observe the differences in the roots after two weeks. In the second experiment they use a weed killer on a selected area of the school playing field to assess its effectiveness at removing the weeds. They need to repeat the observations once a week for a fortnight. Supply students with other resources to research the drawbacks of herbicides. Ask students to list other uses of plant hormones using the information in the student book.	**Extend:** Students should plan to collect quantitative data. **Extend:** Ask students to debate the advantages and disadvantages of using herbicides.	**Practical:** Plant growth hormones

Plenary	Support/Extend	Resources
Writing predictions (10 min) Students write predictions for the two experiments they set up.	**Extend:** Students should use scientific knowledge to explain their predictions.	
Uses of plant hormones (5 min) Students use the interactive to match different plant hormones with their uses.	**Extend:** For each answer, students should state one advantage or disadvantage of using that plant hormone.	**Interactive:** Uses of plant hormones

Homework		
Ask students to prepare a TV or radio advert for selective weed killers, (herbicides) aimed at farmers. The advert should include information on how selective weed killers work, and the benefits of using them.		

kerboodle

A Kerboodle highlight for this lesson is **Extension: Plant hormones and tissue culture**. Refer to the **Content map** on Kerboodle for a full list of resources and assessment.

B11 Hormonal coordination

Overview of B11 Hormonal coordination

In this chapter students have studied the principles of hormonal control and the endocrine system. They should be able to identify the main parts of the endocrine system and recall the hormones they produce.

Students should recall how blood-glucose concentration is controlled, including the role of insulin. Higher-tier students should also be able to explain the role of glucagon, and clearly distinguish between glucose, glycogen, and glucagon. All students should be aware of the causes and treatments of both type 1 and type 2 diabetes. They should link this with work in B2.3 *Stem cells* and with the effect of lifestyle on type 2 diabetes in B7.4 *Diet, exercise, and disease*.

Higher-tier students should understand the process of negative feedback, particularly as applied to the hormones adrenaline and thyroxine.

All students have studied hormones in human reproduction. They should recall the action of hormones in bringing about puberty. They should be aware of the role of oestrogen in the menstrual cycle in females, and of testosterone in males. Higher-tier students should have a more detailed understanding of how hormones interact to control the menstrual cycle. Students should understand how hormones are used in the control of fertility as applied to contraception, and for higher-tier students, to infertility treatments.

Finally students studying *AQA GCSE biology* have studied the role of hormones in plants, and the tropism responses they cause. Higher-tier students should understand the use of plant hormones in agriculture and horticulture.

Required practical

All students are expected to have carried out the required practical:

Practical	Topic
Investigate the effect of light or gravity on the growth of newly germinated seedlings.	B11.9
Record results both as length measurements and as accurate, labelled biological drawings to show the effects.	

MyMaths

You can find additional support for the maths skills covered in this chapter on **MyMaths**, including estimations, working with graphs, data analysis, and collecting quantitative data.

kerboodle

For this chapter, the following assessments are available on Kerboodle:

B11 Checkpoint quiz: Hormone control in humans and plants
B11 Progress quiz: Hormone control in humans and plants 1
B11 Progress quiz: Hormone control in humans and plants 2
B11 On your marks: Hormone control in humans and plants
B11 Exam-style questions and mark scheme: Hormone control in humans and plants

Checkpoint follow-up lesson

A student's route through this lesson can be determined using the Checkpoint assessment. Percentage pass marks are supplied in the Checkpoint teacher notes.

For each successive route through it is assumed that the student can perform to their current route as well as previous routes. For example, students working at Aiming for 6 are assumed to be secure in Aiming for 4 knowledge and understanding and working towards achieving all the learning outcomes for Aiming for 6.

	Aiming for 4	**Aiming for 6**	**Aiming for 8**
Learning outcomes	State some of the functions of the hormones of the endocrine system.	Describe some of the functions of the hormones of the endocrine system.	Explain some of the functions of the hormones of the endocrine system.
	State what happens during the menstrual cycle.	Describe what happens during the menstrual cycle.	Explain what happens during the menstrual cycle.
	State some types of contraceptive methods.	Describe some uses of plant hormones.	Explain some uses of plant hormones.
Starter	**Hormones (5 min)** Student pairs list as many hormones in the body as they can think of. Pairs could compare their list with a neighbouring pair. Summarise the hormones they have listed on the board.		
Differentiated checkpoint activity	Students use the Aiming for 4 follw-up sheet to complete three activties to revise the role of hormones in the human body. Students label a diagram to show glands and the hormones they produce, using the labels provided. They then fill in a table about functions of hormones, analyse a graph on the menstrual cycle, and complete a cut-and-stick exercise on methods on contraception. The activities are all highly-structured, but students may need access to the student book to complete them. and may benefit from a brief introduction from the teacher.	Students use the Aiming for 6 follow-up sheet to complete two activities to revise the role of hormones in the human body and in plants. Students label a diagram to show glands and the hormones they produce, using the hormone labels provided. They then draw a table about functions of hormones, analyse a graph on the menstrual cycle. Students studying *AQA GCSE Biology* could create a visual summary on the uses of plant hormones, in place of one of the other activities, depending on which subject areas they need support with revision. The activities are fairly structured and students should not need any introduction.	Students use the Aiming for 8 follow-up sheet to complete two activities to revise the role of hormones in the human body and in plants. Students label a diagram of the endocrine system, analyse a graph on the menstrual cycle, and students studying *AQA GCSE Biology* can create a visual summary on the uses of plant hormones. The activities have little structure, and students should be working independently.
	Kerboodle resource B11 Checkpoint follow-up: Aiming for 4, B11 Checkpoint follow-up: Aiming for 6, B11 Checkpoint follow-up: Aiming for 8		
Plenary	**Hormone card sort (5 min)** Each small group of students will need cards with hormone names. Ask the groups to sort the cards into different groups, or to select the correct card/s for your description. Examples of groups and descriptions include plant and animal hormones, hormones released by the pituitary gland, menstrual hormones, the hormone that causes eggs to mature, and so on.		
Progression	Provide students with a blank human body diagram so that they can label the positions of the glands. A model of the human body to show gland positions will help them visualise this. When studying the menstrual cycle, you could provide a graph for students to add a different colour to track the changes of each hormone.	Students find out the current numbers of people with type 1 and type 2 diabetes in the UK. Organising a debate about the advantages and disadvantages of fertility treatment should allow students of all abilities to put over their points of view.	Students research how hormones work in terms of their interaction with DNA and protein synthesis, producing diagrams showing the effects of insulin and glucagon. In studying plant hormones there is opportunity to carry out practical work and challenge the more able to investigate other factors.

B — 12 Homeostasis in action
12.1 Controlling body temperature

AQA spec link: 5.2.4 Body temperature is monitored and controlled by the thermoregulatory centre in the brain. The thermoregulatory centre contains receptors sensitive to the temperature of the blood. The skin contains temperature receptors and sends nervous impulses to the thermoregulatory centre.

If the body temperature is too high, blood vessels dilate (vasodilation) and sweat is produced from the sweat glands. Both these mechanisms cause a transfer of energy from the skin to the environment.

If the body temperature is too low, blood vessels constrict (vasoconstriction), sweating stops, and skeletal muscles contract (shiver).

(H) Students should be able to explain how these mechanisms lower or raise body temperature in a given context.

Aiming for	Outcome	Checkpoint Question	Checkpoint Activity
Aiming for GRADE 4 ↓	State that the thermoregulatory centre in the brain monitors and controls body temperature.	2	Main, Homework
	Predict whether certain activities will raise or lower body temperature.		Main, Starter 2
Aiming for GRADE 6 ↓	Describe how body temperature is monitored and controlled.	2, 3, End of chapter 2	Main, Homework
	Describe the mechanisms that take place if body temperature is too high or too low.	4	Main, Plenary 1, Plenary 2
Aiming for GRADE 8 ↓	(H) Explain in detail how mechanisms lower or raise body temperature.	4	Main, Plenary 2, Homework
	Explain why it is dangerous if body temperature is too high or too low.	1, End of chapter 3	Main

Maths
Students use forehead thermometers to measure their temperature. They discuss the reasons for variations in body temperature.

Literacy
Students to use information from the student book to create a flow chart to show what happens if core body temperature gets too high or too low. They also read a news article on hypothermia or heatstroke.

Key words
thermoregulatory centre, vasodilation, vasoconstriction

B12 Homeostasis in action

Starter	Support/Extend	Resources
Taking your temperature (10 min) Provide students with forehead thermometers and ask them to take their temperature. Collect results and calculate the mean of the class.	**Extend:** Discuss how much variation there was, and possible reasons why. Do people have different temperatures, or is it due to the resolution of the thermometers? Discuss how you could tell.	
Up or down? (5 min) Present the class with a series of activities and ask them to predict if each would result in an increase or decrease in body temperature, for example, putting on a jumper, running, taking a cold shower, starting to sweat, shivering.	**Extend:** Students should explain why.	

Main	Support/Extend	Resources
Controlling body temperature (40 min) Discuss the fact that our bodies maintain a body temperature of 37 °C. Ask students to use information in the student book to create a flow chart to show what happens if core body temperature gets too high or too low. Then share a news article about someone who was in a situation where they suffered from heatstroke or hypothermia. Allow students to discuss why this is dangerous, using the student book.	**Support:** Provide the stages in temperature regulation and ask students to arrange them in the correct order. **Extend:** Students should also explain how these mechanisms work. **Support:** Read the article as a class. **Extend:** Provide students with two articles – one about each condition.	**Activity:** Controlling body temperature

Plenary	Support/Extend	Resources
Warming up and cooling down (5 min) Students sort methods of temperature control into different categories to show whether they are ways of warming up or cooling down. **Misconceptions** (10 min) Present the class with a series of misconceptions about controlling body temperature: • Blood capillaries dilate or constrict to control body temperature. • In order to cool the body down, blood vessels move towards the surface of the skin to allow more heat to escape. • Sweating cools the body down because sweat is cold. Students should say why the statements are incorrect, and write them out correctly.	**Extend:** Students should also explain how each method works. **Support:** Students can use the student book for help. **Extend:** Ask students to write their own incorrect statements and share them with a partner.	**Interactive:** Warming up and cooling down

Homework		
Students produce two diagrammatic summaries of how the body changes to control body temperature. One diagram should explain how the body cools itself, and the other should explain how the body warms itself up.	**Extend:** Students should use a context in their summaries.	

kerboodle

A Kerboodle highlight for this lesson is **Extension sheet: Structural adaptations for thermoregulation**. Refer to the **Content map** on Kerboodle for a full list of resources and assessment.

GCSE Biology only

B12.2 Removing waste products

AQA spec link: 5.3.3 Students should be able to explain the effect on cells of osmotic changes in body fluids.

Water leaves the body via the lungs during exhalation.

Water, ions, and urea are lost from the skin in sweat.

There is no control over water, ion, or urea loss by the lungs or skin.

Excess water, ions, and urea are removed via the kidneys in the urine. If body cells lose or gain too much water by osmosis they do not function efficiently.

H The digestion of proteins from the diet results in excess amino acids which need to be excreted safely. In the liver these amino acids are deaminated to form ammonia. Ammonia is toxic and so it is immediately converted to urea for safe excretion.

MS 1c

Aiming for	Outcome	Checkpoint	
		Question	Activity
Aiming for GRADE 4	State that the level of water in the body has to be controlled.		Starter 1, Main 1
	List the ways in which water is lost from the body.	1	Starter 1, Main 1, Plenary 2
	State that excess water, ions, and urea are removed from the body by the kidneys.		Starter 2, Main 1, Plenary 2
Aiming for GRADE 6	Explain why the body needs to get rid of carbon dioxide, urea, excess ions, and water.	2, End of chapter 1	Main 2, Plenary 2
	Describe how the body forms the waste products carbon dioxide and urea.	2	Starter 2, Main 1, Plenary 2
	Describe the difference between urea and urine.	2	Main 1
Aiming for GRADE 8	Calculate percentage changes in volumes of water lost or gained by the body.		Starter 1
	Suggest an effect of liver failure on the body.		Main 1
	Explain the link between high levels of protein in the diet and an increase in urea concentration of urine.		Plenary 1

Maths
Students may calculate volumes of water and percentages (1c).

Literacy
Students work in groups to create health and safety information for participants in extreme sports. They describe and explain the risks to the body.

■ B12 Homeostasis in action

Starter	Support/Extend	Resources
Water in, water out (10 min) Provide students with a diagram showing the volumes of water taken in and lost by the body in each process (e.g., in by eating and drinking, out by sweating, out by breathing out, out in urine). Ask them to suggest what will happen to these volumes in various situations and why, for example, playing football on a hot day without drinking water. **What do they have in common?** (5 min) Show the class images of the kidneys, skin, and lungs. Ask students to discuss in groups what they think the organs have in common. Discuss the fact that they all have a role in removing waste products from the body.	**Extend:** You could leave out one of the volumes lost and ask students to calculate it. **Extend:** Students should calculate percentages. **Support:** Provide words with the images showing one waste product that they remove (lungs – carbon dioxide, skin – water, kidneys – urea). **Extend:** Students should describe how each waste product is made.	**Interactive:** Water in, water out

Main	Support/Extend	Resources
Removing waste (15 min) Introduce students to how water and other waste products are removed from the body. Students then answer Questions 1 and 2 from the student book. **Extreme sports** (25 min) Split the class into groups and give each group two examples of extreme sports, for example, free diving and a marathon in the desert. You can show the class pictures and/or videos that describe these sports if you wish. Ask students to create health and safety information for participants in the sports. This should include why the sport could be dangerous for their health in terms of waste product removal, and what they should do to minimise risks. This can be presented as written or verbal information.	**Extend:** 🄷 Students should find out about the role of the liver and kidneys in removing excess proteins from the body. **Support:** Groups can just do one sport and then share their findings. **Extend:** Students should use correct scientific terminology in their information.	**Activity:** Extreme sports

Plenary	Support/Extend	Resources
Protein and urea (5 min) Show students an example of a high-protein meal and ask them to predict and explain how the urine will change after eating it. **My role** (10 min) Ask students to work in groups of three. Designate each student as the skin, lungs, or kidney. Ask them to present an argument to each other that their role in removing waste products is the most vital in the body.	**Extend:** Use groups of four and ask one student to be the liver.	

Homework		
Students consider the repeatability, reproducibility, and validity of an investigation about antiperspirant.		**Working scientifically:** Sweat-beater: fake or real?

kerboodle

A Kerboodle highlight for this lesson is **Go further: Osmoregulation in Amoeba**. Refer to the **Content map** on Kerboodle for a full list of resources and assessment.

GCSE Biology only

B12.3 The human kidney

AQA spec link: 5.3.3 Students should be able to describe the function of kidneys in maintaining the water balance of the body.

The kidneys produce urine by filtration of the blood and selective reabsorption of useful substances such as glucose, some ions, and water.

Knowledge of other parts of the urinary system, the structure of the kidney, and the structure of a nephron is not required.

Students should be able to translate tables and bar charts of glucose, ions, and urea before and after filtration. Students should be able to describe the effect of ADH on the permeability of the kidney tubules.

H The water level in the body is controlled by the hormone ADH which acts on the kidney tubules. ADH is released by the pituitary gland when the blood is too concentrated and it causes more water to be reabsorbed back into the blood from the kidney tubules. This is controlled by negative feedback.

MS 1d

Aiming for	Outcome	Checkpoint	
		Question	Activity
Aiming for GRADE 4	State the function of the kidneys.	1, End of chapter 4	Starter 1, Main 1, Homework
	List the substances found in urine.		Starter 2, Main 2
	Describe how the amount of liquid you drink affects your urine.	3	Main 2, Plenary 2
Aiming for GRADE 6	Describe the processes of filtering and selective reabsorption in the kidneys.	1	Main 1, Plenary 2, Homework
	Suggest how the composition of the urine will change in given situations.	2	Main 2
	Describe the effect of ADH on the kidneys.		Main 1, Plenary 1
Aiming for GRADE 8	Apply knowledge of the processes of filtering and selective reabsorption to diagnose problems and suggest treatments for patients using results from a urine test.		Main 2
	Explain how the production of ADH will change in given situations.		Main 1, Plenary 2
	Explain how these changes will affect the amount of water in the urine.	4	Main 1, Plenary 2

Maths
Students calculate how much urine on average a person produces in a year. They convert units (1D).

Literacy
Students write creatively and persuasively to create an information profile for a kidney. They follow instructions to carry out urine tests and write diagnoses.

Key words
selective reabsorption, ADH

Practical

Title	'Urine' testing
Equipment	four 750 cm³ beakers or other containers, 2 mol/dm³ hydrochloric acid, 2 dm³ distilled water, yellow food colouring, 1 g glucose powder, 1 g albumin powder, few drops 1 mol/dm³ ammonia solution, four test tubes, test-tube rack, plastic pipettes, Benedict's solution, water bath heated to 40 °C, universal indicator paper

B12 Homeostasis in action

Overview of method	Before the lesson prepare the samples of 'urine'. Put 500 cm³ of distilled water into each beaker. Add hydrochloric acid until a pH of 6 is reached. Label each beaker urine A, urine B, urine C, and urine D. To urine A add a few drops of yellow food colouring to give a pale yellow colour. To urine B add more hydrochloric acid to give a pH of 4 and add yellow food colouring to give a dark yellow colour. Into urine C dissolve 1 g of glucose powder and add yellow food colouring to give a light yellow colour. Into urine D dissolve 1 g albumin powder, add drops of ammonia solution to give a pH of 8, and add yellow food colouring to give a very dark yellow colour. Students take a small sample of each 'urine' and put it into a test tube. They observe each sample and write down its colour. They then test each sample with universal pH paper, test for the presence of glucose using Benedict's solution, and test for the presence of protein by heating a sample in a water bath and noting whether it turns cloudy.
Safety considerations	Wear eye protection. Hydrochloric acid and ammonia solution is corrosive, avoid contact with skin.

Starter	Support/Extend	Resources
Kidney function (10 min) Show students an image of a kidney and ask them what it is. Now, Then ask the class to work in pairs to write down everything they know about the kidneys. Draw out essential facts about the kidneys through discussion. **Urea and urine** (5 min) Ask students to write down the difference between urea and urine. They peer assess each other's answers.	**Support:** Ask the class a series of true or false questions about the kidneys. **Extend:** If you wish you can demonstrate a kidney dissection.	

Main	Support/Extend	Resources
Kidney profile (15 min) Ask students to design a an information profile for a kidney. This should contain facts such as size, mass, position in the body, and function, as well as explaining why the kidney is a useful organ that the body can't do without. They should write using correct scientific language. **Urine testing** (25 min) Provide the class with four 'urine' samples to test from patients. Students observe the colour and then test each sample for pH and for the presence of glucose and protein. They write down their results and give a diagnosis.	**Support:** Provide students with a template that contains different sections to fill in. **Extend:** Students should talk about ADH. **Extend:** Students should suggest a possible treatment for the patients with different diagnoses. **Extend:** Students should complete the Go further activity, which looks into the structure of the kidney in more detail.	**Practical:** Urine testing **Go further:** Close up on the kidney

Plenary	Support/Extend	Resources
Urine mathematics (5 min) Tell the class that, on average, they produce about 1800 cm³ of urine a day. Ask students to calculate how much this is a year in dm³ (litres). **Restoring normal water levels** (10 min) Provide students with a series of statements that describe what happens when water levels in the blood become too high. They use the interactive to put them into the correct order.	**Support:** Students should just use cm³ and not convert units. **Extend:** Statements should include the effects of ADH. **Extend:** Students should be able to explain why the control of water in the blood is an example of negative feedback.	**Interactive:** Restoring normal water levels

Homework		
Ask students to design a poster or model of the kidneys. They should describe the role of the kidneys and the processes they carry out.		

kerboodle

A Kerboodle highlight for this lesson is **Bump up your grade: Negative feedback systems**. Refer to the **Content map** on Kerboodle for a full list of resources and assessment.

GCSE Biology only

B12.4 Dialysis – an artificial kidney

AQA spec link: 5.3.3 People who suffer from kidney failure may be treated by using kidney dialysis. Students should know the basic principles of the operation of a dialysis machine.

MS 1d

Aiming for	Outcome	Checkpoint	
		Question	Activity
Aiming for GRADE 4	State what kidney failure is.		Starter 1, Starter 2 Main
	Describe why kidney failure is a threat to life.	1	Starter 1, Main
	State that kidney dialysis is a way of treating kidney failure.		Starter 2, Main, Homework
Aiming for GRADE 6	Use a diagram to show how kidney dialysis works.	1, 2, End of chapter 4	Main
	List advantages and disadvantages of kidney dialysis.		Starter 2, Main, Homework
	Describe how a model is similar to kidney dialysis.		Main, Plenary 1
Aiming for GRADE 8	Suggest and explain suitable concentrations of substances in dialysis fluid.	4	Main
	Apply knowledge of what affects the rate of diffusion to explain how dialysis is made efficient.	1, 4	Main
	Evaluate in detail a model of kidney dialysis.		Main, Plenary 1

Maths
Students apply their knowledge of how kidney dialysis works by suggesting suitable concentrations of substances in dialysis fluid (1d).

Literacy
Students write from the perspective of a dialysis patient.

Key word
dialysis

Practical

Title	Modelling kidney dialysis
Equipment	three 15 cm lengths of Visking tubing that have been soaked in water, string, dropping pipettes, 1% starch solution, 10% glucose solution, test tube, test-tube rack, three beakers, distilled water, iodine solution, spotting tile for iodine test, Benedict's solution, water bath, labels, marker pen, eye protection
Overview of method	Students place starch solution in the first length of tubing, glucose in the second, and a mixture in the third. They place each in a beaker of water and after 20 minutes test the water for the presence of starch (using iodine solution) and glucose (using Benedict's solution).
Safety considerations	Wear eye protection. Iodine solution is harmful, avoid contact with skin. Take care when using Benedict's reagent. Wash hands after handling chemicals.

B12 Homeostasis in action

Starter	Support/Extend	Resources
Kidney questions (5 min) Ask the class a series of multiple choice questions covering the function of the kidney to recap learning from Topic 12.3. Discuss what would happen to the body if the kidneys stopped working. **Kidney dialysis** (10 min) Introduce how a kidney can fail. Ask students to suggest ways that a failing kidney can be treated. Introduce them to the idea of dialysis, and ask students to suggest how they think a kidney dialysis machine works.	**Extend:** Discuss the advantages and disadvantages of kidney dialysis.	**Interactive:** Kidney questions

Main	Support/Extend	Resources
Modelling kidney dialysis (40 min) Explain how a kidney dialysis machine works, linking it back to the function of the kidney. Students set up the equipment for a practical where they model how kidney dialysis works. This is used to show how a partially permeable membrane can allow the passage of some molecules but not others. Provide students with a diagram of a kidney dialysis machine and ask them to use information from the student book to label it and explain how it works. This can be done whilst the kidney dialysis model is in the water.	**Support:** Set up the Visking tubing for the students prior to the lesson. **Extend:** Ask students to write a prediction based on their scientific knowledge. **Extend:** Tell students the different concentrations of substances in the blood and ask them to suggest suitable concentrations for these substances in dialysis liquid in order to make dialysis efficient.	**Practical:** Modelling kidney dialysis

Plenary	Support/Extend	Resources
Analysing results (10 min) Students test the water surrounding the Visking tubing set up in the Main activity for the presence of starch or glucose, and record their results. They then write a conclusion and explain how the model is similar to what happens in kidney dialysis. **Dialysis diet** (5 min) Ask students to explain why patients with kidney damage are given a reduced-protein diet.	**Extend:** Students should suggest how the model could be improved to be more accurate.	

Homework		
Ask students to write what it is like to be a dialysis patient. This can be in the form of an interview, diary extracts, or an article.	**Support:** Ask students to put themselves into the role of a dialysis patient. Provide them with interview questions to answer.	

kerboodle
A Kerboodle highlight for this lesson is **Bump up your grade: How dialysis machines work**. Refer to the **Content map** on Kerboodle for a full list of resources and assessment.

GCSE Biology only

B12.5 Kidney transplants

AQA spec link: 5.3.3 People who suffer from kidney failure may be treated by organ transplant or by using kidney dialysis. Students should know the basic principles of dialysis.

MS 1d

Aiming for	Outcome	Checkpoint	
		Question	Activity
Aiming for GRADE 4 ↓	Describe what an organ transplant is.		Starter 1
	List some advantages and disadvantages of kidney transplants.	1, End of chapter 4	Main, Plenary 1
Aiming for GRADE 6 ↓	Explain why kidney donors can be living.	2	Starter 1, Plenary 1
	Compare the advantages and disadvantages of treating kidney failure using dialysis or kidney transplant.	3, End of chapter 4	Main, Plenary 2
Aiming for GRADE 8 ↓	Explain why family members are usually a good choice for an organ donor.	2	Main, Plenary 1
	Use economic, social, and ethical arguments to evaluate treating kidney failure by dialysis or kidney transplant.		Main

Maths
Students study information on the costs of kidney dialysis and kidney transplant in the UK. They analyse the data, perform calculations, and comment on which treatment is the best economically. Students study data on the gap between the number of people needing organ transplants and the number of available organs (1d).

Literacy
Students use information from a range of websites to research two systems of organ donation. They discuss in groups what they found out and write up independently which system they think is best and why.

■ B12 Homeostasis in action

Starter	Support/Extend	Resources
Organ transplants (10 min) Ask students to write down as much as they can in five minutes about organ transplants. Gather key ideas from the class and list them on the board. **A third kidney?** (5 min) Show students a diagram to show a donor kidney in place with the patient's two failed kidneys. Ask students to comment on what they think it shows.	**Support:** Allow students to work in groups. **Extend:** Ask the class why donated kidneys can come from a living donor.	

Main	Support/Extend	Resources
Transplant versus dialysis (40 min) Supply students with information on the costs of kidney dialysis and kidney transplant in the UK. Ask students to analyse this data and comment on which treatment is the best economically. Students then use information from the student book to look at social and ethical considerations and write down advantages and disadvantages of each method. Discuss whether they think the most economical choice is the best choice overall.	**Extend:** Ask students to study data on the gap between the number of people needing organ transplants and the number of available organs. **Support:** Read through the information as a class and list the advantages and disadvantages. **Extend:** Students should write a letter of recommendation to the Government, commenting on the financial benefits of transplants versus dialysis. They should use calculations to support their argument.	**Working scientifically:** Transplant versus dialysis

Plenary	Support/Extend	Resources
The treatment of kidney failure (5 min) Supply students with a cloze activity about the treatment of kidney failure, to include information on dialysis and transplants. **The future of transplants** (10 min) Present two possibilities for kidney transplants in the future– the production of new kidneys using a patient's own cells, and the use of animals that have been genetically modified to grow human kidneys. Ask students to discuss the benefits and drawbacks of each method.	**Support:** Provide a choice of words for each gap. **Extend:** Share a news story with the class about developments in this area. **Extend:** Students should discuss the advantages of these alternatives in terms of immune response.	**Interactive:** The treatment of kidney failure

Homework		
Explain that the UK, England, Scotland, and Northern Ireland currently have an 'opt-in' system for organ donation. This means that people have to register as donors. Wales has an 'opt-out' system. This means it is assumed that people want to donate their organs, unless they register to say that they don't want to. Students complete the WebQuest by researching both systems. They should then produce a report on which system they think is best, and why.		**WebQuest:** Kidney transplants

kerboodle

A Kerboodle highlight for this lesson is **Literacy sheet: Kidney donation**. Refer to the **Content map** on Kerboodle for a full list of resources and assessment.

B12 Homeostasis in action

Overview of B12 Homeostasis in action

This chapter is exclusively for students studying GCSE Biology rather than Combined Science. Students have studied homeostasis, starting with why and how the body controls its temperature. They should recall the role of the thermoregulatory centre in the brain and be able to describe the body's responses if the body temperature starts to become too high or too low. Higher-tier students should be able to explain these mechanisms in a given context.

In studying the removal of waste products, students should recall that water, ions, and urea are lost from the skin in an uncontrolled way, and that the removal of excess water, ions, and urea by the kidneys is a controlled process. They should link the removal of carbon dioxide with their studies of breathing and gas exchange in the lungs in B4 *Organising animals and plants*. Higher-tier students should be aware that the digestion of proteins may result in excess amino acids, which are deaminated in the liver to ammonia and then converted to urea for safe excretion.

Students should understand the role and functions of the human kidney, linking with work on diffusion, osmosis, and active transport in B1 *Cells and organisation*. They should recall that the kidneys produce urine by filtration of the blood and selective reabsorption of useful substances such as glucose, some ions, and water. Higher-tier students should recall the action of ADH as a hormone working by negative feedback, linked with B11.4 *The role of negative feedback*.

Finally students have studied treatments for kidney failure. They should understand how dialysis works, and link this with earlier work on diffusion. They should recall the process of kidney transplantation including the problems of rejection, linked with B5.9 *Human defence responses* and B6.1 *Vaccination*. Students should have compared dialysis with transplantation and be able to analyse the advantages and disadvantages of both treatment options.

MyMaths

You can find additional support for the maths skills covered in this chapter on **MyMaths**, including working with volumes, converting units, and data analysis.

kerboodle

For this chapter, the following assessments are available on Kerboodle:

B12 Checkpoint quiz: Homeostasis in action
B12 Progress quiz: Homeostasis in action 1
B12 Progress quiz: Homeostasis in action 2
B12 On your marks: Homeostasis in action
B12 Exam-style questions and mark scheme: Homeostasis in action

Checkpoint follow-up lesson

A student's route through this lesson can be determined using the Checkpoint assessment. Percentage pass marks are supplied in the Checkpoint teacher notes.

For each successive route through it is assumed that the student can perform to their current route as well as previous routes. For example, students working at Aiming for 6 are assumed to be secure in Aiming for 4 knowledge and understanding and working towards achieving all the learning outcomes for Aiming for 6.

	Aiming for 4	**Aiming for 6**	**Aiming for 8**
Learning outcomes	State the substances that are filtered and selectively reabsorbed by the kidney.	State the substances present in the blood entering and leaving the kidney, the kidney filtrate, and the urine.	Describe the substances present in the blood entering and leaving the kidney, the kidney filtrate, and the urine.
	State ways that water enters and leaves the body.	Describe the body's response to high and low water concentration in the blood.	Explain the body's response to high and low water concentration in the blood.
	State some advantages and disadvantages of dialysis and kidney transplants.	Describe the advantages and disadvantages of dialysis and kidney transplants.	Compare the advantages and disadvantages of dialysis and kidney transplants.
Starter	**Controlling conditions (5 min)** Student pairs list as many conditions in the body as they can think of that need to be controlled. Pairs could compare their list with a neighbouring pair. Summarise the conditions they have listed on the board.			
Differentiated checkpoint activity	Demonstrate a kidney dissection. You will need a kidney such as a sheep's kidney and dissection instruments. Ask targeted questions about the function of the kidney and the parts of the kidney.			
	Students then answer questions to summarise how water levels and body temperature are maintained in the human body, before creating a poster on the advantages and disadvantages of using dialysis and kidney transplants to treat kidney failure.			
	The Aiming for 4 follow-up sheet provides highly-structured questions to support students with revising the content of the lesson. Students should work in pairs to create their poster. Students may need access to the student book.	The Aiming for 6 follow-up sheet is fairly structured and provides prompts to support students with revising the content of the chapter. Students should work in pairs to create their posters. Students may need access to the student book.	The Aiming for 8 follow-up sheet provides minimal support for students and they should be aiming to work independently. They should attempt the tasks without the student book.
	Kerboodle resource B12 Checkpoint follow-up: Aiming for 4, B12 Checkpoint follow-up: Aiming for 6, B12 Checkpoint follow-up: Aiming for 8			
Plenary	**Higher or lower? (5 min)** Each student will need two cards of different colours. Read out a series of statements about homeostasis. Students hold up one coloured card if they think the answer is 'higher', and the other colour if the answer is 'lower'. Examples of statements include: concentration of urine if you have consumed a lot of salt; volume of urine after drinking a large amount of water.			
Progression	A debate about kidney transplants and who should receive them would be suitable for all abilities, as would a discussion about an opt-in versus an opt-out donor register.	The concept of how the human kidney works is challenging and diagrams to help explain the filtering of the blood and selective reabsorption of useful substances will aid learning for Aiming for 6 students.	Students can work towards explaining the mechanisms the body uses to raise and lower body temperature in a given context.
			Students could also look further at the concentration gradients set up in the kidney to cause selective reabsorption.

4 Genetics and reproduction

Specification links

AQA specification section	Assessment paper
6.1 Reproduction	Paper 2
6.2 Variation and evolution	Paper 2
6.3 The development of understanding of genetics and evolution	Paper 2
6.4 Classification of living organisms	Paper 2

Maths skills

AQA maths skills	Topic
1b Recognise and use expressions in standard form.	13.6, 15.4, 15.5, 15.6, 15.8
1c Use ratios, fractions and percentages.	13.6, 13.7, 13.8, 14.7, 15.1
1d Make estimates of the results of simple calculations.	13.5, 15.7, 15.9, 15.10
2a Use an appropriate number of significant figures.	15.8, 15.9
2b Find arithmetic means.	14.5
2c Construct and interpret frequency tables and diagrams, bar charts, and histograms.	13.7, 13.8
2e Understand simple probability.	13.2, 13.3, 13.7, 13.9, 13.10
2g Use a scatter diagram to identify a correlation between two variables.	14.3
2h Make order of magnitude calculations.	13.4
3a Understand and use the symbols: =, <, <<, >>, >, ∝, ~.	13.7, 13.8
4a Translate information between graphical and numeric form.	13.7, 14.2, 15.3, 15.7

B4 Genetics and reproduction

KS3 concept	GCSE topic	Checkpoint	Revision
About the nucleus of the cell and the chromosomes it contains	B13.2 Cell division in sexual reproduction	Ask students what the function of the nucleus is	Ask students to use the words 'gene, chromosome, DNA' in a sentence
About mitosis and the cell cycle	B13.1 Types of reproduction	Show students diagrams of the stages of cell division and ask them to describe what it is showing	Ask students to describe how cell division enables an organism to grow
The process of reproduction	B13.1 Types of reproduction	Ask students 'why do we look a bit like both parents?'	Ask students to draw a diagram to show how genetic information from both parents gets passed to offspring
How inheritance works	B14.1 Variation	Ask students what GM organisms are	Ask students to suggest why all offspring from the same parents are not identical
How variation can drive natural selection	B14.2 Evolution by natural selection	Ask students to list examples of variation in humans	Ask students to classify variation as inherited or environmental
How biological ideas develop	B15.2 Theories of evolution	Ask students why our understanding of science has increased over time	Ask students to discuss what they know about the work of Charles Darwin
About the characteristics of eukaryotic and prokaryotic cells, and the differences between animal, bacterial and plant cells	B15.9 Classification	Ask students to list similarities and differences between plant and animal cells	Ask students to group organisms in a method of their choosing
How to interpret scientific diagrams	B15.10 New systems of classification	Give groups a selection of biological diagrams and ask them to discuss what they show	Ask students to define what a scientific model is
About the concept of proportion and probability	P13.7 Inheritance in action	Give students a simple proportion problem e.g. there is a litter of six puppies, 3 are white and 3 are brown. What proportion is white?	Give students a completed genetic cross and ask them questions based on proportion, ratio and probability
That some applications of science can have both positive and negative implications	B14.3 Selective breeding	Ask students to define what 'ethical issues' means.	Ask students if they would want to clone themselves. Ask them to discuss in groups possible uses and issues of this technology

B 13 Reproduction
13.1 Types of reproduction

AQA spec links: 6.1.1 Students should understand that meiosis leads to non-identical cells being formed while mitosis leads to identical cells being formed

Sexual reproduction involves the joining (fusion) of male and female gametes:

- sperm and egg cells in animals
- pollen and egg cells in flowering plants.

In sexual reproduction there is mixing of genetic information which leads to variety in the offspring. The formation of gametes involves meiosis.

Asexual reproduction involves only one parent and no fusion of gametes. There is no mixing of genetic information. This leads to genetically identical offspring (clones). Only mitosis is involved.

6.1.3 Advantages of sexual reproduction:

- produces variation in the offspring
- if the environment changes variation gives a survival advantage by natural selection
- natural selection can be speeded up by humans in selective breeding to increase food production.

Advantages of asexual reproduction:

- only one parent needed
- more time and energy efficient as do not need to find a mate
- faster than sexual reproduction
- many identical offspring can be produced when conditions are favourable.

Aiming for	Outcome	Checkpoint	
		Question	Activity
Aiming for GRADE 4	Define sexual and asexual reproduction.	1	Main 1, Plenary 2
	Name some organisms that use either sexual or asexual reproduction.		Starter 1, Main 1
	Use a model to show why variation is produced in offspring from sexual reproduction but not from asexual reproduction.		Main 2
Aiming for GRADE 6	Describe the differences between sexual reproduction.		Starter 1, Main 1
	Describe the advantages and disadvantages of sexual and asexual reproduction.	3, End of chapter 1	Main 1, Plenary 1
	Design a model to show why variation is produced in offspring from sexual reproduction but not from asexual reproduction.		Main 2
Aiming for GRADE 8	Compare and contrast sexual and asexual reproduction.		Main 1, Plenary 2
	Explain in detail why meiosis is important for sexual reproduction.	End of chapter 2	Main 2
	Evaluate a model to show that variation is produced in offspring from sexual reproduction but not from asexual reproduction.		Main 2

Maths
Students consider the speed of sexual reproduction compared with asexual reproduction.

Literacy
Students organise information from the student book into a table.

Key words
sexual reproduction, asexual reproduction, meiosis

■ B13 Reproduction

Practical

Title	Modelling reproduction
Equipment	two plastic cups containing a mixture of different coloured beads, counters, or beans; two empty cups
Overview of method	Students are told that the beads in the two cups represent different chromosomes in two parent organisms. They use the equipment to model how offspring are produced in sexual and asexual reproduction. For example, they can take around half of the beads from each cup and mix them in the new cup to show sexual reproduction. They then reflect on how the chromosomes, and hence genetic information, of offspring produced by each method differ.

Starter	Support/Extend	Resources
Bacterial reproduction (10 min) Ask students to write a paragraph that describes how bacteria reproduce. Discuss as a class how this compares with how animals reproduce. **DNA, genes, and chromosomes** (5 min) Ask students to draw a diagram that shows DNA, genes, and chromosomes, and how they are related.	**Support:** Show the class an animation or video of bacteria dividing. **Extend:** Students should look for similarities in the reproduction of bacteria and animals.	

Main	Support/Extend	Resources
Sexual and asexual (20 min) Introduce the terms sexual reproduction and asexual reproduction. Students use information in the student book to create a table comparing sexual and asexual reproduction. **Modelling reproduction** (20 min) Students work in groups to carry out a practical modelling why sexual reproduction produces variation in offspring, but asexual reproduction does not.	**Support:** Provide students with a blank table that includes suitable categories to compare (e.g., number of parents, variation in offspring, speed, examples). **Extend:** Students should write a summary of the table, comparing and contrasting sexual and asexual reproduction. **Support:** Show students a model of how asexual reproduction happens and ask them to use the equipment to model sexual reproduction. **Extend:** Students should evaluate the model. For example, it does not show the chromosomes in pairs or show meiosis. **Extend:** Students explain why meiosis is important in sexual reproduction.	**Practical:** Modelling reproduction

Plenary	Support/Extend	Resources
Sexual and asexual reproduction (10 min) Students sort advantages and disadvantages of sexual and asexual reproduction into groups. **Definitions** (5 min) Ask students to write definitions for each type of reproduction and share them with a partner.	**Support:** Show students a definition and ask them to improve it.	**Interactive:** Sexual and asexual reproduction

Homework
Give students an example of an organism that can use both sexual and asexual reproduction. Students suggest why this would be useful to that organism, and suggest situations when the organism might use either type of reproduction.

kerboodle

A Kerboodle highlight for this lesson is **Extension sheet: Comparing different reproductive strategies**. Refer to the **Content map** on Kerboodle for a full list of resources and assessment.

B13.2 Cell division in sexual reproduction

AQA spec link: 6.1.2 Students should be able to explain how meiosis halves the number of chromosomes in gametes and fertilisation restores the full number of chromosomes.

Cells in reproductive organs divide by meiosis to form gametes.

When a cell divides to form gametes:

- copies of the genetic information are made
- the cell divides twice to form four gametes, each with a single set of chromosomes
- all gametes are genetically different from each other.

Gametes join at fertilisation to restore the normal number of chromosomes. The new cell divides by mitosis. The number of cells increases. As the embryo develops cells differentiate.

Knowledge of the stages of meiosis is not required.

WS 1.2
MS 2e

Aiming for	Outcome	Checkpoint	
		Question	Activity
Aiming for GRADE 4	State that gametes (sex cells) are formed by meiosis.	End of chapter 2	Main 1, Plenary 1, Plenary 2, Homework
	State that meiosis halves the number of chromosomes in gametes and fertilisation restores the full number.	1	Starter 1, Main 1, Homework
	Solve simple probability questions.		Main 2
Aiming for GRADE 6	Describe the processes of meiosis and mitosis.		Main 1, Plenary 1
	Explain how meiosis halves the number of chromosomes in gametes and fertilisation restores the full number.	3, End of chapter 2	Main 1, Homework
	Solve simple probability questions.		Main 2
Aiming for GRADE 8	Compare and contrast mitosis and meiosis.		Main 1
	Explain in detail why gametes are all genetically different to each other.	2	Starter 1, Main 1
	Solve complex calculations to determine the number of possible gametes formed during meiosis.		Main 2

Maths
Students work out the number of chromosomes in body and sex cells by doubling or halving numbers. They carry out probability calculations to work out the number of possible unique gametes produced during meiosis. (2e)

Literacy
Students write explanations and answer questions. They extract information from the student book to compare mitosis and meiosis.

Key word
meiosis

B13 Reproduction

Starter	Support/Extend	Resources
How many? (5 min) Ask students how many chromosomes there are in a human body cell and a human gamete (sex cell), and why they are different. Then read out the number of chromosomes in the body cells of different organisms and ask them to say the number in the corresponding gametes (or vice versa).	**Extend:** Students should predict what kinds of organisms they think have the most chromosomes.	
Passing on instructions (5 min) Ask students to write a short answer to the question: Why do we look like our parents? Go through their answers and discuss the fact that, during fertilisation, chromosomes from both parents are paired up.	**Support:** Provide students with useful key words – egg, sperm, genes, chromosomes, fertilisation.	

Main	Support/Extend	Resources
Which one? (20 min) Show students a simple animation that shows the process of meiosis, or go through Figure 1 in the student book with them, describing what happens at each stage. Then provide them with statements about mitosis and meiosis. They use information from the student book to correctly categorise them and place them into a table. Tell students that a way of remembering the difference between mitosis and meiosis is: mitosis – **m**aking **i**dentical **t**wo, meiosis – **m**aking **e**ggs (and sperm).	**Extend:** Students should be able to compare and contrast mitosis and meiosis. **Extend:** Ask students to calculate how many different combinations of unique gametes are possible in humans (2^{23})	**Activity:** Which one?
Probability (20 min) Ask students the question: If siblings have the same parents, why don't the siblings look identical? Use the Maths skills interactive to show the students how to work out how many unique gametes could be produced during meiosis, using probability. Ask the class to use this to answer the original question.		**Maths skills:** Probability in science

Plenary	Support/Extend	Resources
Inheritance (10 min) In this interactive activity students check their understanding by answering questions on mitosis, meiosis, and the differences between sexual and asexual reproduction.		**Interactive:** Inheritance
Simple inheritance in plants and animals (10 min) Provide students with an exam-style question on mitosis and meiosis and/or the difference in chromosome numbers between body cells and gametes.		

Homework		
Students make revision notes about meiosis and fertilisation, focusing on how sexual reproduction produces variation in offspring.		

kerboodle
A Kerboodle highlight for this lesson is **Calculation sheet: Probability**. Refer to the **Content map** on Kerboodle for a full list of resources and assessment.

GCSE Biology only

B13.3 The best of both worlds

AQA spec link: 6.1.3 This topic is synoptic and relates to other sections where more detail is given.

Some organisms reproduce by both methods depending on the circumstances.

- Malarial parasites reproduce asexually in the human host, but sexually in the mosquito.
- Many fungi reproduce asexually by spores but also reproduce sexually to give variation.
- Many plants produce seeds sexually, but also reproduce asexually by runners such as strawberry plants, or bulb division such as daffodils.

Knowledge of reproduction in organisms is restricted to those mentioned, but students are expected to be able to explain the advantages and disadvantages for any organism if given appropriate information.

MS 2e

Aiming for	Outcome	Checkpoint	
		Question	Activity
Aiming for GRADE 4 ↓	Name an organism that can reproduce both asexually and sexually.		Starter 1, Main 1, Main 2, Plenary 1
	Give a simple reason why an organism reproduces sexually or asexually.		Starter 1, Main 2
	State that flowers are a plant's reproductive organs.		Starter 1, Main 1, Plenary 2, Homework
Aiming for GRADE 6 ↓	Describe how malarial parasites and fungi reproduce both asexually and sexually.	2	Main 2
	List the ways in which plants can reproduce asexually.	2, End of chapter 1	Main 1
Aiming for GRADE 8 ↓	Suggest and explain the advantages and disadvantages of using both asexual and sexual methods of reproduction.		Starter 2, Main 2, Plenary 1
	Explain in detail how plants reproduce sexually.	End of chapter 1	Starter 2, Main 1, Homework

Maths
Discuss the advantages and disadvantages of sexual reproduction in terms of probability of offspring surviving to adulthood. (2e)

Literacy
Students use information from the student book to annotate a diagram to show the life cycle of a malarial parasite.

Key words
runners, malarial parasites

Practical

Title	Exploring plants and fungi
Equipment	cut flowers with visible stamens and stigma (e.g., lillies), scalpel, tweezers, scissors, white tile, open cap *Agaricus* species of edible mushroom (can be bought from a supermarket), white paper, beaker, hair spray (optional), light microscopes, glass slides, cover slips
	range of examples of asexual reproduction (e.g., spider plants with plantlets, strawberry plants with runners, daffodil bulbs with lateral bulb growing, sprouting potatoes).

B13 Reproduction

Overview of method	Students dissect the flower and identify the parts. They examine pollen under the microscope.
	Students then set up a fungal spore print. This needs to be left for at least 2 hours, so can be viewed in the next lesson.
Safety considerations	Take care when using scalpels, glass slides, and scissors. Wash hands after handling plant material. Be aware of any students who are allergic to pollen.

Starter	Support/Extend	Resources
Do plants have sex? (5 min) Ask students to discuss this question in pairs. Listen to their ideas and have a class discussion about how plants reproduce sexually.	**Extend:** Ask students for examples of when plants reproduce asexually.	
Some examples (10 min) Ask students to share their findings from the Homework activity for Topic B13.2 about examples of organisms that can reproduce both sexually and asexually. Create a list showing organisms that use both methods, and ask students to suggest why they do this.	**Extend:** Students should add organisms that only use sexual reproduction or only use asexual reproduction.	

Main	Support/Extend	Resources
Exploring plants and fungi (25 min) Students carry out a range of practical tasks looking at reproduction in plants and fungi. They carry out a flower dissection to identify and name the parts and explain their role in sexual reproduction. They also study a range of reproduction methods that plants and fungi use, including studying fungal spores (which needs to be studied in a subsequent lesson).		**Practical:** Exploring plants and fungi
Reproduction in malaria parasites (15 min) Provide students with an unlabelled diagram that shows the life cycle of the malaria parasite (Figure 4 in the student book). Ask them to discuss in pairs where the parasite is using asexual and sexual reproduction, and why it uses both methods. Then ask students to check their answers and add further information about the advantages and disadvantages of each method by referring to information in the student book.		

Plenary	Support/Extend	Resources
Sexual or asexual? (10 min) Read out some information about the reproduction of some unfamiliar organisms that use both asexual and sexual reproduction. Ask students to stand up if you are describing sexual reproduction and sit down if you are describing asexual reproduction.	**Extend:** Discuss why the organisms use both methods.	
Fruit and vegetables (5 min) Show students a variety of images of different fruit and vegetables (e.g., peas in a pod, potatoes, root ginger, strawberries, apples, courgettes). Ask them which are produced by sexual and which by asexual reproduction.	**Support:** Start by discussing which are fruit and which are vegetables. Fruits are always produced from sexual reproduction.	**Interactive:** Fruit and vegetables

Homework		
Breeding plants: Tell the class that a rose breeder is trying to create a new coloured flower by breeding together plants (selective breeding). Ask them to describe the steps the breeder should use to breed together the chosen plants.	**Extend:** Students should explain what is happening at each step in detail.	

kerboodle
A Kerboodle highlight for this lesson is **Bump up your grade: Reproduction**. Refer to the **Content map** on Kerboodle for a full list of resources and assessment.

B13.4 DNA and the genome

AQA spec link: 6.1.4 Students should be able to describe the structure of DNA and define genome. The genetic material in the nucleus of a cell is composed of a chemical called DNA. DNA is a polymer made up of two strands forming a double helix. The DNA is contained in structures called chromosomes.

A gene is a small section of DNA on a chromosome. Each gene codes for a particular sequence of amino acids, to make a specific protein.

The genome of an organism is the entire genetic material of that organism. The whole human genome has now been studied and this will have great importance for medicine in the future.

Students should be able to discuss the importance of understanding the human genome.

This is limited to the:

- search for genes linked to different types of disease
- understanding and treatment of inherited disorders
- use in tracing human migration patterns from the past.

WS 1.1, 1.4
MS 2h

Aiming for	Outcome	Checkpoint	
		Question	Activity
Aiming for GRADE 4 ↓	State that DNA contains a code to build proteins.		Starter 1, Starter 2
	Describe what the the Human Genome Project was.	1	Main
	Give one goal of the Human Genome Project.		Main
Aiming for GRADE 6 ↓	Describe the relationship between DNA, genes, and chromosomes.		Starter 1, Starter 2
	Describe some of the benefits of studying the human genome.	2	Main
	Explain why genome projects are costly and take a long time.		Main
Aiming for GRADE 8 ↓	Explain why the cost of genome sequencing has reduced since it was started.		Main, Plenary 2
	Explain why knowledge of the genomes of other species is useful.	2, 3	Main
	Discuss possible issues surrounding genome sequencing.		Main

Maths
Students use simple estimation to work out how long it would take to read out the entire human genome (1d)

Literacy
Students use information from the student book to write an argument for carrying out genome projects. They also research information on the Internet to create a video to explain the 100 000 genome project.

B13 Reproduction

Starter	Support/Extend	Resources
What do I know about DNA? (10 min) Ask students to work in pairs and write the word DNA in the middle of a sheet of paper. They should then write as much as they know about DNA around it. Ask each pair for one piece of information and collate the information from the whole class.	**Support:** Provide key words to help discussion – nucleus, genes, chromosomes. **Extend:** Ask students to link ideas to form a concept map.	
Order them (5 min) Ask students to place in size order – DNA, nucleus, genes, chromosomes, organism. Ask students to present their order to the class and allow others to comment.	**Support:** Give the class the order – DNA, genes, chromosome, nucleus, organism – and ask them to discuss why you have put them in this order.	

Main	Support/Extend	Resources
Why does the genome matter? (40 min) Tell the class that the Human Genome Project took 12 years and cost around $3 billion. Some people may view this as a waste of time and money. Ask students to use the information in the Student Book to write an argument outlining why the project was important. Ask students to work in small groups and discuss if they would have their genome sequenced and analysed. Tell them that this information could help doctors to work out their risk of developing certain diseases (e.g., cancer or heart disease and possibly prescribe personalised medicines. However, some people are concerned that in the future they could be asked to reveal this information in other situations (e.g., when applying for a job). Furthermore, there is a limit to how useful the information is at the moment. Ask them to discuss these and other issues, think about the advantages and disadvantages of genome sequencing, and come to a personal decision. Share these with the rest of the class.	**Support:** Provide groups with extra information on the pros and cons of genome sequencing.	**Activity:** Why does the genome matter?

Plenary	Support/Extend	Resources
The Human Genome Project (10 min) Students complete the interactive about what the Human Genome Project was and what it achieved.		**Interactive:** The Human Genome Project
Would you sequence your genome? (5 min) Explain that it now only takes a few days to sequence a genome and the technology is getting quicker and cheaper. Ask the students to discuss in groups whether they would want their genome sequenced.		

Homework		
Students complete the WebQuest to research the 100 000 genomes project. They should design an information video on the project to explain to people what it aims to do and why.	**Extend:** Students should discuss concerns including ethical issues.	

kerboodle

A Kerboodle highlight for this lesson is **Go further: The future of the human genome**. Refer to the **Content map** on Kerboodle for a full list of resources and assessment.

GCSE Biology only

B13.5 DNA structure and protein synthesis

AQA spec link: 6.1.5 Students should be able to describe DNA as a polymer made from four different nucleotides. Each nucleotide consists of a common sugar and phosphate group with one of four different bases attached to the sugar.

DNA contains four bases, A, C, G, and T.

A sequence of three bases is the code for a particular amino acid. The order of bases controls the order in which amino acids are assembled to produce a particular protein.

The long strands of DNA consist of alternating sugar and phosphate sections. Attached to each sugar is one of the fourbases.

The DNA polymer is made up of repeating nucleotide units.

(H) Students should be able to:
- recall a simple description of protein synthesis
- explain simply how the structure of DNA affects the protein made
- describe how genetic variants may influence phenotype: a) in coding DNA by altering the activity of a protein: and b) in non-coding DNA by altering how genes are expressed.

In the complementary strands a C is always linked to a G on the opposite strand and a T to an A.

Students are not expected to know or understand the structure of mRNA, tRNA, or the detailed structure of amino acids or proteins.

Students should be able to explain how a change in DNA structure may result in a change in the protein synthesised by a gene.

Proteins are synthesised on ribosomes, according to a template. Carrier molecules bring specific amino acids to add to the growing protein chain in the correct order.

When the protein chain is complete it folds up to form a unique shape. This unique shape enables the proteins to do their job as enzymes, hormones or forming structures in the body such as collagen.

WS 1.2
MS 1d

Aiming for	Outcome	Checkpoint	
		Question	Activity
Aiming for GRADE 4	Describe the structure of DNA.	1	Starter 1, Main, Plenary 1, Plenary 2, Homework
	State that groups of three nucleotides code for an amino acid.	1	Main, Plenary 1, Plenary 2, Homework
Aiming for GRADE 6	Describe how the four bases make up a code.	3	Main, Plenary 1, Plenary 2, Homework
	(H) Explain why the correct folding of a protein is important to its function.	2	Main
Aiming for GRADE 8	(H) Describe the steps involved in producing a protein inside the cell.	3	Main
	Discuss possible issues surrounding genome sequencing.		
	(H) Explain how the order of bases determines the type of protein made.	3	Main, Homework

Maths
Students use their understanding of orders of magnitude to put key terms from the lesson in size order. (2h)

Literacy
Students follow instructions to extract DNA from kiwi fruit. They discuss in pairs what they know about DNA.

Key words
bases, nucleotide

204

B13 Reproduction

Practical

Title	Extracting DNA from kiwi fruits
Equipment	water bath at 60 °C, access to a balance for weighing, 3 g of sodium chloride (table salt), 10 cm³ liquid detergent, distilled water (at least 150 cm³), plastic syringe, two 100 cm³ beakers, two 250 cm³ beakers, glass rod, knife, kiwifruit, pestle and mortar, stopwatch, glass funnel, filter paper, test tube, test-tube rack, small bottle of ice-cold ethanol, dyes
	The ethanol should be supplied to students in tightly-capped plastic bottles containing 50 cm³. These bottles can be kept in the fridge for at least two hours before they are needed. The bottles must be tightly capped to prevent vapour from the ethanol escaping.
Overview of method	Students prepare the extraction solution by mixing salt solution and detergent.
	They then mash up kiwi-fruit flesh and heat with the extraction solution before filtering. Ice-cold ethanol is poured into the filtrate and left to rest. The DNA precipitates out of the solution.
Safety considerations	Take care when handling ethanol (no naked flames)

Starter	Support/Extend	Resources
What do you already know? (10 min) Show students a model or an image of the DNA molecule. Ask if any of them can identify what it is, and if they know anything about it's structure. Create a mind map on the board or on a large piece of paper of what students already know. **Genome sequencing** (5 min) Ask students to read out the bases in one strand of a section of DNA 20 bases long. Then ask them to estimate how long it would take them to read out the entire human genome (3 billion base pairs).		

Main	Support/Extend	Resources
Extracting DNA from kiwi fruits (40 min) Formally introduce the structure of DNA and a nucleotide to all students. (H) Higher-tier students should also be introduced to the complimentary pairing of the A, T, C, and G bases. All students then complete a practical where they extract genetic material from kiwifruit. This could be done as a demonstration with students helping at each stage. (H) Whilst the mixture of kiwifruit and extraction solution is in the water bath, higher-tier students should be introduced to the synthesis of proteins. Students should the use the student book to produce a simple animation story board describing how a protein is produced within a cell.		**Practical:** Extracting DNA from kiwi fruits

Plenary	Support/Extend	Resources
What I now know (10 min) Revisit the mind map created at the beginning of the lesson. Ask students to correct any misconceptions, and then to add any information they have learnt this lesson. **DNA to protein** (10 min) Students fill in the gaps to complete a paragraph about how DNA and protein are connected.	**Extend:** Students should explain that one function is to alter the expression of genes.	**Interactive:** DNA to protein

Homework		
Students draw a diagram of DNA on an A4 piece of paper, and annotate it with their understanding from the lesson. (H) Higher-tier students could also finish their animation storyboard from the Main.	**Support:** Provide students with the key terms that students should use in their annotations.	

kerboodle
A Kerboodle highlight for this lesson is **Progress quiz: Reproduction 1**. Refer to the **Content map** on Kerboodle for a full list of resources and assessment.

GCSE Biology only — Higher tier

B13.6 Gene expression and mutation

AQA spec link: 6.1.5 Mutations occur continuously. Most do not alter the protein, or only alter it slightly so that its appearance or function is not changed.

A few mutations code for an altered protein with a different shape. An enzyme may no longer fit the substrate binding site or a structural protein may lose its strength.

Not all parts of DNA code for proteins. Non-coding parts of DNA can switch genes on and off, so variations in these areas of DNA may affect how genes are expressed.

WS 1.2
MS 1b, 1c

Aiming for	Outcome	Checkpoint	
		Question	Activity
Aiming for GRADE 6 ↓	Describe what a mutation is.		Main, Plenary 1
	Explain why the correct folding of a protein is important to its function.		Starter 2, Main
Aiming for GRADE 8 ↓	Outline the reasons why most mutations are harmless.	3	Main, Plenary 1
	Explain in detail how a mutation can affect the function of a protein.	3	Starter 2, Main, Plenary 1

Maths
Students calculate the percentage of DNA that is non-coding (1c) using standard form in their calculations (1b).

Literacy
Students use information from text, diagrams, and animation to create a storyboard to describe protein synthesis.

Key word
mutation

206

■ B13 Reproduction

Practical

Title	Make your own protein
Equipment	coloured beads, string, diagram of a strand of DNA with around 36 base pairs, table that shows the colour of bead coded for by different codons
Overview of method	Students work out the codons in the DNA strand. They choose which coloured beads to thread onto the string in order to build an amino acid chain. They then fold up the chain to form a protein.

Starter	Support/Extend	Resources
Missing bases (5 min) Students use the interactive to match complementary base pairs in DNA. **Enzyme function** (10 min) Tell students that human DNA contains 3 billion base pairs, but only around 45 million are coding. They work out the percentage of DNA that is non-coding, using standard form.	**Support:** Remind students that T pairs with A and G with C by using the sentence – Tigers Are Great Cats.	**Interactive:** Missing bases

Main	Support/Extend	Resources
Make your own protein (40 min) Provide students with a diagram of a strand of DNA with around 30 base pairs and a table that shows the colour of bead coded for by different codons (three bases that code for one amino acid). Students then use their DNA strand to build an amino acid chain. Tell them which amino acids form bonds with each other so they can fold the chain of beads into the correct shape. Now, make one change to a base in the DNA and ask them to build a new protein. They should explain whether it has affected the protein.	**Extend:** Students should explain why mutations often do not affect the function of a protein.	**Practical:** Make your own protein

Plenary	Support/Extend	Resources
Mutations in the movies (10 min) Show the class images of mutants from movies (e.g., Spiderman, X-Men) or a suitable clip from a movie. Discuss how this is different to what happens in real life, and why. **Non-coding DNA** (5 min) Tell the students that human DNA contains 3 billion base pairs but only 21 000 genes. Ask them to list possible functions for non-coding sections of DNA.	**Extend:** Students should explain that one function is to alter the expression of genes.	

Homework		
Ask students to find an example where a single mutation causes an illness or disorder.	**Extend:** Students should also find out where the mutation is located.	

kerboodle

A Kerboodle highlight for this lesson is **Go further: DNA at work**. Refer to the **Content map** on Kerboodle for a full list of resources and assessment.

B13.7 Inheritance in action

AQA spec link: 6.1.6 Students should be able to explain the terms:

- gamete
- chromosome
- gene
- allele
- dominant
- recessive
- homozygous
- heterozygous
- genotype
- phenotype.

Some characteristics are controlled by a single gene, such as: fur colour in mice; and pendulous or attached ear lobes in humans. Each gene may have different forms called alleles.

The alleles present, or genotype, operate at a molecular level to develop characteristics that can be expressed as a phenotype.

A dominant allele is always expressed, even if only one copy is present. A recessive allele is only expressed if two copies are present (therefore no dominant allele present).

If the two alleles present are the same the person is homozygous for that trait, but if the alleles are different they are heterozygous.

Most characteristics are a result of multiple genes interacting, rather than a single gene.

Students should be able to understand the concept of probability in predicting the results of a single gene cross, but recall that most phenotype features are the result of multiple genes rather than single gene inheritance.

Students should be able to use direct proportion and simple ratios to express the outcome of a genetic cross.

Students should be able to complete a Punnett square diagram and extract and interpret information from genetic crosses and family trees.

Students should be able to construct a genetic cross by Punnett square diagram and use it to make predictions using the theory of probability.

WS 1.2
MS 1c, 2c, 2e, 3a, 4a,

Aiming for	Outcome	Checkpoint	
		Question	Activity
Aiming for GRADE 4 ↓	Recognise examples of inherited traits.	2, End of chapter 6	Starter 1
	Recognise a genotype and a phenotype.		Main 2
	Use a simple diagram to state how offspring have inherited traits.		Main 1
Aiming for GRADE 6 ↓	Use the terms allele, dominant, recessive, homozygous, and heterozygous correctly.	1, End of chapter 6	Main 1, Plenary 2
	Describe a phenotype when given the genotype.		Main 1, Plenary 2
	ⓗ Use a Punnett square diagram to predict the outcome of a monohybrid cross using the theory of probability.	3	Main 1

B13 Reproduction

Aiming for GRADE 8	Use the terms homozygous and heterozygous correctly.	1	Main 1, Plenary 2
	Explain how the genotype affects the phenotype at a molecular level.		Plenary 1
	H Explain why Punnett squares cannot be used to work out possible genotypes in offspring for the majority of human traits.	4	Main 1

Maths
Introduce the idea of working out probabilities using percentages and ratios of offspring with different genotypes and phenotypes. (1c, 2e)

Literacy
Students use the student book to find out the meanings of new terminology. They also spot mistakes in a passage and correct them.

Key words
alleles, homozygous, heterozygous, genotype, phenotype, dominant, recessive

Starter	Support/Extend	Resources
Is it inherited? (5 min) Students use the interactive to sort a series of human traits according to whether they are inherited traits or not. **Mice inheritance** (10 min) Tell the class that two black mice have a litter of offspring. Some are brown. Ask them to discuss in pairs how they think this is possible. The answer will be revealed in Main 1.	**Support:** Tell the class that the gene for fur colour has two versions – black and brown.	**Interactive:** Is it inherited?

Main	Support/Extend	Resources
Explaining inheritance (20 min) Explain how two black mice could have brown offspring (referring back to Starter 2 if appropriate). Assign two alleles to the fur colour gene – dominant black (B) and recessive brown (b). Draw a simple genetic cross to show the possible genotypes and phenotypes of offspring from two heterozygous mice (Bb). As you introduce new terminology, ask students to write the words down. Then, ask them to write definitions using information from the student book. Set the class another example with parent mice of different genotypes for them to practise. **Inheritance card game** (20 min) Students play a card game using dominant and recessive cards for different snake characteristics – length, skin colour, skin pattern, eye shape. They pick cards at random to form offspring and draw the outcome.	**Extend:** Model using a Punnett square. **Extend:** Discuss that the majority of human traits are the result of multiple genes interacting. Ask students to explain why this means that Punnett squares cannot be used to show inheritance of these traits. **Support:** Demonstrate how to play the game first. **Extend:** Give students blank Punnett squares for them to attempt to use.	**Activity:** Inheritance card game

Plenary	Support/Extend	Resources
From genotype to phenotype (5 min) Ask students to create a flow chart to show how the homozygous genotype for black fur in mice (BB) affects the phenotype, using what they know about protein synthesis. **Using a Punnett square** (10 min) Use another example of simple inheritance and demonstrate how to use a Punnett square to work out genotypes and phenotypes of offspring. However, purposely make mistakes and use incorrect terminology. Ask students to shout out when you make a mistake and correct you.	**Extend:** This activity is suitable for more able students only.	

Homework		
Ask students to create a quiz from what they have learnt in the lesson, with ten questions and answers. Questions can be collated and used for revision at the end of the chapter.		

B13.8 More about genetics

AQA spec link: 6.1.8 Ordinary human body cells contain 23 pairs of chromosomes.

22 pairs control characteristics only, but one of the pairs carries the genes that determine sex.

- In females the sex chromosomes are the same (XX).
- In males the chromosomes are different (XY).

Students should to be able to carry out a genetic cross to show sex inheritance.

Students should understand and use direct proportion and simple ratios in genetic crosses.

MS 1c, 2c, 3a

Aiming for	Outcome	Checkpoint	
		Question	Activity
Aiming for GRADE 4 ↓	State that in females the sex chromosomes are XX and in males they are XY.		Starter 2, Main 2, Plenary 1
	Use a family tree to describe how people are related.		Main 3, Plenary 2, Homework
Aiming for GRADE 6 ↓	Carry out a genetic cross to show sex inheritance.	2	Main 2
	Use direct proportion and simple ratios to express the outcome of a genetic cross.	2	Main 1
Aiming for GRADE 8 ↓	Explain why you only get the expected ratios in a genetic cross if there are large numbers of offspring.	2	Main 1, Main 2
	Use a family tree to work out whether an individual is likely to be homozygous or heterozygous for particular alleles.	3	Main 3, Plenary 2, Homework

Maths
Students use direct proportion and ratio to express the outcome of genetic crosses. They record data in a tally table. (2c)

Literacy
Students are given a passage with some correct information about sex inheritance but also some errors. They spot the errors and add corrections.

Key word
sex chromosomes

B13 Reproduction

Starter	Support/Extend	Resources
Gender ratio (10 min) Tell the class the number of students in the school or number of babies born in the UK in a certain year and ask them to estimate the number of boys and girls. Reveal the answer and discuss that on average the ratio will be around 1:1. State that they will be able to explain why by the end of the lesson. **Sex chromosomes** (5 min) Ask students if they have heard of the terms XX chromosomes and XY chromosomes. Collate any existing knowledge students have.	**Extend:** Ask students to suggest why, in the 2011 census, there were more women (28.5 million) than men (27.6 million) registered in the UK.	

Main	Support/Extend	Resources
Proportion and ratio (15 min) Remind students about the genetic cross you used last lesson to show inheritance in two heterozygous mice. Ask students for the ratio of black to brown offspring (3:1). Ask them: if the mice had a litter of four offpsring would it mean that they would definitely have three black and one brown offspring? Discuss why this proportion becomes more apparent the more offspring the mice have. Use this as a springboard to discuss the idea of using proportion and ratio to express the outcome of genetic crosses.	**Support:** The Calculation sheet will help explain the maths. **Extend:** Use a Punnett square for the genetic cross. **Extend:** Students should draw a Punnett square to show the cross and explain why the ratio is 1:1.	**Calculation sheet:** Direct proportion and ratio
Sex determination (15 min) Show the class an image of human chromosomes from a man, in their pairs. Ask them to spot the pair that is different. Introduce this pair as the sex chromosomes. Prepare sets of sperm cards with either an X or a Y on the back, and egg cards all with an X on the back. Working in pairs, students choose pairs of cards at random and turn them over. They record the genotype and phenotype each time and record these in a tally table. They do this for five minutes. Discuss what their evidence shows about the ratio, and how it would change if they repeated this activity 1000 times.	**Extend:** Show the chromosomes from woman and ask students to compare how the sex chromosomes are different.	**Activity:** Sex determination
Family trees (10 min) Show students the tiger family tree from the student book (Figure 3). Ask students a series of questions designed to test their understanding of what it shows (e.g., Which are the youngest tigers? Which is the mother of the youngest tigers? What is the relationship between the tigers on the bottom row and the three on the middle row?).	**Extend:** Also ask questions to test understanding of how fur colour is inherited, for example, which allele (white or orange) do you think is recessive and why?	

Plenary	Support/Extend	Resources
Checking understanding (5 min) Students use the interactive to sort a series of statements about sex inheritance according to whether they are true or false. Students should then correct the false statements. **Colour vision deficiency** (0 min) Show students a family tree that shows the inheritance of colour vision deficiency. Students work in pairs to ask each other questions about what it shows. They should identify that it affects men more than women.	**Extend:** Students should make up their own passages to test a partner. **Support:** Supply suitable questions to each pair.	**Interactive:** Checking understanding

Homework		
Ask students to create a family tree for their family or a famous family using circles for women and squares for men. They should annotate it with the names of the people.	**Extend:** Students should choose a famous family where an inherited disorder or condition has been passed down (e.g., the inheritance of haemophilia in the Victorian royal family). They should annotate it with genotype and phenotypes.	

kerboodle

A Kerboodle highlight for this lesson is **Bump up your grade: Sex linkage**. Refer to the **Content map** on Kerboodle for a full list of resources and assessment.

B13.9 Inherited disorders

AQA spec links: 6.1.7 Some disorders are inherited. These disorders are caused by the inheritance of certain alleles.

- Polydactyly (having extra fingers or toes) is caused by a dominant allele.
- Cystic fibrosis (a disorder of cell membranes) is caused by a recessive allele.

6.2.4 Modern medical research is exploring the possibility of genetic modification to overcome some inherited disorders.

MS 2e

Aiming for	Outcome	Checkpoint	
		Question	Activity
Aiming for GRADE 4 ↓	Describe what is meant by an inherited disorder and recognise examples.		Starter 1, Main 1
	Use secondary sources of information to describe symptoms of an inherited disorder.		Main 1
Aiming for GRADE 6 ↓	Name examples of inherited disorders, such as cystic fibrosis and polydactyly.	1	Starter 1, Main 1, Plenary 2
	Use a genetic cross to explain how inherited disorders are passed on.	1, 2, 3, End of chapter 4	Starter 2, Plenary 1
Aiming for GRADE 8 ↓	Evaluate in detail the use of genetic engineering to cure inherited disorders.		Main 2
	Use a genetic cross to predict the probability of a child inheriting a genetic disorder.		Starter 2, Main 1, Plenary 1

Maths
Students use a genetic cross to make a prediction of the probability of a child inheriting a genetic disorder. (2e)

Literacy
Students use information from books and the Internet to prepare a presentation about inherited disorders. They present an answer to a question to the class.

Key words
polydactyly, cystic fibrosis, genetic engineering

B13 Reproduction

Starter	Support/Extend	Resources
Inherited disorders (5 min) Provide students with a list of disorders – some inherited and some not, for example, colour blindness, cystic fibrosis, sickle cell disease (inherited), anaemia, measles, malaria (not inherited). Ask them to discuss in pairs and categorise the disorders. **Inheritance of colour blindness** (10 min) Remind students of how the inheritance of colour blindness is linked to the XX and XY chromosomes of women and men. Ask students to draw a genetic cross diagram of a colour blind father and unaffected mother. Ask them to interpret their diagram. (Students should find that the parents cannot have an affected child, but could have carrier daughters.)	**Extend:** Use examples that could have an inherited link to promote discussion (e.g., cancer, asthma, heart disease).	

Main	Support/Extend	Resources
Disorder research (30 min) Discuss what is meant by an inherited disorder. Split the class into small groups and ask each to research and present information about the inherited disorders cystic fibrosis and polydactyly. Set students a series of questions that they need to find out about (e.g., how the condition is inherited, the symptoms, possible treatments). Allow them to use the Internet and/or books to find the answers and present them on a poster, presentation, or leaflet. Towards the end of the task set each group a different question that they need to answer to the rest of the class. They then present their answers whilst presenting their findings. **Genetic engineering** (10 min) Set pairs of students the question: How could genetic engineering help cure inherited disorders in the future? Ask them to use information from the student book to find the answer.	**Support:** Student groups could either research cystic fibrosis or polydactyly. **Support:** Provide suitable page numbers and/or webpages for research. **Extend:** Groups should also research how a mutation causes the disorder on a molecular basis. **Extend:** Students should first discuss how they think genetic engineering could help before looking it up.	**Activity:** Inherited disorders

Plenary	Support/Extend	Resources
Genetic disorders and inheritance (10 min) Set students an example of a past exam question on the inheritance of disorders. Provide the mark scheme for them to self-assess their answer. **Test your understanding** (5 min) Ask the class a series of quick questions on inherited disorders to check their understanding.	**Support:** Provide two questions and model how to answer the first one.	**Interactive:** Test your understanding

Homework		
Students choose an inherited disorder and write an information leaflet to educate people on the cause, symptoms, and possible treatments.	**Extend:** Encourage students to investigate how genetic engineering may be used in future treatments.	

kerboodle

A Kerboodle highlight for this lesson is **Working scientifically: Genetic engineering and inherited disorders**. Refer to the **Content map** on Kerboodle for a full list of resources and assessment.

B13.10 Screening for genetic disorders

AQA spec link: 6.1.7 Students should make informed judgements about the economic, social, and ethical issues concerning embryo screening, given appropriate information.

MS 2e

Aiming for	Outcome	Checkpoint	
		Question	Activity
Aiming for GRADE 4 ↓	Give a reason why embryos might be screened.		Starter 2, Main 1, Plenary 1
	Describe one concern about embryo screening.	3	Main 1
Aiming for GRADE 6 ↓	Outline the methods used to screen embryos.	1, 2	Main 2
	List advantages and disadvantages of embryo screening.	3	Main 1, Plenary 1
Aiming for GRADE 8 ↓	Explain how screening shows whether an embryo has a genetic disorder.		Main 2
	Make an informed judgement about embryo screening by evaluating in detail the economic, social, and ethical issues.	3	Main 1, Plenary 1

Maths
Throughout this lesson there are many opportunities for students to role play situations as parents or doctors advising parents on the probabilities of having children with an inherited disorder. (2e)

Literacy
Students use the student book to make notes on the two embryo screening techniques using the correct terminology and their scientific understanding.

■ B13 Reproduction

Starter	Support/Extend	Resources
Genetic disorder (10 min) Tell students to put themselves in the role of a parent who has a child with a serious genetic disorder and who wants to have another child. Ask them to discuss in pairs why this is a big decision for the parent. **Genetic screening for all?** (5 min) Tell the class that it is possible to test embryos to see if they have an inherited disorder before they are born. Ask students if they think all parents should be offered this test. They can vote by moving to different places in the classroom or by a show of hands. Ask some students to explain their opinion.	**Extend:** Tell students that the condition is recessive and that both the parent and their partner are both carriers.	

Main	Support/Extend	Resources
Making a decision (25 min) Ask students to use information from the student book to research the screening options for a couple who are both carriers of a recessive inherited condition and who want a healthy child. Ask students to write down the pros and cons of each screening option. **Screening techniques** (15 min) Ask students to make notes using the student book about the two embryo screening techniques amniocentesis and chorionic villus sampling, plus IVF with embryo screening. They should describe each process.	**Support:** Give students the two options – get pregnant naturally and have the embryo screened or use IVF and screen the embryos. **Extend:** Students should evaluate the economic, social, and ethical issues involved in each method. **Extend:** Students should also explain how genetic screening works.	**Activity:** Making a decision

Plenary	Support/Extend	Resources
What would you do? (10 min) Ask students to put themselves into the role of the parent in Starter 1. They should write what their decision would be, with reasons why. **Screening true or false?** (5 min) Students use the interactive to answer a series of true or false questions about screening for genetic disorders.	**Support:** Students could present their decision verbally.	**Interactive:** Screening true or false?

Homework		
Students use the information gathered in Main 2 to design a leaflet that could be used to inform people about embryo screening options, to include the reasons for screening, how each procedure is carried out, and the issues surrounding each option.		

kerboodle

A Kerboodle highlight for this lesson is **Homework: Inheritance**. Refer to the **Content map** on Kerboodle for a full list of resources and assessment.

B13 Reproduction

Overview of B13 Reproduction

This chapter on reproduction includes some content for students studying GCSE Biology only, as well as some higher-tier content. All students should be able to outline asexual and sexual reproduction, and should be aware of the importance of meiosis, fertilisation, and variation in sexual reproduction. They should link this with work on chromosomes and mitosis and the cell cycle in B2 *Cell division*. *AQA GCSE Biology* students should be able to compare the advantages of each type of reproduction.

AQA GCSE Biology students should recall that fungi, plants, and malaria parasites are able to use both types of reproduction. They should link this with work on the life cycle of the malarial protist in B5.8 *Diseases caused by fungi and protists*.

All students have studied DNA and its role in inheritance. They should be aware of the genetic code and genomes, including how the data produced by genome research can be used. *AQA GCSE Biology* students should be able to outline DNA structure, with higher-tier students recalling the detailed structure of DNA and also studying protein synthesis, including how the genetic code is used to assemble amino acids into proteins. Another higher-tier *AQA GCSE Biology* topic is different types of mutation and their consequences.

All students have studied inheritance, and should be able to use genetic terms and set out a genetic cross with the use of a Punnett square. They should be able to predict ratios of different phenotypes, and apply this to sex determination and family trees. Students should be able to describe the inheritance of genetic disorders as applied to polydactyly and cystic fibrosis. They should be aware of developments in genetic engineering with the aim of curing genetic disorders.

Finally students should be able to discuss screening for genetic disorders and the implications of using this technology. This links in with the *AQA GCSE Biology* topic of monoclonal antibodies in B6 *Preventing and treating disease*.

MyMaths

You can find additional support for the maths skills covered in this chapter on **MyMaths**, including working with chromosome numbers, probability calculations, estimates, and percentages.

kerboodle

For this chapter, the following assessments are available on Kerboodle:

B13 Checkpoint quiz: Reproduction
B13 Progress quiz: Reproduction 1
B13 Progress quiz: Reproduction 2
B13 On your marks: Reproduction
B13 Exam-style questions and mark scheme: Reproduction

Checkpoint follow-up lesson

A student's route through this lesson can be determined using the Checkpoint assessment. Percentage pass marks are supplied in the Checkpoint teacher notes.

For each successive route through it is assumed that the student can perform to their current route as well as previous routes. For example, students working at Aiming for 6 are assumed to be secure in Aiming for 4 knowledge and understanding and working towards achieving all the learning outcomes for Aiming for 6.

	Aiming for 4	**Aiming for 6**	**Aiming for 8**
Learning outcomes	State the advantages and disadvantages of asexual and sexual reproduction.	Describe the advantages and disadvantages of asexual and sexual reproduction.	Explain the advantages and disadvantages of asexual and sexual reproduction.
	State what occurs during the process of meiosis.	Describe what occurs during the process of meiosis.	Explain what occurs during the process of meiosis.
	Describe the structure of DNA.	Describe how the structure of DNA is important for protein synthesis.	Describe the steps involved in protein synthesis.
Starter	**Asexual or sexual? (5 min)** Show images of various organisms, such as fungi, strawberry plants, mammals. Suitable images are readily available on the Internet. Ask if each organism reproduces asexually, sexually, or both.		
Differentiated checkpoint activity	Students work in small groups moving around five stations, spending around 10 minutes at each station. You will need to move students on to the next station at the appropriate time. You will need: • station 1 – student books, scissors, and glue sticks for Aiming for 4 students • station 2 – pictures of various stages of meiosis (these will need to be prepared in advance), and scissors and glue sticks for Aiming for 4 students • station 3 – pink and white marshmallows, jelly babies, and cocktail sticks • station 4 – student books, and Internet access for Aiming for 4 students • station 5 – student books for Aiming for 4 students.		
	The Aiming for 4 sheet is highly structured and involves cut and paste exercises and structured questions.	The Aiming for 6 sheet is fairly structured. Students write lists and flowcharts in their books, and draw a genetic diagram using a Punnett square template.	The Aiming for 8 sheet has very little structure. Students write lists and flowcharts in their books, including explanations, and carry out a genetic cross without prompts.
	Kerboodle resource B13 Checkpoint follow-up: Aiming for 4, B13 Checkpoint follow-up: Aiming for 6, B13 Checkpoint follow-up: Aiming for 8		
Plenary	**Genetic diseases (5 min)** In pairs, students write down the names of as many genetic diseases as they can think of. Aiming for 6 and Aiming for 8 students could also say whether they are caused by a fault on the dominant allele or the recessive allele.		
Progression	Students ork towards answering questions in a non-human context, naming plant gametes as well as human gametes, as well as recalling that chromosome numbers are different in different organisms.	Students ork towards being able to carry out a genetic cross to show sex inheritance, and understanding and using direct proportion and simple ratios in genetic crosses. A good research task is to find out more about what the human genome project has revealed. For issues surrounding the screening of embryos, a class debate would challenge all abilities.	Students ork towards constructing a genetic cross by a Punnett square diagram and use it to make predictions using the theory of probability. Students could be extended by looking at mitosis and meiosis together and seeing at which stages of a life cycle each is involved. The topic of mutations and their effect on the function of the protein coded for is conceptually demanding and students may benefit from looking at some real examples of codes and proteins so that they can practise using the code and learning the consequences of some mutations.

B 14 Variation and evolution
14.1 Variation

AQA spec link: 6.2.1 Students should be able to describe simply how the genome and its interaction with the environment influence the development of the phenotype of an organism. Differences in the characteristics of individuals in a population is called variation and may be due to differences in:

- the genes they have inherited (genetic causes)
- the conditions in which they have developed (environmental causes)
- a combination of genes and the environment.

Aiming for	Outcome	Checkpoint	
		Question	Activity
Aiming for GRADE 4 ↓	List some examples of human variation.		Starter 2
	Categorise some human traits as being due to genetic causes, environmental causes, or both.		Starter 2, Main 1, Plenary
	Describe why identical twins share the same genes.		Starter 1
Aiming for GRADE 6 ↓	List some examples of variation in plants and categorise these as being due to genetic causes, environmental causes, or both.		Main 1, Plenary
	Suggest reasons why identical twins will start to show variation as they get older.	End of chapter 4	Starter 1, Main 2
	Use data to explain why studying identical twins helps scientists investigate which traits have genetic causes.	2, End of chapter 4	Main 2, Homework
Aiming for GRADE 8 ↓	Explain why some traits are only due to genetic causes.		Main 1
	Explain why it is so hard to get valid results from identical-twin studies.	2	Main 2
	Discuss some of the issues scientists face when conducting twin studies.	2	Main 2, Homework

Maths
Students analyse data from twin studies.

Literacy
Students write a list of examples of human variation and then use information from the student book to categorise the causes of each example.

B14 Variation and evolution

Starter	Support/Extend	Resources
Twins (10 min) Show the class images of identical twin babies. Ask students to write down a scientific explanation as to why they look identical. Discuss the fact that identical twins are genetically identical to each other and were formed when a fertilised egg split in half. Ask students to explain why the twins will not look exactly identical as they get older (due to environmental changes).	**Support:** Provide key words to use – egg, sperm, fertilisation, split, genes, traits. **Extend:** Students should also explain why non-identical twins look similar but not identical.	
Human variation (5 min) Ask the students to write down a list of variations in humans. They should think about both traits that can be seen and those that can't. Allow pairs or small groups to discuss their answers so that all students have a list of at least 10 examples.	**Support:** Start by giving the class some examples (e.g., hair colour, height, blood group).	

Main	Support/Extend	Resources
What causes variation? (15 min) Use Starter 2 here if not already used. Students use information from the student book on inherited and environmental causes of variation to categorise the causes of each example of human variation in the list generated in Starter 2. Ask students to repeat the activity using variation in plants.	**Extend:** Students should be able to link knowledge of inheritance to explaining why some traits (e.g., blood group) are only due to inheritance.	
Twin studies (25 min) Tell students to imagine that identical twins are each adopted by different families. They meet up 25 years later. Ask students to discuss in small groups how similar they think the twins would be and why, giving specific examples of traits. After hearing their thoughts, direct students to the student book. They should work alone to study Table 1 and write down conclusions from the data.	**Extend:** Groups should consider why these types of studies are rare (very few twins are raised apart). **Extend:** Ask students why the most valid data results from studies where the twins were separated at birth. They list reasons why.	**Working scientifically:** Twin studies

Plenary	Support/Extend	Resources
Inherited or environmental? (10 min) Give students a range of examples of human traits – some inherited, some environmental, and some due to both. Ask them to categorise the examples.		**Interactive:** Inherited or environmental?
Effects of the environment (5 min) State one example of a lifestyle choice that a person can make (e.g., living in a hot country, smoking, eating fatty food, working hard at school). Choose students to name one example of variation that might be affected by each choice.	**Extend:** Use examples for plants (e.g., wet weather might cause a plant to grow taller).	

Homework		
Ask students to research the work of scientist Thomas Bouchard and write down a bullet-pointed list of his findings.	**Extend:** Students should explain why studies like this cannot be carried out any more.	

kerboodle

A Kerboodle highlight for this lesson is **Bump up your grade: Identifying causes of variation**. Refer to the **Content map** on Kerboodle for a full list of resources and assessment.

B14.2 Evolution by natural selection

AQA spec links: 6.2.1 Students should be able to:

- state that there is usually extensive genetic variation within a population of a species
- recall that all variants arise from mutations and that most have no effect on the phenotype; some influence phenotype; very few determine phenotype.

Mutations are continuous changes in the DNA code. Very rarely a mutation will lead to a new phenotype. If the new phenotype is suited to an environmental change it can lead to a relatively rapid change in the species.

6.2.2 Students should be able to describe evolution as a change in the inherited characteristics of a population over time through a process of natural selection which may result in the formation of a new species.

The theory of evolution by natural selection states that all species of living things have evolved from simple life forms that first developed more than three billion years ago.

Students should be able to explain how evolution occurs through natural selection of variants that give rise to phenotypes best suited to their environment.

If two populations of one species become so different in phenotype that they can no longer interbreed to produce fertile offspring they have formed two new species.

MS 4a

Aiming for	Outcome	Checkpoint	
		Question	Activity
Aiming for GRADE 4	Describe a mutation as a change in the DNA code.	2	Starter 1
	Describe the theory of evolution by natural selection as a process by which living things have evolved from simple life forms.		Main 2, Plenary 1
	State some useful adaptations.	1	Starter 2
Aiming for GRADE 6	Explain how a mutation may lead to a new phenotype.	2	Starter 1
	Describe the steps that take place during evolution by natural selection.	2	Main 1, Main 2, Plenary 1, Plenary 2
	Analyse data from an activity modelling natural selection.		Main 1
Aiming for GRADE 8	Explain why it is rare that a mutation leads to a new phenotype.		Starter 1
	Apply the theory of evolution by natural selection to suggest how a specific organism evolved.	3	Main 2
	Explain how a change in a model can make it useful for explaining something else.		Main 1

Maths
Students can calculate how the numbers of each coloured circle changed during the practical activity. This can be displayed as a results table and bar charts. (4a)

Literacy
Students read through the stages of natural selection from the student book. They then use this information to create an explanation of how an organism has evolved.

Key words
mutation, natural selection

220

B14 Variation and evolution

Practical

Title	Modelling natural selection
Equipment	A4 piece of brightly coloured wrapping paper, circles of paper of a range of different colours (these can be made using a hole-punch), tweezers, Petri dish, stopwatch.
Overview of method	Students work in pairs with one student acting as the referee and the other as the predator. Without the predator looking, the referee should arrange small circles of coloured paper on a piece of patterned wrapping paper. The predator then picks up as many circles as they can in 20 seconds using tweezers. For each of the remaining circles two more of that colour are added, and the process is repeated a further two times. The pair discusses what has happened to the colour of the population, and why.

Starter	Support/Extend	Resources
Albinism (5 min) Show the class a range of albino animals. Tell them that albinism is due to a mutation. Ask students to suggest whether this mutation is an advantage or a disadvantage, and explain why they think this. **Adaptations** (10 min) Ask students to list the adaptations that result in the lion being such a successful predator. Listen to their suggestions and ask them what would happen to a lion cub born without these adaptations.	**Support:** Remind students that a mutation is a change in the DNA code. **Extend:** Students should suggest how a mutation could result in albinism. **Extend:** Students should also explain why a mutation rarely results in a change in phenotype.	

Main	Support/Extend	Resources
Modelling natural selection (20 min) Students play a game to model natural selection. After the game, question students about how they think this relates to real life. Discuss why there is variation in a population, and why this means some organisms are better adapted then others. What happens to the organisms that are poorly adapted? Why does the number of the best-adapted organisms increase? **Real-life examples** (20 min) Introduce evolution as a process by which living things change over time, and natural selection as a theory that explains how this happens. Ask students to read through the stages of natural selection in the Student Book. They then use this to create an explanation of how a mouse evolved to have very good hearing, or how a cheetah evolved to be fast.	**Extend:** Ask students what would happen to their final population if the type of wrapping paper they used changed. Use this as a model of what happens when there is a sudden change to the environment. **Support:** Provide the stages as a storyboard and ask students to draw pictures to show what is happening at each stage.	**Practical:** Modelling natural selection

Plenary	Support/Extend	Resources
Describing natural selection (5 min) Students use the interactive to complete a description of the process of natural selection by filling in the gaps. **Evolution** (10 min) Set students a past exam question on natural selection to complete. Provide the mark scheme to self-assess.	**Support:** Provide the words but in the wrong order.	**Interactive:** Describing natural selection

Homework		
Set the class a series of ramped questions on natural selection for them to complete.		

kerboodle

A Kerboodle highlight for this lesson is **Extension sheet: Antibiotic resistant bacteria**. Refer to the **Content map** on Kerboodle for a full list of resources and assessment.

B14.3 Selective breeding

AQA spec link: 6.2.3 Students should be able to explain the impact of selective breeding of food plants and domesticated animals. Selective breeding (artificial selection) is the process by which humans breed plants and animals for particular genetic characteristics.

Humans have been doing this for thousands of years since they first bred food crops from wild plants and domesticated animals.

Selective breeding involves choosing parents with the desired characteristic from a mixed population. They are bred together. From the offspring those with the desired characteristic are bred together. This continues over many generations until all the offspring show the desired characteristic.

The characteristic can be chosen for usefulness or appearance:

- Disease resistance in food crops.
- Animals which produce more meat or milk.
- Domestic dogs with a gentle nature.
- Large or unusual flowers.

Selective breeding can lead to 'inbreeding' where some breeds are particularly prone to disease or inherited defects.

MS 2g

Aiming for	Outcome	Checkpoint	
		Question	Activity
Aiming for GRADE 4	Describe selective breeding as a process where humans choose which plants or animals to breed together.	1	Main
	Give one example where selective breeding has been used.	1	Starter 1, Starter 2, Main, Homework
	Choose organisms to breed together to result in desired traits in the offspring.		Main
Aiming for GRADE 6	Explain the process of selective breeding.		Main
	Explain why humans have used selective breeding.	1, 2	Starter 2, Main, Plenary 1, Homework
	Explain what inbreeding is, and why it is a problem in dog breeding.	3	Main
Band C to D GRADE 8	Compare and contrast natural and artificial selection.		Plenary 2
	Explain in detail how the variation of alleles in a population is reduced through selective breeding.	2	Starter 2, Main
	Explain in detail why the reduction of variation in a population through selective breeding is a problem.	2	Starter 2, Main, Homework

Maths
Students use data about milk yields and fat percentage in milk to choose cattle to breed. (2g)

Literacy
Students work in groups and research the selective breeding of dogs. They produce an item for a TV show and present it to the rest of the class.

Key word
selective breeding

B14 Variation and evolution

Starter	Support/Extend	Resources
Dog breeds (5 min) Show students an image of different dog breeds. Explain that they are all one species because they can breed with each other to produce fertile offspring. Choose examples and ask students to suggest how the features of that breed make it useful for specific tasks, for example, greyhound is fast so it is good for racing, mastiff is large so it makes a good guard dog.		
Then and now (10 min) Show the class images of ancient and modern wheat. Ask them to list the similarities and differences. Tell the class that over the thousands of years that people have been farming they have kept seeds from the best wheat plants to grow the following year. Introduce this as an example of selective breeding.	**Extend:** Students should suggest why this practice has reduced the variation in wheat, and why this is a problem. You could discuss why ancient wheat seeds are being collected and stored in seed banks.	

Main	Support/Extend	Resources
Developing dog breeds (40 min) Use Starter 1 now if not used already. Tell students that all modern dogs are descended from one species – the wolf. Students work in groups to research and develop an item for a TV programme about the selective breeding of dogs. They should explain to a general audience how people used selective breeding to make all the modern dog breeds, and also discuss the problems inbreeding has caused some breeds. They can choose which breeds to focus on and produce an engaging verbal or computer presentation to present to the rest of the class.	**Support:** Focus on one breed of dog that has obvious advantageous features (e.g., greyhound or husky).	**Activity:** Developing dog breeds

Plenary	Support/Extend	Resources
Wolf to greyhound (10 min) Students use the interactive to order a set of sentences so they describe how people developed greyhounds from wolves by selective breeding.	**Support:** Provide students with the stages in the wrong order for them to sort.	**Interactive:** Wolf to greyhound
Artificial selection (5 min) Tell the class that selective breeding is also called artificial selection. Ask them to suggest why.	**Extend:** Ask students to compare and contrast natural and artificial selection.	

Homework		
Ask students to research one more example of selective breeding. They should explain how and why it has been done.	**Extend:** Students should also evaluate the benefits and drawbacks of selective breeding in this species.	

kerboodle

A Kerboodle highlight for this lesson is **Bump up your grade: Selective breeding techniques**. Refer to the **Content map** on Kerboodle for a full list of resources and assessment.

B14.4 Genetic engineering

AQA spec link: 6.2.4 Students should be able to describe genetic engineering as a process which involves modifying the genome of an organism by introducing a gene from another organism to give a desired characteristic.

Plant crops have been genetically engineered to be resistant to diseases or to produce bigger better fruits.

Bacterial cells have been genetically engineered to produce useful substances such as human insulin to treat diabetes.

Students should be able to explain the potential benefits and risks of genetic engineering in agriculture and in medicine and that some people have objections.

In genetic engineering, genes from the chromosomes of humans and other organisms can be 'cut out' and transferred to cells of other organisms.

Crops that have had their genes modified in this way are called genetically modified (GM) crops. GM crops include ones that are resistant to insect attack or to herbicides. GM crops generally show increased yields.

Concerns about GM crops include the effect on populations of wild flowers and insects. Some people feel the effects of eating GM crops on human health have not been fully explored.

Modern medical research is exploring the possibility of genetic modification to overcome some inherited disorders.

Ⓗ Students should be able to describe the main steps in the process of genetic engineering.

In genetic engineering:
- enzymes are used to isolate the required gene; this gene is inserted into a vector, usually a bacterial plasmid or a virus
- the vector is used to insert the gene into the required cells
- genes are transferred to the cells of animals, plants, or microorganisms at an early stage (egg or embryo) in their development so that they develop with desired characteristics.

Aiming for	Outcome	Checkpoint	
		Question	Activity
Aiming for GRADE 4 ↓	Describe GM organisms as containing a gene from another organism, and order the stages of genetic engineering.	End of chapter 5	Main 1, Main 2
	Give examples of GM organisms and describe why they are useful to humans.	1, 2, End of chapter 3	Starter 2, Main 1, Main 2, Plenary 1
Aiming for GRADE 6 ↓	Describe the steps used in genetic engineering to produce GM organisms.	3, End of chapter 3	Starter 2, Main 2
	Analyse data to describe why growing GM crops may be beneficial to a farmer.		Main 1
Aiming for GRADE 8 ↓	Explain the process of genetic engineering using technical vocabulary (e.g., plasmid, vector, restriction enzymes, marker genes, recombinant DNA).		Main 2
	Explain how genetic engineering could be used to cure people with inherited disorders, and discuss the limitations.	1	Plenary 2

■ B14 Variation and evolution

Maths
Students analyse data about the yields of GM crops compared with normal crops and write conclusions.

Literacy
Students use a diagram to explain how genetic engineering is carried out. They write a letter to a farmer explaining what data about GM crops shows.

Starter	Support/Extend	Resources
GM opinion (5 min) Show the class an image showing a food that contains GM ingredients. Ask them for their immediate thoughts and feelings – would you eat it, and why? **Glow-in-the-dark mouse** (10 min) Show an image of the genetically modified fluorescent mouse. Ask students to discuss in small groups how they think the mouse could have been produced. Explain that the mouse's genome now contains the gene for a glowing protein from a jellyfish.	**Support:** Ask students if they know what GM means. **Extend:** After revealing the science, ask students to write down how the inserted gene results in the mouse glowing.	

Main	Support/Extend	Resources
Genetic engineering (40 min) Explain what is meant by genetic engineering. Ask students to use information from the student book to write a list of examples of genetically engineered organisms. Discuss as a class why scientists have produced GM organisms. Provide students with data that show how crop yields of GM corn and normal corn compare. Ask them to analyse the data and write a letter to a farmer explaining what it shows, and whether they would recommend growing it. Introduce another function of genetic engineering, such as making GM bacteria that produce human insulin. Provide students with an unlabelled diagram showing the principles of genetic engineering and ask them to go through the diagram as a pair, working out between them how the process is carried out. Allow them to use a labelled diagram to check their understanding. Then ask them to write down the stages of how GM corn is produced.	**Support:** Model how to analyse one graph with the class. **Extend:** Students should be aware that there are other issues surrounding the growing of GM crops. These will be covered in Topic B14.7. **Support:** Provide pairs with cards of the stages in the genetic engineering of GM corn, and get them to put them into the correct order. **Extend:** Use a simulation or animation to show the process. **Extend:** Students should complete the Go further activity that looks at genetic engineering in more detail.	**Activity:** Genetic engineering

Plenary	Support/Extend	Resources
Advantages and disadvantages (5 min) Use the interactive where students sort a series of statements, which are either advantages or disadvantages of genetic engineering, by dragging and dropping the statements into one of two boxes. **Genetic engineering for people** (10 min) Remind students that genetic engineering could be used to help cure inherited disorders such as cystic fibrosis. Ask students to suggest how this could be done.	**Extend:** Students should also explain how this will help the farmer. **Support:** Students can read the information from the student book before discussing. **Extend:** Discuss the limitations of this technique.	**Interactive:** Advantages and disadvantages

Homework		
Ask students to do some research into issues surrounding GM crops and find a news article or webpage that is stating an argument for or against GM. They should write bullet points outlining what it says.	**Support:** Point students to suitable webpages (e.g., Monsanto – pro-GM, or Greenpeace anti-GM).	

kerboodle

A Kerboodle highlight for this lesson is **Literacy sheet: GM crops**. Refer to the **Content map** on Kerboodle for a full list of resources and assessment.

GCSE Biology only

B14.5 Cloning

AQA spec link: 6.2.5 Tissue culture: using small groups of cells from part of a plant to grow identical new plants. This is important for preserving rare plant species or commercially in nurseries.

Cuttings: an older, but simple, method used by gardeners to produce many identical new plants from a parent plant.

Embryo transplants: splitting apart cells from a developing animal embryo before they become specialised, then transplanting the identical embryos into host mothers...

MS 2b

Aiming for	Outcome	Checkpoint	
		Question	Activity
Aiming for GRADE 4 ↓	Describe how to take stem and leaf cuttings of plants.		Main 1
	Define the term clone, and use a diagram to describe why embryo transplants are clones.		Main 2, Plenary 1
Aiming for GRADE 6 ↓	Describe the benefits for plant growers of reproduction using cuttings or tissue culture rather than seeds.	End of chapter 1	Main 1, Plenary 2
	Describe how embryo transplants are undertaken, and why they produce clones.	2, End of chapter 1	Main 2
Securnig GRADE 8 ↓	Explain the benefits of embryo transplants over sexual reproduction for farmers.	2	Main 2, Plenary 2
	Compare and contrast tissue culture in plants and embryo transplantation in animals.	2, 3, End of chapter 1	Main 2

Maths
Students could measure the length of the roots of their cuttings after 4–6 weeks of growth and calculate an average. (2b)

Literacy
Students design a leaflet aimed at horse breeders advertising embryo transplantation.

Key word
tissue culture

Practical

Title	Stem and leaf cuttings
Equipment	two plastic plant pots 9 cm in diameter, polythene bags and elastic bands or access to a propagator, compost, geranium or zonal pelargonium plant with several shoots, African violet plant with healthy leaves, scalpel, dibber labels
Overview of method	Students take shoots from a geranium plant and place the cuttings in compost. They also make leaf cuttings from an African violet plant. Both pots are placed in a propagator or on a windowsill and left for 4–6 weeks for roots to develop.
Safety considerations	Take care when handling compost. Wash hands after handling compost (or wear disposable gloves). Take care when using scalpels.

■ B14 Variation and evolution

Starter	Support/Extend	Resources
Using cloning (10 min) Briefly remind students what cloning is. Ask students to suggest some possible uses of cloning. Encourage them to think about uses of both plant and animal cloning. **Identical twins** (5 min) Tell the class that identical twins are clones. Ask students to discuss in pairs what this means.		

Main	Support/Extend	Resources
Stem and leaf cuttings (20 min) Introduce cuttings as a way of cloning plants using asexual reproduction. Students take leaf and stem cuttings from plants. They can take photographs of the cuttings before they are placed in the soil, and then after a period of 4–6 weeks to show any root development. Set a series of questions based on the experiment, testing understanding of the purpose of each step and the advantages of growing plants using cuttings compared with seeds. Remind students about tissue culture as another method of cloning plants (used in Topic B2.2). Ask them to look at the pros and cons of each method and compare them.	**Support:** Demonstrate how to take the cuttings before students carry it out.	**Practical:** Stem and leaf cuttings
Embryo transplants (20 min) Tell the class that they are horse breeders. They have an excellent racehorse that has won them lots of money, and it would be ideal if they could produce more horses like her. Ask students to discuss in pairs what they would do. Listen to their suggestions. They then read through the information from the student book about cloning animals. Ask them to describe how they would use this technique and why each of the embryos produced would be a clone. Then, students put themselves in the role of a company that carries out embryo transplantation. They should write a leaflet aimed at horse breeders explaining how the technique works, and why they should consider using it.	**Support:** Provide students with a template for the leaflet that includes space and instructions for each section. **Extend:** Students should compare and contrast tissue culture in plants and embryo transplantation in animals **Extend:** Allow students to use the Internet and supply the URL of a suitable company's website to gather more information.	

Plenary	Support/Extend	Resources
Key meanings (10 min) Students use the interactive to match definitions and key words from the topic (e.g., tissue culture, cuttings, embryo transplants, cloning).		**Interactive:** Key meanings
Cloning advantages (5 min) Ask each student to write down at least three advantages of cloning plants and animals over using sexual reproduction.	**Support:** Provide advantages and disadvantages and ask them to categorise them.	

Homework		
Students should complete their leaflets on embryo transplants.		

GCSE Biology only

B14.6 Adult cell cloning

AQA spec link: 6.2.5 Adult cell cloning:

- The nucleus is removed from an unfertilised egg cell.
- The nucleus from an adult body cell, such as a skin cell, is inserted into the egg cell.
- An electric shock stimulates the egg cell to divide to form an embryo.
- These embryo cells contain the same genetic information as the adult skin cell.
- When the embryo has developed into a ball of cells, it is inserted into the womb of an adult female to continue its development.

Aiming for	Outcome	Checkpoint	
		Question	Activity
Aiming for GRADE 4 ↓	Describe adult cell cloning as producing a complete clone of an adult animal.		Starter 1, Main 1, Plenary 1
	Describe the process of adult cell cloning using a diagram.	End of chapter 2	Main 1, Plenary 2
	Give one reason why scientists may want to clone an adult animal.		Main 2, Homework
Aiming for GRADE 6 ↓	Explain why the animal produced using adult cell cloning is a clone.		Main 1
	Design a flow chart to describe the process of adult cell cloning.	1	Main 1, Plenary 2
	List some benefits and drawbacks of adult cell cloning.	3, End of chapter 2	Main 2
Aiming for GRADE 8 ↓	Use advanced terminology to explain the process of adult cell cloning.		Main 1
	Compare and contrast the processes of adult cell and embryo cloning.	2	Plenary 2
	Evaluate the possible uses of adult cell cloning.	3	Main 2

Maths
Students can find out how much it costs to clone an animal.

Literacy
Students use information from the student book to produce a flow chart. They use information from a range of sources to find out about possible future uses of adult cell cloning, and discuss their opinions in groups.

Key word
adult cell cloning

B14 Variation and evolution

Starter	Support/Extend	Resources
Dolly (5 min) Ask if any students have heard of Dolly the sheep. Share a video or news article from 1997 when Dolly's birth was announced. **Cloning animals** (10 min) Ask students to recap the process of embryo cloning in one sentence. The ask students to recap the process of plant cutting in on sentence.		

Main	Support/Extend	Resources
How to clone an animal (15 min) Give students a diagram showing the process of adult cell cloning (Figure 2 in the student book). Ask them to study the diagram and then explain to a partner how the process is carried out. Allow them to use information from the student book to design a flow chart to show how adult clones are produced. They should then explain why the baby that is born is a clone.	**Extend:** Students should use the terms somatic cell, surrogate mother, enucleation, and mitosis in their description. Define these words for them.	
Future uses? (25 min) Split the class into groups and give each group one possible future use of adult cell cloning. For example, bringing back extinct animals, cloning cows/sheep that produce useful substances in their milk, cloning dead pets, or cloning humans. Provide students with information on each potential use (or direct them to suitable webpages) and ask them to discuss whether they think it is a good idea or not. Ask groups to present their thoughts and then ask the class to stand in continuum lines to show how they feel about each use of cloning (with one end of the line being 'not acceptable' and the other end 'good idea').	**Support:** Students could just use information from the student book. **Extend:** Students should use information from the presentations to list the benefits and drawbacks of adult cell cloning.	**Working scientifically:** Future uses of adult cell cloning

Plenary	Support/Extend	Resources
Cloning words (10 min) Write a list of words associated with cloning on the board, but leave out the vowels (e.g., CLNNG, NCLS, GNS, SRRGT, MBRY – CLONING, NUCLEUS, GENES, SURROGATE, EMBRYO). Ask students to write out the words.	**Support:** Indicate where the vowels should go by using dashes. **Extend:** Students should write a definition of each word and explain how it is linked to adult cell cloning.	
Order the process (5 min) Students use the interactive to arrange the stages of adult cell cloning into the correct order.	**Extend:** Students should compare and contrast the processes of adult and embryo cloning.	**Interactive:** Order the process

Homework		
Students can find out about the plot of the film *Jurassic World* and suggest how scientists could have cloned dinosaurs.	**Extend:** In the film a genetically engineered dinosaur is produced. Students should also explain how this could be done.	

kerboodle

A Kerboodle highlight for this lesson is **Literacy sheet: Advantages and disadvantages of adult cell cloning**. Refer to the **Content map** on Kerboodle for a full list of resources and assessment.

B14.7 Ethics of genetic technologies

AQA spec links: 6.2.4 Students should be able to explain the potential benefits and risks of genetic engineering in agriculture and in medicine and that some people have objections.

Concerns about GM crops include the effect on populations of wild flowers and insects. Some people feel the effects of eating GM crops on human health have not been fully explored.

MS 1c

Aiming for	Outcome	Checkpoint	
		Question	Activity
Aiming for GRADE 4 ↓	Give one concern people may have about growing GM crops.	2, End of chapter 5	Starter 2, Main 2, Plenary 2
	Describe why some people are against the cloning of animals.	2	Starter 2, Main 1, Plenary 2
Aiming for GRADE 6 ↓	Outline the potential benefits and risks of genetic engineering.	1	Starter 2, Main 2
	Describe economic and ethical concerns that people may have about cloning animals.	2	Starter 2, Main 1
Aiming for GRADE 8 ↓	Evaluate the potential benefits and risks of genetic engineering.	2	Main 2
	Explain in detail the significance of events in the field of genetics.	1, 2	Homework

Maths
Students use facts that include figures to present data against the use of adult cell cloning. They can calculate percentage success rates (1c).

Literacy
Students write a balanced article about genetic engineering and peer assess each other's work.

■ B14 Variation and evolution

Starter	Support/Extend	Resources
Definitions (5 min) Ask students to work in pairs. One student should define genetic engineering and the other should define cloning. Ask them to read out their definitions to each other and suggest changes until they are happy with their definitions. **Black and white** (10 min) Read out the following statement to the class: Some people agree with genetic engineering and cloning and some people do not. Discuss as a class whether students think opinions are always as black-and-white as this. Talk about the grey areas (e.g., the genetic engineering of bacteria to produce human insulin is generally seen to be a good use of the technology, but the genetic modification of mammals is not).	**Support:** Provide pairs with several definitions of the terms and ask them to pick out the ones that they think are best.	

Main	Support/Extend	Resources
Cloning concerns (10 min) Present the class with a range of numerical facts about cloning: The process that produced Dolly in 1996 used 277 fertilised eggs, which formed 29 viable embryos, which produced three lambs at birth, one of which lived. Dolly died young (at 6 years old – most sheep live until they are 12). She had lung problems and arthritis. In 2001 it took 188 attempts to make Cc, the first cloned cat, producing 87 cloned embryos, only one of which resulted in a kitten. You can clone your dog for £60 000. Ask students to use these figures to present data to support the argument against the use of adult cell cloning. **Benefits and risks of genetic engineering** (30 min) Provide students with resources that outline arguments for and against genetic engineering in agriculture and medicine. Students may have their own resources, having completing the homework in Topic B14.4. Ask them to write a balanced article for a newspaper or news website on genetic engineering.	**Extend:** Students should consider both economic and ethical issues. For example, it costs money to clone animals, and the success rate is low. This could be seen as wasting money that could be used for other pursuits. Also, many embryos will die during the process. **Extend:** Students should calculate the percentage success rates of adult cell cloning. **Support:** Students could just use information from the student book. **Support:** Use the Literacy interactive to go through how to write a balanced article. **Support:** Provide students with a template to help them write the article.	**Working scientifically:** Viewpoints: Genetically modified crops

Plenary	Support/Extend	Resources
Peer assessment (10 min) Ask students to peer assess each other's articles from Main 2, giving one positive comment about the work and one comment giving suggestions on how it could be improved. **For or against?** (5 min) Students categorise a range of arguments for and against cloning and genetic engineering.	**Extend:** Students should go on to categorise them as economic, ethical, or social arguments.	**Interactive:** For or against?

Homework		
Provide students with a range of events for them to order into a timeline (e.g., Watson and Crick publish DNA double helical structure, human insulin first produced by GM bacteria, Chinese scientists clone a fish, GM tomatoes are available to buy, Dolly the sheep is born, Human Genome Project is completed, first synthetic cells are produced).	**Extend:** Students should state why each event is significant.	

kerboodle

A Kerboodle highlight for this lesson is **Extension sheet: Genetic history**. Refer to the **Content map** on Kerboodle for a full list of resources and assessment.

B14 Variation and evolution

Overview of B14 Variation and evolution

This chapter on variation and evolution includes some content for *AQA GCSE Biology* students only, as well as some higher-tier content. All students should be able to discuss the causes of variation in terms of genetic, environmental, or a combination of both. They should link environmental variation with the effect of alcohol on a fetus in B7.5 *Alcohol and other carcinogens*.

In studying evolution by natural selection, students should understand the role of mutation in variation, understand the theory of evolution by survival of the fittest and natural selection, and be able to give examples. They should link this with previous studies on sexual reproduction and meiosis in B13.2 *Cell division in sexual reproduction*.

Students have studied the process of selective breeding. They should understand this as an example of artificial selection, and be aware of its limitations. In studying genetic engineering, all students should understand what is meant by the term, and be able to give examples of its use and consider the potential benefits and problems. They should link this with work on diabetes treatment using human insulin in B11.3 *Treating diabetes*, and with the treatment of cystic fibrosis in B13.9 *Inherited disorders*. Higher-tier students should be able to recall the steps involved in the process of genetic engineering.

Finally, *AQA GCSE Biology* students have studied cloning as applied to both plants and animals. They should recall different ways of creating clones, and be able to describe why they are useful. They should link cloning plants with work in B11.10 *Using plant hormones*. They should understand the processes of embryo transplants and adult cell cloning in animals, and be able to discuss the choices that need to be made about all genetic technologies.

MyMaths

You can find additional support for the maths skills covered in this chapter on **MyMaths**, including data analysis, finding means, and working with percentages.

kerboodle

For this chapter, the following assessments are available on Kerboodle:

B14 Checkpoint quiz: Variation and evolution
B14 Progress quiz: Variation and evolution 1
B14 Progress quiz: Variation and evolution 2
B14 On your marks: Variation and evolution
B14 Exam-style questions and mark scheme: Variation and evolution

Checkpoint follow-up lesson

A student's route through this lesson can be determined using the Checkpoint assessment. Percentage pass marks are supplied in the Checkpoint teacher notes.

For each successive route through it is assumed that the student can perform to their current route as well as previous routes. For example, students working at Aiming for 6 are assumed to be secure in Aiming for 4 knowledge and understanding and working towards achieving all the learning outcomes for Aiming for 6.

	Aiming for 4	**Aiming for 6**	**Aiming for 8**
Learning outcomes	Describe the mechanisms involved in natural selection and selective breeding.	Explain the mechanisms involved in natural selection and selective breeding.	Compare the mechanisms involved in natural selection and selective breeding.
	State what genetic engineering is.	Describe the mechanisms involved in genetic engineering.	Explain the mechanisms involved in genetic engineering.
	State examples of the different types of cloning.	Describe the different types of cloning.	Compare the different types of cloning.
Starter	**Genetic or environmental? (5 min)** Read out a series of characteristics, for example eye colour, weight, language spoken. Students write down whether the variation in this characteristic is genetic, environmental, or both.		
Differentiated checkpoint activity	The activity students complete depends on the specification they are studying. Activities 1 and 2 are appropriate for all students. Activity 3 is only appropriate for students studying *AQA GCSE Biology*. Students studying *AQA GCSE Biology* should be encouraged to choose two of the three activities to complete, based on what they perceive to be their weakest subject areas. If they complete both activities within the lesson time, they should then be encouraged to complete the other activity.		
	The Aiming for 4 sheet is highly-structured and students may require an introduction to the activities. Students either create a comic strip to describe natural selection and selective breeding, complete a pragraph to describe genetic engineering, or complete a cut-and-stick activitiy to describe the process of cloning. Students will need A4 paper, colouring pencils, scissors, and glue, and may need access to the student book.	The Aiming for 6 sheet is fairly structured and should not require any introduction from the teacher. Students either create a comic strip to describe the processes of natural selection and selective breeding, draw a flow chart to describe the process of genetic engineering, or create a visual summary to summarise the process of cloning. Students will need A3 paper and colouring pencils. Students could be given an opportunity to peer assess each other's work.	The Aiming for 8 follow-up sheet provides minimal prompts for students. Students create two visual summarises on either natural selection and selective breeding, genetic engineering, or cloning. Aiming for 8 students may need to be reminded to move on to the next section of their visual summary. They should be given an opportunity to peer assess each other's work.
	Kerboodle resource B14 Checkpoint follow-up: Aiming for 4, B14 Checkpoint follow-up: Aiming for 6, B14 Checkpoint follow-up: Aiming for 8		
Plenary	**Making choices (5 min)** Students will need mini-whiteboards and pens. Read out a series of scenarios, such as cloning pets, or genetically engineering crops to be drought resistant. Ask students to vote on their mini-whiteboards to show whether they agree or disagree with cloning being used for this purpose.		
Progression	Students can look at different types of characteristics that are controlled by genes to extend their learning. A practical of taking cuttings will aid understanding of cloning.	Students can consider more examples of natural selection such as that of the peppered moth. They could find out different examples of pedigree breeding in terms of the health problems they cause. The topic of making choices about genetic technologies would lend itself to a class debate which would be suitable for all abilities.	Students could plan an investigation where they grow cuttings and then change the conditions that each cutting is exposed to once established. They should include predictions in their plans, using scientific knowledge to justify them. .

B GCSE Biology only

15 Genetics and evolution

15.1 The history of genetics

AQA spec link: 6.3.3 Students should be able to:

- describe the development of our understanding of genetics including the work of Mendel
- understand why the importance of Mendel's discovery was not recognised until after his death.

In the mid-19th century Gregor Mendel carried out breeding experiments on plants. One of his observations was that the inheritance of each characteristic is determined by 'units' that are passed on to descendants unchanged.

In the late 19th century behaviour of chromosomes during cell division was observed.

In the early 20th century it was observed that chromosomes and Mendel's 'units' behaved in similar ways, leading to the idea that the 'units', now called genes, were located on chromosomes.

In the mid-20th century the structure of DNA was determined and the mechanism of gene function worked out.

This scientific work by many scientists led to the gene theory being developed.

WS 1.1
MS 1c

Aiming for	Outcome	Checkpoint	
		Question	Activity
Aiming for GRADE 4 ↓	Use an example to describe the results from Mendel's experiments.	1	Starter 1, Main
	Describe some important discoveries in gene theory.		Main, Homework
Aiming for GRADE 6 ↓	Discuss why the importance of Mendel's work was not recognised until after his death.	2	Plenary 2
	Correctly order important discoveries in gene theory.		Main
Aiming for GRADE 8 ↓	Use a Punnett square to draw conclusions from the results of Mendel's experiments.	1	Starter 1
	Suggest why Mendel's work was not recognised during his lifetime, but the work of Watson and Crick was.	2	Plenary 2

Maths
Students can describe the results of Mendel's crosses using ratios (1c).

Literacy
Students use information from the student book plus their own research to design a social media profile for Gregor Mendel.

B15 Genetics and evolution

Starter	Support/Extend	Resources
Pea parents (10 min) Tell the class that peas come in two colours – green and yellow. Ask them to suggest how two plants with green peas can have offspring with yellow peas. They can check their answers by referring to Figure 1 in the student book.	**Extend:** Students should use a Punnett square to show this.	**Interactive:** Genetic definitions
Genetic definitions (5 min) Students use the interactive to match genetics terms with their definitions.	**Support:** Use the terms DNA, gene, allele, chromosome, and nucleus. **Extend:** Also use recessive, dominant, homozygous, and heterozygous.	

Main	Support/Extend	Resources
Gene theory timeline (40 min) Provide students with cards showing major discoveries in gene theory from Mendel's work to the modern day (refer to the student book for examples). Ask them to work in groups to create a time line of the development of gene theory. Students should annotate their time line with further details on each stage, using the student book or the Internet.	**Extend:** Students should also explain how each discovery was important to our current understanding of gene theory.	**Activity:** Gene theory timeline

Plenary	Support/Extend	Resources
Hot seat (10 min) Ask a confident student to take the role of Gregor Mendel and to sit in front of the class while the rest of the class ask questions about his life, his work, and his thoughts about how ideas about heredity have developed since his death.	**Support:** Have a tick list of the key points to cover. Give one copy of this to a student to tick off, and do some prompting if necessary.	
Recognition (5 min) Students write down possible reasons why Mendel's work was not recognised during his lifetime, but the work of Watson and Crick was. Gather ideas as a class to create an agreed list.		

Homework		
Ask students to research how the work of Rosalind Franklin was important in the development of gene theory.	**Extend:** Students should also find out the name of one other person whose work led to gene theory being developed. They should include what they discovered, when, and why it is important. Students should also justify why they think this discovery was important.	

GCSE Biology only

B15.2 Theories of evolution

AQA spec link: 6.3.1 Charles Darwin, largely as a result of observations on a round the world expedition, linked to developing knowledge of geology and fossils, proposed the theory of natural selection:

- Individual organisms within a particular species show a wide range of variation for a characteristic.
- Individuals with characteristics most suited to the environment are more likely to survive to breed successfully.
- The characteristics that have enabled these individuals to survive are then passed on to the next generation.

Other theories, including that of Jean-Baptiste Lamarck, are based mainly on the idea that changes that occur in an organism during its lifetime can be inherited. We now know that in the vast majority of cases this type of inheritance cannot occur.

A study of creationism is not required.

WS 1.1, 1.3

Aiming for	Outcome	Checkpoint	
		Question	Activity
Aiming for GRADE 4	Define the term evolution.	1	Starter 1
	State that Charles Darwin proposed the theory of evolution by natural selection.		Starter 1, Main 2, Plenary 1
	Describe the stages of evolution by natural selection.	1, End of chapter 2	Starter 2
Aiming for GRADE 6	Compare and contrast Darwin and Lamarck's theories of evolution.	End of chapter 1	Plenary 1
	Describe the theory of inheritance of acquired characteristics proposed by Jean-Baptiste Lamarck.	2, End of chapter 1	Main 1, Plenary 1
	Design a storyboard to highlight important events that helped Darwin develop his theory.		Main 2
Aiming for GRADE 8	Explain why Lamarck's theory is no longer accepted in the vast majority of cases.		Main 1
	Describe an example of where Lamarck's theory could be correct.		Main 1
	Explain how and why theories, such as how evolution takes place, change over time.		Main 1, Homework

Maths
Students can use dates in the information about Darwin's life to work out how old he was when each event occurred, and how many years elapsed between each event.

Literacy
Students use information from the student book and other sources to design a storyboard that highlights key events in Darwin's life.

236

■ B15 Genetics and evolution

Starter	Support/Extend	Resources
How much do you already know? (10 min) Write each of the following terms – evolution, natural selection, Charles Darwin – in the centre of a large piece of paper. Place the sheets around the classroom and invite groups of students to come up and write one thing that they already know about the term on each sheet.		
Natural selection (5 min) Students use the interactive to put the stages of natural selection into the correct order.	**Support:** Allow students to use information from the student book.	**Interactive:** Natural selection

Main	Support/Extend	Resources
Lamarck's theory (15 min) Review previous knowledge about evolution then explain that over time scientists have proposed different theories for how it occurs. Introduce Lamarck as a scientist who proposed a theory of how evolution takes place. Ask students to read through the information about his theory in the student book and then use it to explain how cheetahs have evolved to run faster. Ask students to use evidence to discuss why this theory is no longer recognised as correct in the majority of circumstances.	**Support:** Students can use the example of how the neck of the giraffe got longer, which is in the student book.	
Darwin's theory (25 min) Students learnt about natural selection in Topic B 14.2. Ask students to complete a storyboard for an animation or film on the work of Charles Darwin. As a class, use information from the student book to agree on the different scenes. As well as drawing the scene (or describing it in words), students should write a narration that explains what it is showing and why this was important in the development of Darwin's theory of natural selection.	**Support:** Show students an example of an animation about Darwin's journey and discoveries.	**Activity:** Darwin's theory

Plenary	Support/Extend	Resources
Lamarck or Darwin? (5 min) Read out a series of statements or key words from each scientist's theory and ask students to write down L for Lamarck, D for Darwin, or LD for both. Suitable examples are: fountain of life (L), natural selection (D), organisms change over time (LD), inheritance of acquired characteristics (L), survival of the fittest (D), life on Earth evolved from simple life forms (LD).	**Extend:** Students should suggest one more example and read it out to the rest of the class.	
What do you know now? (10 min) Review Starter 1 by creating another sheet of paper with the word Lamarck on it. Ask students to write one comment on this and on each of the sheets from Starter 1 to show what they know now.		

Homework		
Ask students to find another example of a theory that has changed over time as scientists collect more evidence.	**Extend:** Students should explain how and why the theory selected was changed.	

kerboodle

A Kerboodle highlight for this lesson is **Bump up your grade: How Darwin arrived at his theory**. Refer to the **Content map** on Kerboodle for a full list of resources and assessment.

GCSE Biology only

B15.3 Accepting Darwin's ideas

AQA spec link: 6.3.1 Darwin published his ideas in *On the Origin of Species* (1859). There was much controversy surrounding these revolutionary new ideas.

The theory of evolution by natural selection was only gradually accepted because:

- the theory challenged the idea that God made all the animals and plants that live on Earth
- there was insufficient evidence at the time the theory was published to convince many scientists
- the mechanism of inheritance and variation was not known until 50 years after the theory was published.

WS 1.1, 1.3
MS 4a

Aiming for	Outcome	Checkpoint	
		Question	Activity
Aiming for GRADE 4	Describe how finches have different-shaped beaks so they can eat different foods.		Main 1
	Give one piece of evidence that support's Darwin's theory of natural selection.	2, End of chapter 5	Main 1
	State one reason why most people did not accept Darwin's theory when it was first published.	3	Starter 2, Main 2, Plenary
Aiming for GRADE 6	Explain how finches on different islands evolved different-shaped beaks by natural selection.		Main 1
	Describe several reasons why most people did not accept Darwin's theory when it was first published.	3	Starter 2, Main 2, Plenary 2
	Explain why it was important that Darwin collected a variety of evidence.	2	Main 2, Plenary 1
Aiming for GRADE 8	Explain how the finch species on the different Galapagos Islands are evidence for evolution by natural selection.	2, End of chapter 2	Main 1
	Discuss why Darwin was conflicted over publishing his theory.		Starter 2
	Explain why scientists eventually accepted Darwin's theory.	3, End of chapter 3	Main 2

Maths
As an addition to the practical activity students can time how many sweets they can eat in 20 seconds and record this in a results table. You can also present students with data including graphs to show correlation between height and intelligence. (4a)

Literacy
Students carry out a fishbowl activity where they role-play a meeting between Charles Darwin and a member of public at the time.

Practical

Title	Darwin's finches
Equipment	sets of 'beaks' – pegs, straws, teaspoons, cocktail stick chopsticks; sweets representing food sources – marshmallows (easily picked up by cocktail stick), sugar-coated chocolate beans (easily picked up by peg and spoon), sherbet (easily picked up by straw), jelly sweets (easily picked up by peg and cocktail stick), paper plates as 'islands' to hold foodstuffs

238

■ B15 Genetics and evolution

Overview of method	Each student should be given one of the four 'beak' options.
	Four 'islands' should be set up around the classroom, with different sweets on each island.
	In groups, students move around the islands with their different beaks and try to eat (or pick up) the sweets on the different islands.
	Students should find that there is one island on which the sweets are easy to eat (or pick up) and others where they are harder.
Safety considerations	If the aim of the practical is for students to eat sweets then this practical should be carried out in a suitable room, not a laboratory. If the practical is carried out in a laboratory, students should not be allowed to eat the sweets. Non-edible alternatives could be used.

Starter	Support/Extend	Resources
Darwin cartoon (5 min) Show students the famous cartoon of Charles Darwin with an ape's body. Ask students to suggest what it shows, and why it was published. **Creation clip** (10 min) Ask students whether they think Darwin's theory of evolution is correct. Then ask students to suggest why they think Darwin's theory was so controversial at the time it was first published.		

Main	Support/Extend	Resources
Darwin's finches (30 min) Use an Internet map service to show the location of the Galapagos Islands, which Charles Darwin visited on his journey. Discuss how they are separated from each other and from the mainland. Then, show students images of the different finch species that live on each island. Ask them to suggest features that they share and features that are different. Students then carry out the practical activity where they try to eat or pick up sweets using different-shaped 'beaks'. After completing the practical, ask students to state on which 'island' they would survive, and on which they would become extinct. **Accepting a theory** (10 min) Tell students that there is a theory that taller people are more intelligent than shorter people (this is based on a real study – you can show them a news article). Discuss with them what they think, and what evidence they would need in order to accept the theory. Link this to how people reacted when Darwin published his theory of evolution by natural selection, and why it gradually came to be accepted.	**Extend:** Tell students that the finches all have a common ancestor and ask them to explain how they evolved into different species, using ideas about natural selection. **Extend:** Present students with evidence to support this theory, including graphs to show correlation. Ask students to propose scientific explanations for this correlation.	**Practical:** Darwin's finches

Plenary	Support/Extend	Resources
Darwin fishbowl (10 min) Invite a confident pair of students to role-play a meeting between Charles Darwin and a member of public at the time. The member of the public should question Darwin on his theory and ask for evidence. The rest of the class observe the meeting. Discuss why it was so important that Darwin had a variety of evidence to support his theory.	**Extend:** Allow observing students to join the central pair if they feel that they have something important they can add to the conversation.	
Why was Darwin's theory not accepted? (5 min) Students use the interactive to sort a series of statements according to whether or not they were reasons why Darwin's theory of evolution was not immediately accepted. They then sort evidence according to whether it supports Darwin's theory of evolution or not.	**Support:** Allow students to work in groups and use the information in the student book to help them.	**Interactive:** Why was Darwin's theory not accepted?

Homework		
Set the class an exam question on evolution, or the summary questions from the student book.		

kerboodle

A Kerboodle highlight for this lesson is **Bump up your grade: Objections to Darwin's ideas**. Refer to the **Content map** on Kerboodle for a full list of resources and assessment.

GCSE Biology only

B15.4 Evolution and speciation

AQA spec link: 6.3.2 Students should be able to:

- describe the work of Darwin and Wallace in the development of the theory of evolution by natural selection
- explain the impact of these ideas on biology.

Alfred Russel Wallace independently proposed the theory of evolution by natural selection. He published joint writings with Darwin in 1858 which prompted Darwin to publish *On the Origin of Species* (1859) the following year.

Wallace worked worldwide gathering evidence for evolutionary theory. He is best known for his work on warning colouration in animals and his theory of speciation.

Alfred Wallace did much pioneering work on speciation but more evidence over time has led to our current understanding of the theory of speciation.

Students should be able to describe the steps which give rise to new species.

WS 1.1
MS 1b

Aiming for	Outcome	Checkpoint	
		Question	Activity
Aiming for **GRADE 4** ↓	Describe what a species is.		Starter 2
	Define speciation as the process by which new species form.		Main 2
	Give an example of an important discovery by Wallace.	3, End of chapter 3	Main 1
Aiming for **GRADE 6** ↓	Describe the steps in the process of speciation.	1	Main 2, Plenary 2
	Explain why there are species living on Madagascar that share some similarities with species found elsewhere.	1	Starter 1, Main 2
	Carry out research to describe other examples of speciation.		Homework
Aiming for **GRADE 8** ↓	Explain the relationship between the length of isolation and the number of unique species that evolve.		Homework
	Suggest how new species of organisms evolved.	1, 2, End of chapter 6	Main 2, Homework
	Explain why Wallace's work prompted Darwin to publish *The Origin of Species*.	End of chapter 3	Main 1

Maths
Students can calculate for how long Madagascar was part of Gondwana, and for how long it has been separated. (1b)

Literacy
Students read through the information about Wallace in the student book and summarise it by writing down five bullet points.

Key word
speciation

B15 Genetics and evolution

Starter	Support/Extend	Resources
Madagascar (10 min) Show the class images of animals that are only found in Madagascar. These could include the aye-aye, various other lemurs including bamboo, black-and-white ruffed, ring-tailed, and mouse lemurs, Verreaux's sifakas, fossa, tomato frog, giant leaf-tailed gecko, satanic leaf-tailed gecko, giraffe weevil, and miniature chameleons *Brookesia micra*. Ask students to make notes on their features and on similarities and differences between these and other related animals not found on Madagascar.	**Extend:** Students should be asked to think about possible reasons why unique species are found on Madagascar.	
What is a species? (5 min) Ask students to review their understanding of what a species is by writing down what they already know. Listen to suggestions, and come up with an agreed definition.	**Support:** Provide students with three definitions, only one being correct. They should choose the correct one.	

Main	Support/Extend	Resources
Wallace (10 min) Ask students to read through the information about Alfred Russel Wallace in the student book and write down five bullet points that they think summarise the most vital information about who he was, and his work.	**Extend:** Ask students to explain how his work prompted Darwin to publish *On the Origin of Species*.	
The process of speciation (30 min) Describe speciation as the process by which new species evolve. Provide students with diagrams that show the process of speciation. They should put them into the correct order and explain what is happening in each. Students use their knowledge to complete a cloze paragraph to explain how lemurs evolved through the process of speciation.	**Support:** Students can use information from the student book to explain what the diagrams show.	**Activity:** Speciation

Plenary	Support/Extend	Resources
How organisms change through time (5 min) Students use the interactive to answer a series of true or false questions about the information covered in the lesson.		**Interactive:** How organisms change through time
Old and new species (10 min) Provide students with the mock exam question: Describe how new species may arise. (6 marks) Students spend 5 minutes writing an answer, before a brief class discussion on the key points they included in their responses.	**Support:** Allow students to use information from their notes to answer the question.	

Homework		
Ask students to prepare a presentation on another example where speciation has occurred through isolation. Examples of suitable locations include Australia and Costa Rica. They should include the type of isolation, examples of unique species found there, and an explanation of how they evolved.	**Extend:** Ask students to consider why Great Britain has very few unique species compared with Australia, even though they are both islands.	

kerboodle
A Kerboodle highlight for this lesson is **Extension sheet: A Madagascan mystery**. Refer to the **Content map** on Kerboodle for a full list of resources and assessment.

B15.5 Evidence for evolution

AQA spec links: 6.3.4 Students should be able to describe the evidence for evolution including fossils and antibiotic resistance in bacteria.

The theory of evolution by natural selection is now widely accepted.

Evidence for Darwin's theory is now available as it has been shown that characteristics are passed on to offspring in genes. There is further evidence in the fossil record [and the knowledge of how resistance to antibiotics evolves in bacteria.]

6.3.5 Fossils are the 'remains' of organisms from hundreds of thousands of years ago, which are found in rocks.

Fossils may be formed:

- from parts of organisms that have not decayed because one or more of the conditions needed for decay are absent
- when parts of the organism are replaced by other materials as they decay
- as preserved traces of organisms, such as footprints, burrows, and rootlet traces.

Many early forms of life were soft-bodied, which means that they have left few traces behind.

What traces there were have been mainly destroyed by geological activity. This is why scientists cannot be certain about how life began on Earth.

WS 1.3
MS 1b

Aiming for	Outcome	Checkpoint	
		Question	Activity
Aiming for GRADE 4 ↓	Describe what a fossil is and give an example.	End of chapter 5	Starter 1
	Recognise that fossils are evidence for evolution by natural selection.	1	Main 1, Plenary 1
	Order geological events.		Main 2
Aiming for GRADE 6 ↓	Describe how fossils are formed.	2, End of chapter 5	Main 1, Plenary 2
	Describe how fossils are evidence for evolution by natural selection.	1, 3, End of chapter 5	Main 1, Plenary 1
	Explain why the fossil record is not complete.		Main 1
Aiming for GRADE 8 ↓	Evaluate the use of fossils as evidence for evolution by natural selection and how life first formed.	1, End of chapter 5	Main 1, Plenary 1
	Use standard form to discuss the large timescales used when considering the evolution of life.		Main 2
	Create a geological timeline to scale.		Main 2

Maths
Students convert between thousands, millions, and billions and use standard form to discuss large timescales. (1b)

Literacy
Students write down why fossils are evidence for evolution by natural selection.

■ B15 Genetics and evolution

Starter	Support/Extend	Resources
What is it? (10 min) Set up a display of fossils around the classroom, ideally some real and some photographs. They should be a range of different types of fossils (e.g., those in rock/ice/ash, footprints, burrows). Number each one for referencing. Ask students to try and identify each fossil. Make sure you talk through the incorrectly identified fossils. **Frozen mammoth** (5 min) Show the class an image of a mammoth preserved in ice (see Figure 1 in the student book). Discuss what scientists could learn from studying the mammoth.	**Support:** Provide students with a sheet with the identities of the fossils. Ask them to match the name to the numbered fossil.	

Main	Support/Extend	Resources
Fossil evidence (10 min) Show a series of images to show how fossils form in rock (Figure 2 in the student book). Discuss what can be learnt about evolution from studying fossils. Ask students to read through the section An incomplete record in the student book and to write down three reasons why the fossil record is not complete. **History of the Earth timeline** (30 min) Provide students with some major events in the evolution of life on Earth. Ask them to use the Internet to research when they happened and to place them into the correct order: Earth formed (4.6 billion years ago), oceans and continents start to form (4.4 billion years ago), first evidence of life (3.5 billion years ago), atmospheric oxygen forms (2.4 billion years ago), evolution of eukaryotic life (1.8 billion years ago), plants move on to land (450 million years ago), animals move on to land (430 million years ago), Permo-Triassic mass extinction (251 million years ago), evolution of mammals (195 million years ago), extinction of the dinosaurs (65 million years ago), evolution of humans (200 000 years ago), extinction of the woolly mammoth (10 000 years ago).	**Support:** Show students how to convert between thousands, millions, and billions. **Extend:** Students should express the timescales in standard form. **Extend:** Students should create a scale timeline using a piece of string 4.6 metres long. They should work out the scale used.	**Maths skills:** Geological timescales **Activity:** History of the Earth timescale

Plenary	Support/Extend	Resources
Fossil evaluation (10 min) Ask students to write down why fossils are evidence for evolution by natural selection. **Fossil formation** (5 min) Students use the interactive to put the stages of fossil formation into the correct order.	**Extend:** Students should evaluate the use of fossils as evidence for evolution and how life started on Earth.	**Interactive:** Fossil formation

Homework		
Ask students to make notes on what they have learnt about fossils and speciation.		

kerboodle

A Kerboodle highlight for this lesson is **Calculation sheet: Questions on geological timescales**. Refer to the **Content map** on Kerboodle for a full list of resources and assessment.

B15.6 Fossils and extinction

AQA spec links: 6.3.5: We can learn from fossils how much or how little different organisms have changed as life developed on Earth.

Students should be able to extract and interpret information from charts, graphs, and tables such as evolutionary trees.

6.3.6 Extinctions occur when there are no remaining individuals of a species still alive.

Students should be able to describe factors which may contribute to the extinction of a species.

WS 1.3
MS 1b

Aiming for	Outcome	Checkpoint	
		Question	Activity
Aiming for GRADE 4 ↓	Describe what is meant by extinction.		Starter 1
	Describe one way that an animal could become extinct.		Starter 1, Main, Plenary
	Order fossil diagrams to show the evolution of the horse.		Main
Aiming for GRADE 6 ↓	Describe how other organisms can cause an animal or plant to become extinct.		Main, Plenary
	Suggest a hypothesis for why an organism became extinct.	3	Main
	Explain how fossil diagrams show how the horse has evolved.	2	Main
Aiming for GRADE 8 ↓	Suggest alternative hypotheses for why an organism became extinct.	3	Main
	Evaluate in detail the need to conserve endangered plants.		Plenary 2
	Apply knowledge of speciation to explain why dodos were only found on one island.		Main

Maths
Groups can interpret data about the numbers of each species left in the wild. (1b)

Literacy
Students use information about the dodo and its habitat to suggest hypotheses for why it became extinct.

Key word
extinction

244

■ B15 Genetics and evolution

Starter	Support/Extend	Resources
Least favourite way to go (10 min) Ask the class to work in small groups to discuss and list the ways in which organisms become extinct. Go through their ideas and produce the following list – asteroid impact, climate change, competition with other species, new diseases, new predators. Highlight the causes associated with other organisms and tell the class that this is what they will be focusing on in this lesson.	**Support:** Use images as visual clues for the methods of extinction.	
Fossil review (5 min) Students use the interactive to complete a series of statements on fossils. they then sort statements about fossils according to whether they are true or false.	**Support:** Give students the endings for them to match up.	**Interactive:** Fossil review

Main	Support/Extend	Resources
Fossils and extinction (40 min) Give students a set of pictures showing the evolution of the horse, but with no labels and in an incorrect sequence (Figure 1 from the student book). Ask students to put them into the correct sequence and explain what they show. They can then use the student book to check their work.	**Support:** Allow students to use the student book to complete the task.	**Activity:** Fossils and extinction
Then introduce students to the extinct bird, the dodo. (A video clip from the Internet may be useful here.) Discuss what scientists can deduce about the bird using its skeleton. Tell them that the dodo became extinct when humans and their livestock settled for the first time on the island of Mauritius, where they lived. Ask groups to work together to propose several hypotheses for why the dodo became extinct.	**Support:** Provide the hypotheses and ask groups to decide which are more likely, with reasons. **Extend:** Students should apply their knowledge of speciation to explain why dodos were only found on one island.	

Plenary	Support/Extend	Resources
Endangered animals (10 min) Give groups of students a set of images of different endangered animals (e.g., polar bear, black rhino, orangutan, giant panda), and ask them to discuss the reasons why they are endangered.	**Support:** Provide the reasons for students to choose from. **Extend:** Give groups data about the numbers of each species left in the wild for them to interpret.	
Plant extinction (5 min) Ask students to suggest what could cause the extinction of a plant species.	**Extend:** Ask students to discuss whether they think conserving plants is equally as important as conserving endangered animals.	

Homework		
Set the class the summary questions from the student book.		

kerboodle

A Kerboodle highlight for this lesson is **Go further: Using fossils to reconstruct the past**. Refer to the **Content map** on Kerboodle for a full list of resources and assessment.

B15.7 More about extinction

AQA spec link: 6.3.6 Extinctions occur when there are no remaining individuals of a species still alive.

Students should be able to describe factors which may contribute to the extinction of a species.

MS 1d, 4a

Aiming for	Outcome	Checkpoint Question	Checkpoint Activity
Aiming for GRADE 4	Describe what a mass extinction is.	1	Starter 1
	State that environmental change and a catastrophic event are two possible causes of mass extinction.	1	Starter, Main 1, Main 2, Plenary 2
	Describe one theory that explains why the dinosaurs became extinct.		Main 2
Aiming for GRADE 6	Suggest the effects of an asteroid, comet, or meteorite strike on Earth.	3	Starter 2, Main 2
	Explain how environmental change can cause mass extinctions.		Main 1, Plenary 2
	Identify strengths and weaknesses in two different theories of mass extinction.	3	Main 2, Homework
Aiming for GRADE 8	Link ideas to give a scientific explanation of why an asteroid could have caused the dinosaurs to become extinct.	3	Starter 2, Main 2
	Suggest why mass extinctions are important for the evolution of life on Earth.	2	Plenary 1
	Evaluate two theories to come to a conclusion about which is more believable, and explain why scientists are not sure what caused the extinction of dinosaurs or mammoths.		Main 2, Homework

Maths
Students use calculations to estimate the volume of rock thrown up by a meteor impact (1d). You could also use the average density of rock (about 2.5 tonnes per m^3) to ask students to work out the mass of rock. Students interpret a graph that shows how Earth's temperature has changed over time. (4a)

Literacy
Students use information from the student book and/or webpages to evaluate the evidence that supports theories on why the dinosaurs became extinct. They then discuss their ideas in small groups, and then as a class.

■ B15 Genetics and evolution

Starter	Support/Extend	Resources
Human extinction (5 min) Ask students to discuss whether they think humans will become extinct. and, if so, when and how. Introduce the term mass extinctions and use Figure 2 in the student book to show when these have occurred.	**Support:** Provide possible events for groups to discuss – virus, climate change, meteorite/asteroid strike.	
Deep impact (10 min) Show students the trailer for the movie *Deep Impact* and discuss what effects an asteroid, comet, or asteroid strike would have on Earth. Explain that this happened at Chicxulub in Mexico at the end of the Cretaceous period, and that the crater formed was 180 km in diameter and 10 km deep.	**Extend:** Using the dimensions of the Chicxulub crater, ask students to work out how many cubic kilometres of rock were thrown into the air, and to compare this with published estimates (4660 km^3).	

Main	Support/Extend	Resources
Extinction (40 min) Show the class a graph that shows how average temperatures on Earth have varied. Ask students to use Figure 2 in the student book to see whether there is a link between changes in temperature and mass extinctions. They can then use the information in the student book to explain why there is a link.	**Extend:** Remind students that scientists agree that global temperatures are rising. Ask them to summarise how this is affecting organisms such as the polar bear.	**Activity:** Extinction
Then ask students to read through the section *What destroyed the dinosaurs* in the student book, which outlines popular theories. Ask them to evaluate the evidence and to identify strengths and weaknesses in each case. They then discuss their ideas in small groups, and then as a class. Discuss the fact that theories are ideas supported by evidence that become accepted, and are then often superseded over the years. Explain why scientists are not sure what caused the extinction of the dinosaurs.	**Support:** Ask students to work in groups just looking at one theory. **Extend:** Students should use their knowledge of asteroid strikes, photosynthesis, and energy flow through food chains and webs to produce a concept map linking all of these factors to the mass extinction of the dinosaurs.	

Plenary	Support/Extend	Resources
What do you think? (5 min) Introduce to the class the opinion that, in the long term, mass extinction is beneficial to the development of life. Discuss thoughts as a class.	**Support:** A more accessible discussion may be to present the opinion that giant pandas should not be saved from extinction.	
Extinction causes (5 min) Students use the interactive select the correct cause of extinction for different creatures.		**Interactive:** Extinction causes

Homework		
Tell students that there are two theories to explain why mammoths became extinct – climate change and human hunters. Ask them to research both, and list the evidence for and against each theory.	**Support:** Students can just investigate one theory.	**WebQuest:** What killed the mammoths?

kerboodle

A Kerboodle highlight for this lesson is **Homework: Fossils, evolution, and extinction**. Refer to the **Content map** on Kerboodle for a full list of resources and assessment.

B15.8 Antibiotic resistant bacteria

AQA spec link: 6.3.7 Bacteria can evolve rapidly because they reproduce at a fast rate.

Mutations of bacterial pathogens produce new strains. Some strains might be resistant to antibiotics, and so are not killed. They survive and reproduce, so the population of the resistant strain rises. The resistant strain will then spread because people are not immune to it and there is no effective treatment.

MRSA is resistant to antibiotics.

To reduce the rate of development of antibiotic resistant strains:

- doctors should not prescribe antibiotics inappropriately, such as treating non-serious or viral infections
- patients should complete their course of antibiotics so all bacteria are killed and none survive to mutate and form resistant strains
- the agricultural use of antibiotics should be restricted.

The development of new antibiotics is costly and slow and is unlikely to keep up with the emergence of new resistant strains.

MS 1b, 2a

Aiming for	Outcome	Checkpoint	
		Question	Activity
Aiming for GRADE 4	Describe what is meant by an antibiotic resistant bacteria.	2	Starter 1
	Describe why scientists want to slow down the rate of development of new strains of antibiotic resistant bacteria.		Starter 1, Main 2
	List some ways in which scientists can slow down the development of new strains of antibiotic resistant bacteria.	2	Main 2
Aiming for GRADE 6	Describe how antibiotic resistant bacteria evolve.	1	Main 1, Plenary 1
	Explain why scientists need to develop new antibiotics.		Starter 1, Main 2, Homework
	Create an information sheet outlining important facts about antibiotic resistant bacteria to the public.		Main 2
Aiming for GRADE 8	Explain how a fast reproduction rate is linked to the development of antibiotic resistance strains of bacteria.		Starter 2, Main 1
	Explain how antibiotic resistant bacteria are evidence for evolution.		Plenary 2
	Summarise the reasons why the development of new antibiotics is unlikely to keep up with the emergence of new strains of antibiotic resistant bacteria.		Homework

Maths
Students calculate the number of bacteria in a colony after a day. They use standard form and significant figures. (1b, 2a)

Literacy
Students use information from the student book to summarise how to reduce the rate of development of antibiotic resistant bacteria. They then create an information sheet for the general public outlining important facts.

B15 Genetics and evolution

Starter	Support/Extend	Resources
Please wash your hands (5 min) Show students images of antibacterial hand gel for public use in hospitals or hand-washing stations for medical professionals. Ask them why these are important. Introduce the fact that some strains of bacteria are especially dangerous because they cannot be controlled by antibiotics. **How many?** (10 min) Ask students to calculate how many bacteria would be present after one day if a colony of 100 bacteria reproduced once every hour (224 × 100 = 1 677 721 600). As a class, use this information to discuss why bacteria evolve much quicker than animals.	**Extend:** Show students news articles about 'super gonorrhea' – a strain of gonorrhea that has developed antibiotic resistance. **Support:** Simplify the calculation so there is one starting bacteria and a division time of 5 hours. **Extend:** Students should use 3 significant figures and standard form to present their answer (1.68×10^9).	

Main	Support/Extend	Resources
Public information (40 min) Provide students with images that show how bacteria become antibiotic resistant, but put these in the wrong order (see Figure 1 in the student book). Ask students to rearrange them and then describe to a partner what they show. After checking their ideas by using the student book, they can stick the diagrams into their books and write down what each shows. Then ask students to use information from the student book to summarise their top three things the public should understand about how to reduce the rate of development of antibiotic resistant bacteria. Students then share their lists with a partner before deciding on a shared list. Ask students to then create an information sheet for the general public outlining these.	**Support:** Students can use the student book information from the start of the task. **Extend:** Students should use the stages of natural selection to explain the process. **Support:** Decide the top three facts as a class. Students can just write about one fact.	**Activity:** Public information

Plenary	Support/Extend	Resources
Order the stages (5 min) Give students the interactive with the stages of the development of antibiotic resistant bacteria in the wrong order. Ask them to arrange them correctly. **Evidence for evolution** (10 min) Ask students to write an explanation for how antibiotic resistant bacteria are evidence for evolution.	**Support:** Provide this as a cloze passage for students to complete.	**Interactive:** Order the stages

Homework		
Set the class a series of questions about the search for new antibiotics (e.g., Why are new antibiotics needed?). Describe one example of work being carried out by scientists investigating the development of new antibiotics. Why is this work costly and slow? Describe how you would find out if any potential antibiotics in development could be used to treat antibiotic resistant infections.	**Extend:** Students should search the Internet for an interesting example of research being carried out in this area.	

kerboodle

A Kerboodle highlight for this lesson is **Progress quiz: Genetics and evolution 2**. Refer to the **Content map** on Kerboodle for a full list of resources and assessment.

B15.9 Classification

AQA spec link: 6.4 Traditionally living things have been classified into groups depending on their structure and characteristics in a system described by Carl Linnaeus.

Linnaeus classified living things into kingdom, phylum, class, order, family, genus, and species. Organisms are named by the binomial system of genus and species.

Students should be able to use information given to show understanding of the Linnaean system.

MS 1d, 2a

Aiming for	Outcome	Checkpoint	
		Question	Activity
Aiming for GRADE 4 ↓	Describe what classification is.	1, End of chapter 4	Starter 2
	Classify animals into groups based on their shared characteristics.		Starter 2
	Write an organism's name correctly using the binomial system.		Plenary 1
Aiming for GRADE 6 ↓	Describe the classification system developed by Carl Linnaeus, to include the order of the taxonomic groups.	2	Main 1, Main 2
	Identify genus and species from a scientific name.		Main 2, Plenary 1
	Explain why a binomial naming system is useful.	4	Plenary 2
Aiming for GRADE 8 ↓	Use the Linnaean system to name the groups that given organisms belong to.		Main 2
	Suggest why hybrids are not assigned scientific names using the binomial system.		Starter 1

Maths
During Starter 1 you can ask students to estimate how many known species there are (at least 1.75 million, with an estimated 3–10 million yet to be discovered). (1d, 2a)

Literacy
Students summarise key points about the Linnaean system in their own words. They learn the rules of writing binomial names.

Key words
classification, archaea, species

250

■ B15 Genetics and evolution

Starter	Support/Extend	Resources
Name that species! (5 min) Tell the class that they need to name the species of animal that you are going to show them. Show them images of a lion, a tiger, and a liger or tigron. Discuss that lions and tigers are different species but they can breed to produce infertile offspring.	**Extend:** Share the binomial (scientific) names of each species. Ask students to suggest why ligers and tigrons aren't given these names (because they are hybrids of two species).	
Classify (10 min) Give groups of students a range of images of different animal species. Ask students to classify them into groups based on their shared characteristics. Allow groups to share their method with the class and use this as a basis for a discussion about why it is a good idea for everyone to use the same system.	**Extend:** Students should be given images of other living organisms (species of plants, fungi, and single-celled organisms). Ask students to first organise them into large groups, and then smaller ones.	

Main	Support/Extend	Resources
Linnaeus (20 min) Introduce students to the work of Carl Linnaeus. Ask students to read through the section *How are organisms classified?* in the student book on his classification system, and write down at least five key points in their own words.	**Support:** Tell students that a good way to remember the order of the groups in the classification system (Kingdom, Phylum, Class, Order, Family, Genus and Species) is King Prawn Curry Or Fried Greasy Sausage.	
Classifying animals (20 min) Provide pairs of students with cards that contain the Linnaean classification for some different animal species. For example, for a lion there would be seven cards stating: Kingdom – Animalia (animals), Phylum – Chordata (vertebrate), Class – Mammalia (mammals), Order – Carnivora (meat eaters), Family – Felidae (all cats), Genus – Panthera (great cats), Species – Leo. Students should correctly order the cards and suggest the common name of the animal. You can provide different pairs with different animals, each pair with several animals, or all pairs doing the same animal. Go through the correct answers and introduce the term binomial system, including why it is useful to scientists.		**Activity:** Classifying animals

Plenary	Support/Extend	Resources
Classifying humans (10 min) Students use the interactive to put the taxonomic groups in the correct order. They then put the classification of humans into the correct order.		**Interactive:** Classifying humans
Why use the binomial system? (5 min) Ask students to write down why this system is useful for scientists.	**Support:** Give students a clue by reminding them that scientists of different nationalities share their findings in publications.	

Homework		
Set the class an exam question on classification, or the summary questions from the student book.		

kerboodle

A Kerboodle highlight for this lesson is **Homework: Classification**. Refer to the **Content map** on Kerboodle for a full list of resources and assessment.

B15.10 New systems of classification

AQA spec link: 6.4 Students should be able to use information given to show understanding of the Linnaean system.

As evidence of internal structures became more developed due to improvements in microscopes, and the understanding of biochemical processes progressed, new models of classification were proposed.

Due to evidence available from chemical analysis there is now a 'three-domain system' developed by Carl Woese. In this system organisms are divided into:

- Archaea (primitive bacteria usually living in extreme environments)
- Bacteria (true bacteria)
- Eukaryota (which includes protists, fungi, plants, and animals).

Evolutionary trees are a method used by scientists to show how they believe organisms are related. They use current classification data for living organisms and fossil data for extinct organisms.

WS 1.1, 1.2
MS 1d

Aiming for	Outcome	Checkpoint	
		Question	Activity
Aiming for GRADE 4	Name the three domains.	1	Main 1
	Recognise that ideas about classification have changed over time.		Main 1
	Draw a conclusion from a simple evolutionary tree.		Starter 1, Main 2, Plenary 2
Aiming for GRADE 6	Describe how organisms are divided in the three-domain system.	1	Main 1, Plenary 1
	Describe why the three-domain system was proposed.	1	Starter 2, Main 1, Homework
	Draw several conclusions from a simple evolutionary tree.		Starter 1, Main 2, Plenary 2
Aiming for GRADE 8	Compare and contrast the Linnaean system with the three-domain system.	End of chapter 4	Main 1
	Outline how ideas about classification have developed over time.	2, End of chapter 4	Starter 2, Main 1, Homework
	Draw conclusions from a more complex evolutionary tree.		Starter 1, Main 2, Plenary 2

Maths
In Starter 2 ask students to estimate the range of pressure and temperature at which most bacteria on Earth can survive. (1d)

Literacy
Students summarise information from the student book into a diagram. They outline how classification systems have changed over time.

Key words
domain, evolutionary trees

■ B15 Genetics and evolution

Starter	Support/Extend	Resources
The tree of life (10 min) Print out copies of an example of a tree of life from an Internet search. Let pairs study the diagram and discuss what they think it shows before opening it up as a class discussion. **Extreme organism** (5 min) Tell the class that a single-celled organism has been found living in a hydrothermal vent on the ocean floor at pressures of more than 200 atmospheres and temperatures above 85 °C. It survives without oxygen and produces methane as a product of its metabolism. Tell students that scientists cannot place it into any of the five kingdoms proposed by Linnaeus, and suggest why.	**Support:** A simple tree can be found at spindriftpress.com by searching for 'tree of life'. **Extend:** Discuss the theory that eukaryotes evolved because of a symbiosis between two forms of prokaryote.	
Main	**Support/Extend**	**Resources**
The three-domain system (20 min) Ask students to use information from the student book to draw a simple diagram to show how the three-domain system is subdivided up into six kingdoms. Students should also give an example of a species that belongs to each kingdom, and explain the common characteristics of each. **Evolutionary trees** (20 min) Allow students to use the Internet to research what evolutionary trees show, and print off an example. Allow them to share these examples with other students in a group and explain what they show about evolution.	**Support:** Provide a template of the diagram for students to fill in. **Extend:** Students should compare the three-domain system to the Linnaean system. **Extend:** Students should write binomial names for each example. **Extension:** Students should create an instruction sheet on how to read evolutionary trees.	**Activity:** Evolutionary trees
Plenary	**Support/Extend**	**Resources**
Which kingdom? (10 min) Students use the interactive to classify a list of organisms as archaebacteria, eubacteria, protista, fungi, plants, or animals. **Thumbs up** (5 min) Review the evolutionary tree shown in Figure 2 in the student book. Ask students questions to check their understanding (e.g., Do the giant and red panda have a common ancestor? How long ago did it live? Did this ancestor have 'wrist thumbs?' Why have both species evolved to have them?).	**Support:** Use images to show each organism. **Extend:** Ask students to write one question and present this to the rest of the class.	**Interactive:** Which kingdom?
Homework		
Ask students to summarise how ideas about classification have changed over time, and why.	**Support:** Students can use information from the student book to complete sentence starters. **Extend:** Students should do their own research to include work from scientists other than Linnaeus and Woese.	

B15 Genetics and evolution

Overview of B15 Genetics and evolution

This chapter includes the theory of evolution, which is for *AQA GCSE Biology* students only. These students have studied Mendel and his discoveries, and should understand how later understanding of the mechanism of inheritance and genetics applies to his findings. They should be able to describe several theories of evolution including the work of Lamarck and Darwin, focusing on Darwin's theory of natural selection. They should link this with B14.2 *Evolution by natural selection*. *AQA GCSE Biology* students should also be able to outline the reasons why Darwin's ideas were not accepted for some time. They should be familiar with Wallace's ideas on evolution and how he established our current theory of speciation. Students should understand that each part of a divided population undergoes natural selection separately and therefore differently, and over a long period of time can end up being very different from each other.

All students should be aware of evidence for evolution, including the fossil record and reasons for extinction. They should be able to describe antibiotic resistant bacteria and their fast evolution, in particular the problem of MRSA. They should link this with work in B6 *Preventing and treating disease* on antibiotics and the discovery and development of drugs.

Finally all students should understand how living organisms are classified. They should recall the natural system designed by Linnaeus, and be able to give the rules of the binomial system of naming living things. They should be familiar with the three-domain system developed in the light of recent technological advances. They should link this with B1.3 *Eukaryotic and prokaryotic cells*.

MyMaths

You can find additional support for the maths skills covered in this chapter on **MyMaths**, including using ratios, data analysis, using standard form to discuss large time scales, and estimating.

kerboodle

For this chapter, the following assessments are available on Kerboodle:

B15 Checkpoint quiz: Genetics and evolution
B15 Progress quiz: Genetics and evolution 1
B15 Progress quiz: Genetics and evolution 2
B15 On your marks: Genetics and evolution
B15 Exam-style questions and mark scheme: Genetics and evolution

Checkpoint follow-up lesson

A student's route through this lesson can be determined using the Checkpoint assessment. Percentage pass marks are supplied in the Checkpoint teacher notes.

For each successive route through it is assumed that the student can perform to their current route as well as previous routes. For example, students working at Aiming for 6 are assumed to be secure in Aiming for 4 knowledge and understanding and working towards achieving all the learning outcomes for Aiming for 6.

	Aiming for 4	**Aiming for 6**	**Aiming for 8**
Learning outcomes	State different theories of evolution.	Describe different theories of evolution.	Explain different theories of evolution.
	State some causes of extinction.	Describe some causes of extinction.	Explain some causes of extinction.
	Describe how antibiotic resistance develops in bacteria.	Explain how antibiotic resistance develops in bacteria.	Explain how antibiotic resistance in bacteria is a growing issue.
Starter	**Unscramble (5 min)** Scramble the names of famous scientists in this topic: Mendel, Darwin, Wallace, Lamarck, and Linnaeus. Write the on the board and ask students to unscramble the names.		
Differentiated checkpoint activity	The activity students complete depends on the specification they are studying. Activities 2 and 3 are appropriate for all students. Activity 1 is only appropriate for students studying *AQA GCSE Biology*. Students studying *AQA GCSE Biology* should be encouraged to choose two of the three activities to complete, based on what they perceive to be their weakest subject areas. If they complete both activities within the lesson time, they should then be encouraged to complete the other activity		
	The Aiming for 4 sheet is highly structured. Students either complete a cut-and-stick activity to summarise the development of the theory of evolution, .create fossil impressions, or complete a cut-and-stick activity to describe the development of antibiotic resistance. Students may need a brief introduction from the teacher. They will need scissors and glue sticks for the cut and paste activities.	The Aiming for 6 sheet is fairly structured and should not require any introduction from the teacher. Students either complete a table to summarise what each scientist (Lamarck, Darwin, and Wallace) contributed to the development of the theory of evolution, create a fossil impression before escrbing how fossils are made, or create a flow chart to describe how bacteria develop antibiotic resistance.	The Aiming for 8 sheet has very little structure. Students should be able to complete their task with no introduction from the teacher. Students either describe the contributions of Lamarck, Darwin, and Wallace to the developmentof the theory of evolution, create a fossil impression before describing how fossils form, or draw a flow chart to explain how bacteria develop antibiotic resistance.
	For students who choose to complete activity 2, show them a range of fossils or images of fossils and give a brief description on how they form. Sources of fossils or pictures of fossil are readily available on the Internet. Students could then make fossil impressions using modelling clay and fossils with the teacher.		
	Kerboodle resource B15 Checkpoint follow-up: Aiming for 4, B15 Checkpoint follow-up: Aiming for 6, B15 Checkpoint follow-up: Aiming for 8		
Plenary	**The big idea (5 min)** Ask targeted questions – what was each of the scientists in the starter famous for? Students could make up their own mnemonic for the seven levels of classification.		
Progression	Give students' Aiming for 6 work to peer-assess. They should then add any information they missed to their own notes from the lesson.	Give students Aiming for 8 work to peer-assess. They should then add any information they missed to their own notes from the lesson.	To progress, students should write an explanation on how the development of antibiotic resistant bacteria can be used as evidence for evolution. They could evaluate this evidence, adding one reason why this is a good piece of evidence for the theory fo evolution, and one piece of evidence why it may not be a good piece of evidence for the theory of evolution.

5 Ecology

Specification links

AQA specification section	Assessment paper
7.1 Adaptations, interdependence and competition	Paper 2
7.2 Levels of organisation	Paper 2
7.3 Biodiversity and the effect of human interaction on ecosystems	Paper 2
7.4 Trophic levels in an ecosystem	Paper 2
7.5 Food production	Paper 2

Required practicals

AQA required practicals	Practical skills	Topic
Measure the population size of a common species in a habitat. Use sampling techniques to investigate the effect of a factor on the distribution of this species.	AT 1 – use appropriate apparatus to record length and area. AT 3 – use transect lines and quadrats to measure distribution of a species. AT 4 – safe and ethical use of organisms and response to a factor in the environment. AT 6 – application of appropriate sampling techniques to investigate the distribution and abundance of organisms in an ecosystem via direct use in the field. AT 8 – use of appropriate techniques in more complex contexts including continuous sampling in an investigation.	B16.3
Investigate the effect of temperature on the rate of decay of fresh milk by measuring pH change.	AT 1 – use appropriate apparatus to record temperature and pH. AT 3 – the use of appropriate apparatus to measure anaerobic decay. AT 4 – safe use of microorganisms. AT 5 – measurement of rate of decay by pH change.	B7.2

Maths skills

AQA maths skills	Topic
1a Recognise and use expressions in decimal form.	18.11
1b Recognise and use expressions in standard form.	17.3, 18.1
1c Use ratios, fractions and percentages.	17.4, 18.3, 18.8, 18.9
2a Use an appropriate number of significant figures.	18.11
2b Find arithmetic means.	16.3
2c Construct and interpret frequency tables and diagrams, bar charts, and histograms.	16.1, 16.2, 16.4, 16.5, 18.3, 18.5, 18.8
2f Understand the terms mean, mode and median.	16.3, 18.1
2h Make order of magnitude calculations.	18.12
4a Translate information between graphical and numeric form.	16.1, 16.2, 16.3, 16.4, 16.5, 16.8, 17.1, 17.4, 18.3, 18.6, 18.7
4c Plot two variables from experimental or other data.	16.3, 16.5, 17.4
5c Calculate areas of triangles and rectangles, surface areas, and volumes of cubes.	16.3, 16.7, 17.2, 18.4

B5 Ecology

KS3 concept	GCSE topic	Checkpoint	Revision
How food webs show the interdependence on organisms in an ecosystem	B17.1 Feeding relationships	Present students with a food web and ask them to write down 5 facts about what it shows	Ask students the affects of changing the populations of organisms in a food web, how does each affect other organisms?
That plants and animals have different requirements from their environments	B16.3 Distribution and abundance	Ask students to consider how the amount of light available in different places on a field affects the distribution of plants	Ask students to suggest why the species of plants found changes as you walk inland away from a shoreline
That organisms compete for resources	B16.4 Competition in animals	Ask students to name resources that animals and plants compete for	Ask students why a faster cheetah or a tree with long roots will be more likely to survive in the wild
That plants need mineral ions and water from the soil as well as carbon dioxide from the air and light to make the chemicals they need	B17.2 Materials cycling	Ask students why farmers use fertilisers	Ask students to suggest why decay is an important part of a food web
Factors that affect the growth of bacterial populations	B17.2 Materials cycling	Ask students to suggest how to slow down the decay of food in the kitchen	Ask students what the function of a plastic compost bin is and suggest why it is black
What population means	B16.1 The important of communities	Ask students to define the term population	Show students a graph of human population since the 1800s and ask them to interpret it
Draw a pyramid of numbers for a food chain	B18.8 Trophic levels and biomass	Give students a simple food chain e.g. grass→ rabbit → fox and ask them to draw a pyramid of numbers	Present students with different pyramids of number (some not pyramid shaped) and ask them to interpret what they show
The types of food people need to keep them healthy and the impact of poor diet on non-communicable diseases	B18.10 Factors affecting food security	Ask students to suggest examples of poor diets	Ask students to list the ways a poor diet can affect health
How pollution affects organisms	B18.2 Land and water pollution	Ask students to name examples of water and air pollutants	Ask students to discuss n groups the impact of rising carbon dioxide levels in the atmosphere
The importance of biodiversity and why gene banks are used	B18.7 Maintaining biodiversity	Ask students to define the term biodiversity	Ask students to list ways that humans impact on biodiversity and ways that we are trying to conserve it

B 16 Adaptations, interdependence, and competition

16.1 The importance of communities

AQA spec link: 7.1.1 Students should be able to describe:

- different levels of organisation in an ecosystem from individual organisms to the whole ecosystem
- the importance of interdependence and competition in a community.

Students should be able to, when provided with appropriate information:

- suggest the factors for which organisms are competing in a given habitat
- suggest how organisms are adapted to the conditions in which they live.

An ecosystem is the interaction of a community of living organisms with the non-living (abiotic) parts of their environment.

To survive and reproduce, organisms require a supply of materials from their surroundings and from the other living organisms there...

Plants in a community or habitat often compete with each other for light and space, and for water and mineral ions from the soil.

Animals often compete with each other for food, mates, and territory.

Within a community each species depends on other species for food, shelter, pollination, seed dispersal, etc. If one species is removed it can affect the whole community. This is called interdependence. A stable community is one where all the species and environmental factors are in balance so that population sizes remain fairly constant.

Students should be able to extract and interpret information from, charts, graphs, and tables relating to the interaction of organisms, within a community.

WS 2.6
MS 2c, 4a

Aiming for	Outcome	Checkpoint	
		Question	Activity
Aiming for GRADE 4 ↓	Describe what is meant by ecosystem, population, and community.	1, End of chapter 1	Starter 1, Plenary 1
	List some resources that living things need.		Main
	Use a given example to describe why one species relies on another.		Main, Plenary 2
Aiming for GRADE 6 ↓	Define the terms community, population, habitat, ecosystem, abiotic factor, biotic factor.	1, End of chapter 1	Starter 1, Plenary 1
	Describe what a stable community is and give an example.	3	Main
	Suggest how one species relies on another.	2, End of chapter 1	Main, Plenary 2
Aiming for GRADE 8 ↓	Link key words to explain why a community is stable and important.		Main
	Use evidence to write hypotheses about why populations have changed in a community.		Main, Homework
	Explain why interdependence is important in maintaining a stable community.	3	Main, Plenary 2

B16 Adaptations, interdependence, and competition

Maths
Students can analyse and interpret data showing bee population change. (4a)

Literacy
Students use information from books or the Internet to research stable ecosystems. They complete a Webquest where they use evidence from websites to write hypotheses about why populations changed in Lake Victoria.

Key words
communities, interdependence

Starter	Support/Extend	Resources
Ecological words (5 min) Students use the interactive to match key words with their definitions (e.g., community, population, habitat, ecosystem, distribution, abiotic factor, biotic factor). **Ecosystems** (10 min) Ask the class to suggest names of different ecosystems. Choose one that has high biodiversity and challenge students to spend 2 or 3 minutes listing as many organisms as they can think of that might be found in that community. Students can then peer assess and see who came up with the most organisms.	**Extend:** Only give students the key words and ask them to work in pairs to come up with definitions. **Support:** Make sure students understand what an ecosystem is – a group of living and non-living things interacting with each other. Give an example, (e.g., rainforest).	**Interactive:** Ecological words

Main	Support/Extend	Resources
A country garden (20 min) Assign each student a biotic or abiotic factor found in a garden. Biotic factors could include, for example, rose, ladybird, bee, goldfish, hedgehog, algae, grass, or soil bacteria. Abiotic elements could include, for example, water, sunlight, air, soil, or wind. Ask students to think about their role in the ecosystem and list ideas. Then, ask them to get into groups of four and work out how each biotic element in their group is dependent on all the other factors, and how they work together to create a stable community. For example, the bee is dependent on the soil because it provides plants with water and minerals to grow flowers to provide nectar for the bee. As a class, talk through some of the examples of interdependence that were discussed.	**Support:** Students can work in pairs at first and then join to form groups of four.	**Activity:** A country garden

Plenary	Support/Extend	Resources
Concept mapping (10 min) Give students the key words used in Starter 1. Ask them to link them together to create a concept map (a spider diagram with words/sentences linking the boxes) to outline what they learnt in the lesson. **The importance of bees** (5 min) Ask students to explain why bees are so important in maintaining a stable community.	**Support:** Students can just create a spider diagram. **Support:** Give students sentence starters' to guide their writing (e.g., Bees are pollinators. This means…). **Extend:** Provide students with data showing the change in bee population to interpret. This can be found by going to the Natural History Museum's website and searching for 'bumblebees'.	

Homework		
Ask students to find a simple food web. (They studied food webs at KS3). Students should choose three organisms from the food web and write an explanation of what would happen to the food web if that organism was removed from the community.	**Extend:** Students choose three abiotic factors and explain what affect changing them would have on the food web.	

B16.2 Organisms in their environment

AQA spec links: 7.1.2 Students should be able to explain how a change in an abiotic factor would affect a given community given appropriate data or context.

Abiotic (non-living) factors which can affect a community are:

- light intensity
- temperature
- moisture levels
- soil pH and mineral content
- wind intensity and direction
- carbon dioxide levels for plants
- oxygen levels for aquatic animals.

Students should be able to extract and interpret information from charts, graphs and tables relating to the effect of abiotic factors on organisms within a community.

7.1.3 Students should be able to explain how a change in a biotic factor might affect a given community given appropriate data or context.

Biotic (living) factors which can affect a community are:

- availability of food
- new predators arriving
- new pathogens
- one species outcompeting another so the numbers are no longer sufficient to breed.

Students should be able to extract and interpret information from charts, graphs, and tables relating to the effect of biotic factors on organisms within a community.

WS 1.2
MS 2c, 4a

Aiming for	Outcome	Checkpoint	
		Question	Activity
Aiming for GRADE 4 ↓	Identify factors as biotic or abiotic.	1	Starter 1, Starter 2, Plenary 1
	Use an instrument to measure an abiotic factor.		Main
Aiming for GRADE 6 ↓	Describe how a factor influences the distribution of organisms.	2, 3, 4, End of chapter 2, 4	Main, Plenary 2
	Record measurements of abiotic factors.		Main
Aiming for GRADE 8 ↓	Describe in detail how to measure the pH and water content of soil.		Main, Plenary 2
	Analyse data in detail and draw appropriate conclusions.		Main, Plenary 2, Homework

Maths
Students suggest ranges and units for different abiotic factors (e.g., air temperature). They use instruments to measure abiotic factors and record and analyse data. Students analyse a chart to make conclusions. (4a)

Literacy
Students work in groups to research an abiotic factor and produce a report.

260

■ B16 Adaptations, interdependence, and competition

Practical

Title	Measuring abiotic factors
Equipment	rain gauges, maximum–minimum thermometers, oxygen meters
Overview of method	Students measure the dissolved oxygen concentration and water temperature in different locations in a pond or stream. They place thermometers and rain gauges in different locations in the school grounds.
Safety considerations	Careful handling needs to be stressed as the instruments may be expensive to replace if damaged. Follow local rules on working in an outside environment and wash hands after lesson. When any fieldwork is undertaken, students should work in groups and be aware of hazards. Sensible footwear and clothing should be worn. If the weather is hot and sunny, sunscreen and hats are required. Follow school guidelines for outside activities.

Starter	Support/Extend	Resources
Abiotic factors (10 min) Ask students to list as many abiotic factors as they can. Then ask them to choose some of their factors and estimate the range of values (with their units) that they would expect to find on Earth. On completion, ask students to compare and contrast their list with those of other students. **What will be different?** (5 min) Show students images of two highly contrasting environments such as rainforest, desert, tundra, or savannah. Ask them in pairs to compare them in terms of their abiotic factors and suggest biotic factors for each.	**Support:** Ask students to estimate ranges for air temperature only. **Extend:** Discuss which factors are hardest to estimate due to difficulties in measuring accurately.	

Main	Support/Extend	Resources
Abiotic and biotic factors (20 min) Ask students to consider a local ecosystem, for example, a local woodland or park. Students work through the abiotic and biotic factors given in the student book, and create a table that explains what affect each factor may have on the community of the chosen ecosystem, giving specific examples where relevant. **Measuring abiotic factors** (40 min) Students carry out fieldwork and measure the dissolved oxygen concentration and water temperature in different locations in a pond or stream. If you do not have a suitable location in the school grounds then they can use the oxygen probe on tap water. They could compare still water and water flowing from a tap, or water at different temperatures. Students could also record rainfall and temperature in suitable locations in the school grounds. Time will need to be allocated during the next lesson for analysing the results, or this could be done as homework.	**Support:** Demonstrate to students how to use the equipment. Students could simply use data loggers to measure light and temperature around the school. **Extend:** Students could also collect soil from different areas and measure the percentage water content by measuring mass before and after heating.	**Practical:** Measuring abiotic factors

Plenary	Support/Extend	Resources
Sorting factors (5 min) Students use the interactive to sort a list of factors according to whether they are abiotic factors or biotic factors. **Soil pH** (10 min) Show the class a diagram that shows the pH range of soil that different crops can tolerate. Ask students to draw conclusions.	**Extend:** Ask pairs to discuss how each of the factors could affect a population of native red squirrels. **Support:** Ask questions (e.g., what crops can grow in acidic soil?). **Extend:** Ask students why farmers sometimes add lime to their soil.	**Interactive:** Sorting factors

Homework		
Students can analyse their data from Main 2 and draw conclusions.	**Support:** Set specific questions for students to answer in order to analyse their data.	

kerboodle

A Kerboodle highlight for this lesson is **Bump up your grade: Understanding biotic and abiotic factors**. Refer to the **Content map** on Kerboodle for a full list of resources and assessment.

B16.3 Distribution and abundance

AQA spec link: 7.2.1 Students should understand that photosynthetic organisms are the producers of biomass for life on Earth.

Feeding relationships within a community can be represented by food chains. All food chains begin with a producer which synthesises molecules. This is usually a green plant or alga which makes glucose by photosynthesis.

A range of experimental methods using transects and quadrats are used by ecologists to determine the distribution and abundance of species in an ecosystem.

In relation to abundance of organisms students should be able to:
- understand the terms mean, mode, and median
- calculate arithmetic means
- plot and draw appropriate graphs selecting appropriate scales for the axes.

Producers are eaten by primary consumers, which in turn may be eaten by secondary consumers and then tertiary consumers. Consumers that kill and eat other animals are predators, and those eaten are prey. In a stable community the numbers of predators and prey rise and fall in cycles.

Interpret graphs used to model predator-prey cycles.

Students should be able to interpret graphs used to model these cycles.

Required practical: measure the population size of a common species in a habitat. Use sampling techniques to investigate the effect of a factor on the distribution of this species.

WS 1.2
MS 2b, 2f, 4a, 4c, 5c

Aiming for	Outcome	Checkpoint	
		Question	Activity
Aiming for GRADE 4	Describe the function of a quadrat and a transect.	End of chapter question 4a	Main
	Follow a method to estimate a population using a sampling technique.		Main
	Calculate the mean of a set of results.	2	Main
Aiming for GRADE 6	Explain how to use a quadrat and a transect to estimate population sizes.	2, 3 End of chapter 3, 4	Main, Plenary 2
	Design a method to estimate a population using a sampling technique.		Main
	Calculate range, mean, median, and mode in order to analyse results.	2 End of chapter 3	Main, Homework
Aiming for GRADE 8	Discuss what factors determine the size of the quadrat used.		Plenary 1
	Design independently an investigation based around a question or hypothesis.		Starter 2, Main
	Evaluate in detail the use of sampling to estimate population size.	1, 2	Homework

Maths
During the investigation students measure area (5c) and calculate means (2b). They are also reminded about how to calculate range, mode, and median and how these can be used to analyse fieldwork data. (2f)

Literacy
Students design a method to help them investigate the population size of organisms in a habitat.

Key words
abundance, distribution, quadrat, sample size, mean, quantitative sampling, range, median, mode, transect

Required practical

Title	Investigating population size
Equipment	two 20 m measuring tapes, table of random numbers or other generator of random numbers, 50 cm × 50 cm gridded quadrat frame, notebook and pencil, identification sheet

■ B16 Adaptations, interdependence, and competition

Overview of method	Measure out an area 20 m × 20 m in the chosen location. Students then choose random coordinates to place their quadrats. They count the number of species and repeat.
Safety considerations	Follow local rules on working in an outside environment and wash hands after lesson. When any fieldwork is undertaken, students should work in groups and be aware of hazards. Sensible footwear and clothing should be worn. If the weather is hot and sunny, sunscreen and hats are required. Follow school guidelines for outside activities.

Starter	Support/Extend	Resources
Sampling (10 min) Display the lyrics of a popular song for a five seconds and ask students to estimate the number of words. Invite students to reveal their estimates and the technique they used (e.g., counting the number of lines and how many words are in the few first lines). Discuss this as a form of sampling technique. **Distribution** (5 min) Ask students to suggest examples where the distribution of an organism in an ecosystem differs within a certain area. Discuss how they would count the population in order to check their hypothesis.	**Extend:** Discuss how to improve their methods to make their estimates more accurate. **Support:** Give an example (e.g., the amount of grass on a field). There will be less under trees and in areas with high footfall. **Extend:** Students should explain why the distribution is different.	

Main	Support/Extend	Resources
Investigating population size (40 min to plan in this lesson plus 1–2 extra lessons to complete) Show students images of the distribution of organisms, (e.g., daisies on a field, barnacles on a rock). Discuss why biologists might want to estimate the number of these organisms within an ecosystem. Ask students to use information from the student book to make notes on different techniques used to measure distribution. Choose a suitable location (e.g., the school field). Let students study the area and choose an organism to investigate. Discuss how to use a quadrat, how to choose random coordinates, why this is important, and how many samples to take. Pairs should then write their plan to include equipment, method, and a suitable results table. Go through with the class how to calculate mean, median, and mode, and how these could be used to analyse their results.	**Support:** Provide students with ideas of locations and suitable population to estimate (e.g., daisies in different areas of the school field). **Extend:** Students should write a question or hypothesis to investigate. They could compare different distinct areas or choose to use a line transect to study how the population changes gradually.	**Required practical:** Investigating population size **Calculation sheet:** Mean, median, and mode

Plenary	Support/Extend	Resources
Equipment (5 min) Use the interactive in which students link the names of pieces of apparatus to organisms that they are used to sample. **Quadrat calculation** (10 min) Set the class a question: Students are estimating the number of dandelions on a field that is 20 m × 20 m. They are using 50 × 50 cm square quadrats. – How many quadrats would cover the whole area? (1600) – If they wanted to cover 2%, how many samples would they need to take? (32) – The mean number of dandelions in a quadrat is 2.2. Estimate the number in the whole field. (3520)		**Interactive:** Equipment

Homework
Students can complete the planning section of the practical for homework.

kerboodle

A Kerboodle highlight for this lesson is **Maths skills: Sampling**. Refer to the **Content map** on Kerboodle for a full list of resources and assessment.

B16.4 Competition in animals

AQA spec link: 7.1.1 Students should be able to describe:

- different levels of organisation in an ecosystem from individual organisms to the whole ecosystem
- the importance of interdependence and competition in a community.

Students should be able to, when provided with appropriate information:

- suggest the factors for which organisms are competing in a given habitat
- suggest how organisms are adapted to the conditions in which they live.

An ecosystem is the interaction of a community of living organisms (biotic) with the non-living (abiotic) parts of their environment. To survive and reproduce, organisms require a supply of materials from their surroundings and from the other living organisms there.

WS 2.6
MS 2c, 4a

Aiming for	Outcome	Checkpoint	
		Question	Activity
Aiming for GRADE 4	Recognise that animals compete with each other for resources.		Starter 1
	List resources that animals compete with each other for.		Starter 2, Main 1
	Describe what will happen to an animal if it cannot compete for resources.	1	Main 1, Main 2, Plenary 1
Aiming for GRADE 6	Use information to suggest factors that animals are competing for in a given habitat.		Starter 2, Main 2
	Explain tactics that help an animal compete for a resource.	2, End of chapter question 6	Main 2, Plenary 2
	Describe how the distribution of a species has changed because of competition.		Main 2, Plenary 1
Aiming for GRADE 8	Evaluate a model of competition between organisms.		Main 1
	Use the terms inter-specific and intra-specific competition, and give examples of each.	1, End of chapter questions 1, 6	Starter 1
	Suggest and explain how animals are adapted to compete for resources.	3	Main 2, Homework

Maths
Students analyse maps that show how the distribution of red and grey squirrels has changed.

Literacy
Students write an explanation as to why there are many more non-native grey squirrels now living in the UK compared with native red squirrels.

Key word
competition

B16 Adaptations, interdependence, and competition

Starter	Support/Extend	Resources
Grass eaters (5 min) Give students one minute to write a list of as many animals they can think of that eat grass. Ask them to swap lists with another student to count how many they found, and announce the winner. Use this to introduce the idea of competition between animals for food. **Food web** (10 min) Show the class a food web for a certain ecosystem. Ask them to discuss in pairs what resources the animals will be competing for. As a class, write a list of these resources.	**Extend:** Introduce the terms inter-specific and intra-specific competition. **Support:** Explain the concept of competition first. **Extend:** Students can suggest how the animals are adapted to compete.	

Main	Support/Extend	Resources
Survival rivals (15 min) Print small cards, each showing one of the following words – food, territory, water, mate. Make enough cards so most, but not all members of the class will have a full set. Before the lesson, place the cards around the room. Ask the students to move around and collect cards to get a full set. The rules are that they can only hold one of each type at a time, they must not take any by force, and they can't swap. Give a time limit of 2 minutes. At the end, those without the full set did not 'survive'. As a class, discuss how this models real life, why each of these resources is needed, and how they could have increased their chances of survival. Then provide students with information about competition between red and grey squirrels in the UK (or ask them to use the Internet to do their own research). Ask them to write down an explanation as to why there are many more non-native grey squirrels now living in the UK than native red squirrels, using ideas about competition.	**Extend:** Repeat the game but this time let students share if they wish. Discuss whether this happens in real life, and why (e.g., mothers giving up their share of food for their offspring). **Extend:** Students can also evaluate the model – how well did it represent real life? **Support:** Set students questions that lead to the explanation.	**Activity:** Survival rivals

Plenary	Support/Extend	Resources
Panda problems (5 min) Remind the class that the giant panda only eats bamboo. Ask them to discuss in pairs how this links to the fact that pandas are endangered, using ideas about competition. **Name the resource** (10 min) Use the interactive to show the students a range of tactics that different animals use when competing for resources (e.g., a peacock using feathers to attract a mate, a male robin fighting another in his territory, an owl hunting at night). Students choose the resource that each tactic helps them to compete for.	**Support:** Give students two resources to choose from. **Extend:** Ask students how this adaptation helps the animals to survive.	**Interactive:** Name the resource

Homework		
Ask students to research other examples of competition between animals (e.g., non-native animals outcompeting native animals, inter-specific competition between animals in a habitat). They should explain how the animals compete successfully.	**Extend:** Students should explain how the adaptations animals have make them better competitors.	

B16.5 Competition in plants

AQA spec link: 7.1.1 Plants in a community or habitat often compete with each other for light and space, and for water and mineral ions from the soil.

Animals often compete with each other for food, mates and territory. Within a community each species depends on other species for food, shelter, pollination, seed dispersal etc. If one species is removed it can affect the whole community. This is called interdependence. A stable community is one where all the species and environmental factors are in balance so that population sizes remain fairly constant.

Students should be able to extract and interpret information from charts, graphs, and tables relating to the interaction of organisms within a community.

WS 2.6
MS 2c, 4a, 4c

Aiming for	Outcome	Checkpoint	
		Question	Activity
Aiming for GRADE 4 ↓	List resources that plants compete with each other for.		Starter 1
	Describe what seed dispersal is and give some ways in which plants carry it out.	2	Starter 2
	Make measurements of seedlings.		Main 1
Aiming for GRADE 6 ↓	Suggest factors that plants are competing for in a given habitat.	End of chapter 2	Starter 1, Plenary 1
	Explain why plants use seed dispersal.	2	Starter 2, Main 2
	Describe the methods plants use to outcompete others or avoid competition.	1, 3	Main 2, Plenary 2
Aiming for GRADE 8 ↓	Plan a method to investigate competition between cress seeds.		Main 1
	Analyse data to explain the effects of overcrowding.	End of chapter 2, 6	Main 1, Homework
	Suggest the problems caused by plants that can easily outcompete others.		Main 2, Plenary 1

Maths
Students make measurements of seedlings (length and mass). They record these and use them to draw conclusions about the effects of overcrowding. (4c)

Literacy
Students summarise information from the student book. They write explanations about why some plants outcompete others.

Practical

Title	Density of sowing
Equipment	four seed trays filled with compost, radish seeds, transparent plastic rulers, balances
Overview of method	Plant two sets of seeds using the seed manufacturer's recommendations for seed spacing. This is the control group. Plant two additional sets of seeds using 5 times the number of seeds per recommended spacing requirements. Leave all trays in identical growing conditions (light exposure, heat) and water each with the same amount of water. The plants will take around a month to grow. Students work in pairs to measure and observe one seedling from each set of trays.
Safety considerations	Wash hands after handling soil and seeds.

■ B16 Adaptations, interdependence, and competition

Starter	Support/Extend	Resources
What do plants compete for? (5 min) Remind the class that animals compete for food, mates, and territory. Show them an image of plants growing in a forest. Students use the interactive to list the resources they think the plants are competing for. **Spreading the seeds** (10 min) Ask students what methods of seed dispersal they can remember from KS3. (Show images to prompt if necessary.) Ask students to use their understanding on competition to explain why plants use seed dispersal methods.	**Support:** Provide students with a list of resources for them to choose from.	**Interactive:** What do plants compete for?

Main	Support/Extend	Resources
Density of sowing (25 min) Let students study seed packets for information on how to sow seeds. Ask them why the packet gives information on how far apart to sow the seeds and why this is different for each species of plant. Allow them to study seedlings that have been set up in advance to show the effects of density of sowing on seedlings. Split the class into pairs. Each pair should make observations and measure the length of shoot, length of root, and mass of one seedling from each set of trays. They can share results in order to analyse the data and draw conclusions. **Invasive plants** (15 min) Ask students to read the section *Coping with competition* in the student book and make bullet points of the adaptations plants have to avoid competition. Then show images of invasive plants to show their fast growth rate, (e.g., Japanese knotweed and kudzu). Ask students to suggest why these plants are so successful.	**Extend:** Students can plan and set up their own experiment using cress seeds. **Extend:** Students should also suggest why invasive plants can be a problem to humans.	**Practical:** Density of sowing

Plenary	Support/Extend	Resources
Weed removal (5 min) Ask students to explain why farmers want to remove weeds from their crop fields, using ideas about competition. **Plant adaptations** (10 min) Show the class a series of images of familiar plants that are well-adapted for competition, for example, dandelion (spreads seeds), ivy (climbs towards light), clover (makes nitrates), snowdrop (grows in winter). Ask students to suggest how each is adapted in terms of competition.	**Support:** Create a cloze exercise on this.	

Homework		
You may wish students to analyse the data collected in Main 1 and draw conclusions as a homework task.		

kerboodle

A Kerboodle highlight for this lesson is **Extension: Investigation of the distribution of species**. Refer to the **Content map** on Kerboodle for a full list of resources and assessment.

B16.6 Adapt and survive

AQA spec link: 7.1.4 Students should be able to explain how organisms are adapted to live in their natural environment, given appropriate information.

Organisms have features (adaptations) that enable them to survive in the conditions in which they normally live. These adaptations may be structural, behavioural, or functional.

Some organisms live in environments that are very extreme, such as at high temperature, pressure, or salt concentration. These organisms are called extremophiles. Bacteria living in deep sea vents are extremophiles.

Aiming for	Outcome	Checkpoint	
		Question	Activity
Aiming for GRADE 4 ↓	Describe one example of how an organism is adapted.	3	Starter 2, Plenary 1
	Define an extremophile.	1	Main 2
Aiming for GRADE 6 ↓	Suggest features that an organism may have in order to survive in a given habitat.	3	Main 1, Main 2, Plenary 1
	Explain how adaptations allow an organism to survive in its habitat.	3	Starter 2, Main 1, Main 2, Plenary 1
Band C to D GRADE 8 ↓	Suggest and explain in detail how an organism in an extreme location might evolve to become better adapted to its habitat.		Main 1
	Apply knowledge of extremophiles to discuss why scientists believe there could be life on other planets (or moons).		Plenary 2

Maths
Student use measurements and SI units to describe the extreme conditions that extremophiles live in (e.g., temperatures over 80°C).

Literacy
Students use the Internet to research an extremophile. They present their findings to the rest of the class.
They may also use the names of extremophiles to suggest what type of habitat they live in by using the root of the word (e.g., **therm**ophiles live in very hot temperatures).

Key words
adaptations, extremophiles

■ B16 Adaptations, interdependence, and competition

Starter	Support/Extend	Resources
What do microorganisms need? (5 min) Ask pairs to discuss what resources they think microorganisms compete for. As a class, discuss that they need a range of things. Some are similar to plants and animals and some don't need oxygen or light to survive.	**Support:** Students can list resources that plants and animals compete for.	
Pick an organism (10 min) Students are shown a range of plants and animals with different structural, behavioural, and functional adaptations. Students use the interactive to select the strategy each organism is showing. They should describe these strategies as adaptations.	**Extend:** Students should try to group the organisms in terms of their survival strategies.	**Interactive:** Pick an organism

Main	Support/Extend	Resources
Making a living organism (20 min) Ask students to name some extreme environments that would be difficult for an organism to live in (e.g., inside a volcano, the top of Everest, deep ocean trenches, the surface of Mars). Ask them to explain why it would be difficult to live there. Then students should pick one location and design an organism that has adaptations to help it to survive there. They draw the organism, label the adaptations, and explain how they help it to survive.	**Support:** As a class choose one suitable location. **Extend:** Students should explain in detail how their organisms evolved to have these adaptations.	**Activity sheet:** Making a living organism
Extremophiles (20 min) Give students some examples of extremophiles (organisms that live in extreme conditions) – red flat bark beetle (*Cucujus clavipes*), Sahara desert ant (*Cataglyphis bicolor*), Himalayan jumping spider (*Euophrys omnisuperstes*), Pompeii worm (*Alvinella pompejana*), *Aquifex* genus of bacteria, or the bacteria *Halobacterium halobium*. Ask them to use the Internet to research one of them. They should find out where it lives, why this is an extreme environment, how it is adapted, and how this helps it to survive. They can present their findings to the rest of the class.	**Support:** Students can work in small groups. **Extend:** Ask students to suggest what each of these types of extremophile are tolerant to, using their existing knowledge of scientific terms – acidophile, alkaliphile, anaerobe, halophile, thermophile, xerophile. Students can choose their own extremophile to study.	

Plenary	Support/Extend	Resources
The life of blister beetles (10 min) Show the class a video of how blister beetle larvae get food (search for 'blister beetle' on the BBC website). Ask them to describe why the beetle's habitat is extreme, why getting food is difficult, and how the larvae are adapted to find food.	**Extend:** Discuss how this behavioural adaptation of the larvae is an example of an instinct.	
Life on Europa? (5 min) Tell the class that Europa is a moon of Jupiter that is covered with a thick layer of ice underneath which is liquid water. Use what students have found out about extremophiles to discuss why scientists believe that there may be organisms living here.	**Extend:** Students should suggest what the organisms may be like.	

Homework		
Students complete the WebQuest where they research extremophiles.		**WebQuest:** Life at the extreme

B16.7 Adaptations in animals

AQA spec link: 7.1.4 Students should be able to explain how organisms are adapted to live in their natural environment, given appropriate information. Organisms have features (adaptations) that enable them to survive in the conditions in which they normally live. These adaptations may be structural, behavioural, or functional.

MS 5c

Aiming for	Outcome	Checkpoint	
		Question	Activity
Aiming for GRADE 4	Describe one example of an animal adaptation.		Starter 1, Main 2, Homework
	Describe why it is important that most animals maintain the correct body temperature.	1, End of chapter question 5	Starter 2
↓	Describe why fur or feathers can be used to maintain a warm body temperature.	2	Main 2
Aiming for GRADE 6	Classify adaptations as structural, behavioural, or functional.		Starter 1
	Calculate surface area to volume ratio.		Main 1
↓	Describe how animals are adapted to live in hot, dry, and cold habitats.	1, 2, 3, End of chapter question 5	Main 2, Homework
Aiming for GRADE 8	Suggest structural, behavioural, or functional adaptations.		Starter 1
	Explain and illustrate how surface area to volume ratio is linked to maintaining the correct body temperature.	2, 3, End of chapter question 5	Main 1
↓	Discuss how and why climate change is affecting the distribution of animals.		Plenary 2

Maths
Students calculate surface area to volume ratios. (5c)

Literacy
Students use books and/or the Internet to research animals that live in hot and cold habitats. They present their findings to the rest of the class.

Key word
predators

■ B16 Adaptations, interdependence, and competition

Starter	Support/Extend	Resources
What type of adaptation? (5 min) Provide students with a list of animal adaptations and ask them to sort them into structural, behavioural, or functional adaptations. **Temperature regulation** (10 min) Discuss why it is important that animals maintain a constant body temperature.	**Support:** Students can use information from the student book to help them. **Extend:** Students should suggest one other adaptation to fit into each category. **Extend:** Discuss how mammals and birds can regulate their body temperature, but other animals cannot.	**Interactive:** What type of adaptation?

Main	Support/Extend	Resources
Surface area to volume ratio (15 min) Review what is meant by surface area to volume ratio and how to calculate it (students could use the Maths skills activity from B4.5 to recap this). Ask students to use information from the student book to find out how surface area to volume ratio, and insulation, is important for the temperature regulation of animals. **Hot and cold** (25 min) Ask half the class to research animals that live in cold conditions in polar regions, and half to research those that live in hot, dry deserts. They should use books and/or the Internet to list animals that live there, the problems they face, and their adaptations. Invite students from each side to present one thing they found out. You can award prizes for the most interesting facts. Allow all students to make notes on adaptations of animals that live in these extremes of temperature. They can supplement these with information from the student book.	**Extend:** Students should complete the Working scientifically exercise. They analyse data from an insulation experiment. **Support:** Ask students to either research the polar bear or the camel. **Extend:** Encourage students to find examples of unusual animals.	**Maths skills:** Surface area to volume ratio **Working scientifically:** Insulation

Plenary	Support/Extend	Resources
Camouflage (5 min) Show the class some examples of camouflaged animals in their habitat, and ask students to spot them. Use one example and ask them to write down how this adaptation aids the animal's survival. **Polar problem** (10 min) Discuss the fact that the Arctic is getting warmer. Ask students to suggest why this is affecting the population of polar bears.	**Extend:** Discuss how climate change is affecting the distribution of animals, and why.	

Homework		
Set the class an example of an exam question on animal adaptation.	**Extend:** Also set a question on plant adaptation so students can apply their knowledge.	

B16.8 Adaptations in plants

AQA spec link: 7.1.4 Students should be able to explain how organisms are adapted to live in their natural environment, given appropriate information.

MS 4a

Aiming for	Outcome	Checkpoint	
		Question	Activity
Aiming for GRADE 4 ↓	Describe one example of a plant adaptation.		Main, Plenary 1
	Describe why plants need a constant supply of water.	1	Starter 1
	Draw a graph to display data, with guidance.		Main
Aiming for GRADE 6 ↓	Explain how a plant adaptation allows it to survive in its habitat.	3	Main, Plenary 1
	Explain why plants need to reduce water loss by transpiration.	2	Starter 2
	Display data using a graph and describe what it shows.		Main
Aiming for GRADE 8 ↓	Explain how an unfamiliar plant is adapted and give reasons for its adaptations.		Plenary 1
	Link and explain rate of transpiration to leaf structure.		Main, Plenary 1
	Suggest and explain why a cactus would not survive in a cold climate.		Plenary 2

Maths
Students display data showing rate of transpiration as a graph and analyse it in order to draw conclusions. (4a)

Literacy
Students carry out research and label a diagram with plant adaptations. They explain how each helps it to survive.

B16 Adaptations, interdependence, and competition

Starter	Support/Extend	Resources
The need for water (10 min) Ask students to list reasons why water is important for plants. Pairs of students can then compare lists and feed back their ideas to the class. Discuss how plants are adapted to take up water efficiently. **Transpiration** (5 min) Review knowledge about transpiration by asking students to work in groups to complete a spider diagram showing everything they already know.	**Extend:** Discuss how plants lose water by transpiration, and adaptations that some have to reduce this.	

Main	Support/Extend	Resources
Analysing transpiration data (40 min) Provide students with a method and raw data from an investigation into the rate of transpiration using shoots from different species of plant. Ask students to analyse the data using methods of their choosing. Show the students images of each plant and ask them to explain why the rate was different based on the structure of their leaves, and why these plants might have these adaptations.	**Support:** Guide students through how to analyse the data (e.g., what type of graph to use).	**Activity:** Analysing transpiration data

Plenary	Support/Extend	Resources
Plant adaptations (5 min) Ask students to match images of different plants to the correct description of the adaptation and the reason for the adaptation. For example, an image of marram grass should be matched to curled leaves and to reduce water loss. **Why wouldn't you find...** (10 min) Ask students to explain why you wouldn't find a cactus in the Arctic.	**Extend:** Use examples that were not used in Main 1 so students have to apply their knowledge. **Extend:** Students should write their own examples and swap with a partner.	**Interactive:** Plant adaptations

Homework		
Ask students to summarise the learning in this chapter. They can create a glossary, create revision cards, design a poster, or create a script for a revision podcast.	**Support:** Provide students with key words for them to include in their summary.	

kerboodle

A Kerboodle highlight for this lesson is **Homework: Plant and animal adaptations**. Refer to the **Content map** on Kerboodle for a full list of resources and assessment.

B16 Adaptations, interdependence, and competition

Overview of B16 Adaptations, interdependence, and competition

In this chapter students have studied communities, environments, adaptations, and competition. There are a number of ecological terms including community, population, habitat, ecosystem, abiotic factor, and biotic factor, and students should recall the precise meaning of each.

Students should understand the importance of communities including the interdependence of all the species present, and be able to give real examples to illustrate interdependence. In studying organisms in their environments, students should recall the effects of abiotic and biotic factors on populations. They should link this with the importance of temperature and pH on the action of enzymes in B3 *Organisation and the digestive system*. Students should have measured the distribution of organisms with quadrats and transects, and carried out a practical to investigate the population size of a common species in a habitat.

Students have studied competition in animals and plants and should recall what factors they compete for and how they compete, and how they become successful in their environments.

Students should understand how organisms are adapted to survive in many different conditions. They should be able to give examples of the ways in which animals and plants are adapted to their environments. In studying animals in cold climates students should make the link to surface area to volume ratio in their work on diffusion in B1 *Cells and organisation*.

Required practical

All students are expected to have carried out the required practical:

Practical	Topic
Measure the population size of a common species in a habitat. Use sampling techniques to investigate the effect of a factor on the distribution of this species.	B16.3

MyMaths

You can find additional support for the maths skills covered in this chapter on **MyMaths**, including data analysis, measuring abiotic factors using the correct units, calculating means, ranges, modes, and medians, and using surface area to volume ratios.

kerboodle

For this chapter, the following assessments are available on Kerboodle:

B16 Checkpoint quiz: Adaptations, interdependence, and competition
B16 Progress quiz: Adaptations, interdependence, and competition 1
B16 Progress quiz: Adaptations, interdependence, and competition 2
B16 On your marks: Adaptations, interdependence, and competition
B16 Exam-style questions and mark scheme: Adaptations, interdependence, and competition

Checkpoint follow-up lesson

A student's route through this lesson can be determined using the Checkpoint assessment. Percentage pass marks are supplied in the Checkpoint teacher notes.

For each successive route through it is assumed that the student can perform to their current route as well as previous routes. For example, students working at Aiming for 6 are assumed to be secure in Aiming for 4 knowledge and understanding and working towards achieving all the learning outcomes for Aiming for 6.

	Aiming for 4	**Aiming for 6**	**Aiming for 8**
Learning outcomes	State some abiotic and biotic factors.	Describe some abiotic and biotic factors.	Understand how abiotic and biotic factors interact in an ecosystem.
	State some things that animals and plants compete for.	Describe some things that animals and plants compete for.	Explain why animals and plants compete for certain resources.
	State some adaptations of animals and plants to their environment.	Describe some adaptations of animals and plants to their environment.	Explain some adaptations of animals and plants to their environment.
Starter	**Interdependence (5 min)** Show an image of an ecosystem, for example, a pond. Pictures of various ecosystems are readily available on the Internet. Ask targeted questions such as – what would happen if there was a drought? What would happen if a new predator arrived and ate the fish? Use this as a stimulus to introduce the idea of interdependence.		
Differentiated checkpoint activity	Students work in small groups moving around five stations, spending around 10 minutes at each station. Students work in pairs. You will need to move students on to the next station at the appropriate time. You will need: • station 1 – scissors and glue sticks for Aiming for 4 students, A3 paper • station 2 – calculators • station 3 – scissors for Aiming for 4 students, mini-whiteboards and pens • station 4 – pictures of a camel, a polar bear, and a cactus • station 5 – animal skulls or pictures of different animals' teeth including a range of herbivores and carnivores. Some omnivores can be included for Aiming for 8 students.		
	The Aiming for 4 sheet is highly structured, including a cut and paste exercise.	The Aiming for 6 sheet is fairly structured and should not require introduction from the teacher.	The Aiming for 8 sheet has very little structure. Students should be able to complete their task with no introduction from the teacher.
	Kerboodle resource B16 Checkpoint follow-up: Aiming for 4, B16 Checkpoint follow-up: Aiming for 6, B16 Checkpoint follow-up: Aiming for 8		
Plenary	**Review (5 min)** Ask the students to stand up. They may sit when they have answered a question correctly. Ask targeted questions, such as: 1. Is this factor abiotic or biotic? 2. What was the population? 3. Name a factor that plants/animals compete for. 4. Name an adaptation of a camel/polar bear/cactus. 5. Is this skull from a herbivore or a carnivore?		
Progression	To progress, students should create a glossary of the ecological terms they have met in the chapter.	To progress, students should give real examples to illustrate interdependence.	To progress, students should research other examples of of adaptation for competition and general adaptations for surviva..

B 17 Organising an ecosystem
17.1 Feeding relationships

AQA spec link: 7.2.1 Students should understand that photosynthetic organisms are the producers of biomass for life on Earth.

Feeding relationships within a community can be represented by food chains. All food chains begin with a producer which synthesises molecules. This is usually a green plant which makes glucose by photosynthesis.

Producers are eaten by primary consumers, which in turn may be eaten by secondary consumers and then tertiary consumers.

Consumers that eat other animals are predators, and those eaten are prey. In a stable community the numbers of predators and prey rise and fall in cycles.

Students should be able to interpret graphs used to model these cycles.

WS 1.2
MS 4a

Aiming for	Outcome	Checkpoint	
		Question	Activity
Aiming for GRADE 4	State the meaning of the terms producer, consumer, predator, and prey, and give examples of each.	1, End of chapter 1	Starter 1, Plenary 1
	Identify producers, consumers, predators, and prey in a food chain.		Starter 2, Main 1
	Describe what a graph shows about how the numbers of predators and prey change over time.	3, End of chapter 1	Main 2, Plenary 2
Aiming for GRADE 6	Identify producers, primary consumers, secondary consumers, tertiary consumers, predators, and prey in a food web.		Main 1, Homework
	Describe what happens to a population in a food web when another population changes.		Main 1
	Plot data as a line graph and explain the pattern of predator and prey populations.	3, End of chapter 1	Main 2, Plenary 2
Aiming for GRADE 8	Explain in detail why all living things depend on producers.	1	Starter 1, Main 1
	Evaluate in detail food chains/webs as models to show feeding relationships.	2	Main 1
	Make predictions based on data on a predator–prey relationship.	3	Main 2, Plenary 1

Maths
Students display data as a graph. They interpret the graph and explain what it shows about predator–prey relationships. (4a)

Literacy
Students use and define key words to explain feeding relationships.

Key words
biomass, producers, primary consumers, secondary consumers

276

■ B17 Organising an ecosystem

Starter	Support/Extend	Resources
Producers (5 min) Show the class images of different plants and algae. Ask students to write down why they think they are called producers. After hearing their ideas, discuss the fact that plants and algae are able to produce their own food by photosynthesis.	**Support:** Include images of animals feeding on plants when asking students why plants are called producers. **Extend:** Students should explain why all living things depend on producers.	
Food chains (10 min) Ask students to work in groups and give each group an example of a food chain on a large sheet of paper. Ask them to annotate it with as much scientific terminology as they can (e.g., label the plant as a producer).	**Support:** Provide students with the words to use – producer, primary consumer, secondary consumer, predator, prey, herbivore, carnivore, energy.	

Main	Support/Extend	Resources
Food webs (15 min) Provide students with an example of a food web. Set them a series of questions on categorising the different organisms and on how a change in the population of one organism can affect an other.	**Extend:** Students should write questions for a partner and then peer assess the answers. **Extend:** Discuss the limitations of food chains/webs as models.	**Working scientifically:** Predator/prey relationship
Predator/prey relationship (25 min) Give students data showing changes in the population of a prey and predator. Ask them to plot the data on a suitable graph (both populations should be on the same set of axes). Then ask students to explain the shape of the graph. They can use the explanation of the predator–prey cycle in the corresponding student book to assess their answer.	**Support:** Provide ready-drawn axes and guide students on how to plot the data. **Extend:** Students should make predictions based on the data.	

Plenary	Support/Extend	Resources
Feeding relationship key words (10 min) Students complete the interactive to revise key words and their definitions.	**Support:** Read out a definition and ask students to say the key word.	**Interactive:** Feeding relationships key words
Predator and prey (5 min) Ask students to suggest what would happen to a predator/prey graph when the following variables are changed: • prey birthrate • predator effectiveness. Students should justify their answers.		

Homework		
Ask students to design a food web for organisms found in their garden, a local park, or the school field.	**Support:** Students can just draw out some examples of simple food chains found in one of the locations.	

kerboodle

A Kerboodle highlight for this lesson is **Calculation sheet: Predator–prey relationship numbers**. Refer to the **Content map** on Kerboodle for a full list of resources and assessment.

B17.2 Materials cycling

AQA spec link: 7.2.2 Students should:
- recall that many different materials cycle through the abiotic and biotic components of an ecosystem
- explain the importance of the carbon and water cycles to living organisms.

All materials in the living world are recycled to provide the building blocks for future organisms...The water cycle provides fresh water for plants and animals on land before draining into the seas. Water is continuously evaporated and precipitated.

Students are not expected to study the nitrogen cycle.

Students should be able to explain the role of microorganisms in cycling materials through an ecosystem. Decay of dead plants and animals by microorganisms returns carbon to the atmosphere as carbon dioxide and mineral ions to the soil.

WS 1.2
MS 5c

Aiming for	Outcome	Checkpoint	
		Question	Activity
Aiming for GRADE 4 ↓	Describe what a decomposer is and give examples.	1	Main 2
	Name some substances that are recycled in the living world.		Main 1, Homework
	Describe the events in the water cycle.	2	Starter 2
Aiming for GRADE 6 ↓	Explain why decomposers are important to a stable ecosystem.	5	Starter 1
	Explain the importance of recycling substances.	3, 6	Starter 1, Plenary 2
	Describe the events in the decay cycle.		Main 1
Aiming for GRADE 8 ↓	Explain how detritivores increase the rate of decay using ideas about surface area.		Main 2
	Explain how substances change as they decay.		Main 2
	Comment on the limitations of a simple model of decay.		Plenary 1

Maths
Tell the class that 97% of the world's water is found in salty oceans, and ask them to calculate how much is fresh water (3%). Discuss the implications of this for accessible drinking water for life on Earth. (5c)

Literacy
Students write a narration for a time-lapse video to explain the process of decay. They also arrange the parts of the decay cycle and use correct terminology to describe the water cycle.

Key word
decomposers

■ B17 Organising an ecosystem

Starter	Support/Extend	Resources
A world without decay (10 min) Ask students to form groups and discuss what the world would be like if there was no decay. Ask groups to feed back their ideas and draw out the idea that decay is useful for recycling materials. **The water cycle** (5 min) Students use their prior knowledge to label a diagram of the water cycle on the interactive.	**Support:** Provide groups with stimulus images showing decay (e.g., mouldy fruit). **Support:** Provide the words to use – condensation, evaporation, precipitation, respiration, transpiration.	**Interactive:** The water cycle

Main	Support/Extend	Resources
The decay cycle (20 min) Provide students with cards that describe the parts of the decay cycle (Figure 2 in the student book. Ask students to arrange the cards to create a cycle that shows how carbon atoms and mineral ions are recycled. They can check their answers against the diagram in the student book. **Explaining decay** (20 min) Ask students to work in pairs to write a suitable narration that explains what is happening in Figure 1 of the student book. Their narration should include which organisms are carrying out the process of decay and why decay is vital for the survival of other organisms in the ecosystem. They should use the information in the student book to help them.	**Support:** Provide a cycle with boxes on an A3 piece of paper. Students can place the cards in the correct box. **Extend:** Students should give scientific explanations for the change in appearance of the decaying organism. **Extend:** Encourage students to explain how detritivores such as worms and maggots increase the rate of decay, using ideas about surface area.	**Activity:** The decay cycle

Plenary	Support/Extend	Resources
Modelling decay (10 min) Provide students with simple models made out of interlocking plastic blocks. Ask them to rearrange the blocks to build something else, and then explain how this models the decay cycle. **Importance of the water cycle** (5 min) Go round the class and ask each student to state one thing that would happen if there was no water cycle. Discuss how important it is to life on Earth.	**Extend:** Students should comment on the limitations of this model for decay (e.g., it does not show how some carbon is converted into carbon dioxide during respiration by decomposers).	

Homework		
Ask students to find out the names of other substances that are recycled in nature (e.g., oxygen, nitrogen).	**Extend:** Students should complete the Go further activity to find out about the nitrogen cycle in more detail.	

kerboodle

A Kerboodle highlight for this lesson is **Go further: The nitrogen cycle**. Refer to the **Content map** on Kerboodle for a full list of resources and assessment.

B17.3 The carbon cycle

AQA spec link: 7.2.2 The carbon cycle returns carbon from organisms to the atmosphere as carbon dioxide to be used by plants in photosynthesis.

WS 1.2
MS 1b

Aiming for	Outcome	Checkpoint Question	Checkpoint Activity
Aiming for GRADE 4	Recognise that carbon atoms are moved around the Earth (recycled).	1	Starter 1, Main 1, Main 2
	Give one reason why we need to recycle carbon.		Main 1
	Use a diagram of the carbon cycle to describe the main processes involved.		Starter 1, Plenary 2, Homework
Aiming for GRADE 6	Describe the events in the carbon cycle.	1, End of chapter 4	Starter 1, Main 1, Main 2, Plenary 1, Homework
	Explain why the carbon cycle is vital to life on Earth.	1, End of chapter 4	Main 1
	Write word equations for photosynthesis, respiration, and combustion.		Main 1
Aiming for GRADE 8	Explain in detail why the concentration of carbon dioxide in the atmosphere is rising, and why this is an issue.	End of chapter 4	Main 2
	Explain the links between photosynthesis, respiration, and combustion in the carbon cycle.	3	Starter 2, Main 1
	Write balanced symbol equations for photosynthesis, respiration, and combustion.		Starter 2, Main 1

Maths
Provide students with data that shows how the concentration of carbon dioxide in the atmosphere has changed. Tell the class that every year about 166 gigatonnes of carbon are cycled through the living world. Ask them convert this into tonnes (166 000 000 000) and express this in standard form (1.66×10^{11}). (1b)

Literacy
Through discussion and research, students work out the structure of the carbon cycle. They write a story explaining how a carbon atom is recycled.

■ B17 Organising an ecosystem

Starter	Support/Extend	Resources
Study the cycle (10 min) Split the class into groups of four to five students, and give each group a piece of A4 paper. One student from each groups comes to the front and has 30 seconds to study an image of the carbon cycle. They then return to their group and describe what they saw, with the rest of the group drawing it. The next student from each group comes up and gets 30 seconds to study the image, before returning to the group and adding to their image. This continues until each member of the group has studied the image and reported back. Invite each group to share their diagram for the rest of the class to judge which group re-created the carbon cycle the most accurately.	**Support:** Provide groups with partially completed diagrams.	
Fossil fuel combustion (5 min) Light a Bunsen burner and ask students to suggest how this links to photosynthesis. You may wish to give hints, for example, what is burning? (methane/natural gas), what gas is produced from the burning of methane? (carbon dioxide).	**Support:** Give students a choice of three answers – one being correct. **Extend:** Students should write word and balanced symbol equations for the combustion of methane.	

Main	Support/Extend	Resources
Processes in the carbon cycle (30 min) Split the class into groups and give each group a process of the carbon cycle to study in more detail (photosynthesis, respiration, combustion, decay and decomposition, feeding). Ask each group to research how their process moves carbon from one place to another, name the places, write down any word equations for the process, and draw a picture to represent it. Then ask them to present their findings and use them to compile a class diagram of the carbon cycle. Use an animation of the carbon cycle to check and reinforce students' understanding.	**Extend:** Students should write balanced symbol equations as well.	**Activity:** Processes in the carbon cycle
Pass the carbon (10 min) Provide groups of five students with a soft ball to represent a carbon atom. Give students roles as parts of the carbon cycle (the atmosphere, plant, animal, fossil fuel, decomposer). Ask the group to pass the ball around to model how carbon is recycled, and to name each process that they are showing.	**Extend:** Students should use their model to explain why the concentration of carbon dioxide in the atmosphere is rising, and why this is an issue.	

Plenary	Support/Extend	Resources
Jurassic carbon (10 min) Tell the class that a carbon atom in their body might have been part of a dinosaur million of years ago. Ask students to discuss in pairs how this could be true.	**Support:** Tell students to use their copy of the carbon cycle to trace different ways in which a carbon atom could move from one animal into the body of another. **Extend:** Students could write the movement of a carbon atom through the cycle down as a story and complete for homework.	
Carbon cycle sort (5 min) Students are shown the main parts of the carbon cycle and have to arrange them in the correct order.		**Interactive:** Carbon cycle sort

Homework		
Either set the summary questions from the student book spread, a past exam question, or completion of the story from Plenary 1.		

kerboodle

A Kerboodle highlight for this lesson is **Homework: The carbon cycle**. Refer to the **Content map** on Kerboodle for a full list of resources and assessment.

GCSE Biology only

B17.4 Rates of decomposition

AQA spec link: 7.2.3 Students should be able to explain how temperature, water, and availability of oxygen affect the rate of decay of biological material.

Students should be able to:

- calculate rate changes in the decay of biological material
- translate information between numerical and graphical form
- plot and draw appropriate graphs selecting appropriate scales for the axes.

Gardeners and farmers try to provide optimum conditions for rapid decay of waste biological material. The compost produced is used as a natural fertiliser for growing garden plants or crops.

Anaerobic decay produces methane gas. Biogas generators can be used to produce methane gas as a fuel.

Required practical: Investigate the effect of temperature on the rate of decay of fresh milk by measuring pH change.

MS 1c, 4a, 4c

Aiming for	Outcome	Checkpoint	
		Question	Activity
Aiming for GRADE 4 ↓	List the factors that affect the rate of decay.		Starter 2
	Choose a suitable independent variable and a way of changing it.		Main
	Plot a line graph with more than one line plotted on the same axes, with guidance.		Main
Aiming for GRADE 6 ↓	Identify factors that speed up or slow down decay.		Starter 1, Plenary 1, Homework
	Choose a suitable dependent variable and plan a way to measure it accurately.		Main
	Plot a line graph with more than one line plotted on the same axes.		Main
Aiming for GRADE 8 ↓	Explain why factors speed up or slow down decay.	End of chapter 5	Starter 2, Plenary, Homework
	Apply factors which affect the rate of decay to real life situations (e.g., compost making, preserving food).	1, 2, End of chapter 2, 5	Plenary 2, Homework
	Calculate percentage change and rate of decay.		Main

Maths
Students plan how to collect quantitative data. They make measurements and then display data as a line graph where more than one independent variable is plotted. They may extend this and use their graph to calculate rate of decay. (4c)

Literacy
Students write a plan for an investigation, to include an equipment list and method.

282

■ B17 Organising an ecosystem

Required practical

Title	The rate of decay
Equipment	sample of milk measuring cylinders (10 cm^3), balances, small beakers, thermometers, waterproof pens or sticky labels, mobile device/camera (optional)
Overview of method	Students place milk samples in beakers. They should choose an appropriate method to maintain the temperature of their milk sample (e.g., in fridge or laboratory oven). They choose the dependent variable and measure it in subsequent lessons.
Safety considerations	Ensure that no food is eaten. Wear gloves when handling food. Wash hands when set-up is complete. Waste should be disposed of in an appropriate manner. Students must not open the containers once mould has started to form.

Starter	Support/Extend	Resources
What happens when food decays? (5 min) Show students a series of images of food before and after it has decayed (e.g., milk, bread, fruit). Ask students to suggest what has happened, and why.	**Extend:** Students should also suggest how they would measure the decay so it can be compared to the same food in different conditions.	
What affects the rate of decay? (10 min) Students sort conditions (warm temperature, cold temperature, lots of oxygen, no oxygen, moist conditions, dry conditions, no carbon dioxide, lots of carbon dioxide) into groups of what will speed up, slow down, or have no effect on decay.	**Extend:** Students should explain why each condition has this effect.	**Interactive:** What affects the rate of decay?

Main	Support/Extend	Resources
The rate of decay (40 min to plan in this lesson, plus time in subsequent lessons to take measurements and a further lesson to analyse data) Ask students to work through the questions in the Required practical box in the student book spread to help them plan their investigation. They should produce an equipment list and a method. Discuss how they will collect quantitative data. One idea is to measure the mass of the milk each day and calculate the percentage loss. Check methods and allow students to set up their experiment. Students should use time in subsequent lessons to collect data. This should be represented as a line graph with more than one line plotted (e.g., the different temperatures they used) with time on the x-axis and decay (measured using mass or other quantitative technique) on the y-axis.	**Support:** Place the equipment on a desk so students can choose what to use (include different examples of organic material). **Extend:** Students should use their line graph to calculate the rate of decay.	**Required practical:** The rate of decay **Maths skills:** Calculating rate

Plenary	Support/Extend	Resources
Ice mammoth (5 min) Show students an image of a mammoth preserved in ice. Ask them to explain why it hasn't decayed, using ideas about what affects the rate of decay.	**Support:** Provide students with an explanation as a cloze paragraph for them to complete.	
Decay in recycling (10 min) Show the class an image of a compost heap/bin. Ask them what it is, what it is used for, and how it links with what they have learnt in the lesson. They should discuss what conditions are needed.	**Extend:** Students should explain why these conditions are needed.	

Homework		
Students should list the techniques used to preserve food and stop it from decaying.	**Extend:** Students should explain in detail how each technique works, using scientific terminology.	

kerboodle
A Kerboodle highlight for this lesson is **Bump up your grade: Champion rotters**. Refer to the **Content map** on Kerboodle for a full list of resources and assessment.

B 18 Biodiversity and ecosystems
18.1 The human population explosion

AQA spec links: 7.3.1 Biodiversity is the variety of all the different species of organisms on earth, or within an ecosystem.

A great biodiversity ensures the stability of ecosystems due to the interdependencies of one species on another for food, shelter, and the maintenance of the physical environment.

The future of the human species on Earth relies on us maintaining a good level of biodiversity. Many human activities are reducing biodiversity and only recently have measures been taken to try to stop this reduction.

7.3.2 Rapid growth in the human population and an increase in the standard of living mean that increasingly more resources are used and more waste is produced. Unless waste and chemical materials are properly handled, more pollution will be caused.

7.3.3 Humans reduce the amount of land available for other animals and plants by building, quarrying, farming, and dumping waste.

WS 1.4
Ms 1b, 2f

Aiming for	Outcome	Checkpoint	
		Question	Activity
Aiming for GRADE 4	Describe what biodiversity means.		Main 1
	List some resources that humans are using up.	2	Starter 2, Main 2
	Describe some ways that air, water, and land are polluted.		Starter 2, Plenary 2
Aiming for GRADE 6	Describe why a good level of biodiversity is important to the future of the human species.		Main 1
	Describe some effects of human population growth.	1, 2, 3	Starter 2, Main 2, Plenary 2
	Analyse and interpret data and information concerning human population growth.		Starter 1, Main 2
Aiming for GRADE 8	Explain in detail why a high level of biodiversity is important to the stability of ecosystems.		Main 1
	Explain why human population change differs from population change of other animals.	1	Starter 1
	Suggest and evaluate solutions to the problems caused by human population growth.		Plenary 1

B18 Biodiversity and ecosystems

Maths
Students estimate human population, using standard form. They may also calculate the range, median, and mean of the estimates and analyse data showing population changes. (1b, 2f)

Literacy
Students organise information as lists and concept maps. They prepare and give presentations on the impact of population growth.

Key word
biodiversity

Starter	Support/Extend	Resources
Estimating human population (10 min) Ask students to write on a piece of paper their estimation of the number of people in the world. Ask them to stand in a line so their estimates are in numerical order. Reveal whose estimate is the closest. You can show students a population counter (found online) that shows the current population changing. **Resource issues** (5 min) Show the class a series of stimulus images showing the problems surrounding human population growth, e.g., air and water pollution, landfill sites, deforestation, shanty towns. Ask them to discuss in groups what each image is showing in terms of how humans are affecting the environment, and examples of consequences.	**Extend:** Students can use standard form to express population number. They could also calculate the range, median, and mean of the estimates given. **Support:** Ask each group to look at one image and collate ideas as a class. **Extend:** Ask groups to suggest reasons for the issues.	

Main	Support/Extend	Resources
Biodiversity (15 min) Tell the class that a rainforest has a high level of biodiversity, and ask students to suggest what this means. Ask pairs of students to list possible reasons why a high level of biodiversity is important to: a) other plants and animals in the same ecosystem, and b) the entire human population. **The problem with human population** (25 min) Ask students for examples of resources that humans need, e.g., air, clean water, food. Discuss where we get each of these things. Divide the class into small groups and give each a topic to research – air, water, land, natural resources (e.g., minerals/fossil fuels), biodiversity. Ask them to prepare a short presentation on how the growth in human population is impacting negatively on their resource, and why. Students can use information from the student book, other books and the Internet.	**Support:** Students can use the information in the student book. **Support:** Give students a clear brief to follow by giving them specific subheadings for their presentation or specific questions to answer. **Extend:** Students could find data to support their presentation.	**Activity:** The problem with human population

Plenary	Support/Extend	Resources
Solutions (10 min) For each of the problems presented in Main 2, ask students to suggest solutions. For example, the depletion of fossil fuels can be reduced by using more renewable energy resources. **Land, air, or water** (5 min) Present different ways in which we are polluting the Earth. Ask students to classify them as air, water, or land pollution.	**Extend:** Choose one solution and evaluate the suggestion in detail.	**Interactive:** Land, air, or water?

Homework
Students research one effect of pollution from global warming, global dimming, smog, or acid rain.

kerboodle
A Kerboodle highlight for this lesson is **Working scientifically: Human population**. Refer to the **Content map** on Kerboodle for a full list of resources and assessment.

B18.2 Land and water pollution

AQA spec link: 7.3.2 Pollution can occur:
- in water, from sewage, fertiliser, or toxic chemicals
- on land, from landfill and from toxic chemicals such as pesticides and herbicides, which may be washed from land into water.

Pollution kills plants and animals which can reduce biodiversity.

Aiming for	Outcome	Checkpoint	
		Question	Activity
Aiming for GRADE 4 ↓	List some substances that pollute water and land.	1	Starter 1
	Describe some effects of rubbish, pesticides, and sewage on land and water.	1	Main 1, Homework
	Display data appropriately with guidance.		Main 2
Aiming for GRADE 6 ↓	Describe how sewage, fertilisers, pesticides, and herbicides pollute the land and water.	2	Starter 1, Main 1, Plenary 1
	Describe the processes of eutrophication and bioaccumulation.		Main 2, Homework
	Draw conclusions from data.		Main 2, Plenary 2
Aiming for GRADE 8 ↓	Explain in detail how pollution affects biodiversity.		Main 2
	Explain how pesticides in water can kill top predators in food chains.		Homework
	Consider a land- or water-based pollution issue, stating opinions with reasoning.	2	Main 2, Homework

Maths
Students collect results and analyse data in order to draw conclusions.

Literacy
Students use information from the student book to describe how different substances cause water and land pollution.

Practical

Title	Eutrophication
Equipment	beakers, tap water, *Lemna* (duckweed) plants, commercial fertiliser
Overview of method	Fill five beakers with tap water and add different concentrations of the fertiliser to four of them, leaving one as the control. Use the manufacturer's instructions to decide on the concentrations to use, use a range above and below the recommended concentration. Mark the beakers with the concentration. Mix the water and fertiliser together, then place ten plants in each beaker. Count and record the number of leaves on the plants in each beaker. Place the beakers in the same conditions for three weeks. During the lesson ask the students to count the leaves in each beaker and record the results. They can compare the increase in number of leaves in each beaker.
Safety considerations	Take care when handling fertiliser.

B18 Biodiversity and ecosystems

Starter	Support/Extend	Resources
Water pollution key words (10 min) Ask students to work in pairs to write down definitions of the key words – pesticide, sewage, herbicide, fertiliser. Ask them to share their definitions, and state what they all have in common. Discuss that they can all pollute water. **Waste** (5 min) Ask students to list the things that get thrown away from their house every day. Discuss the fact that these include paper, metal, plastic, and food waste as well as sewage and waste water from washing machines, etc.	**Support:** Provide cards with the word and definition to match up. **Extend:** Students should suggest the effects of each pollutant on water.	**Interactive:** Water pollution key words

Main	Support/Extend	Resources
Impact of waste (15 min) Ask students to consider where waste from homes ends up, and to use information from the student book to describe how it can cause water and land pollution. **Water pollution** (25 min) Set up in advance the demonstration to show the effect of extra nitrates and phosphates in the water supply on the growth of plants. Students then collect data and analyse the results. Ask them to link this to the problem of eutrophication, using the information in the student book.	**Support:** Set students a cloze paragraph that describes the different ways in which land is polluted. **Support:** Provide students with cards that show the events in eutrophication. They can arrange them into the correct order. **Extend:** Students should explain how eutrophication affects biodiversity.	**Practical:** Eutrophication

Plenary	Support/Extend	Resources
Effects of farming (10 min) Give small groups of students a substance that is used or produced by farms (e.g., fertilisers, herbicides, pesticides, sewage, etc). Ask them to discuss how it can damage ecosystems. **Chernobyl** (5 min) Show students the map in the student book (Figure 1). Ask them to analyse what it shows, and come up with one conclusion.	**Support:** Give groups three possible impacts and ask them to pick out the correct one. **Extend:** Students should link this to the effects of ionising radiation on the body (Topic B7.5).	

Homework		
Ask students to draw a diagram that summarises bioaccumulation.	**Support:** Give students a copy of Figure 2 from the student book to add annotations to. **Extend:** Students should explain how it shows that pesticides in water can kill top predators in food chains. Ask students to research one example of bioaccumulation that occurred in the past. They can describe why it happened, and the effects. A suitable example is the use of DDT as an insecticide in the 1950s and 60s.	

B18.3 Air pollution

AQA spec link: 7.3.2 Pollution can occur:
- in air, from smoke and gases such as sulfur dioxide, which contributes to acid rain.

MS 1c, 2c, 4a

Aiming for	Outcome	Checkpoint	
		Question	Activity
Aiming for GRADE 4	State that acid rain is caused as a result of burning some fuels.	1	Starter 1, Main 1, Plenary 2
	List some effects of acid rain on plants and animals.		Main 2
	Analyse observations and data, with guidance.		Starter 2, Main 2
Aiming for GRADE 6	Describe how acid rain is formed.	2, End of chapter 2	Starter 1, Main 1, Plenary 2
	Plan an investigation to find out how acid rain affects the germination of seeds.		Main 2
	Choose a suitable method for analysing data.		Main 2
Aiming for GRADE 8	Use word and symbol equations to show how burning some fuels produces acidic gases.		Starter 1, Main 1
	Explain what causes global dimming and smog, and describe their effects.		Main 2
	Analyse in detail data showing sulfur emissions over the last 30 years, and suggest reasons for the trend.	3, 4, End of chapter 2	Plenary 1

Maths
Students analyse results by calculating the percentage germination (1c) and displaying the results in a suitable chart or graph. (2c, 4a)

Literacy
Students use information from the student book to complete a diagram showing how acid rain is formed, and list its effects. They also write a plan for an investigation.

Key word
acid rain

Practical

Title	Production of acidic gases
Equipment	Bunsen burner, gas jar, fuel (coal or splints), deflagrating spoon (optional), universal indicator
Overview of method	Set light to the coal in the deflagrating spoon and place in a gas jar with indicator in the bottom. Shake and see the colour change.
Safety considerations	Carry out in a fume cupboard. Wear eye protection.

■ B18 Biodiversity and ecosystems

Title	The effect of acid rain on plants
Equipment	Petri dishes with lids, filter paper circles, water, 0.01 mol/dm³ HCl, 0.1 mol/dm³ HCl, 0.5 mol/dm³ HCl, 1 mol/dm³ HCl, cress seeds, measuring cylinders or syringes (10 cm³), beakers for making solutions (optional)
Overview of method	Place filter paper into each Petri dish. Moisten one with water and the others with different concentrations of acid. Place cress seeds into each dish (controlling the number), cover and keep in the same conditions (out of direct sunlight to prevent them drying out). Count the number of germinated seeds daily.
Safety considerations	Wear eye protection. Hydrochloric acid is corrosive, avoid contact with skin.

Starter	Support/Extend	Resources
Production of acidic gases (10 min) Demonstrate that the burning of a fuel (produces acidic gases. Discuss where coal is burnt, and ask students to suggest why burning coal has an impact on the environment. **Testing rainwater** (5 min) Supply students with a test tube of rainwater. Ask them to use universal indicator paper to test the sample and write a conclusion. It will be slightly acidic but students shouldn't conclude that it can be classed as acid rain.	**Extend:** Ask students to construct word and symbol equations to show how the carbon and/or sulfur in the fuel produces acidic oxides. **Support:** Supply students with pH charts to remind them of the colours with universal indicator.	

Main	Support/Extend	Resources
The effect of acid rain (10 min) Supply students with a diagram that shows the steps in the production of acid rain but has labels missing. Ask them to complete the diagram using information from the student book. Discuss that rain is naturally slightly acidic because carbon dioxide reacts with rainwater to form an acid, but the addition of nitrogen oxides and sulfur dioxide from burning fuels has made rainwater more acidic. Ask students to use information from the student book to list the effects of acid rain on living organisms. Students then plan an investigation into the effect of acid rain on the germination of cress seeds. Ask students to write a method and prediction, then allow them to carry out the investigation. Time will be needed in subsequent lessons to gather results and analyse them. Students can calculate the percentage germination and display the results in a suitable chart or graph.	**Extend:** Students can include word and symbol equations. **Support:** Supply students with a suitable method to follow. **Extend:** Students can dilute acid to make up their own choice of different concentrations. **Extend:** Students can also describe the effects of smog and global dimming.	**Practical:** The effect of acid rain

Plenary	Support/Extend	Resources
The reduction in sulfur emissions (10 min) Show the class data that shows how sulfur emissions have fallen in the UK over the last 30 years. Ask them to analyse the data, and then suggest reasons for the trend. **Acid rain** (5 min) Use the interactive in which students order the stages in the production of acid rain.	**Extend:** Ask students why some countries that have strict controls on sulfur emissions still suffer acid rain damage.	**Interactive:** Acid rain

Homework		
Ask students to create a storyboard for a revision video to explain the effects of acid rain.		

kerboodle

A Kerboodle highlight for this lesson is **Go further: Improving air quality**. Refer to the **Content map** on Kerboodle for a full list of resources and assessment.

B18.4 Deforestation and peat destruction

AQA spec links: 7.3.3 Humans reduce the amount of land available for other animals and plants by building, quarrying, farming, and dumping waste.

The destruction of peat bogs, and other areas of peat to produce garden compost, reduces the area of this habitat and thus the variety of different plant, animal, and microorganism species that live there (biodiversity). The decay or burning of the peat releases carbon dioxide into the atmosphere.

7.3.4 Large-scale deforestation in tropical areas has occurred to:
- provide land for cattle and rice fields
- grow crops for biofuels.

WS 1.4, 1.5
MS 5c

Aiming for	Outcome	Checkpoint	
		Question	Activity
Aiming for GRADE 4	Define deforestation.	1	Starter 1, Main 1, Homework
	Describe an effect of deforestation.	1, 2	Starter 1, Main 1, Homework
	Give a use for peat.	3	Starter 2, Main 2
Aiming for GRADE 6	Explain the effects of deforestation and peat removal.	1, 2, 3, End of chapter 2	Main, Homework
	Categorise reasons for and effects of deforestation as environmental, social, economic, and/or political.		Main 1
	Describe why there is a conflict between using peat to increase food production and the need to conserve peat bogs.	4	Main 2, Plenary 1
Aiming for GRADE 8	Explain in detail how deforestation and peat removal increase the amount of carbon dioxide in the air.	2, 3, End of chapter 2	Starter 1, Main 2
	Analyse data to describe a trend in deforestation rate, and give an explanation.		Plenary 2
	Explain the conflict between using peat to increase food production and the need to conserve peat bogs.	4	Main 2, Plenary 1

Maths
Students analyse data to describe a trend in deforestation rate. They could also use units of area to estimate how much forest is cut down each year. (5c)

Literacy
Students use information from books and/or the Internet to research the reasons for, and effects of, deforestation. They present this as a mind map. They write a persuasive email.

Key words
deforestation, biodiversity

■ B18 Biodiversity and ecosystems

Starter	Support/Extend	Resources
Looking at deforestation (5 min) Show the class an image of deforestation. Ask them why it is considered a bad thing. Then ask if there are any benefits. **For peat's sake!** (10 min) Let students study samples of compost that contains peat and peat-free compost, or show them samples yourself. Students should wear gloves when handling the samples. Ask them to write down their observations about the differences. Ask them to suggest why gardeners often use peat in their compost (it improves the properties of the soil by increasing mineral content and helping with water retention).	**Extend:** Students should consider who benefits from deforestation.	

Main	Support/Extend	Resources
Deforestation mind map (20 min) Let students use information from the student book spread, other books, and/or the Internet to study the reasons for, and effects of deforestation. Ask them to organise this information as a visual summary with diagrams and pictures as well as text. They should categorise the reasons and effects as environmental, social, economic, and/or political, and show how they are linked together. **Peat problems** (20 min) Give the class a series of true or false statements on peat – what it is, where it comes from, what it is used for, problems with its use. Ask students to use information from the student book to help them decide which are true and which are false. They should write down the true statements and correct versions of the false ones. Discuss the conflict between using peat to increase food production and the need to conserve peat bogs.	**Extend:** Ask students to write their own statements to test a partner.	**Activity:** Deforestation mind map

Plenary	Support/Extend	Resources
Put the peat down (10 min) Ask students to write an email to a gardener, persuading them to use peat-free compost. **Deforestation rates** (5 min) Use the interactive, in which students look at a chart of deforestation of time and answer a multiple choice question about possible reasons for increased deforestation rates.	**Support:** Provide key points that students should include.	**Interactive:** Deforestation rates

Homework		
Ask students to write down bullet points to describe how deforestation is linked to global warming.	**Support:** Students can carry out their own research into global warming. There are many suitable animations on the Internet which they can use.	

kerboodle

A Kerboodle highlight for this lesson is **Homework: Population, pollution, and deforestation**. Refer to the **Content map** on Kerboodle for a full list of resources and assessment.

B18.5 Global warming

AQA spec link: 7.3.5 Students should be able to describe some of the biological consequences of global warming.

Levels of carbon dioxide and methane in the atmosphere are increasing, and contribute to 'global warming'.

WS 1.3, 1.6
MS 2c

Aiming for	Outcome	Checkpoint	
		Question	Activity
Aiming for GRADE 4 ↓	Describe how global warming is caused by increased levels of carbon dioxide and methane in the atmosphere.	2	Main 1
	Give one biological consequence of global warming.	2, 3	Starter 2, Main 2, Plenary 1
Aiming for GRADE 6 ↓	Use the terms greenhouse effect, global warming, and climate change correctly.	1	Main 1, Plenary 2
	Describe in detail the biological consequences of global warming.	2, 3	Main 1, Plenary 1
Aiming for GRADE 8 ↓	Produce scale diagrams showing some of the contributors to the greenhouse effect.		Main 1
	Explain in detail the causes and effects of rising carbon dioxide and methane levels in the atmosphere.	End of chapter 2	Starter 1, Main 1, Homework

Maths
Share data with the class showing the change in average temperatures or the predicted rise in sea level over time. Ask students to interpret the data. Students produce scale diagrams showing some of the contributors to the greenhouse effect. (2c)

Literacy
Students summarise written information on global warming into flow charts and spider diagrams.

■ B18 Biodiversity and ecosystems

Starter	Support/Extend	Resources
Carbon cycle review (10 min) Ask students to help you compile a diagram of the carbon cycle on the board by thinking about ways in which carbon dioxide is removed from the atmosphere, and ways in which it is added. Discuss that for thousands of years these processes were in balance and the amount of carbon dioxide in the air remained relatively constant. **Polar bear peril** (5 min) Show the class an image or video clip of an ice sheet breaking up. Ask them to share what this image means to them.	**Extend:** Students can compile their own carbon cycle diagram.	

Main	Support/Extend	Resources
Global warming (20 min) Use a diagram of the greenhouse effect to show how greenhouse gases (methane and carbon dioxide) in the atmosphere help maintain the Earth at a temperature suitable for life. Discuss how human activity has increased the volume of these gases in the air. Ask students to use the information in the student book to summarise this as a flow chart. **Changing conditions** (20 min) Tell the class about the two main consequences of global warming – rising sea levels and climate change. Use a map from the Internet to show predictions for flooding in areas of the UK as sea levels rise. Ask students to divide a sheet of paper in two and write 'rising sea levels' in the middle of one side of the page and 'climate change' in the middle of the other. They can use information from the student book to draw a spider diagram to show how each will affect living organisms.	**Support:** Supply students with cards that they can put in order. **Extend:** Ask students to provide scientific definitions of the terms greenhouse effect, global warming, and climate change. **Extend:** Students complete the Extension activity where they produce scale diagrams showing some of the contributors to global warming. **Extend:** Allow students to do extra research on specific examples of living organisms that are thought to be already affected by global warming.	**Activity:** Global warming **Extension:** Just the facts

Plenary	Support/Extend	Resources
Effects on food production (10 min) Ask the class to consider how global warming will impact on food production in the UK. How would it affect the types of crops farmers could grow? Can they think of negative and positive changes? **What is happening to Earth?** (5 min) Students use the interactive to complete a cloze paragraph to explain the greenhouse effect and global warming.	**Extend:** Ask students to explain the greenhouse effect and global warming to a partner without using the student book.	**Interactive:** What is happening to Earth?

Homework		
Students complete the WebQuest where they research why the oceans are becoming more acidic, what effect this has, and what is being done to prevent it.	**Support:** Set a series of simple questions based on the video.	**WebQuest:** Acidic oceans

kerboodle

A Kerboodle highlight for this lesson is **Calculation sheet: Global warming**. Refer to the **Content map** on Kerboodle for a full list of resources and assessment.

GCSE Biology only — Higher tier

B18.6 The impact of change

AQA spec link: 7.2.4 Students should be able to evaluate the impact of environmental changes on the distribution of species in an ecosystem given appropriate information.

Environmental changes affect the distribution of species in an ecosystem. These changes include:
- temperature
- availability of water
- composition of atmospheric gases.

The changes may be seasonal, geographic, or caused by human interaction.

WS 1.4
MS 4a

Aiming for	Outcome	Checkpoint	
		Question	Activity
Aiming for GRADE 6	State some examples of environmental changes that affect the distribution of species in an ecosystem.	1	Main, Plenary 2
	Explain how humans can cause environmental changes.		Starter 2
	Describe an example of how environmental change has affected the distribution of a species.	1, 2	Main, Homework
Aiming for GRADE 8	Categorise environmental changes as due to seasonal changes, geographical changes, human interaction, or a combination.		Plenary 2
	Explain how people are attempting to reduce the problems caused by a change in distribution of organisms.		Main
	Predict and explain how an environmental change will affect the distribution of an organism.		Starter 1, Main, Plenary 1

Maths
Students study data in the form of graphs and maps that show how the distribution of organisms have changed. (4a)

Literacy
Students extract information from a newspaper article to summarise abiotic factors that have affected the distribution of a bird.

■ B18 Biodiversity and ecosystems

Starter	Support/Extend	Resources
What lives where? (10 min) Split the class into small groups. Give each group an image of a different environment, e.g., polar region, African savannah, rainforest, UK woodland. Ask students to describe the abiotic factors and suggest organisms that live in each. As a class, discuss why different organisms are found in different environments.	**Extend:** Ask students to predict what would happen to the organisms in the environment if the abiotic factors were to change.	
How humans change the environment (5 min) Read out a list of abiotic factors (air temperature, water temperature, atmospheric gases, pH of water, light levels). Ask students to describe how each factor can be changed by human activity. This links to previous lessons on pollution.	**Extend:** Students can also discuss how these may be influenced by seasonal and geographical changes.	

Main	Support/Extend	Resources
Changing birds of Britain (40 min) Supply students with a newspaper article on the changes to the distribution of birds in Britain and ask students to summarise the information. They should include what abiotic factors affect their distribution, how this is changing, why it is changing, the effect on the bird populations, and what is being done to prevent any further disruption to their distribution. Alternatively, use the example of the Dartford warbler from the corresponding section in the student book.	**Extend:** Provide students with a variety of articles from different sources.	**Activity:** Changing birds of Britain

Plenary	Support/Extend	Resources
What would happen? (10 min) Give students examples of organisms in their habitat, e.g., rabbit in a UK field. Present possible environmental changes (e.g., increase in rainfall over the summer or a very cold winter). Ask them to predict how the organisms' distribution might change, with reasons.		
Types of environmental change (5 min) Use the interactive, in which students categorise environmental changes into whether they are due to seasonal changes, geographical changes, or human interaction.		**Interactive:** Types of environmental change

Homework		
Ask students to find another example of how the distribution of an organism has changed. They should include the reasons for the change, and any impact on the species.		

B18.7 Maintaining biodiversity

AQA spec link: 7.3.6 Students should be able to describe both positive and negative human interactions in an ecosystem and explain their impact on biodiversity.

Scientists and concerned citizens have put in place programmes to reduce these negative effects on ecosystems and biodiversity.

These include:

- breeding programmes for endangered species
- protection and regeneration of rare habitats such as coral reefs, mangroves, and heathland
- reintroduction of field margins and hedgerows in agricultural areas where farmers grow only one type of crop
- reduction of deforestation and carbon dioxide emissions by some governments
- recycling resources rather than dumping waste in landfill.

WS 1.4, 1.5
MS 4a

Aiming for	Outcome	Checkpoint	
		Question	Activity
Aiming for GRADE 4 ↓	List some ways in which people can help maintain biodiversity.		Main 1, Main 2, Plenary 1
	Describe the reasons why some habitats are at risk.		Main 1, Main 2
Aiming for GRADE 6 ↓	Describe programmes to reduce negative effects on ecosystems and explain how they work.	1, 2, 3	Main 1, Main 2, Plenary
	Use information to explain the conflicting pressures on maintaining biodiversity.		Main 2, Plenary 1
Aiming for GRADE 8 ↓	Evaluate the conflicting pressures on maintaining biodiversity in some habitats.		Main 2, Plenary 1
	Link ideas to suggest why recycling can help protect habitats.		Plenary 2

Maths
Students could analyse a graph that shows the relationship between landfill tax and amount of material put into landfill (Figure 4 in the student book). (4a)

Literacy
Students use information from a range of sources to describe, explain, and evaluate reasons why habitats are at risk, and how protective methods help.

B18 Biodiversity and ecosystems

Starter	Support/Extend	Resources
Odd one out (5 min) Ask students to choose which is the odd one out from – orangutan, polar bear, blue whale, and bottlenose dolphin. The bottlenose dolphin is the only animal in the list that is not currently an endangered species.	**Support:** Make sure students realise that plants can be endangered, too. **Extend:** Discuss the reasons why these animals are endangered.	
Biodiversity (10 min) Use the interactive, in which students select the correct definition of biodiversity. Discuss previous learning that covered why maintaining a high level of biodiversity is important.		**Interactive:** Biodiversity

Main	Support/Extend	Resources
Protecting endangered species (20 min) Discuss reasons why some species are at risk from extinction and why this has an impact on other organisms, including humans. Ask students to work in groups of four and give them some sticky notes (preferably of different colours). Ask them to use information from the student book to write down the four ways to protect biodiversity (breeding programmes, protection of rare habitats, reintroduction of hedgerows, reduction of deforestation), one on each note, and stick them to the desk. Then, ask students to choose one method and work alone. They should find one example of an organism that is being protected in this way, one place in the world it is being used, and summarise how the method can help maintain biodiversity. They should write each piece of information on a sticky note and place it with the protection method. Each person can then explain their protection method, with the example, to the rest of the group.	**Support:** Consider photocopying the information in the student book and allowing students to highlight relevant parts.	
Heathland restoration (20 min) Show the class a map of the UK showing areas of heathland. Locate the nearest area of heathland. Provide the class with information on heathlands. They should find out about species that live in heathlands, the reasons why the habitat is under threat, problems this can bring, and methods that are being used to maintain the areas. This can be written as a report, presentation, or leaflet that could be completed for homework.	**Extend:** Students should consider conflicting interests, e.g. the need for housing for a growing population versus the need to protect unique habitats.	**Activity:** Heathland restoration

Plenary	Support/Extend	Resources
he class that zoos carry out breeding programmes. Divide the class into two and ask one half to argue that keeping animals captive in zoos should not be allowed, and one to argue the opposite side.	**Support:** Ask students to work in pairs and give them statements for and against zoos. They can sort them into for and against.	
How can recycling help? (5 min) Ask students to write down at least two reasons why recycling can help protect biodiversity.		

Homework		
Students complete their report, presentation, or leaflet from the lesson.		

kerboodle

A Kerboodle highlight for this lesson is **Literacy sheet: Maintaining and rebuilding biodiversity**. Refer to the **Content map** on Kerboodle for a full list of resources and assessment.

GCSE Biology only

B18.8 Trophic levels and biomass

AQA spec links: 7.4.1 Students should be able to describe the differences between the trophic levels of organisms within an ecosystem.

Trophic levels can be represented by numbers, starting at level 1 with plants and algae. Further trophic levels are numbered subsequently according to how far the organism is along the food chain.

Level 1: Plants and algae make their own food and are called producers.

Level 2: Herbivores eat plants/algae and are called primary consumers.

Level 3: Carnivores that eat herbivores are called secondary consumers.

Level 4: Carnivores that eat other carnivores are called tertiary consumers. Apex predators are carnivores with no predators.

Decomposers break down dead plant and animal matter by secreting enzymes into the environment. Small soluble food molecules then diffuse into the microorganism.

7.4.2 Pyramids of biomass can be constructed to represent the relative amount of biomass in each level of a food chain. Trophic level 1 is at the bottom of the pyramid.

Students should be able to construct accurate pyramids of biomass from appropriate data.

WS 1.2
MS 1c, 2c

Aiming for	Outcome	Checkpoint	
		Question	Activity
Aiming for GRADE 4	Identify a producer, primary consumer, and secondary consumer from a food chain and pyramid of biomass.		Starter 1, Main 1
	Identify organisms using a chart and group organisms into feeding types.		Main 2
	Draw a pyramid of biomass, with guidance.	2	Main 2, Homework
Aiming for GRADE 6	Number the trophic levels in a food chain, food web, and pyramid of biomass.		Main 1, Plenary 2
	Describe how decomposers feed.		Plenary 1
	Use data to draw a pyramid of biomass and explain what it shows.		Main 2, Homework
Aiming for GRADE 8	Explain why pyramids of biomass are always pyramid shaped.	2, End of chapter 1	Plenary 2
	Evaluate a method for collecting information about biomass.	1	Main 2
	Calculate the percentage of biomass passed between trophic levels.	3, End of chapter 1	Main 2, Homework

Maths
Students measure mass, draw pyramids of biomass to scale, and calculate percentages. (1c, 2c)

Literacy
Students label food chains, food webs, and pyramids of biomass using the terms producer, primary consumer, secondary consumer, tertiary consumer, decomposer, and apex predator.

Key word
trophic levels

300

■ B18 Biodiversity and ecosystems

Practical

Title	Leaf litter investigation
Equipment	quadrat, trays, fine mesh, pooters, tweezers, sorting trays and small beakers, identification charts, balances
Overview of method	Before the lesson place the quadrat on an area of ground. Collect all leaf litter, plants, and soil to a depth of around 2 cm. Place into a tray and cover with fine mesh to prevent any animals from escaping. During the lesson, place a section of the material into a tray for each group. Allow students to search for and carefully remove all animals present. Smaller animals can be removed using a pooter, larger ones with tweezers. They can use identification charts to identify and sort the animals as herbivores, detrivores, or carnivores. They then measure the mass of the plants and animals. Gather class results.
Safety considerations	Cover any open wounds on hands. Wash hands after the investigation. Treat all creatures with care and return to original site after the lesson.

Starter	Support/Extend	Resources
1, 3, or 5 (5 min) Ask students to write down either 1, 3, or 5 examples of producers, consumers, predators, and prey.	**Support:** Students can write one example of each. **Extend:** Students can write five examples.	
Pyramids of number (10 min) Show the class the food chain oak tree → aphids → ladybirds. Ask students to draw a pyramid of numbers. Reveal the answer (see Figure 4 in student book).	**Support:** Do this activity as a class. **Extend:** Discuss why pyramids of number are not always a pyramid shape.	

Main	Support/Extend	Resources
Trophic levels (10 min) Ask students to write down a food chain with four organisms. Then ask them to label it using the terms producer, primary consumer, secondary consumer, and tertiary consumer. Use a food chain chosen by a student as an example to introduce the term 'trophic levels'. Ask students to label each of their trophic levels with a number, starting from the bottom.	**Extend:** Ask students to construct a simple food web that contains decomposers, producers, and an apex predator.	
Leaf litter investigation (30 min) Students can either identify the organisms in leaf litter and measure their mass to construct pyramids of biomass (see practical instructions) or you can provide students with a method and results from a similar investigation. Students can use squared paper to construct pyramids using a suitable scale. They should explain what the pyramid shows about the habitat.	**Support:** Students will need support choosing a scale and converting mass into suitable widths for the pyramids. **Extend:** Students should calculate the percentage mass passed on between trophic levels. **Extend:** Students should evaluate the accuracy of the data collected e.g., wet mass was used, not dry mass.	**Practical:** Leaf litter investigation **Maths skills:** Constructing a pyramid of biomass

Plenary	Support/Extend	Resources
Decomposers (10 min) Ask students to use the information in the student book to find out how decomposers feed, including bacteria. They can then show this using a labelled diagram.	**Support:** Supply the start of the diagram to show bacteria in the soil. **Extend:** Discuss whether detrivores should be placed in a food chain or pyramid of biomass.	
Spot the pyramid (5 min) Use the interactive, in which students are shown a food chain and asked to select the correct pyramid of biomass for it.	**Extend:** Students should explain why pyramids of biomass are always pyramid shaped.	**Interactive:** Spot the pyramid

Homework		
Supply students with data from other habitats so they can practice drawing pyramids of biomass to scale.		

kerboodle
A Kerboodle highlight for this lesson is **Literacy skills: Trophic levels diagrams**. Refer to the **Content map** on Kerboodle for a full list of resources and assessment.

GCSE Biology only

B18.9 Biomass transfers

AQA spec link: 7.4.3 Students should be able to:
- describe pyramids of biomass
- explain how biomass is lost between the different trophic levels.

Producers are mostly plants and algae which transfer about 1% of the incident energy from light for photosynthesis.

Only approximately 10% of the biomass from each trophic level is transferred to the level above it.

Losses of biomass are due to:
- not all the ingested material is absorbed, some is egested as faeces
- some absorbed material is lost as waste, such as carbon dioxide and water in respiration and water and urea in urine.

Large amounts of glucose are used in respiration.

Students should be able to calculate the efficiency of biomass transfers between trophic levels by percentages or fractions of mass.

Students should be able to explain how this affects the number of organisms at each trophic level.

MS 1c

Aiming for	Outcome	Checkpoint	
		Question	Activity
Aiming for GRADE 4	Describe the energy transfer that occurs during photosynthesis.		Starter 1
	Calculate the percentage of biomass passed between trophic levels, with guidance.	End of chapter question 1	Main 1
	Give a reason why not all biomass is passed from one trophic level to the next.	1, 2	Main 1, Plenary 1
Aiming for GRADE 6	Calculate the percentage of biomass passed between trophic levels.	End of chapter question 1	Main 1, Homework
	Calculate the efficiency of transfers, with guidance.		Main 1
	Explain how the loss of biomass at each trophic level affects the number of organisms at each level.	End of chapter question 1	Main 1, Homework
Aiming for GRADE 8	Calculate the efficiency of energy transfers.		Main 1
	Explain in detail the reasons why not all biomass is passed from one trophic level to the next.	1, 2	Main 1, Main 2, Plenary 1
	Link the reduction in biomass to energy transfers, and evaluate a model used to represent this.	End of chapter question 1	Starter 1, Starter 2, Main 2, Plenary 2

Maths
Students calculate percentage efficiency of energy transfer between trophic levels (1c).

Literacy
Students summarise information from the student book. They may write a plan for a practical investigation.

Key word
incident energy

B18 Biodiversity and ecosystems

Practical

Title	Energy released by respiration
Equipment	two vacuum flasks; thermometers or probes for data loggers; one batch of live, germinating peas; one batch of boiled, dead peas that have been cooled; cotton wool. Both batches of peas should be rinsed in disinfectant to kill microorganisms.
Overview of method	Into one flask add live germinating peas and a thermometer. Close the mouth of the flask with cotton wool. In the second flask, repeat with the same quantity of dead peas.

Starter	Support/Extend	Resources
Photosynthesis (5 min) Remind students that plants use photosynthesis to produce glucose from carbon dioxide and water, and that light is needed. Ask them to write down the energy transfer taking place (light energy transferred to chemical energy store). Discuss the fact that only around 1% of the light falling on producers (plants and algae) is transferred. **Dung energy** (10 min) Inform students that cow pats can be burnt and explain how this shows that dung is a source of energy. Ask the class to suggest where this energy comes from.	**Extend:** Ask students to suggest what happens to the rest of the light (absorbed by other parts of the leaf (not chloroplasts), reflected, passes through the leaf)	

Main	Support/Extend	Resources
Biomass efficiency (15 min) Show the class a pyramid of biomass and ask students to calculate the percentage of biomass passed between each trophic level. Then they can calculate the efficiency of transfer for each. Ask students to use information from the student book to summarise the reasons why biomass decreases as you go up a food chain. **Modelling biomass transfers** (25 min) Use a model to show biomass loss through trophic levels. One example is an outside activity. Arrange a course with four posts about 10 m apart. Post 1 represents a producer and has two large containers of water next to it. Post 2 represents a primary consumer and has two buckets with holes in the bottom – this is the same for post 3, which represents a secondary consumer. Post 4 represents a tertiary consumer and has an empty container next to it. Pairs of students stand at posts 2 and 3. Students at the second post collect water from the producer and run to post three. They pass the water on to students at post 3, who tip the water into the container. The water represents biomass. Discuss how this models what happens in real food chains.	**Support:** Show students how to calculate the percentage efficiency of energy transfer from producer to primary consumer and allow students to calculate this between primary and secondary consumer. **Extend:** Students should evaluate the model used and discuss its limitations. **Extend:** Students should also be able to use ideas about energy transfer to explain why biomass is lost at each trophic level.	**Calculation sheet:** Efficiency of energy transfer **Activity:** Modelling biomass transfers

Plenary	Support/Extend	Resources
Energy released by respiration (10 min) Prior to the lesson set up the practical investigation. Record the temperature and discuss the results in terms of respiration. **Marine food chains** (5 min) Use the interactive, in which students answer a multiple choice question about why marine food chains can be a lot longer than those on land.	**Extend:** Allow students to plan the investigation themselves following the instructions in the student book.	**Interactive:** Marine food chains

Homework		
Set students an exam-style question (or past paper question) that assesses their understanding of pyramids of biomass and energy transfers.		

kerboodle

A Kerboodle highlight for this lesson is **Bump up your grade: Energy loss between trophic levels**. Refer to the **Content map** on Kerboodle for a full list of resources and assessment.

GCSE Biology only

B18.10 Factors affecting food security

AQA spec link: 7.5.1 Students should be able to describe some of the biological factors affecting levels of food security.

Food security is having enough food to feed a population.

Biological factors which are threatening food security include:

- the increasing birth rate has threatened food security in some countries
- changing diets in developed countries means scarce food resources are transported around the world
- new pests and pathogens affect farming
- environmental changes affect food production, such as widespread famine occurring in some countries if rains fail
- cost of agricultural inputs
- conflicts have arisen in some parts of the world over the availability of water or food.

Sustainable methods must be found to feed all people on Earth.

WS 1.4

Aiming for	Outcome	Checkpoint	
		Question	Activity
Aiming for GRADE 4	Describe what food security and malnutrition mean.	1, End of chapter question 3	Starter 2, Main 1, Plenary 1
	List some factors that reduce food security.	2, End of chapter question 3	Main 2, Plenary 2, Homework
	Present information in a debate.		Main 2
Aiming for GRADE 6	Define sustainable food production and describe how it could help increase food security.	2, End of chapter question 3	Main 2, Plenary 1
	Explain how factors affect food security.	2, 3	Main 2, Homework
	Present information based on research.	4	Main 2, Homework
Aiming for GRADE 8	Suggest and explain how events could affect food security.		Main 2, Plenary 2, Homework
	Consider whether malnutrition is just a problem in developing countries.		Starter 2
	Present information clearly with supporting evidence.	4	Main 2

Maths
As part of the research into food security in different countries, students from each country could find data to present.

Literacy
Students describe food security using diagrams. Students research information and plan how to present it during a convention. They discuss and debate food security issues in a group.

304

B18 Biodiversity and ecosystems

Starter	Support/Extend	Resources
Reasons for world hunger (10 min) Tell the class that around 1 in 9 people in the world do not have enough food to lead a healthy life. Ask students to discuss in small groups and list the possible reasons why. Use their ideas to collate a class list.		
Malnutrition (5 min) Ask students to discuss in pairs and come up with a definition of the word malnutrition.	**Extend:** Ask students to consider if this is just a problem in developing countries.	

Main	Support/Extend	Resources
Defining food security (10 min) Introduce the term food security. Ask students to use the student book to find the three main aspects of food security and draw a picture to illustrate each one.		
Food security convention (30 min) Split the class into seven groups. Six of the groups contain delegates from countries where food security is an issue: • Uganda – increasing birth rate • Bolivia – changing diet (quinoa being exported) • Cuba – new pests (banana disease Black Sigatoka) • Pakistan – environmental changes (floods) • Kenya – high costs of agricultural inputs • Afghanistan – conflict. Ask students to research the problems they face using the student book and the Internet if available. They should find out the problem, how it affects food security, and what they need from other countries to help them solve it. The seventh group contains food security experts. They should research how sustainable solutions can help. After researching, ask students from each group to form new groups containing one delegate from each group. Each delegate from a country should present their food security problem, the factors that have caused it, and explain the impact on their country. The food security experts can present possible solutions. The groups should debate these solutions and suggest others.	**Support:** Instead of small group debates, hold a class debate. The teacher can represent the food security experts. **Extend:** Students should collect evidence (either on what problem the country has or on what would help) supported by their reasoning to use in the convention.	**Activity:** Food security convention

Plenary	Support/Extend	Resources
Definitions (5 min) Use the interactive in which students match the keywords food security, malnutrition, and sustainable food production to their definitions.	**Support:** Provide three definitions for each, only one being correct. Ask students to spot the correct definitions.	**Interactive:** Definitions
Refugee crisis (10 min) Discuss that conflict results in people moving away in search of safety in other countries. Ask students to consider how this impacts on food security.	**Extend:** Students can read news stories linked to food security (e.g., a natural disaster).	

Homework		
Ask students to find out whether food security is/could be a problem in the UK, and the reasons why.		

GCSE Biology only

B18.11 Making food production efficient

AQA spec link: 7.5.2 The efficiency of food production can be improved by restricting energy transfer from food animals to the environment. This can be done by limiting their movement and by controlling the temperature of their surroundings.

Some animals are fed high protein foods to increase growth.

WS 1.3, 1.4
MS 1a, 2a

Aiming for	Outcome	Checkpoint	
		Question	Activity
Aiming for GRADE 4 ↓	Describe the difference between free-range and factory farming of chickens.		Starter 2, Main 1, Main 2
	List some advantages and disadvantages of free-range and factory farming of chickens.	3	Main 2
Aiming for GRADE 6 ↓	Explain why there could be more food for everyone if we ate less meat.	2	Starter 1, Plenary 2, Homework
	Explain why there are ethical objections to some factory farming techniques.	3	Main 2, Plenary 1
	Explain how factory farming techniques increase rate of growth.	3, End of chapter 4	Main 1, Plenary 1
Aiming for GRADE 8 ↓	Use viewpoints from a range of people during a debate on farming.	3	Main 2
	Explain in detail why, in terms of food production efficiency, it is a good idea to reduce meat in the diet or replace it with insects.		Starter 1, Plenary 2, Homework

Maths
Students consider the difference in price between free-range and intensively reared chicken. They could calculate the price per 100 g to compare them. (1a, 2a)

Literacy
Students write speeches in support of battery farming of chickens and against. They present their findings in a class debate.

B18 Biodiversity and ecosystems

Starter	Support/Extend	Resources
Meat-free Monday (10 min) Tell the class that eating less meat could mean more food for everyone. Ask them to explain why in terms of biomass loss by presenting them with food chains for plants and meat, for example, wheat → person, wheat → chicken → person). **Free-range or not?** (5 min) Tell the class the price of a free-range eggs compared to caged ones. Ask them which they would choose to buy with their own money, and why.	**Support:** Supply sentence starters to help students construct an explanation. **Extend:** Discuss why there is a price difference.	

Main	Support/Extend	Resources
Increasing efficiency (15 min) Remind students that biomass is lost as animals use it for respiration and energy release for movement and controlling body temperature. Ask them to consider how caged hens are kept, and explain why this increases the rate of growth. Students can use information from the student book for guidance. **Chicken speech** (25 min) Students write a short speech in support of factory farming of chickens, and one against it. They should include the advantages and disadvantages of both, and use scientific facts and data as evidence. Then ask students to draw lots as to which side to present during a class debate. You could open up the discussion to debate views on the raising of calves in pens to produce veal.	**Support:** Set clear prompt questions, for example, how are battery hens kept warm? How does this reduce the amount of biomass used in respiration? **Extend:** Present viewpoints from different people, e.g., battery hen farmer, parent on a low income.	**Activity:** Increasing efficiency **Extension:** Chicken out viewpoints

Plenary	Support/Extend	Resources
Fish farming (10 min) Use the interactive in which students are presented with ways that growth is increased in farmed fish (e.g., small cages and feeding with high protein food) and match the techniques to explanations of how they work. **Eating insects** (5 min) Ask the class how they feel about eating insects and why, in terms of food production efficiency, it is a good idea. Information about eating insects can be found on the Internet. You could even consider having samples of insects for students to try.	**Extend:** Provide students with data comparing the amount of resources (water, space, etc.) that insects need compared with large animals, as well as information about pollution caused by each. They can use this to write a clear argument with evidence to support it.	**Interactive:** Fish farming

Homework		
Students can write advice for meat eaters on how they could reduce the amount of meat in their diet but still get a balanced diet. They could design some example menus.	**Extend:** Students should also explain why eating plants rather than meat is more energy-efficient.	

GCSE Biology only

B18.12 Sustainable food production

AQA spec links: 7.5.3 Fish stocks in the oceans are declining. It is important to maintain fish stocks at a level where breeding continues or certain species may disappear altogether in some areas.

Control of net size and the introduction of fishing quotas play important roles in conservation of fish stocks at a sustainable level.

7.5.4 Students should be able to describe and explain some possible biotechnical and agricultural solutions, including genetic modification, to the demands of the growing human population.

Modern biotechnology techniques enable large quantities of microorganisms to be cultured in industrially controlled vats for food.

The fungus *Fusarium* is useful for producing mycoprotein, a protein-rich food suitable for vegetarians. The fungus is grown on glucose syrup, in aerobic conditions, and the biomass is harvested and purified.

A genetically modified bacterium produces human insulin. When harvested and purified this is used to treat diabetics.

GM crops could provide more food or food with an improved nutritional value such as golden rice.

WS 1.4
MS 2h

Aiming for	Outcome	Checkpoint	
		Question	Activity
Aiming for GRADE 4 ↓	Give one reason why fish stocks in the oceans are decreasing.	1	Main 1
	Describe one reason why a reduction in fish stocks is a problem.		Main 1, Plenary 2
	Describe what mycoprotein is.		Main 2
Aiming for GRADE 6 ↓	Describe the reasons why fish stocks in the oceans are decreasing.		Starter 1
	Describe the techniques used to conserve fish stocks.	1, 2	Main 1
	Describe how mycoprotein is produced.	3	Main 2
Aiming for GRADE 8 ↓	Explain the negative impacts of fishing restrictions on communities.	1	Main 1
	Compare and contrast the production of mycoprotein with intensive farming.		Main 2
	Explain the advantages of eating mycoprotein for the individual and for society as a whole.	3	Main 2, Plenary 1

Maths
Students analyse data on changes to fish stocks. (2h)

Literacy
Students use a range of information to create a leaflet on mycoprotein.

B18 Biodiversity and ecosystems

Starter	Support/Extend	Resources
Remembering GM crops (5 min) Give students 2 minutes to write down what they can remember about genetically modified crops. Spend a few minutes sharing ideas and correcting any misconceptions. **Increasing food production** (5 min) Remind students that the human population is rapidly increasing. Use the interactive, in which students answer questions about how food production can be improved and made more sustainable.	**Support:** Support: Students work in pairs. **Support:** Present a number of options to increase food production (e.g., using more chemicals on crops, eating less meat, using GM crops). Ask students to order them to show how useful they think they are.	**Interactive:** Increasing food production

Main	Support/Extend	Resources
Sustainable fishing (20 min) Discuss the problem with overfishing and why it is necessary to conserve fish stocks. Present the restrictions used to increase fish stocks – fishing quotas, controlling the size of holes in the nets, bans on fishing during breeding seasons. Ask students to use information from the student book to explain how each works. **The role of biotechnology** (20 min) Search the Internet for information about the production of mycoprotein (e.g., Quorn), such as diagrams and flow charts about how it is produced, and nutritional information. You can also show the class video of adverts for mycoprotein meat substitutes. Ask students to use this, plus the information in the student book, to create an information leaflet on mycoprotein.	**Extend:** Students should also explain the negative impacts of these restrictions on fishing communities. **Support:** Create a template that shows what kind of information should be included. **Extend:** The leaflet should persuade people to eat mycoprotein rather than meat. **Extend:** Students should compare and contrast the production of mycoprotein with intensive farming.	**Activity:** The role of biotechnology

Plenary	Support/Extend	Resources
Consequences spider diagram (10 min) Ask students to consider what might happen if the Government decided that the eating of animals should be banned and the nation should eat more mycoprotein. Ask students to write 'ban animal farming' in the middle of a sheet of paper and write consequences around it that are linked (e.g., there would be fewer farms, which would lead to people losing jobs). **Bluefish tuna** (5 min) Ask students to write one sentence that they could use to persuade someone to stop eating bluefin tuna, a species endangered due to overfishing.	**Extend:** Students should distinguish between positive and negative consequences by using different coloured pens.	

Homework		
Ask students to summarise learning about food production by producing a short quiz with answers to test a partner.		

kerboodle

A Kerboodle highlight for this lesson is **Progress quiz: Biodiversity and ecosystems 2**. Refer to the **Content map** on Kerboodle for a full list of resources and assessment.

B18 Biodiversity and ecosystems

Overview of B18 Biodiversity and ecosystems

In this chapter students have studied biodiversity and ecosystems, starting with the reasons for and the effects of the human population explosion. Students should understand the effect of different types of pollution including land, water, and air pollution.

Students should be able to outline the processes of deforestation and peat destruction. They should link this with how materials are cycled in B17.3 *The carbon cycle*. Students should understand what is meant by the greenhouse effect, global warming, and its predicted effects. Students should be able to distinguish greenhouse gases from those that cause acid rain.

GCSE Biology higher-tier students have studied the impact of environmental change and should be able to recall how changes in the distribution of organisms can be evaluated.

On the topic of maintaining biodiversity, all students should understand how waste, deforestation, and global warming affect biodiversity, and be able to give examples of some of the actions being taken to stop the reduction in biodiversity.

GCSE Biology students have studied trophic levels, how biomass is transferred from one trophic level to the next, pyramids of biomass, and the efficiency of this energy transfer. They have also studied some of the factors that affect global food security. They should be able to outline ways of improving the efficiency of food production, discuss the ethics of factory farming, and understand the concept of sustainable food production with a focus on fisheries.

Finally GCSE Biology students should be familiar with biotechnological methods of food production including the production of mycoprotein and the use of genetically modified organisms.

MyMaths

You can find additional support for the maths skills covered in this chapter on **MyMaths**, including estimating, working with standard form and percentages, data analysis, and plotting graphs and pyramids of biomass.

kerboodle

For this chapter, the following assessments are available on Kerboodle:

B18 Checkpoint quiz: Biodiversity and ecosystems
B18 Progress quiz: Biodiversity and ecosystems 1
B18 Progress quiz: Biodiversity and ecosystems 2
B18 On your marks: Biodiversity and ecosystems
B18 Exam-style questions and mark scheme: Biodiversity and ecosystems

Checkpoint follow-up lesson

A student's route through this lesson can be determined using the Checkpoint assessment. Percentage pass marks are supplied in the Checkpoint teacher notes.

For each successive route through it is assumed that the student can perform to their current route as well as previous routes. For example, students working at Aiming for 6 are assumed to be secure in Aiming for 4 knowledge and understanding and working towards achieving all the learning outcomes for Aiming for 6.

	Aiming for 4	**Aiming for 6**	**Aiming for 8**
Learning outcomes	State ways in which human activity decreases biodiversity.	Describe ways that human activity decreases biodiversity.	Explain ways that human activity decreases biodiversity.
	State the causes and effects of land, water and air pollution.	Describe the causes and effects of land, water, and air pollution.	Explain the causes and effects of land, water and air pollution.
	State the ways the humans can maintain biodiversity.	Describe the ways the humans can maintain biodiversity.	Explain the ways the humans can maintain biodiversity.
	State the factors that affect food security and ways the food production can be maximised.	Describe the factors that affect food security and ways the food production can be maximised.	Explain the factors that affect food security and ways the food production can be maximised.
Starter	**Humans and the environment (5 min)** Student groups write down as many ways as they can think of that humans use the environment we live in. Examples include quarrying, fishing, road building, etc. Summarise on the board. Ask targeted questions about the effect of some of these things on the environment – pollution, loss of habitat, and so on.		
Differentiated checkpoint activity	Students produce a series of revision visual summaries for the content of the chapter. Students will require access to A3 paper, coloured pencils, and the student book. There are five topics for students to create a visual summary on. Assign two to three topics per student, then provide an opportunity at the end of the lesson for the class to peer-assess their visual summaries. The best visual summary for each topic could be displayed or photocopied for each student to take a copy.		
	The Aiming for 4 activity is a highly structured guide. The teacher may need to introduce the task and advise students on parts of their visual summary. Students are given five sections on pollution, deforestation and peat bog destruction, global warming and the greenhouse effect, maintaining biodiversity, and food security.	The Aiming for 6 activity is a reasonably structured guide. The teacher may need to introduce the task. Students are given five sections on pollution, deforestation and peat bog destruction, global warming and the greenhouse effect, maintaining biodiversity, and food security.	The Aiming for 8 activity has very little structure. Students are given six sections on pollution, deforestation and peat bog destruction, global warming and the greenhouse effect, maintaining biodiversity, biomass, and food security.
	Kerboodle resource B18 Checkpoint follow-up: Aiming for 4, B18 Checkpoint follow-up: Aiming for 6, B18 Checkpoint follow-up: Aiming for 8		
Plenary	**Review (5 min)** Students spend the plenary session peer assessing each other's work. Students can work on this in differentiated pairs or small groups. Guidance is given in question 2 on the differentiated worksheets.		
Progression	To progress, students should peer-assess Aiming for 6 visual summaries, identifying any content they have not included on their own visual summary and adding it.	To progress, students should peer-assess Aiming for 8 visual summaries, identifying any content they have not included on their own visual summary and adding it.	Aiming for 8 students are expected to evaluate the impact of environmental change on the distribution of species in an ecosystem. Provide lots of data examples to help them practise their interpretation and evaluation skills.

Answers

B1.1

1a advantages: relatively cheap, can be used almost anywhere, magnification up to around ×2000 [1]; disadvantages: limited magnification and resolution [1]

b advantages: high magnification (up to around ×2 000 000), high resolution, can give 3D images [1]; disadvantages: expensive, can only be used in temperature, pressure, and humidity-controlled rooms [1]

2a size of real object = $\frac{\text{size of image}}{\text{magnification}}$

capillary diameter = $\frac{5}{1000}$ = 0.005 mm = 5.0 µm [4]

b magnification = $\frac{\text{size of image}}{\text{size of real object}}$

magnification = $\frac{800}{20}$ = ×40 [3]

3 electron microscopes: magnify up to around ×2 000 000, [1] have a resolving power of about 10 nm (scanning electron microscope) or 0.2 nm (transmission electron microscope), [1] may be used to examine subcellular structures (e.g., chromosomes during cell division) [1]; light microscopes: magnify up to around ×2000, [1] have a resolving power of about 200 nm, [1] may be used to look at cells dividing (e.g., stained onion cells) [1]

B1.2

1a nucleus, [1] cytoplasm, [1] cell membrane, [1] mitochondria, [1] ribosomes [1]

b cell wall, [1] chloroplasts, [1] permanent vacuole [1]

c cell wall strengthens cell and provides support, [1] chloroplasts for photosynthesis, [1] permanent vacuole keeps cells rigid to support plant [1]

2 nucleus: controls all cell activities, [1] contains instructions for making new cells or new organisms [1]; mitochondria: site of aerobic respiration, [1] releasing energy for the cell [1]

3 Any two from root cells – no exposure to light, cells in centre of tree trunk – no exposure to light, cells in flowers of plants – their function is not to photosynthesise. [4] Any other valid suggestion.

B1.3

1a Genetic material in a prokaryotic cell isn't contained in a nucleus [1] and may include extra rings of DNA (plasmids) separate from main genetic material. [1]

b i long protein strand that lashes about [1]

ii movement [1]

2a small animal cell length around 10 µm

$\frac{10}{6}$ = 1.7

Length of small animal cell is same order of magnitude as cell nucleus. [2]

b large plant cell length around 100 µm

$\frac{100}{6}$ = 16.7

Length of large plant cell is an order of magnitude (10^1) bigger than cell nucleus. [2]

3 All cells have cell membranes [1] and cytoplasm [1] and both prokaryotes and eukaryotes can have cell wall. [1] Prokaryotes have no nucleus [1] and no chloroplasts [1], whilst eukaryotes have no plasmids. [1]

B1.4

1a Any one from lots of dendrites – to make connections to other nerve cells, long axons – to carry nerve impulse, synapses – to pass impulse to another cell or between nerve cell and muscle using transmitter chemicals. [2]

b Any one from special proteins – that slide over each other to contract fibres, many mitochondria – to produce energy for movement, glycogen storage – for cellular respiration. [2]

c Any one from long tail – to move sperm towards egg, many mitochondria – to produce energy for movement, acrosome – stores digestive enzymes for breaking down outside layers of egg, large nucleus – to contain genetic material to be passed on. [2]

2 Transmitter chemicals [1] are required to pass impulse from cone cell to another nerve cell and then on to brain. [1] The many mitochondria [1] supply energy from cellular respiration needed to make transmitter chemicals. [1]

3 Any three from mitochondria – number of mitochondria indicates how much energy cell uses, flagella or cilia – presence indicates whether cell moves around or moves substances such as mucus, nucleus – presence indicates whether cell is capable of reproduction, storage materials such as fat or starch – presence indicates whether cell stores materials it can use for respiration. [6] Any other valid feature.

B1.5

1a Any one from increased surface area – to promote water uptake, large permanent vacuole – to speed up movement of water by osmosis, many mitochondria – to produce energy for active transport of minerals. [2]

b Any one from cells die forming long hollow tubes – to allow water and mineral ions to move easily through them, lignin spirals formed – to help cells withstand pressure of water moving up plant and to support plant stem. [2]

c Any one from cell walls break down to form sieve plates – to enable water and dissolved food to pass through, companion cells – to support phloem cells and provide energy to move substances up and down in phloem. [2]

d Any one from chloroplasts – contain chlorophyll to trap light needed for photosynthesis, positioned in leaves and outer layers of stem – to absorb as much light as possible, large permanent vacuole – to keep cell rigid and support leaf and stem to capture light. [2]

2 Cell not exposed to sunlight and therefore not adapted to photosynthesise (not photosynthetic). [2]

3 Any three from chloroplasts – presence indicates whether cell is photosynthetic, large vacuole – presence indicates role in osmosis/rigid support, lignin spirals – presence indicates strengthening and transport of water, sieve plates/companion cells – presence indicates transport of dissolved food, mitochondria – presence indicates active movement of substances. [6]

B1.6

1 Spreading out of particles of a gas or a substance in solution along a concentration gradient (from area of higher concentration to area of lower concentration). [1] This takes place as a result of random movement of particles. When particles are concentrated, there are more collisions. [1]

2a Heating makes particles move more quickly, [1] speeding up diffusion as particles collide more often and harder, [1] and spread out faster. [1]

b Folded membranes provide increased surface area. [1] The greater the surface area, the more diffusion of dissolved substances can take place across it. [1]

3a Digested food molecules move from gut (high concentration) into bloodstream (low concentration) down a concentration gradient. [1] Large surface area of small intestine lining increases rate of diffusion. [1] Rich blood supply maintains concentration gradient. [1]

b Carbon dioxide moves from blood (high concentration) into air in the alveoli of the lungs (low concentration) down a concentration gradient. [1] Large surface area of alveoli increases rate of diffusion. [1] Rich blood supply maintains concentration gradient. [1]

c Chemicals produced by female moth spread out into air around her down concentration gradient. [1] Chemicals more concentrated close to female moth (high concentration) than further away (low concentration). [1] Male moth flies up concentration gradient, following chemical to reach female moth. [1]

B1.7

1a In diffusion all particles move freely down concentration gradients. [1] In osmosis only water (solvent) molecules move across a partially permeable membrane from a dilute solution to a concentrated solution. [1]

b If cells use up water in chemical reactions and cytoplasm becomes too concentrated, water moves into cells by osmosis. [1] If cells make water during chemical reactions and cytoplasm becomes too dilute, water moves out of cells by osmosis. [1]

2a i solution with same concentration of solutes as inside of cell [1]

  ii solution with lower concentration of solutes than inside of cell [1]

  iii solution with higher concentration of solutes than inside of cell [1]

b If solute concentration outside body cells is more dilute than cell contents, water will move into cells by osmosis – cells will swell and may burst. [1] If solute concentration outside body cells is higher than cell contents, water will leave cells by osmosis – cells will shrink and stop working properly. [1] Solute concentration outside body cells must be as constant as possible to minimise changes in size and shape of cells, [1] keeping them working normally. [1]

3 Cytoplasm of *Amoeba* is more concentrated than fresh water. [1] Its cell membrane is partially permeable, so water constantly moves into *Amoeba* from its surroundings by osmosis. [1] If this continued without stopping, the organism would burst. [1] Water is moved into special vacuole by active transport, and vacuole then bursts to remove excess water. [1]

B1.8

1 movement of water (solvent) molecules across a partially permeable membrane from dilute solution to concentrated solution [1]

2 mass gained: surrounding sugar solution hypotonic to beetroot cells, [1] so water moved into cells by osmosis [1]; mass lost: surrounding sugar solution hypertonic to beetroot cells, [1] so water moves out of cells by osmosis [1]; mass constant: surrounding sugar solution isotonic to beetroot cells, [1] so no net movement of water into or out of cells by osmosis [1]

3 Plants rely on osmosis to support stems and leaves. [1] Water moves into plant cells by osmosis. [1] Vacuole swells and presses cytoplasm against plant cell walls. [1] Turgor pressure is reached when pressure is so great that no more water can physically enter cell. [1] This makes cells hard and rigid (turgid), [1] preventing wilting. [1]

B1.9

1 Useful molecule binds to transport protein in cell membrane. [1] Transport protein changes shape and moves useful molecule across membrane into cell [1] against concentration gradient. [1] Useful molecule is released, transport protein returns to original position. [1]

2a active transport: substances moved against concentration gradient across partially permeable membrane, [1] process uses energy supplied by cellular respiration [1]; osmosis and diffusion: substances moved down concentration gradient, no requirement for energy from respiration [1]

b Cellular respiration in mitochondria releases energy needed for active transport. [1] Cells that carry out a lot of active transport often have many mitochondria to meet their energy requirements. [1]

3a Marine birds are exposed to salt water in the sea. [1] They use active transport to remove excess salt from the body against a concentration gradient. [1]

b Plants need to move mineral ions from soil into their roots. [1] Mineral ion solutions in soil are much more dilute than the solution in plant root hair cells, [1] so they are moved against a concentration gradient using active transport. [1]

B1.10

1 Any two from large surface area, being thin, having an efficient blood supply (in animals), being ventilated (in animals). [2]

2 Fish have gills and turtle has specialised excretory opening. [1] Both gas exchange systems have large surface area, [1] rich blood supply, [1] and are ventilated by flow of water for steep concentration gradient. [1] Main difference is location of gas exchange surface (fish gills on side of head, excretory opening on underside of turtle). [1]

3a affects how quickly organism can exchange materials with outside world, [1] smaller ratio means diffusion alone cannot provide sufficient gas and food molecules to cells and metabolic waste cannot be removed quickly enough [1]

b large surface area – greater area over which exchange can take place, thin membrane/being thin – short diffusion path, efficient blood supply – maintains steep concentration gradient, being ventilated – maintains steep concentration gradient [6]

Answers

B2.1

1a structures made of DNA found in pairs in the nucleus of cells that contain inherited material [1]

b small packet of information (section of DNA) that controls a characteristic, or part of a characteristic, of your body [1]

c unique chemical that makes up genetic material [1]

2 stage 1: chromosomes replicated and all sub-cellular structures such as mitochondria and ribosomes reproduced [2]; stage 2: (mitosis) nucleus divides to form two identical daughter nuclei [2]; stage 3: cytoplasm and cell membranes divide to make two independent cells [2]

3a New cells needed for growth and development, and worn out or damaged cells must be replaced with identical cells. [1] Mitosis produces cells with same chromosomes and identical genetic material, which fulfil same function as original cells. [1]

b Mitosis forms two identical daughter cells. [1] Two copies are made of each original chromosome before cell division and daughter cells each hold a copy of the full set of chromosomes. [1] Mitosis is important for forming identical cells needed for growth or tissue replacement. If chromosome number did not stay the same, new cells would not work properly and organism might die. [1]

B2.2

1a process by which cells become specialised and adapted to carry out a particular function [1]

b All cells in an early animal or plant embryo are unspecialised (stem cells). [1] Differentiation fulfils organisms' requirements for different cells to carry out different roles (e.g., muscle cells, sperm cells, gut lining cells). [1]

2 In animals, differentiation occurs during embryo development and is permanent. [2] In plants, it occurs throughout life and can be reversed or changed. [2]

3 order of magnitude = factor of 10
adult human has approximately 3.72×10^{13} cells
fertilised ovum is one cell
Adult human is around 13 orders of magnitude bigger than the original cell. [4]

4 In plants differentiation can be reversed and mitosis induced. Conditions can be changed to induce more mitosis. [1] Cells redifferentiate into different plant tissues needed to form a new clone plant, [1] so plants can be cloned relatively easily. [1] In animals differentiation cannot be reversed (cells differentiate permanently), [1] so clones cannot be made easily. [1] In order to make animal clones, embryos have to be cloned. [1]

B2.3

1a stem cell: undifferentiated cell [1] with potential to divide by mitosis, differentiate, and form different specialised cells in the body [1]; normal body cell: specialised for a specific function, [1] division by mitosis can only form cells with same specialisation [1]

b bone marrow, [1] embryos, [1] plant meristems [1]

2 embryonic stem cells can make any type of adult cell [1] to repair or replace damaged tissues, [1] could grow organs for transplants as needed, [1] organs grown from stem cells could cause fewer rejection issues if right techniques are used [1] Any other valid advantage.

3a In research it is important as far as possible to change only one variable. [1] Ability to produce large numbers of identical plant clones enables researchers to change a variety of different variables and see effects on genetically identical individuals. [1] Any differences will be due to variables under investigation, not genetic differences between plants. [1]

b Single rare plant specimen may not reproduce or researchers may not understand conditions needed for it to thrive. [1] If specimen dies or does not make seeds, species will be lost. [1] Cloning allows scientists time to find out about the plant and to find other specimens to introduce long-term genetic variation. [1]

B2.4

1 Any three from spinal cord damage, diabetes, heart damage after heart attack, eyesight in the blind, bone and cartilage repair, growing organs for transplant. [3] Any other valid suggestion.

2 for: potential to cure many currently untreatable diseases/ injuries, grow new organs for transplant, prevent organ rejection; against: use of human embryos problematic for some, risk of side effects (e.g., cancer, viral infection), patients may need immunosuppressant drugs, development of treatments slow and expensive, difficult to control stem cells [4] Any other valid evidence-based argument.

3 using embryonic stem cells from umbilical cord blood [1] and amniotic fluid [1] rather than embryos, using adult stem cells where possible, [1] developing therapeutic cloning [1] in which cells originate from patient so no reproductive embryo and no immune problems [1] Any other valid point.

B3.1

1a collection of cells of similar structure and function all working together [1]

b collection of different tissues working together to carry out a specific function [1]

2a specialised cell (found individually) [2]

b organ (several tissues working together) [2]

c organ (several tissues working together) [2]

3 Layer of muscular tissue contracts to churn up food, [1] mixing it with digestive juices to help physical and chemical digestion. [1] Glandular tissue produces enzymes to break down food. [1] Folded lining provides increased surface area. [1] Tough epithelial tissue covers and protects inside and outside of organ. [1] Any other valid point.

B3.2

1 **A – 3**, [1] **B – 4**, [1] **C – 1**, [1] **D – 2** [1]

2 organ is a collection of several different tissues that work together to carry out a particular function (any two examples) [2]; organ system is a number of organs working together to carry out a major function (any two examples) [2]

3 Each part of digestive system relies on preceding parts. [1] Stomach relies on mouth, teeth, and salivary glands to deliver chunks of chewed food, [1] small intestine depends on stomach to continue digestive process [1] and on enzymes made by pancreas to help with the digestive process. [1] Large intestine can only deal with remains of food already digested in the small intestine (soluble molecules absorbed into blood, leaving waste material and water), [1] absorbing water and removing faeces from body. [1]

Answers

B3.3

1a molecule made up of long chains of amino acids [1]

b structural components, [1] hormones, [1] antibodies, [1] enzymes (catalysts) [1]

2 similarities: vital components of a balanced diet, contain carbon, hydrogen, and oxygen, large molecules made up of smaller molecules joined together [3]; differences: carbohydrates made up of sugar units, lipids made up of fatty acids and glycerol, proteins made up of long chains of amino acids, lipids insoluble in water, proteins contain nitrogen [3] Any other valid point.

3a iodine test (yellow-red iodine solution turns blue-black if starch present) [2]

b ethanol test (ethanol added to solution gives cloudy white layer if lipid present) [2]

4 Lipids are made up of three molecules of fatty acids joined to a molecule of glycerol. [1] Different combination of fatty acids [1] determines whether lipid is solid (fat) or liquid (oil). [1]

5 Complex carbohydrates are made up of long chains of simple sugars (e.g., glucose, sucrose) [1] joined together. [1] Simple sugars are basic units of complex carbohydrates. [1]

B3.4

1a substance that speeds up a chemical reaction but is not used up or involved in the reaction and can be used many times over [1]

b large protein molecule that acts as biological catalyst [1]

c area in structure of enzyme with unique shape that binds to specific substrate [1]

2a protein [1]

b Substrate of reaction to be catalysed fits into active site of enzyme like a lock and key. [1] Once in place, enzyme and substrate bind together. [1] Reaction takes place rapidly [1] and products are released from active site. [1] Enzyme then ready to catalyse another reaction. [1]

3a building large molecules from smaller ones, [1] changing one molecule into another, [1] breaking down large insoluble molecules into smaller soluble ones [1] Any other valid example.

b Chemical reactions needed for life could not take place fast enough without enzymes to speed them up. [1] Each reaction controlled by specific enzyme [1] so that many metabolic reactions can take place in same small space without interfering with one another. [1] Enzymes enable cells to perform basic reactions (e.g., respiration) [1] and specific reactions to carry out particular functions, [1] simultaneously. [1]

B3.5

1 Rate of enzyme-controlled reaction initially increases as temperature increases, up to optimum temperature. [1] Once temperature exceeds 40 °C, protein structure of enzyme starts to break down. [1] Rate of reaction slows and ultimately stops when enzyme is denatured (stops working). [1]

2 Both change shape of active site, [1] both change rate of enzyme-controlled reaction and ultimately stop it. [1] Temperature permanently denatures most enzymes over about 40 °C. [1] Different enzymes work best at different pH levels. [1]

3 If body temperature increases too much (e.g., over 40 °C), proteins making up cell structure start to be damaged and shape of protein molecules making up enzymes is affected. [1] This changes shape of active sites, [1] making enzymes less effective and ultimately denaturing them, preventing chemical reactions necessary for life. [1] Reducing temperature in ill person represents balancing act between damaging harmful microorganisms and damaging ill person's own cells. [1]

B3.6

1a amylase: salivary glands, pancreas [1]; protease: stomach, pancreas, small intestine [1]; lipase: pancreas, small intestine [1]

b amylase: carbohydrate to sugar [1]; protease: proteins to amino acids [1]; lipase: lipids to fatty acids and glycerol [1]

c amylase: mouth, small intestine [1]; protease: stomach, small intestine [1]; lipase: small intestine [1]

2a about pH 2 [1]

b about pH 8 [1]

c Activity levels increase up to optimum pH, [1] then fall fast. [1]

d Increase in pH affects shape of active site of enzyme, [1] so it no longer bonds to the substrate. [1] Enzyme ultimately denatured [1] and no longer catalyses reaction. [1]

3 Large insoluble molecules in food cannot be absorbed into the blood [1]. They have to be broken down to form small insoluble molecules that can be absorbed. [1] Role of enzymes is to catalyse breakdown of food [1] so food can be digested at the right speed [1] and in the right region of the gut [1] to be absorbed and used by the body. [1]

B3.7

1a acidic [1]

b Hydrochloric acid is made in glands in the stomach lining [1] to produce low pH (acidic conditions). [1]

c alkaline [1]

d Liver produces bile, stored in gall bladder and released when food enters small intestine. [1] Bile is alkaline, neutralising stomach acid to create a slightly alkaline environment in small intestine. [1]

2a Bile emulsifies fats, [1] breaking large fat droplets into smaller droplets. [1]

b Fats do not mix with other liquids in digestive system, staying as large globules that are hard for lipase enzymes to act on. [1] Larger surface area produced by bile action [1] allows enzymes to reach more fat molecules and break them down more quickly. [1]

3 Any six from: Bread taken into mouth, broken up, and coated in saliva to start digestion of starch using amylase from salivary glands. Stomach muscles churn bread and mix it with pepsin and hydrochloric acid. Bread passed from stomach into first part of small intestine.

Bile added from gall bladder via bile duct to emulsify fats, provide larger surface area for digestive enzymes to work on, and neutralise acid from stomach to provide alkaline pH for optimum enzyme action. Digestive enzyme amylase added from pancreas to break down carbohydrates (bread) to glucose. Semi-digested food squeezed on to rest of small intestine. Lining covered with villi giving large surface area so products of digestion can be absorbed into blood as efficiently as possible. Indigestible food remains pass into large intestine where water is absorbed. Faeces pass out of body through anus. [6]

Answers

B4.1

1. Any three from transport of blood cells, transport of dissolved gases, transport of food, transport of hormones, removal of waste products, defence against infection, preventing blood loss through clotting. [3]
2. a Blood is made up of plasma (yellow liquid containing dissolved substances) [1] in which red blood cells are suspended. [1]
   b red blood cells [1]
   c Any three from transports waste products to kidneys as urea, transports soluble products of digestion to cells, transports waste carbon dioxide to lungs, transports oxygen around body in red blood cells. [3]
3. white blood cells: relatively large blood cells with nuclei, [1] protect against invasion of harmful microorganisms, [1] some (lymphocytes) form antibodies or antitoxins, [1] some (phagocytes) actively engulf and digest bacteria and viruses [1]; platelets: fragments of larger cells with no nuclei, [1] help with clotting to keep microorganisms out [1]

B4.2

1. a carry blood away from the heart, [1] thick wall of muscle (to contain blood under pressure) [1] and elastic fibres (to allow stretch as blood is forced through by heartbeat as pulse) [1]
   b carry blood towards the heart, [1] relatively thin walls (blood not under pressure), [1] have valves (to keep blood flowing towards heart) [1]
   c link arteries and veins, [1] very thin walls (to promote diffusion of substances in and out) [1]
2. a Arteries carry blood from heart to organs, veins return blood to heart, [1] capillaries link arteries and veins. [1]
   b Oxygen and dissolved food substances diffuse from blood into cell [1] and waste products such as carbon dioxide diffuse out of cell into blood. [1]
3. In fish blood leaves the capillaries of the gas exchange organ slowly, at low pressure, and without a pulse. [1] Active land mammals require lots of food and oxygen to supply muscles and organs for movement and warmth. They also produce a lot of waste materials such as carbon dioxide that must be removed. [1] Single circulation system would not be able to supply tissues or remove waste fast enough as blood would travel around body too slowly. [1] Double circulation system much more efficient because blood is pumped to gas exchange organ, then returns to heart and is pumped around body quickly at pressure. [1]

B4.3

1. flow chart should include: deoxygenated blood from body enters right atrium through vena cava → oxygenated blood from lungs enters left atrium through pulmonary vein → atria contract together and force blood down into ventricles (lower chambers) → right ventricle sends deoxygenated blood to lungs through pulmonary artery → left ventricle pumps oxygenated blood around the body through aorta [4]
2. a prevent blood flowing backwards, [1] making heart more efficient [1]
   b supply heart muscle cells with oxygenated blood [1] for aerobic respiration and efficient contraction [1]
   c allows heart to pump blood around body very efficiently, [1] enables blood to leave heart at high pressure, [1] right ventricle only has to send blood to the lungs (where high pressure would be damaging) [1]
3. Pulmonary artery carries blood away from heart. [1] Blood carried from heart to lungs is deoxygenated blood from the body, [1] which is dark red until it picks up oxygen in the lungs. [1]
4. a metal mesh placed in artery and opened up by inflation of tiny balloon [1] to hold narrowed blood vessel open so blood can flow freely [1]
   b

	Stent	Bypass surgery
advantages	no anaesthetic required, relatively cheap, effective	very effective against severe blockages
disadvantages	ineffective against severely blocked or narrowed arteries	general anaesthetic required, expensive

[4]

B4.4

1. group of cells in right atrium of heart [1] producing regular electrical signal that spreads through heart and makes it contract [1]
2. electrical device implanted into chest producing regular electrical signals to stimulate heart to contract and beat, [1] often inactive if heart beating normally and activated by change in heart rhythm [1], may measure additional demands increase heart rate during exercise [1]
3. a Valves prevent backflow of blood in heart. [1] Leaky valve can allow blood to flow backwards, [1] which means full amount of blood does not leave heart [1] and blood coming into heart chamber mixes with blood that hasn't left, making heart less efficient. [1]
   b i advantage: work well/no medication needed [1]; disadvantage: limited lifespan (12–15 years) [1]
     ii advantage: lasts a long time [1]; disadvantage: lifetime medication required to prevent clotting [1]
4. Can be used to keep patient alive until suitable heart for transplant becomes available. [1] Can be used in some cases to rest patient's own heart and allow it to recover. [1] May be used to replace the natural heart in the long term. [1] Very expensive, [1] not effective over long periods, [1] could be overtaken by organs grown from stem cells. [1] Any other valid evidence-based argument.

B4.5

1. Intercostal muscles between ribs and diaphragm contract and relax, [1] changing chest volume and pressure [1] and forcing air in or out. [1]
2. a exchange of oxygen and carbon dioxide gases in lungs [1]
   b Oxygen needed by cells for cellular respiration to provide energy, carbon dioxide poisonous waste product that must be removed. [1] Gaseous exchange supplies oxygen to blood and removes carbon dioxide. [1]
3. a Award marks for well-drawn bar chart correctly labelled. [3]
   b Bar chart shows we breathe in air containing mainly nitrogen with oxygen and a tiny bit of carbon dioxide, and breathe out air containing mainly nitrogen but with less oxygen and more carbon dioxide. [1] We take oxygen from air breathed in and

pass carbon dioxide into air breathed out, but we breathe in and breathe out air. [1]

c ventilation and rich blood supply for steep concentration gradient, [2] clusters of alveoli/spherical alveolus shape for large surface area, [2] thin alveolus walls to minimise diffusion distances [2]

B4.6

1a cover surfaces and protect them, may secrete waxy substance for waterproofing [1]

b contains lots of chloroplasts for photosynthesis [1]

c contains some chloroplasts for photosynthesis [1]

2 Tightly packed palisade mesophyll cells at top of leaf contain many chloroplasts for photosynthesis [1] and are protected by epidermis. [1] Spongy mesophyll cells also photosynthesise and have large air spaces and surface area to maximise gas exchange. [1] Xylem supply water for photosynthesis [1], phloem transport food from photosynthesis around plant. [1] Stomata can be opened or closed by guard cells to let gases in and out. [1]

B4.7

1 transport of food made in leaves and water and mineral ions taken from soil to rest of plant [1]

2 Mature xylem cells are dead, phloem cells are living. [1] Xylem transport water and mineral ions from soil, phloem transport dissolved sugars from photosynthesis. [1] Xylem found on inside of vascular bundles, phloem on outside. [1]

3 Phloem in trees found in a ring just underneath bark. [1] Soft bark of young trees vulnerable to damage by animals. [1] If complete ring of bark is eaten, transport of water from roots and sugars from leaves stops and young tree will die. [1] Plastic covers protect young bark from animals. [1] Covers can be removed once trees are more mature and bark is harder. [1] If covers aren't used, most of young trees are likely to be destroyed and woodland will eventually die as old, mature trees are not replaced. [1]

B4.8

1a small openings all over leaf surface surrounded by guard cells [1]

b Stomata open to allow air into the leaves to provide carbon dioxide for photosynthesis, [1] and close to control loss of water. [1]

2 Water vapour evaporates from cells lining air spaces [1] and diffuses out of leaf through stomata [1] down a concentration gradient. [1]

3 As water evaporates from leaf surface, more water is pulled up through xylem to replace it. [1] Water moves into roots by osmosis to replace water moving up xylem. [1] Transpiration stream is constant movement of water molecules through xylem from roots to leaves. [1]

4 sum of readings = 1,855
divide by number of readings = $\frac{1855}{7}$
mean number of stomata = 265 per mm^2 of leaf [3]

B4.9

1a waxy cuticle, [1] guard cells [1]

b Rate of transpiration would increase because rapid air movement across leaf would remove water vapour from near leaf surface and increase concentration gradient for diffusion of water out of the leaf [1], which would increase rate of evaporation from leaf cells, [1] increasing water uptake. [1]

2a rate of transpiration slightly reduced [1]

b rate of transpiration greatly reduced [1]

c Petroleum jelly on top surface has little effect as few stomata covered. Most stomata are found on underside of leaves and would be unaffected. [1] Petroleum jelly on bottom surface greatly reduces transpiration as most of stomata would be covered, allowing little diffusion to take place. [1] Rate of evaporation from cell surfaces would be reduced as surrounding air would become saturated with water vapour (decreasing concentration gradient). [1]

3a Stomata on underside would be under water and water could not be lost through them. [1] Stomata on top surface enable effective gas exchange for photosynthesis through direct exposure to sunlight. [1]

b Excess transpiration not a risk as plants live in water. [1] No shortage of water to bring up from roots to replace that lost in transpiration. [1]

B5.1

1 State of complete physical and mental well-being, not just absence of disease. [1]

2a Any three from pathogens (bacteria, viruses), non-communicable diseases, poor diet, stress, lack of clean water. [3] Any other valid factor.

b pathogens: tuberculosis, flu; non-communicable diseases: heart disease, arthritis; poor diet: obesity, starvation, rickets; stress: heart disease, mental health problems; lack of clean water: diarrhoeal diseases, sickness [3] Any other valid example.

3a Bacterial infection with tuberculosis, viral infection with HIV, injecting drug use [2]

b i increases chances [1]
ii $0.2 - 0.006 = 0.194$, $\frac{0.194}{0.2} \times 100 = 0.97$, [1] 97% more likely to be infected [1]

c HIV positive injecting drug users [1]

d $1.5 - 0.2 = 1.3$, $\frac{1.3}{1.5} \times 100 = 86.67$ [1], 87 times more likely [1]

4 Many diseases more prevalent in overcrowded situations as transmission is easier. [1] Poor cities in less developed countries have this problem. [1] Injecting drug abuse increases risk of transmission of many blood-borne diseases. [1] This problem is more common in wealthy countries. [1] Poor diet linked with non-communicable diseases (e.g., heart disease) in all countries [1] and to poor immune system and more communicable diseases in less developed countries. [1] Any other valid explanation.

B5.2

1a microorganisms known as pathogens [1]

b as a result of reaction to toxins produced, [1] or damage caused to cells [1]

2a Any two from by air, direct skin contact, direct contact of body fluids, by contaminated water, by undercooked or contaminated food. [2]

b Any two from by air, direct contact, by contaminated water. [2]

317

Answers

   c people: by air (droplet infection – droplets full of pathogens expelled in coughing, sneezing, or talking, droplets breathed in by others), direct skin contact (pathogens spread from skin of one person to skin of another), direct contact of body fluids (pathogens pass directly from inside one person's body into another), by contaminated water (taking in pathogen through digestive system), by undercooked or contaminated food (taking in pathogen through digestive system) [2]; plants: by air (fungal spores carried in air from one plant to another), by direct contact (pathogens on traces of plant material come into contact with new plants in the soil and infect them), by contaminated water (fungal spores carried in splashes of water from one plant to another) [2]

3 Bacteria are single-celled organisms much smaller than plant and animal cells. [1] Viruses are even smaller than bacteria. [1] Bacteria divide rapidly by splitting in two (binary fission). [1] Viruses take over body cells and reproduce inside them. [1] Bacteria may produce toxins or directly damage body cells. [1] Viruses damage and destroy cells. [1]

B5.3

1a To find out what nutrients they need to grow [1] and to investigate which chemicals are best at killing them. [1]
 b Agar gel is a culture medium [1] giving microorganisms everything they need to grow. [1]
2a reduces risk of growing dangerous pathogens [1]
 b To prevent contamination of culture by microorganisms from the environment [1] and to prevent release of potentially harmful microorganisms that might grow. [1]
 c Higher temperatures enable microorganisms to grow much more rapidly [1] so that they can be identified sooner (e.g., in hospital labs) [1] or to produce products more quickly in industry (e.g., insulin-producing GM bacteria). [1]
3 Petri dish has limited supplies (nothing new added), [2] bacteria use up available food and oxygen (limiting growth), [2] Petri dish has no mechanism for removal of waste products (build-up of carbon dioxide and other toxins can poison bacteria and stop growth). [2] Any other valid limiting factor.

B5.4

1a Disinfectants are used to kill bacteria in environment but are toxic to people, [1] antiseptics are disinfectants that kill bacteria and are safe to use on human skin, [1] antibiotics are chemicals that can be used inside body to kill bacteria or prevent them from growing. [1]
 b These rooms contain most bacteria [1] and are where people are most careful about hygiene. [1]
2 Bacteria will grow rapidly to begin with as they have everything they need [1] (plenty of food, plenty of oxygen, few waste products). [1] Conditions are optimal for growth and division. [1] As time passes, food and oxygen are used up [1] and waste products build up that cannot escape. [1] Lack of resources and build-up of toxins slows down and eventually stops growth, colony dies. [1]
3a A: (radius of A = 2.5 mm) area = $3.142 \times 2.5^2 = 19.6$ mm^2 [1]
    B: (radius of B = 5.05 mm) area $3.142 \times 5.05^2 = 81.7$ mm^2 [1]
    C: (radius of C = 7.9 mm) area $3.142 \times 7.9^2 = 196.1$ mm^2 [1]
 b $\frac{196.092 \text{ mm}^2}{19.638 \text{ mm}^2} = 9.985$ [1]

Highest concentration approximately 10 times more effective than lowest concentration (an order of magnitude more effective). [1]

B5.5

1 Any three from wiping work surfaces with disinfectant, cleaning toilets, keeping raw meat away from food eaten uncooked, using tissues to blow nose, washing hands before handling food. [3] Any other valid example.
2 wiping work surfaces with disinfectant: destroys microorganisms present after preparing raw food; cleaning toilets: destroys bacteria from faecal material; keeping raw meat away from food eaten uncooked: prevents spread of pathogens that will not later be destroyed by cooking, allowing the pathogens into the gut; using tissues to blow nose: contains pathogen-filled mucus for disposal; washing hands before handling food: prevents spread of pathogens onto food [6] Any other valid explanation.
3 Pathogens are very small, so before development of microscopes people had no way of seeing bacteria or viruses. [1] Inability to see microorganisms made it very difficult to understand how diseases spread. [1] Evidence (e.g., improved hygiene reducing the deaths from childbed fever) was seen as challenging normal practice. [1] Difficult to convince people whose ideas are entrenched. [1] Need people prepared to take a chance (e.g., Pasteur, Lister). [1] Takes time for evidence of effectiveness of new idea to build up. [1]

B5.6

1a fever, [1] red skin rash [1]
 b improved living standards (less overcrowding) have reduced spread of disease by droplet infection, [1] vaccination programme for babies and children has reduced pool of infection [1]
2a HIV is virus that causes AIDS. [1]
 b HIV attacks immune cells, causing only a mild, flu-like illness initially. [1] Without treatment the virus remains hidden after initial mild illness, [1] damaging the immune system to the extent that it cannot defend the body against infections and certain cancers. [1] These diseases kill the patient. [1]
3a i 4,200,000 + 4,400,000 + 4,100,000 + 3,800,000 + 3,300,000 + 3,100,000 = approx. 22,9000,000 cases [3]
   ii 800,000 + 800,000 + 550,000 + 700,000 + 500,000 + 600,000 = approx. 3,950,000 cases [3]
 b 1980–1985: $\frac{22\,900\,000}{100} \times 5 = 1\,145\,000$ people [2]
    2000–2005: $\frac{3\,950\,000}{100} \times 5 = 197\,000$ people [2]
 c Between 1980 and 1990, vaccination rates go up and cases of measles fall dramatically. [1] During 1990s vaccination rates and number of cases of measles plateau. [1] From around 2000 onwards, global vaccination rates increase again and cases of measles show another fall. [1] As vaccination coverage continues to increase, number of cases continues to fall. [1]
4 similarities: red rash in measles and mosaic discolouration pattern in tobacco mosaic virus (TMV), no treatment for either virus; differences: measles spread by droplet infection, TMV spread by direct contact and insect vectors, measles prevented by improved nutrition/living standards/vaccination, TMV prevented by good field hygiene and pest control [6]

B5.7

1. kill bacteria OR prevent growth of bacteria [1]
2. **a** Most common causes are eating either undercooked food contaminated with *Salmonella* [1] or food prepared in unhygienic conditions that becomes contaminated by *Salmonella* bacteria raw meat. [1]
   b Any three from doesn't last long (only a few days), unpleasant but not serious for most people, antibiotics would be lost from system through sickness and diarrhoea, risks development of antibiotic resistance. [3] Any other valid suggestion.
3. **a** sexually transmitted disease, [1] pathogens passed from one partner to another during unprotected sexual contact [1]
   b bacterial infection, [1] so could be treated with antibiotics [1]
   c Any three from being celibate, having a single sexual partner, limiting number of sexual partners, always using barrier method of contraception (e.g., condom). [3]
   d Gonorrhoea will become much more difficult or impossible to treat. [1] It is not serious in the early stages [1] but if not treated can lead to long-term problems (e.g., abdominal pain, infertility, damage to eyes of babies born to infected mothers). [1] These long-term problems will increase as bacteria become more resistant. [1]
4. Look for articulate writing and clear explanation. Main points could include: details of *Salmonella* poisoning and symptoms, *Salmonella* can be found on contaminated meat or mayonnaise made with raw eggs, bacteria killed by thorough cooking, salads often contaminated when prepared with chicken for barbecues, meat not always cooked thoroughly on barbecues, check meat is piping hot in middle, no pink juices. [6]

B5.8

1. **a** Any three from spores carried in air, spores in water splashes, contaminated plant material in soil, direct contact between healthy and diseased leaves. [3]
   b Fungus causes black spots on leaves that then turn yellow and fall early, [1] reducing leaf area for photosynthesis [1] and limiting food available to make flowers. [1]
2. **a** Through bite of female *Anopheles* mosquito [1] infected with malaria parasite from another blood meal. [1]
   b nets prevent mosquito bites, [1] insecticide kills mosquitoes [1]
3. awareness: avoid malarial areas if possible, be aware if malaria is in intended region of travel; bite prevention: precautions such as insecticide-treated mosquito nets to sleep under, mosquito netting at windows and doors, use of insect repellent, keeping skin covered; chemoprophylaxis: take antimalarial drugs that kill parasites in blood; diagnosis: early malaria treatment more likely to be effective, have blood test for early diagnosis if ill after travel to malarial area. [6]

B5.9

1. **a** prevents pathogens transferring from hands to food [1]
   b prevents pathogens coming into contact with other people or your hands [1]
   c prevents pathogens from gut being taken in with drinking water [1]
2. **a** Clotted blood prevents pathogens getting into body through cuts in skin. [1] If blood won't clot properly, pathogens may get in through open cuts. [1]
   b White blood cells destroy pathogens. [1] If number of white blood cells falls, fewer pathogens will be destroyed, [1] increasing likelihood of infection. [1]
3. to include detail on ingestion and digestion (destruction) of microorganisms, [2] production of antibodies to target and destroy particular pathogens, [2] production of antitoxins to counteract toxins released by pathogens [2]

B5.10

1. **a** plant growth stunted [1] as insufficient nitrate to convert sugars from photosynthesis into proteins for protein synthesis [1]
   b leaves yellow [1] as insufficient magnesium to make chlorophyll so plant can't photosynthesise effectively [1]
2. Plant attacked by fungal or bacterial pathogen, [1] or by nematode worms or other plant pest, [1] damaging roots [1] so they cannot absorb mineral ions from soil effectively. [1]
3. Basic table shown below – students should focus on different approaches depending on chosen audience.

Common symptoms	Pathogen/pest type	Example of disease
stunted growth	n/a	nitrate deficiency
areas of decay or rotting	fungi	black spot
growths	bacteria	crown gall
damaged roots, malformed stems/leaves	nematodes, aphids	root knot disease
yellow leaves (chlorosis)	n/a	magnesium deficiency
mosaic patterns	viruses	tobacco mosaic virus
presence of visible pests	aphids, caterpillars	n/a

[4]

B5.11

1. **a** Any three from cellulose cell walls, waxy cuticle, bark, leaf fall, antibacterial chemicals. [3]
   b Any three from poisons, thorns, hairy stems/leaves, drooping or curling when touched, mimicry [3]
2. cellulose cell walls: resist invasion by microorganisms; waxy cuticle: barrier to pathogens; bark: protective layer hard for pathogens to penetrate; leaf fall: pathogens removed when leaves fall; antibacterial chemicals: kill bacterial pathogens; poisons: make herbivores unwell so deter eating; thorns: make plant unpleasant/painful to eat; hairy stems/leaves: deter eating and egg laying; drooping or curling when touched: dislodges insects, frightens small animals; mimicry: mimic unhealthy plants or existing eggs [6]
3. similarities: internal and external defences, antibacterial chemicals, protective layers [3]; differences: people have immune system making specific antibodies to particular pathogens, people have few defences against attack by predators (no thorns, little hair), people do not produce poisons [3] Any other valid point.

Answers

B6.1

1a unique protein found on surface membrane of cell [1]

b protein made by white blood cells in response to specific antigens [1]

c bacterial: tuberculosis, tetanus, diphtheria [1]; viral: polio, measles, whooping cough. [1] Any other valid example.

2a Every cell has unique proteins on its surface called antigens. [1] Immune system recognises that antigens on microorganisms entering the body are different from those on body's own cells. [1] White blood cells make antibodies to target antigens and destroy pathogens. [1] Memory cells remember precise antibody needed to destroy particular pathogen [1] and can produce this antibody very quickly if same pathogen gets into body again, providing immunity to that disease. [1]

b Small amount of dead or inactive form of pathogen introduced into body, [1] stimulating white blood cells to produce antibodies [1] needed to fight pathogen and prevent illness. [1] If same, live pathogen is encountered later, body can respond rapidly to make correct antibodies [1] just as if you had already had the disease, conferring protection. [1]

3 vaccines are effective against both bacterial and viral diseases because they stimulate the immune system [1] to target both bacterial and viral pathogens. [1] Either bacterial or viral pathogens can be grown in a laboratory for use in vaccines. [1] It is difficult to develop vaccines for certain viruses (e.g., those causing the common cold) [1] as the viruses mutate quickly, changing their format by the time a vaccine is developed. [1]

B6.2

1 Paracetamol is a very useful painkiller but will have no effect on the disease-causing pathogen (treats symptoms, not disease). [1] Penicillin is an antibiotic that kills the disease-causing bacteria (treats disease). [1]

2 Viral pathogens reproduce inside body cells [1], so it is very difficult to develop drugs that destroy them without destroying body cells, too. [1] Bacteria exist outside body cells and are different from human cells, [1] so antibiotics can target bacterial cells without hurting body cells. [1]

3a 1930: 680 deaths per 100 000 live births [1]; 1940: 380 deaths per 100 000 live births [1]; 1950: 90 deaths per 100 000 live births [1]

b i $680 - 380 = 300$, [1] $\frac{300}{680} \times 100 = 44.1$, [1] 44% fall [1]

ii $380 - 90 = 290$, [1] $\frac{290}{380} \times 100 = 76.3$, [1] 76% fall [1]

c Deaths fell between 1930 and 1940 due to improved hygiene standards. [1] Deaths fell sharply between 1940 and 1950 due to the introduction of antibiotics (infection could be treated and cured). [1] Hospital births increasingly common, doctors on hand to spot symptoms of infection and prescribe antibiotics. [1]

d Antibiotics have reduced rate of deaths from maternal septicaemia to very low levels. [1] Emergence of antibiotic resistant bacteria renders antibiotics ineffective. [1] Without effective antibiotics rate of deaths could return to 1920–1930 levels and thousands of women could die from infections after giving birth. [1] Any other valid point.

B6.3

1 He noticed a clear ring in jelly around some spots of mould growing on bacterial culture plates. [1] He realised that a chemical in the mould must have killed the bacteria in the culture, [1] leaving the jelly clear. [1]

2 Plant extracts may be impure, or they may be found only in very tiny amounts in a plant, [1] meaning huge amounts of plant material would be needed to extract the drug. [1] Synthetic drugs can be made industrially in large amounts and chemists can change the molecules to change the properties of the medicine. [1] Chemists can make drugs that are more effective and have fewer side effects than natural products. [1]

3 advantages: anecdotal evidence of medicinal properties saves trying many different plants, long and widespread usage suggests few side effects; disadvantages: may be difficult to source the living material, concentrations may be very low, may be difficult to isolate the chemical that has caused the antibiotic effect [6] Any other valid point.

B6.4

1 efficacy: whether a drug does the job it is designed to do [1]; toxicity: whether a drug is toxic and, if so, how much of it is has to be given to have a toxic effect [1]; dosage: dose of a drug that is effective in treating a disease [1]

2a flow chart should include: identify pathway in disease that needs cure → identify new chemical (in living organisms or lab) → preclinical testing on cells, tissues, and animals → phase 1 clinical trials check for side effects → phase 2 clinical trials check efficacy and safety → phase 3 clinical trials check efficacy, safety, and dosage → licencing → phase 4 clinical trials monitor safety throughout life of drug [6]

b If there is already a drug available for treating a disease it would be unethical to deprive patients of treatment by giving a placebo that would have no clinical effect. [1] If new drug is for a condition where there is a current treatment, patients will be given best current treatment as placebo. [1] This is ethical and provides comparison between new drug and current best practice. [1]

3 Florey and Chain successfully treated their patient although drug ran out before he was fully cured. The next patient they tried it on was cured. Thalidomide resulted in the birth of many thousands of babies with no limbs or very much shortened limbs. Trial process has changed over time (more treatments are now available, allowing luxury of time to fully test new ones, which was not the case for Florey and Chain). Thalidomide outcomes show that it is important to test new drugs on pregnant animals as well as healthy adults. Any other valid point demonstrating understanding of different outcomes and consideration of change in attitudes. [6]

B6.5

1a group of genetically identical cells or organisms [1]

b protein made by an immune system cell in response to presence of foreign antigen [1]

c proteins produced from a single clone of cells to target specific body cells or chemicals [1]

2a cell that divides to make large number of identical cells [1] that all produce specific antibodies, [1] formed by fusing a mouse lymphocyte with a tumour cell [1] b To make hybridoma cells mouse lymphocytes are stimulated to make a specific type of antibody and then fused with special tumour cells. Lymphocytes can make antibodies but cannot divide, [1] tumour cells don't make antibodies but can divide rapidly. [1] Hybridoma cells both make required antibodies and divide to make clone of identical cells, meaning they can be used to make very large amounts of specific monoclonal antibodies. [1]

3 Monoclonal antibodies in pregnancy tests make pregnancy diagnosis possible from the very early stages of pregnancy, [1] detecting human chorionic gonadotropin (HCG) in the urine within days of conception. [1] Monoclonal antibodies in pregnancy test bind to HCG hormone if present in urine [1], producing colour change signalling positive test result. [1]

B6.6

1 Because monoclonal antibodies can identify and bind to specific cell types, [1] it was thought that they could be used to carry drugs to specific cancers and treat them, [1] producing much more targeted means of treating cancer than therapies such as radiotherapy. [1]

2 Monoclonal antibodies initially created more side effects than expected, [1] partly because mouse cells were used in formation of hybridoma cells, triggering an immune response in people. [1] Developments such as production of mouse/human hybrid cells [1] and use of fractions of antibodies to carry drugs to target cells are reducing side effects. [1] Doctors are now prepared for side effects and can treat symptoms. [1] Ongoing development of new skills and technologies to create monoclonal antibodies and attach them to drugs and other compounds means they are being used in more and different ways. [1] Any other valid point.

B7.1

1a non-infectious disease that cannot be passed from one individual to another [1]

b Communicable diseases caused by pathogens (e.g., bacteria, viruses, fungi), [1] whilst non-communicable diseases affect people as a result of genetic makeup, lifestyle, or environmental factors. [1]

2a 7.4 + 6.7 + 3.1 + 1.6 + 1.5 + 1.3 + 1.1 = 22.7 million [2]

b Total number of deaths from 10 leading causes = 28.8 million [1] Total number of deaths from non-communicable diseases = 22.7 million [1]

c $\frac{22.7}{28.8} \times 100 = 78.8 = 79\%$ [2]

3 Risk factors are factors that increase your risk of developing a particular disease. [1] They may be something you cannot change (e.g., inherited genes), lifestyle factors (e.g., smoking increases risk of heart disease and lung cancer), or environmental factors (e.g., ionising radiation). [1] Correlations are apparent links between two factors (e.g., between number of people who smoke and number of people with throat and lung cancer). [1] However, correlation does not mean one thing necessarily causes another. [1] If a correlation is seen, further work is needed to determine a causal mechanism. [1] Causal mechanisms explain how one factor influences another through a biological process (e.g., smoking has been shown to increase risk of lung cancer because chemicals in smoke increase risk of mutation in cells). [1]

B7.2

1a mass of abnormally growing cells [1] formed when normal control of cell cycle is lost [1] and cells divide rapidly without growing and maturing. [1]

b Benign tumour grows in one place, is usually contained in a membrane, and does not invade other tissues. [1] Malignant tumour invades neighbouring healthy tissues and can also split, [1] releasing small clumps of cells that spread around the body in the blood and invade different healthy tissues. [1]

c Benign tumour can grow very large and compress/damage organs, which can be life-threatening (e.g., brain tumour). [1] Malignant tumour may split into pieces that are carried around the body in the blood or lymph [1] where uncontrolled cell division continues to form secondary tumours. [1] These tumours disrupt normal tissue and often cause death if untreated. [1]

2a either stop cancer cells dividing, [1] or make them self-destruct [1]

b Cancer drugs are designed to target rapidly dividing cancer cells. [1] They also tend to affect other rapidly dividing cells. [1] Cells of hair follicles, skin, stomach lining, and blood-forming bone marrow are always dividing rapidly [1] so are more likely than other body cells to be affected by chemotherapy. [1]

3 radiotherapy: cancer cells destroyed by targeted doses of radiation, [1] stops mitosis in cancer cells but can also damage healthy cells [1]; chemotherapy: chemicals used to stop cancer cells dividing or make them self-destruct, [1] aim to target cancer cells as specifically as possible [1]

B7.3

1a nicotine, carbon monoxide, tar [3]

b nicotine: addictive/produces sense of calm/increases heat rate [1] carbon monoxide: poisonous/taken up by blood instead of oxygen [1] tar: carcinogenic/damages lung tissue causing COPD [1]

2a Award marks for well-drawn chart correctly labelled. [4]

b the more cigarettes smoked, the greater the risk of dying from cardiovascular disease (CVD) [1]

c Smoking narrows blood vessels, which can increase blood pressure. [1] Nicotine in cigarette smoke increases heart rate. [1] Other chemicals in cigarette smoke damage lining of arteries, making atherosclerosis more likely, or increase blood pressure. [1] All of these effects increase the risk of CVD.

3 Scientists have several causal mechanisms that work together to explain link between smoking and lung cancer. [1] Cigarette smoke contains tar and other carcinogens. The higher the concentration of these chemicals in the lungs, the more likely they are to affect cells and turn them malignant. [1] Cilia that would naturally filter out tar are anaesthetised by chemicals in cigarette smoke so they do not work, [1] allowing tar and other carcinogenic chemicals to build up in delicate lung tissue. [1]

4 Smoking causes blood to carry poisonous carbon monoxide rather than oxygen, reducing oxygen-carrying capacity of blood. [1] In pregnant women this can lead to oxygen shortage for developing fetus. [1] Oxygen shortage can lead to premature births, [1] low birthweight babies, [1] and stillbirths. [1]

Answers

5 Smoking causes many different diseases (e.g., heart disease, stroke, cancers of breathing system) [1] as well as premature births, low birthweight babies, stillbirths, and increased risk of other diseases (e.g., bronchitis, COPD). [1] This has a human cost [1] as individuals may lose the ability to work, their health, and potentially their life, or the life of a loved one. [1] Loss of working time, cost of hospital treatment, and cost of supporting people affected by loss of family income are a significant financial burden to nations, [1] but nations also get money from tax on cigarettes. [1] Any other valid point.

B7.4

1 Exercise builds cardiovascular fitness, so people who exercise are likely to have healthier hearts and bigger lungs than people who don't exercise. [1] People who exercise are less likely to be obese than people who don't exercise [1] and are less likely to suffer diseases such as type 2 diabetes, [1] high blood pressure, [1] and heart disease.

2 If excess food is consumed, it is stored as fat and you may become obese. [1] Exercise uses up some of the energy [1] produced during respiration from the food you eat. [1] As a result, less food is stored as fat, reducing risk of obesity. [1]

3 relative risk in men who exercise least: 4.5 [1]; relative risk in men who exercise most: 1.2 [1]

4 Risk of developing type 2 diabetes is much higher in women than in men with the same body mass index (BMI). [1] At BMI of just over 25 – just overweight – risk for men is 2.2% and for women 8.1%. At BMI of over 35, risk for men is 42% and for women 93%. This is evidence for statement that type 2 diabetes is an epidemic that particularly affects women. [1] Women may be less likely to do exercise whatever their BMI (need more data). [1] Epidemic could be controlled by helping people to eat a balanced diet, [1] take more exercise, [1] and lose weight, [1] to restore normal blood glucose balance and reduce risk of type 2 diabetes.

B7.5

1a agent that increases risk of cancer developing [1]
 b Any three from tar from cigarette smoke, sunlight, X-rays, alcohol. [3] Any other valid suggestion.

2a men: 9 per 100 000 [1]; women: 5 per 100 000 [1]
 b men: 18–19 per 100 000 [1]; women: 8–9 per 100 000 [1]
 c Any three from drinking more socially acceptable and therefore more common, cost of alcohol lower/incomes higher, younger people drinking, people drinking more at a time (binge drinking), more people addicted to alcohol. [3]
 d Points may include: very popular, part of culture, generates revenue for government, enjoyed by many sensibly, hard to change legal status after so many years, many people in authority use alcohol themselves, prohibition tried and failed (led to criminal activity). [3] Accept any thoughtful point.

B8.1

1a carbon dioxide from air, [1] water from soil [1]
 b carbon dioxide and water from water in which it lives, [2] light from Sun or electric light [1]

2 Carbon atom moves from air into air spaces in leaf, [1] into plant cells, [1] into chloroplasts, [1] joins with water to make glucose, [1] and is converted to starch for storage. [1]

3 Leaf kept in light photosynthesises, making glucose from carbon dioxide and water using energy from light. [1] Glucose converted to starch to be stored and used for respiration when leaf is in dark and cannot photosynthesise. [1] Iodine solution turns blue-black in presence of starch. Carrying out an iodine test on a leaf kept in light for 24 hours will give positive blue-black colour for starch because plant has been photosynthesising for a long time and glucose will have been stored as starch. [1] If leaf is then kept in dark for 24 hours it cannot photosynthesise so cells will use stored starch for respiration. Little or no starch left in the leaves so iodine solution unaffected. [1]

4a carbon dioxide + water $\xrightarrow{\text{light}}$ glucose + oxygen [2]

$6CO_2 + 6H_2O \xrightarrow{\text{light}} C_6H_{12}O_6 + 6O_2$ [2]

 b It needs bigger input of energy from environment [1] to break bonds holding carbon dioxide and water together [1] than is released when new bonds form in glucose and oxygen. [1]

B8.2

1 carbon dioxide, [1] light, [1] temperature [1]

2a As light intensity increases, so does rate of photosynthesis. [1] This indicates that light intensity is limiting factor. [1]
 b Increase in light intensity has no effect on rate of photosynthesis, [1] so light intensity is no longer limiting factor (something else probably is). [1]
 c Temperature acts as a normal limiting factor to begin with, in that increase in temperature increases rate of photosynthesis. [1] This is consistent with light and carbon dioxide concentrations (Figures 1 and 4). [1] Increasing light intensity and carbon dioxide concentration cause rate of photosynthesis to rise and then plateau when another factor becomes limiting. [1] Above a certain temperature, enzymes in cells are denatured so no photosynthesis can take place at all. [1]

3 tropical rainforest: high light intensity, warm temperature, plenty of moisture, carbon dioxide from decaying material (relatively few limiting factors and rapid growth conditions available all year round, allowing plants and even individual leaves get very large); [2] UK woodland: low light intensity, short days in winter, cold temperature (most growth takes place in spring and summer with plenty of light and warmth but temperatures still lower temperatures than tropical rain forest, less time for growth so plants smaller); [2] Arctic tundra: no light all winter but lots of light in summer, lack of water due to frozen ground (low temperatures limiting factor on photosynthesis for most of year, so plants much smaller and slower-growing than tropical rainforest or UK woodland) [2]

B8.3

1 Any three from respiration, energy for cell functions, growth, reproduction, building up smaller molecules into bigger molecules, conversion into starch for storage, making cellulose, making amino acids, building up fats and oils for food store in seeds. [3]

2a leaves, [1] stems, [1] roots, [1] storage organs [1]
 b Glucose is soluble and would affect movement of water into and out of plant cells [1] by osmosis. [1] Starch is insoluble and does not disturb plant's water balance. [1]

c Accept any appropriate suggestion involving a slice of potato and dilute iodine solution. [3]

3 Left-hand leaf has been in sunlight and has made starch. [1] When tested with iodine this stains the leaf blue-black. Right-hand leaf has been in dark, has used up its starch stores in respiration [1] and hasn't been exposed to light to photosynthesise and make more starch. [1] Iodine remains yellow-brown in iodine test indicating no starch present. [1]

4 Bogs are wet and peaty and soil contains very few minerals, [1] especially nitrates. [1] Plants need nitrates from soil to make amino acids and build them into proteins. [1] Many plants cannot grow well in bogs. Carnivorous plants trap insects and digest their bodies, [1] which provide good supply of nitrates and other minerals. [1] These plants can grow and thrive in bogs as they do not rely on bog soil for minerals. [1]

B8.4

1a garden greenhouse: temperature changes with sunlight unless heated, light levels change year-round, plants not affected by wind, gardener can water with added food; hydroponics growing system: temperature/light/carbon dioxide levels controlled, plants grown in mineral enriched water rather than soil [3]

b can eliminate limiting factors and promote maximum rate of photosynthesis so plants grow as fast and as large as possible, [1] maximising profit [1] and allowing us to grow more crops in and out of season [1]

2a i light levels low until sunrise – not enough light for photosynthesis, temperature falls overnight – low temperatures affect enzyme activity and slow rate of photosynthesis [3]

ii carbon dioxide will limit photosynthesis – not enough carbon dioxide to make glucose as fast as other conditions would allow [3]

iii days shorter in winter but no leaves on trees so light will reach woodland floor – light limiting factor for trees but not woodland floor plants, carbon dioxide levels normal or higher than normal as fewer leaves absorbing – not limiting, temperature colder – enzyme activity reduced by low temperature, so temperature most likely limiting factor [3]

iv leaves on trees will limit light but light intensity high and days long, temperature warm, carbon dioxide levels most likely limiting factor – insufficient for maximum rate of photosynthesis [3]

b Each case is within natural environment [1] where light, temperature, and carbon dioxide levels change constantly and can interact, [1] meaning that any factor may be limiting factor for photosynthesis at any time. [1]

3 20 °C is a temperature that can be achieved easily in the UK during spring and summer with relatively little or no heating. [1] 30 °C is much higher than ambient temperature all year round so greenhouse would need almost constant heating. [1] Rate of photosynthesis with plenty of carbon dioxide is higher at 30 °C than at 20 °C but cost of constant heating very high (profit from one extra crop annually might not outweigh year-round heating cost). [1] Investing in removable insulation helps maintain a temperature of 20 °C or more for much of year with little or no heating. [1] When greenhouse is heated insulation retains warmth. [1] Minimising heating minimises carbon footprint. [1] Any other valid point.

B9.1

1a glucose + oxygen → carbon dioxide + water (energy transferred to environment) [2]

b $C_6H_{12}O_6 + 6O_2 \rightarrow 6CO_2 + 6H_2O$ (energy transferred to environment) [2]

c Muscle cells are very active and need a lot of energy. [1] They need large numbers of mitochondria to supply energy as aerobic respiration takes place in mitochondria. [1] Fat cells use very little energy [1] so need very few mitochondria. [1]

2a movement, [1] building new molecules, [1] heat generation [1]

b People become thin because stored energy is used up [1] and growth stops as new proteins are not made for lack of energy and raw materials. [1] People lack energy for movement as there is insufficient fuel for respiration in mitochondria. [1] People feel cold as there is insufficient fuel for respiration in mitochondria, which transfers energy to the body to warm it up. [1]

3 Accept any appropriate suggestion for practical investigation. [6]

B9.2

1a i Increases before exercise starts as a result of anticipation, rises rapidly as exercise begins, followed by steady rise and then sharp fall as exercise finishes. [1] Increased heart rate supplies muscles with extra blood needed to bring glucose and oxygen to muscle fibres [1] and to remove increased amounts of carbon dioxide. [1]

ii Increases more slowly and evenly than heart rate but remains high for some time after exercise. [1] Increased heart rate supplies enough oxygen initially, then breathing rate needs to increase to meet demand. [1] When exercise stops, breathing rate remains high until oxygen debt paid off. [1]

b Unfit person has lower heart volume at rest than fit person [1] and is not able to pump as much blood out of heart during each beat at rest as fit person is. [1] This means unfit person's heart has to work harder to deliver same volume of blood to muscle cells and remove waste. [1] Heart rate will therefore be faster in unfit person than fit person. [1]

2a complex carbohydrate [1] stored in muscles [1]

b Glycogen can be converted rapidly into glucose [1] to provide fuel for aerobic respiration, providing body cells with energy. [1] Muscle tissue often needs sudden supply of energy for rapid contraction in a way that most other tissues do not, [1] so muscle needs a glycogen store. [1] Other tissues don't need energy in the same way so have not evolved to have glycogen stores. [1]

3a Award marks based on ideas presented and method produced. Look for sensible ideas, safe investigation, clear instructions, realistic expectations, appropriate methods of recording and analysis, awareness of weakness in investigation, and understanding of variables. [6]

b Results will depend on method chosen and fitness parameter investigated. Look for awareness that fitness will vary (can be affected by age, lifestyle, or health issues). [4]

B9.3

1 After long period of exercise muscles become short of oxygen and switch from aerobic to anaerobic respiration, which is less efficient. [1] Glucose molecules are not broken down completely, [1] so less energy is released than during aerobic respiration. [1] End products of anaerobic respiration are lactic acid and a small amount of energy, resulting in muscle fatigue. [1]

323

Answers

2a cellular respiration without oxygen [1]

b animals: anaerobic respiration takes place in muscles when not enough oxygen, produces lactic acid [1] and relatively small amount of energy, [1] allows animal to continue running even when they cannot breathe fast enough to supply the oxygen they need [1]; plants and yeast: anaerobic respiration forms ethanol and carbon dioxide, [1] allows plant/yeast to continue to respire in low-oxygen atmospheres, [1] rare in plants as they form oxygen during photosynthesis but more common in yeasts, where fermentation is used in baking and brewing [1]

c animals: glucose → lactic acid (energy transferred to environment) [1]

plants and yeast: glucose → ethanol + carbon dioxide (energy transferred to environment) [2]

3 Waste lactic acid produced during exercise as a result of anaerobic respiration has to be broken down to produce carbon dioxide and water. [1] This needs oxygen, and amount of oxygen needed to break down lactic acid is known as oxygen debt. [1] Even though muscles have stopped working, heart rate and breathing rate stay high [1] to supply extra oxygen until all lactic acid broken down and oxygen debt paid off. [1]

B9.4

1a sum of all the reactions in a cell or in the body [1]

b Any four from conversion of glucose to starch, glycogen, and cellulose; formation of lipid molecules from a molecule of glycerol and three fatty acid molecules; use of glucose and nitrate ions to form amino acids used to make proteins; respiration; photosynthesis; breakdown of excess proteins to form urea. [4]

2a waste product [1] formed when excess amino acids broken down in liver [1]

b Excess amino acids carried to liver in bloodstream. [1] Liver removes amino group from amino acids by deamination. [1] This forms ammonia, [1] which is converted into urea. [1] Urea passes into blood and is filtered out by kidneys for excretion. [1]

3 Liver involved in a number of processes requiring a lot of energy, [1] including removal of lactic acid produced during anaerobic respiration (blood carries lactic acid from muscles to liver, where it is converted back to glucose for aerobic respiration in cells), [1] conversion of glucose to glycogen when in excess, [1] and conversion of glycogen back to glucose when needed for respiration. [1] Liver consequently carries out a lot of aerobic respiration to provide energy needed for these reactions. [1]

B10.1

1 regulation of internal conditions of cell or organism [1] to maintain optimum functional conditions [1] in response to internal and external changes [1]

2 receptors: cells that detect changes in internal or external environment, may be part of nervous or hormonal control systems [2]; coordination centres: areas that receive and process information from receptors and coordinate body's response, may be part of nervous or hormonal control systems [2]; effectors: bring about response to signal from coordination centres, may be muscles or glands [2]

3 Any three from temperature increase – warming body, temperature decrease – cooling body, levels of sunlight increase – burning skin, wind levels increase – increasing cooling from skin surface, lack of food – hunger. [6] Any other valid suggestion.

B10.2

1a to take in information from external and internal environment [1] and coordinate body's response [1] so you can react to surroundings [1]

b neurone: single nerve cell; nerve: bundle of hundreds or thousands of neurones [1]

c sensory neurone: carries impulses from sense organs to central nervous system (CNS); motor neurone: carries information from CNS to body's effector organs (muscles and glands) [3]

2a eye, [1] ear, [1] skin, [1] nose, [1] tongue [1]

b eye: light [1]; ear: sound, pressure [1]; skin: touch, pressure, pain, temperature, vibration [1]; nose: smell [1]; tongue: taste [1]

3 light from fruit detected by sensory receptors in eyes, [1] impulse travels along sensory neurone to brain, [1] information processed in brain, [1] impulse sent along motor neurone [1] to muscles of arm and hand [1] so you pick up fruit and put it in mouth [1]

B10.3

1a They enable you to avoid damage and danger because they happen very fast. [1] They control many vital bodily functions, such as breathing, without need for conscious thought. [1]

b This would slow process down, making it less effective at preventing damage. It would be very difficult to consciously control all bodily functions and still be able to do anything else. [1]

2 Reflex actions (e.g., breathing, swallowing) need to happen constantly and operate automatically, even when you are asleep, [1] so cannot rely on conscious thought processes. [1] Speaking and eating require coordination of different areas of body [1] so need to be under conscious control. [1]

3 stimulus (pinprick) → receptor → sensory neurone (electrical impulse) → synapse (chemical impulse) → relay neurone (electrical impulse) → synapse (chemical impulse) → motor neurone (electrical impulse) → muscles in leg lift foot [6]

B10.4

1a millions of interconnected neurones [1] arranged in different regions [1] to carry out different functions [1]

b takes in all sensory information [1] and coordinates responses [1] as well as allowing conscious thought, intelligence, and emotions [1]

2 cerebral cortex: consciousness, intelligence, memory, language [2]; cerebellum: coordinating muscular activity and balance [2]; medulla: unconscious activities (e.g., gut movements, breathing) [2]

B10.5

1a Any three from: sclera, cornea, iris, pupil, lens, suspensory ligaments, ciliary muscles, retina, optic nerve, blind spot, fovea [3]

b Answer should match components given in part a. Up to two marks per component.

sclera: white outer layer of eye, relatively tough and strong so eyeball not easy to damage; cornea: transparent area at front of eyeball that admits light, curved surface to help focus light coming into eye on retina; iris: muscular structure to control size of pupil; pupil: hole in iris through which light enters eye; lens: clear disc to help finely focus light onto retina; suspensory ligaments: attach ciliary muscles to eyeball, involved in changing shape of lens; ciliary muscles: contract and relax to change shape of lens and focus light on retina; retina: layer at back of eye containing light receptor cells, optic nerve: carries impulses from light-sensitive cells of retina to brain; blind spot: where optic nerve leaves eyeball; fovea: area of cones where light is brought into clear focus on retina [6]

2   Longitudinal muscles of iris contract [1] and circular muscles relax [1] in dim light, making pupil as large as possible to let in maximum light. [1]

3   Vision involves much more than lens and retina. Light enters eye through cornea, [1] which focuses it towards the iris and retina. [1] Light passes through the iris, then lens. [1] Lens changes shape to focus light onto retina. [1] Light-sensitive cells of retina stimulated by light and send impulses along neurones. [1] Impulses travel along optic nerve and are translated by brain into visual images. [1]

B10.6

1   When ciliary muscles contract, [1] suspensory ligaments loosen [1] and lens becomes thicker. [1] When ciliary muscles relax, [1] suspensory ligaments pulled tight [1] and lens pulled thin. [1]

2a close objects: ciliary muscles contract, [1] suspensory ligaments loosen, [1] lens becomes thicker and refracts light rays strongly [1]; far away objects: ciliary muscles relax, [1] suspensory ligaments pulled tight, [1] lens pulled thin and only slightly refracts light rays [1]

b   When doing close work ciliary muscles are contracted [1] to keep lens thick [1] and able to focus light from close objects. [1] When looking at distant objects ciliary muscles relax. [1] Looking up into distance regularly when doing close work rests ciliary muscles. [1]

3a myopia: can see close objects in clear focus but distant objects look blurred, [1] as lens too curved or eyeball too long [1]; hyperopia: can focus clearly on distant objects but close objects appear blurred, [1] as lens too flat and thin or eyeball too short [1]

b   glasses: relatively cheap, very effective, don't damage eyes, last a long time, can be nuisance or get lost, some people don't like look of them [3]
laser eye surgery: only available to adults once eyes have stopped growing and vision has stabilised, vision permanently corrected (nothing to take on and off/in and out), good for playing sport and general activities, risk of errors and infections during surgery [3]

B11.1

1a large molecule produced in endocrine gland that provides body's chemical coordination, carried around body in blood to target organs where it produces an effect [1]

b   gland that produces hormones and secretes them directly into the blood [1]

2   hormones: chemicals that control the processes of the body, released from glands into blood, some act quickly but many act more slowly, all are slower than nervous control [3]; nervous system: electrical impulses passed from receptors to brain, transmitted along neurones, can be very fast (especially reflexes), transmission from one neurone to another involves chemical substances [3]

3   Pituitary gland is small endocrine gland in brain that controls many different body processes as well as controlling secretions of many other endocrine glands in the body. [1] It produces a number of different hormones that give it this control. [1] Pituitary gland called master gland because so many other endocrine glands rely on it to function. [1]

4a Child would not grow properly/would be short, may look younger than their age, and may have delayed tooth development. [2] Any other valid suggestion.

b   Adult would have acromegaly (chin, nose, ears, hands, and feet continue to grow). If it happened before puberty they would become unusually tall. [2] Any other valid suggestion.

B11.2

1a hormone made in pancreas that causes glucose to pass from blood into cells, where it is needed for respiration [1]

b   condition under which pancreas cannot make enough insulin to control blood sugar or body cells stop responding to insulin made by pancreas [1]

c   insoluble carbohydrate stored in liver [1]

2a Pancreas detects rise in blood glucose levels and secretes insulin. [1] Insulin triggers conversion of glucose to glycogen by liver, [1] which causes glucose to move out of blood into body cells, lowering blood glucose levels. [1]

b   Pancreas detects fall in blood glucose levels and secretes glucagon. [1] Glucagon triggers conversion of glycogen to glucose by liver, [1] increasing blood glucose levels. [1]

c   Glucose needed for cellular respiration, [1] releasing energy for body's metabolic reactions. [1] Too much or too little glucose in blood causes problems with respiration. [1]

3   type 1: condition under which pancreas does not make enough/ any insulin, treated by insulin injections to help control blood glucose levels, needs carefully controlled diet with regular meals and careful monitoring of carbohydrate intake, usually appears in children and young adults [3]; type 2: condition under which body cells do not respond properly to insulin produced by pancreas, linked to obesity/old age/lack of exercise, treated by improving diet/increasing exercise/losing weight as well as by insulin injections [3]

4   insulin: secreted and released by pancreas when blood glucose levels rise above ideal range, enables glucose to move from blood into body cell where it is needed, triggers conversion by liver of excess glucose into glycogen stored in liver and muscles, lowers blood glucose levels [3]; glucagon: secreted and released by pancreas when blood glucose levels fall below ideal range, triggers conversion by liver of glycogen into glucose released back into blood, raises blood glucose levels [3]

B11.3

1   Any three from: type 1 caused by pancreas making insufficient insulin, type 2 caused by body cells not responding properly to insulin from pancreas; type 1 usually appears in children and young adults, type 2 usually affects older or overweight people; type 1 requires insulin injections, type 2 requires insulin injections only if improved diet/increased exercise/losing weight/ drugs not effective; type 1 can be managed but not cured, type 2 may be cured. [3]

Answers

2a Type 1 diabetes treated by careful monitoring and control of food intake [1] as well as by insulin injections. [1] Pancreas transplant can remove need for insulin injections. [1]

b Type 2 diabetes treated, controlled, or even cured by eating a carefully controlled balanced diet, weight loss, and regular exercise. [1] It may also be treated by drugs that help make insulin made by pancreas more effective on body cells, help pancreas make more insulin, or reduce amount of glucose absorbed from gut. [1] Insulin injections used only if none of these treatments works. [1]

3 pancreatic transplant: complex surgery, high risk, expensive, patients have to be on immunosuppressant drugs for the rest of their lives, not enough donors [2]; insulin injections: widely available, self-administered, relatively cheap [2]

4 type 1: regular meals and monitoring of carbohydrate intake to keep blood glucose levels steady – as body produces insufficient insulin to control blood glucose levels, insulin injections to keep blood glucose steady – as body produces insufficient insulin to control blood glucose levels; [3] type 2: carefully controlled balanced diet to restore normal blood glucose balance – as body cells do not respond to insulin produced by body; weight loss – as type 2 diabetes is linked to obesity; regular exercise – as type 2 diabetes is linked to lack of exercise; drugs to help insulin work better/help pancreas make increase/reduce glucose absorption from gut – to improve effectiveness of insulin on body cells [3]

B11.4

1 If a factor in internal environment increases, [1] changes take place to reduce it and restore original level. [1] If a factor in internal environment decreases, [1] changes take place to increase it and restore original level. [1]

2 thyroxine: controls body's basic metabolic rate (in adults) and growth and development (in children), controlled in negative feedback loop by thyroid stimulating hormone (TSH) from pituitary gland [2]; adrenaline: increases heart and breathing rates, triggers conversion of stored glycogen to glucose, stimulates pupil dilation, heightens mental awareness, diverts blood from digestive system to limb muscles, secreted by adrenal glands upon nervous stimulation (no negative feedback loop) [2]

3 Points may include: how iodine levels affect thyroxine production, effects of lack of iodine on health (stunted growth/developmental problems in children, problems including fatigue/immune system damage in adults), effect on people's ability to fight other communicable diseases and work/care for family, impact of adding iodine to diet (allows body to make thyroxine and overcome health problems related to thyroxine deficiency), ease of adding iodine to diet through iodised salt. [6]

B11.5

1 Any three from involvement in different development of boys and girls in uterus, involvement in body changes at puberty, control of ovulation in menstrual cycle, control of sperm production. [3]

2 Any three similarities from adolescent growth spurt (slightly later in boys), growth of pubic and body hair, external genitalia grow and skin darkens, brain matures. [3] Any three differences from boys develop muscles and male body shape/girls develop female pattern of fat deposits, testes grow and start producing sperm in boys/ovaries start to form mature ova monthly in girls, boys develop facial hair, girls develop breasts, male larynx grows and voice breaks, uterus grows and becomes active in girls, menstruation begins in girls [3]

3a Follicle stimulating hormone (FSH) causes eggs to mature, [1] luteinising hormone (LH) stimulates release of egg at ovulation, [1] oestrogen and progesterone stimulate build-up and maintenance of uterus lining. [2]

b Ovaries contain all the eggs a woman will ever have at birth. [1] Eggs mature after puberty, stimulated by FSH [1] and are released monthly for 35–40 years (except in pregnancy) [1] until supply runs out (menopause). [1] Testes begin producing sperm after puberty, stimulated by testosterone [1] and sperm production continues throughout a man's life. [1]

B11.6

1a follicle stimulating hormone (FSH), [1] luteinising hormone (LH), [1] oestrogen, [1] progesterone [1]

b to provide protection and food for developing embryo if pregnancy occurs [1]

2a 0–5 [1]

b FSH levels rise in first part of cycle, stimulating eggs to mature in ovary and stimulating ovary to produce more oestrogen. [2] LH levels rise sharply around ovulation, triggering release of mature ovum, then fall again rapidly. [2]

c oestrogen [1]

3 Oestrogen stimulates thickening of uterus lining. [1] FSH stimulates egg maturation in ovaries. [1] LH stimulates release of mature egg from ovary (ovulation) after about 14 days. [1] Progesterone maintains uterus lining for about 14 days. [1] Hormone levels then drop and uterus lining and egg are shed in monthly period. [1] Pregnancy is most likely if egg is fertilised between days 14 and 28 while uterus lining is ready to receive developing embryo. [1]

B11.7

1 control of fertility to prevent pregnancy by preventing egg and sperm meeting or preventing implantation of fertilised egg in uterus [1]

2a All are forms of hormone-based contraception. [1]

b one mark per contraceptive.
progesterone-only pill must be taken very regularly
contraceptive implant is placed under the skin, contraceptive implant lasts for up to three years but can be removed at any time the woman wants to get pregnant
contraceptive patch applied to skin every seven days.

c contraceptive implant: most effective, no room for human error, hormones not lost through illness (e.g., vomiting); contraceptive patch: very effective, people may forget to replace them, may occasionally come off; progesterone-only pill: not so effective, easy to forget, very low dose so must be taken regularly, hormones may be lost through illness (e.g., vomiting)

3 hormone-based: relatively effective (0–10% failure rate per Figure 2), open to human error [1] barrier: less effective (12–18% failure rate per Figure 2), open to human error or damage [1] surgical: very effective, not open to human error following successful surgery [1]

B11.8

1 A form of fertility treatment used if oviducts damaged or blocked by infection, if donor egg is needed, or in case of long-term infertility without obvious cause [1]. Mature eggs are collected from mother and fertilised *in vitro* using sperm from father. When fertilized eggs have become tiny embryos, one or two are inserted back into mother's uterus. [1]

2a Artificial FSH can be used to stimulate egg maturation [1] and oestrogen production [1] in ovaries so uterus lining builds up. Artificial LH can then be used to trigger ovulation if necessary. [1]

b Artificial FSH can be used to stimulate maturation of many eggs in ovaries. [1] Artificial LH can then be used to bring them to the point of ovulation [1] for harvesting for IVF. [1]

3a Award marks for well-drawn graph correctly labelled. [4]

b for: people have the right to have children when they want them (ageism), people still considered young at 40 now life expectancies have increased, may not meet right person until later in life, career demands for women make it difficult to have children earlier; against: chances of successful pregnancy very low, cost may exceed benefit, older parents will be old as children grow up, stress and physical risk associated with pregnancy increases with age [6] Also consider any other valid argument.

4 advantages: ability to control when to have a family or how many children to have, ease of starting and stopping contraception, ability to help infertile couples have children; disadvantages: use of female hormones in contraception or infertility treatments may have side effects, can give false sense of security (may forget to use other methods of contraception if sick), can lead to false expectation that you can have a baby whenever you want, can lead to multiple births if dosage not controlled properly. [6] Any other valid point.

B11.9

1a response of plant to light [1]

b response of plant to gravity [1]

2 Plants need to respond to surroundings [1] so that roots grow down into soil when a seed germinates and shoots grow up towards light for photosynthesis. [1] Shoots need to be able to grow into light if something shades them, whilst roots need to be able to grow towards water. [1] Trophic responses enable plants to respond to light and gravity. [1]

3a In light from one side only, exposed shoots would grow and bend towards light. [1] Auxin moves to unlit side of shoots, stimulating cells on unlit side to grow faster and causing shoots to bend towards light until they are effectively illuminated evenly again. [1] Sensitivity to one-sided light is in shoot tip, so covered shoots would continue to grow straight up as there is no change in auxin concentration. [1]

b Newly exposed shoots would start to bend towards light [1] because shoot tips would be exposed and auxin would move to unlit side. [1] Newly exposed shoots wouldn't bend as much as permanently exposed shoots [1] as they would have had less time to grow. [1]

B11.10

1a chemical that coordinates and controls growth and development in plant and help it respond to changes in environment [1]

b Hormone rooting powders contain auxin, plant hormone that stimulates root growth in cut stem. [1] Use of hormone rooting powders by gardeners make it more likely that cuttings will develop roots and grow well, making plant propagation easier. [1]

2 When sprayed onto leaves, [1] hormones such as auxin can stimulate uncontrolled rapid growth that kills plants. [1] More spray is absorbed by broad-leaved plants (e.g., weeds) [1] than by narrow-leaved plants (e.g., cereals and grasses). [1]

3 auxin: used in hormone rooting powders to help cuttings grow into new plants – making crop plant propagation easier, used in weed killer to stimulate uncontrolled growth and plant death – reducing competition to cereal crops from weeds, used in plant tissue cultures to stimulate growth and cell division – promoting plant cloning to produce many identical crop plants; gibberellins: used as a spray to replace natural gibberellins missing in seedless fruit – increasing size of fruit; ethene: used as a gas to control ripening of fruit – fruit can be stored unripe for longer and ripened when needed. [6] Any other valid point.

B12.1

1 Enzymes work best at 37 °C. [1]

2a Thermoregulatory centre is sensitive to temperature of blood flowing through it. [1] It also receives information about skin temperature from receptors in skin [1] and coordinates body's responses to keep core temperature at 37 °C. [1]

b Temperature sensors in skin send impulses to thermoregulatory centre in brain [1] giving information about skin temperature [1] and temperature of things skin touches. [1] If skin and external surroundings are cold, body will tend to conserve energy to keep core temperature up, and vice versa. [1]

3 Blood flows through thermoregulatory centre in brain, which monitors temperature and sends impulses to lower body temperature. [1] Blood vessels supplying capillaries in skin dilate, increasing volume of blood in capillaries and increasing cooling by radiation from skin surface. [1] More sweat produced by sweat glands, cooling skin surface as sweat evaporates. [1] Thermoregulatory centre monitors blood temperature and stops cooling mechanisms when it returns to normal. [1]

4a Thermoregulatory centre in brain recognises loss of body heat to cold environment and sends impulses to raise body temperature. [1] Muscles pull feathers erect [1] to trap an insulating layer of air around the body to reduce cooling. [1] Blood vessels close to skin surface constrict, [1] reducing volume of blood in capillaries to minimise cooling by radiation, conduction, or convection from skin surface. [1] As insulating layer of air is warmed, less cooling will occur as temperature gradient between skin and surroundings will be reduced. [1]

b Thermoregulatory centre in brain recognises that muscles have been contracting hard, respiring a lot and warming the body up, and sends impulses to lower body temperature. [1] Muscles controlling hairs relax to flatten hair, [1] minimising any insulating effect so cooling can take place. [1] More sweat produced by sweat glands, cooling skin surface as sweat evaporates. [1] Blood vessels close to skin surface dilate, [1] increasing volume of blood in capillaries to maximise cooling by radiation and convection from skin surface. [1]

Answers

B12.2

1a exhalation, [1] sweating, [1] excretion in urine [1]

b controlled: excretion in urine [1]; uncontrolled: exhalation, [1] sweating [1]

2a nitrogenous waste product formed from breakdown of excess amino acids in liver [1]

b Urea is poisonous to body cells [1] in high concentrations. [1]

c Excess amino acids carried to liver in bloodstream. [1] Liver removes amino group from amino acids by deamination. [1] This initially forms ammonia, [1] which is converted into urea. [1]

3a Balance of water, mineral ions, and nitrogenous waste (urea) in body important because of effect solute concentrations in cells, tissue fluid, and blood have on osmosis. [1] If solute concentration outside body cells is higher than cell contents, [1] water will leave cells by osmosis and cells will shrink and stop working. [1] If solute concentration outside body cells is lower than cell contents, [1] water will enter cell by osmosis and cells will swell and may burst. [1] Balance enables body cells to retain shape and work efficiently. [1]

b Water loss from lung surfaces during breathing or from skin surface in sweating is uncontrolled. [1] It is vital that there is a system by which loss of water and mineral ions can be controlled to maintain correct osmotic balance between body cells and body fluids [1] and remove poisonous urea, [1] regardless of body's water needs. [1] Urea, excess water, and excess mineral ions are removed from body via kidneys and excreted in urine. [1] This process is very tightly regulated to maintain water and mineral ion content of blood within narrow limits, and to remove urea. [1]

B12.3

1a To filter out urea and balance water and mineral ion levels in blood. [1]

b Sugar, mineral ions, amino acids, urea, and water are filtered out of blood into kidney tubule, [1] then selectively reabsorbed back into blood as liquid travels along tubule. [1] All sugar is taken back into blood but amounts of mineral ions and water vary with body's needs. [1] Some urea returns to blood down concentration gradient. [1]

2 Salt affects concentration of body fluids, balance of which must be maintained for optimal cell function. [1] Kidney is involved in balancing body's salt levels. [1] If salt levels go up, kidneys remove salt and excrete it in urine. [1] Hot day will cause a lot of uncontrolled water loss through sweating, so kidneys will need to conserve water as well as remove excess salt. [1]

3a After drinking large volume of water there is a slight delay and then volume of urine produced increases steadily for more than 60 minutes. [1] Over the next 60–90 minutes urine volume returns to normal. [1] After drinking, concentration of salt in urine falls below normal levels [1] before gradually returning to normal over same time period. [1]

b Drinking large volume of water dilutes blood and body fluids. Body detects this and amount of water passing through kidneys without being reabsorbed increases. [1] Body's mineral ion concentration, including salt levels, has not increased. Body reabsorbs same amount of mineral ions as before. [1] This means that urine contains more water but same amount of mineral ions, so concentration of mineral ions in given volume of water falls. Body removes excess water but maintains levels of mineral ions needed in blood. [1]

4a Blood would become diluted. [1] Receptor cells in brain would detect reduced blood concentration [1] and pituitary gland would release less ADH into blood. [1] Kidney tubules would absorb less water, so you would produce lots of very dilute urine. [1]

b Salt and water would be lost in sweat and water would not be replaced. [1] Receptor cells in brain would detect increased concentration of urea in blood (even with loss of mineral ions in sweat) [1] and pituitary gland would release more ADH into blood. [1] Kidney tubules would absorb more water, conserving both salt (being lost in sweat) and water, so you would produce small quantities of urine containing concentrated urea but a relatively low concentration of mineral ions. [1]

B12.4

1a Toxins such as urea build up in the body and balance of water and mineral ions is not maintained, which can cause cell damage. [1]

b diffusion [1] down concentration gradient [1]

2 Blood passes out of artery via pump. [1] Blood thinners added to prevent clotting. [1] Blood passes between dialysis membranes where excess salt and urea are removed by diffusion down a concentration gradient. [1] Clean blood passes through bubble trap before returning to vein. [1]

3a People with kidney failure cannot remove excess mineral ions such as salt [1] or get rid of urea produced by the breakdown of excess amino acids from proteins, [1] so they have to limit intake to keep levels in body as low as possible to remain feeling well between dialysis sessions. [1]

b Any excess salt and urea [1] are removed during dialysis. [1]

4a No urea ensures steep concentration gradient between blood and dialysis fluid [1] to maximise removal of urea from blood into fluid by diffusion. [1] Normal plasma levels ensure that any excess salt, glucose, and mineral ions in blood diffuse into fluid down concentration gradient to give ideal blood concentration upon completion of dialysis. [1]

b To help maintain optimum concentration gradients. [1] Dialysis process relies on diffusion down concentration gradients (no active transport), maintained by flow of fluid. [1]

B12.5

1 Transplanted kidney takes on functions of failed kidneys, balancing blood chemistry and removing urea. [1]

2a live organs have no tissue damage, [1] family donors often a close tissue match [1]

b Taking organs from a healthy, living person can threaten their health. [1] Surgery always carries a risk. [2]

3 dialysis: machines available, no problem with tissue matching, time-consuming, lifetime commitment, expensive in long-term, diet must be carefully controlled

transplant: shortage of donors, need tissue match, limited transplant lifespan, immunosuppressant drugs post-transplant relatively cheap, permits relatively normal life [6] Personal choice must be justified by rational argument.

B13.1

1a no fusion of gametes, only one parent, no variation [1]

b sex cell containing only a single set of chromosomes, made as a result of meiosis (cell division) [1]

c fusion of gametes from two parents, variation [1]

d differences between individuals as a result of their genetic material [1]

2 Asexually produced offspring formed by mitosis from cells of one parent, [1] with no joining of gametes and no mixing of genetic information, hence no variation. [1] Sexually produced offspring formed by meiosis, [1] with fusing of male and female gametes from two parents, [1] hence offspring genetically different from both parents and from each other. [1]

3 Points may include: asexual offspring identical to parents so if conditions change and one individual cannot survive, none of them can; sexual reproduction introduces variation so if conditions change some offspring may survive; change in conditions may make it more difficult for sexually reproducing organisms to meet and mate, so may be less likely to survive than asexual organisms that can reproduce regardless. [6] Any other valid point.

B13.2

1a 23 [1]

b 23 [1]

c 46 [1]

2 Sexual reproduction involves fusing of two gametes, bringing genetic information from two individuals together and introducing variation. [1] Gametes result from meiosis, [1] during which each gamete receives random mixture of original chromosome pairs, [1] so gametes are all different from original cells as well as from each other. [1]

3a Meiosis. [1] After chromosomes are copied, [1] cell divides twice, [1] resulting in sex cells each with single set of chromosomes. [1]

b reproductive organs (ovaries or testes) [1]

c It halves number of chromosomes in gametes so that when two gametes fuse during sexual reproduction, new individual has full set of chromosomes. [1] It introduces variation as each gamete receives random mixture of original chromosomes. [1]

B13.3

1 Any one similarity from: continue a species, pass on genes, can be sped up by humans (cloning in asexual reproduction, selective breeding in sexual reproduction). [1] Any one difference from: one parent in asexual reproduction, two in sexual reproduction; asexual reproduction faster; asexual reproduction results in identical offspring, sexual reproduction in varied offspring. [1]

2a Flowering plants commonly reproduce sexually but can reproduce asexually (e.g., strawberry runners), [1] enabling formation of new plants even when sex organs (flowers) destroyed or eaten. [1] Fungi commonly reproduce asexually but can reproduce sexually when conditions are unfavourable (e.g., too dry). [1]

b Malaria parasites reproduce differently at different stages of life cycle – asexually in human liver and blood cells, [1] sexually inside red blood cells in mosquito. [1] Both sexual and asexual reproduction are part of life cycle [1] (asexual reproduction is not an alternative for bad conditions, as it is in fungi). [1]

3 Points may include: if organism can reproduce asexually in favourable conditions (e.g., fungi), variation is not needed – organism can reproduce fast and safely with genetic makeup that works; if conditions become more difficult, reproducing sexually can introduce variation to increase chances of survival (e.g., to produce spores better adapted to adverse conditions); reproducing sexually as fixed part of life cycle guarantees continuous variation, which can be an advantage to a pathogen (e.g., malaria parasite) – makes it harder for body to identify and reject it, and harder to make vaccines against it. [6] Any other valid point.

B13.4

1a entire genetic material [1]

b Human cells can use same genes in different ways [1] and switch parts of genes on or off, changing proteins made by a single gene, [1] so humans can make many more chemicals than they have genes. [1]

2a major project to sequence entire human genome [1]

b Any three from: involved scientists from all over the world working together, results shared freely between teams and all other scientists, finished ahead of schedule, cost less than expected. [3]

c i To find out as much as possible about human genome, [1] to identify common differences and similarities in sequences between individuals, [1] to identify genes associated with particular diseases, [1] and to discover more about human evolution. [1] Any other valid point.

ii To find similarities and differences between humans and other organisms, [1] to identify evolutionary relationships between different organisms, [1] and to identify organisms with genetic similarities to people that may be useful in models of disease. [1] Any other valid point.

3 All living humans originate from ancestors who migrated from Africa around 60 000 years ago. [1] Genome analysis enables scientists to map genetic markers in modern humans [1] to trace human migration patterns throughout history. [1] DNA samples are collected from different ethnic groups [1] and genetic differences are identified. [1] More closely related groups will have fewer genetic differences. [1] Any other well-researched point.

B13.5

1a one of four different compounds known as A, C, G, and T that are key to DNA structure [1]

b single unit of DNA made up of sugar, phosphate, and base [1]

2 When the protein chain is completed on the ribosome, [1] it folds up. [1] Shape made depends on sequence of amino acids. [1] Unique shape enables it to carry out specific job as an enzyme, hormone, or structural protein. [1]

Answers

3 Template is produced that reflects sequence of bases in DNA of a single gene. [1] Template is small enough to leave nucleus through pores in nuclear membrane, and binds to surface of ribosome. [1] Carrier molecules in cytoplasm, each attached to specific amino acid, attach themselves to template in order given by DNA until template completed. [1] Amino acids join together to form specific protein. [1] Protein detaches from carrier molecules, which detach from template and return to cytoplasm to pick up more amino acids. [1] Once protein chain is complete molecule folds up to form unique shape that will enable it to carry out its functions in cell. [1]

B13.6

1a gene expressed when protein it codes for is produced in cell [1]

b Non-coding regions of DNA [1] involved in switching genes on so they are expressed, [1] switching them off so they are not expressed, [1] or switching only part of gene on so different protein is expressed. [1]

2 Order of bases in DNA controls proteins made on ribosomes in cell. If mutation alters DNA bases, this may change amino acids joined together to form protein. [1] This affects way in which protein folds and functions. [1] If an enzyme cannot work, certain chemicals will not be made and this can affect organism appearance. [1] If mutation affects non-coding DNA, gene expression is affected, which would also affect appearance. [1]

3 Points may include: most mutations have no effect – every organism contains many mutations that have no observable effect; changes in order of amino acids/shape of protein may have bad effect – active site of enzyme changed so it no longer fits normal substrate, structural protein may lose its strength; mutation may cause changes in molecules controlling rate of cell cycle – causing cancer; mutation may mean organism doesn't compete well – leading to death of affected organism; mutation may cause production of enzyme with different-shaped active site – enabling it to produce different colour/better camouflage; may cause production of enzyme that allows breakdown of different food source – enabling survival when normal food is scarce; may cause production of enzyme that is faster or more efficient catalyst – improving cell function; mutation in bacteria may alter biochemistry to cause antibiotic resistance – advantage to bacteria if not to people; mutation may affect gene expression rather than changing product of particular gene – effect may be neutral, positive, or negative. [6] Any other valid point.

B13.7

1a allele controlling development of characteristic even when present on only one chromosome [1]

b allele controlling development of characteristic only if present on both chromosomes [1]

c homozygous: both alleles for particular characteristic are the same; [1] heterozygous: individual has two different alleles for particular characteristic [1]

2

Gametes	A	a
A	AA	Aa
a	aA	aa	[5]

3a Black fur in mice is dominant phenotype. Black mice may be BB or Bb. [1] Brown mouse has recessive phenotype with genotype bb. [1] Crossing black mouse with brown mouse can help work out genotype of black mouse. [1] Any brown mice in litter show black adult mouse is heterozygote. If offspring are all black, black mouse may be homozygous but not proven as all offspring could be black by chance. [1]

b i

Gametes	B	B
B	BB	BB
b	Bb	Bb	[5]

ii

Gametes	B	b
B	BB	Bb
b	Bb	bb	[5]

B13.8

1a XX [1]

b XY [1]

2 Gametes meeting is a random event. [1] Lots and lots of genetic crosses are needed for patterns to emerge, to overcome the random element of mating. [1]

3a People think that the more times you have a girl, [1] the greater the chance that the next child will be a boy. [1]

b Every time an egg or a sperm meet it is a random event. [1] Whether the sperm is carrying an X or a Y chromosome is completely random, [1] so the chances of any baby being a boy or a girl are 1:1 or 50% that it will be a boy (XY) or a girl (XX). [1] Also accept Punnett square demonstrating this.

4a

Gametes	G	g
g	Gg	gg
g	Gg	gg	[5]

b 1:1 ratio, [2] Gg:gg [2]

B13.9

1a inherited disorder that causes extra fingers or toes [1]

b polydactyly phenotype [1] is dominant [1]

2a A Pp, [1] individual had polydactyly but had unaffected child (must have recessive allele) [1]

  B Pp, [1] individual had polydactyly but had two unaffected children (must have recessive allele) [1]

  C PP or Pp, [1] both parents have polydactyly so each could have passed on dominant allele P, and both parents are heterozygotes as have unaffected children, so each could have passed on recessive allele p [1]

b Carriers have an allele for the normal dominant phenotype, [1] so their body works normally. [1]

c Cystic fibrosis caused by recessive allele, [1] which must be inherited from both parents for child to have disease. [1] If both parents had the disease themselves they would almost certainly be infertile, [1] so parents must be carriers (heterozygotes). [1]

3 Couple must both be carriers (heterozygotes):

Gametes	S	s
S	SS	Ss
s	Ss	ss	[5]

B13.10

1 amniocentesis: taking some fluid from around the developing fetus at around 15–16 weeks of pregnancy [2]; chorionic villus sampling of embryonic cells: taking small sample of tissue from developing placenta at around 10–12 weeks of pregnancy [2]

2a Ultrasound used to show position of fetus and needle, which is inserted through body wall into amniotic fluid. [1] Amniotic fluid sample containing fetal cells drawn up into syringe. [1] DNA isolated from fetal cells and tested for particular genetic disorders. [1]

b Early embryo tested before implantation in mother. [1] DNA isolated from embryonic cells and tested for particular genetic disorders. [1]

3 advantages: screening could reduce high societal cost of health care and support for children with genetic problems, screening could avoid children being born into pain/suffering caused by genetic disorders; disadvantages: collecting cells from fetus increases risk of miscarriage, screening can give false positive or negative result, screening necessitates decisions about termination, screening is expensive, screening could give rise to 'designer babies', no current cures for genetic disorders identified in screening, number of children born with genetic disorders relatively low so screening every fetus may not be cost-effective. [6] Any other valid point.

B14.1

1a Any one from eye colour, nose shape, sex, dimples. [1]

b Any one from scarring, language, suntan, religion. [1] Any other valid example.

2a For comparison with normal population. [1] Studying identical twins reared together and reared apart allows comparison of impact of different environments on genetically identical humans. [1] Identical twins reared together are subject to same environmental conditions, meaning environmental variables are controlled. [1]

b Height seems mostly controlled by genes [1] as there is least difference in height between identical twins whether reared together or apart. [1] Mass seems mostly affected by environment as identical twins brought up apart are no more identical than ordinary siblings. [1]

3 Award marks for any sensible suggestion demonstrating awareness of good experimental design. [6]

B14.2

1 Individuals within particular species may show wide phenotypic and genetic variation. [1] individuals with characteristics most suited to environment more likely to survive to breed successfully [1]. Alleles (variables) enabling survival passed on to next generation. [1]

2a New variant/form of a gene/new allele [1] resulting from change in organism's DNA.

b Mutations occur naturally through mistakes made in copying DNA when cells divide. [1] Mutation may produce adaptation making organism better suited to changed environment. [1] Competitive advantage makes organism more likely to survive and breed, new variant rapidly becomes more common in population. [1]

3a Mutations gave some deer larger antlers, making them more successful in battles with other stags and more attractive to females. [1] Stags with largest antlers mated most successfully, [1] spreading alleles for large antler size within population. [1]

b Mutations gave some seals thick fur and thick blubber, making them more likely to survive and breed in very cold habitat. [1] Seals with thickest fur and blubber mated most successfully, [1] spreading alleles for thick fur and blubber within population. [1]

c Mutations gave some moths colouration like birch twigs that provided better camouflage from predators, [1] making them more likely to survive and mate successfully. [1] Moths with this colouration passed on alleles for it and eventually formed new species. [1]

B14.3

1a animals or plants with desired characteristic chosen [1] and used as breeding stock [1] to produce offspring with same desirable characteristic over time [1]

b to produce animals and plants with useful or desirable characteristics [1] such as: increased yield or disease resistance in crops, [1] increased milk, meat, and wool yield in animals; [1] gentle nature in domestic animals and pets [1]

2a Breeding for particular characteristics [1] means only individuals with alleles for chosen characteristics are allowed to breed, [1] reducing variation in alleles for characteristic. [1]

b If conditions change, variation means some organisms in a population are likely to survive. [1] They will breed [1] and their useful alleles will become more common in the population. [1]

c If conditions change (e.g., new disease, climate change) lack of variation within population reduces the chance of at least some of the organisms containing useful variant allowing them to survive [1] and breed, [1] threatening population's survival. [1]

3 Award marks for explanation using any appropriate example. [6]

B14.4

1 Modifying organism's genetic material [1] to produce a new, desirable characteristic [1] by cutting gene for desirable characteristic out of one organism [1] and transferring it to genetic material of another. [1]

2 Any three from pest resistance – reducing crop vulnerability to pests and increasing yield, improved food value – changing crop composition to make crop more nutritionally valuable, flood resistance – reducing crop vulnerability to flooding and protecting yield, disease resistance – reducing crop vulnerability to common diseases and increasing yield. [6] Any other valid example.

3 flow chart should include: use enzyme to cut out short stem gene from plant → use enzyme to remove plasmid from bacterium → insert short stem gene into bacterial plasmid → insert bacterial plasmid containing short stem gene into target plant [6]

B14.5

1a individual produced asexually [1] that is genetically identical to parent [1]

b only one parent, no joining of gametes, [1] offspring genetically identical to parent [1]

Answers

c use of few cells from desirable plant to make big mass of identical plant cells, [1] each of which can produce tiny identical plant [1]

d splitting apart developing embryo cells before specialisation [1] to produce several identical embryos [1]

2a allows production of far more calves from best cows, [1] allows transport of high-quality embryos worldwide, [1] allows rapid replication of genetically engineered animals [1]

b flow chart should include: cow given hormones to produce large number of eggs → cow inseminated with sperm/eggs collected and fertilised in laboratory → embryos collected and taken to the lab → embryos split to make more identical embryos → embryos transferred to host mothers [6]

c economic: only wealthy farmers/countries can afford cloning technology; ethical: cloning decreases cattle biodiversity, how far should humans be able to interfere in production of new life [6] Any other valid suggestion.

3a Use mixture of plant hormones [1] to make small group of cells from desirable plant. [1] These cells produce mass of identical plant cells (callus). [1] Use different mixture of hormones [1] and conditions [1] to stimulate production of many identical plantlets. [1]

b Commercial use to produce identical plants for homes and gardens quickly and easily. [1] Conservation use to preserve rare plant species [1] by using single specimen to produce many new plants. [1]

B14.6

1 production of new whole animal from cell of another adult animal [1]

2 nucleus removed from unfertilised egg cell and nucleus taken from adult body cell, [1] nucleus from adult cell inserted in empty egg cell, [1] new egg cell given tiny electric shock, [1] new egg cell divides to form embryo cells, [1] ball of cells (embryo) inserted into womb of adult female to continue development [1]

3 advantages: enables cloning of genetically engineered animals, could save animals from extinction, could clone pets or prized animals, could help infertile couples; disadvantages: concerns about human cloning, reduces variety in population [6] Any other valid point.

B14.7

1 Any three from improved plant growth rates of plants, increased crop food value, ability to grow crops in adverse conditions, ability to produce plants that make own pesticide, herbicide-resistant crops. [3]

2 Points may include: cost of genetically engineered products may be too high for those they are designed to benefit (e.g., golden rice), genetically modified crops have previously been made infertile forcing farmers in poor countries to buy new seed each year. [6] Any other valid point.

B15.1

1 He found that characteristics were inherited in clear and predictable patterns, [1] that some characteristics were dominant over others, [1] and that they never mixed together. [1]

2a People couldn't see units of inheritance, [1] so no proof of their existence. [1] People were unused to studying careful records of results. [1]

b Microscopes enabled people to see chromosomes cell nucleus [1] and observe chromosome movement in meiosis. [1] This proved mechanism for Mendel's principles of inheritance, promoting their acceptance. [1]

3 Wilkins and Franklin [1] examined structure of DNA using X-rays. [1] Watson and Crick [1] worked on 3-D DNA model to explain how it works. [1] Watson and Crick ultimately developed double helix structure for DNA molecule [1] based on Franklin's X-ray results. [1]

B15.2

1a development of all species of living and extinct organisms [1] from simple life forms [1] developed more than 3 billion years ago, [1] through a process of natural selection [1]

b Process by which evolution takes place. [1] Every population contains great variation. [1] More offspring are produced than can survive. [1] Only animals and plants best adapted to environment (the 'fittest') [1] will survive to breed and pass on their characteristics. [1]

2 Points may include: helped pave way for Darwin's ideas, stimulated Darwin's thinking, first theory to challenge creation of world by God, instigated debate on origins of life, flaws in Lamarck's theory made Darwin's theory more plausible. [5] Any other thoughtful point.

3a Different types of same bird lived in slightly different areas, [1] making Darwin question how they came about. [1]

b Species varied from island to island, [1] making Darwin wonder how differences arose. [1]

c Gave Darwin time to collect many specimens [1] then make observations and consider theories. [1]

d Gave Darwin time to review specimens, drawings, and observations [1] before developing theories and ideas [1] and gathering evidence to support them. [1]

B15.3

1 Finches had adapted to differing environments [1] by natural selection. [1] Adaptations evolved for particular environments [1] made finch species look different. [1]

2 Breeding experiments with pigeons [1] to show how features could be artificially selected, as evidence for natural selection seen in Galapagos finches. [1] Examination of different barnacle types and their habitats to show adaptation of organisms to environment. [1]

3 Points may include: Darwin's ideas challenged popular and longstanding belief that God made animals and plants, Darwin's evidence was insufficient to convince some scientists, Darwin's theory lacked obvious mechanism for inheritance. [6] Any other valid point.

B15.4

1a geographical isolation: populations physically isolated by geographical feature,[1] such as new mountain range, river, or island [1]; environmental isolation: organisms separated by climate change in a particular area [1]

b Conditions in different isolated areas differ. [1] Different characteristics confer advantages in different environments [1] and will be selected for. [1] Organisms become increasingly specialised for isolated environment until they cannot interbreed [1] and new species evolve (speciation). [1]

Answers

2 Part of population becomes isolated under new environmental conditions. [1] Alleles for characteristics enabling organisms to survive and breed successfully in changed environment will be selected for. [1] These are likely to differ from the alleles selected for in original environment. [1] Selection of different alleles for success in new environment causes characteristics of isolated organisms to change. [1] Eventually, isolated organisms can no longer interbreed with original organisms [1] and new species forms (speciation). [1]

3 similarities: both avid naturalists, both made many observations in the wild in isolated areas of the world, both developed basic model of evolution by natural selection, both published initial papers simultaneously; differences: Darwin rich whilst Wallace relatively poor, Wallace had bad luck and lost specimens whilst Darwin didn't, Darwin formulated and refined his ideas over many years whilst Wallace wrote idea down immediately and sent it to Darwin [6] Any other valid point.

B15.5

1a no one there to see it, [1] early organisms soft-bodied so few fossils formed and most early fossils destroyed by geological activity [1]

b demonstrate how plants and animals have changed over time, [1] how different organisms have developed, [1] and that some no longer exist [1]

2a rock fossils [1]

b millions of years [1]

c when animal or plant does not decay after death [1] as preserved in ice or peat [1]; when hard parts of animal or plant replaced by other minerals, forming part of rock (rock fossil) [1]; when impression of organism made in mud becomes fossilised (mould fossil) [1]; when mould is filled in by minerals (cast fossil) [1]; when traces (footprints, burrows, droppings) are preserved [1]

3a Animal or plant buried in ice [1] where conditions for decay are absent (temperature too low), [1] so does not decay after death. [1]

b animals and plants preserved almost intact, giving clear insight into what organism looked like [1]; very rare and often thousands of years old [1]; can show what animal had been eating or colour of long-extinct flower [1]; DNA can be extracted and compared to DNA of modern organisms [1]

B15.6

1 shows how tall they were, [1] what their feet were like, [1] what terrain they walked on, [1], how fast they moved [1]

2 Complete record gives clear picture of how species evolves over time [1] in response to changing environmental conditions. [1] Some organisms have changed little – fossil sharks very similar to modern sharks as they evolved early into a form almost perfectly adapted to their environment. [1] Records not always complete. [1]

3a rapid population decline [1] as prey population unable to adapt quickly enough [1] to avoid new predators [1]

b rapid population decline [1], especially where whole population is close together (e.g., on island), [1] as disease spreads more rapidly than population can adapt to survive it [1]

c competitive advantage (from mutation or due to newly introduced species) [1] of one organism over another can cause rapid population decline [1] in species unable to adapt quickly enough to compete effectively [1]

B15.7

1a Any four from new predators, new diseases, successful competition, environmental changes. [4] Any other valid point.

b Any two from massive volcanic eruption, collision of giant asteroids with the Earth, major climate change. [2] Any other valid point.

2 Without extinction, unsuccessful species would not die out [1] and there would be too much competition for resources. [1] Evolution of new species would be difficult as no niches to exploit. [1] Any other valid point.

3a crater, [1] layer of rock debris, [1] mineral formed when massive force hits rocks, [1] age of rocks suggest impact happened immediately before dinosaur mass extinction event [1]

b i Asteroid impact would have blasted lots of dust and debris into atmosphere [1] and triggered fires, earthquakes, and landslides [1] generating more smoke and dust. [1]

   ii Levels of light reaching Earth would have been much reduced, [1] which would have stopped plants growing [1] and caused very low temperatures. [1] This global winter would have caused mass extinctions through starvation and freezing. [1]

B15.8

1a bacterium [1]

b MRSA has developed resistance to many antibiotics, including methicillin, [1] as a result of extensive non-essential antibiotic use in hospitals. [1] Small colonies of antibiotic resistant bacteria have survived and reproduced, leading to antibiotic resistance. [1]

2a flow chart should include: colony of bacteria treated with antibiotic A → 5% survive through mutation → surviving bacteria form new colony resistant to antibiotic A and no longer affected by it → colony of bacteria treated with antibiotic B → 5% survive through mutation → surviving bacteria form new colony resistant to antibiotics A and B and no longer affected by them [6]

3a antibiotic resistance caused by increased use of antibiotics/lower hygiene standards in hospitals/spread of bacteria via hands and clothing of medical staff [1]

b Any four from: reduction in prescription of antibiotics, treating specific infections with specific antibiotics, reminders to medical staff to wash hands/use alcohol gel between patients, reminders to patients and visitors to wash hands/use alcohol gel on entering and leaving medical facilities, increasing hygiene standards in hospitals, treating patients affected by antibiotic resistant strains of bacteria in isolation. [4] Any other valid point.

B15.9

1 organisation of living organisms into groups according to their similarities and differences [1]

2a i animals, [1] plants [1]

   ii archaea, [1] eubacteria, [1] protista, [1] fungi, [1] plants, [1] animals [1]

Answers

b Fewer organisms known when Linnaean system developed, [1] all classification based on observation of organism appearance. [1] Many more organisms have since been discovered observed using new techniques. [1]

3a smallest main group in classification, [1] group of organisms that can interbreed and produce fertile offspring [1].

b Any five examples. [5]

4a system by which organisms are named, [1] with two names indicating genus and species [1]

b Enables scientists globally [1] to discuss huge variety of living and extinct organisms [1] by common names, preventing confusion. [1]

B15.10

1a archaea, [1] bacteria, [1] eukaryota [1]

b archaea: primitive forms of bacteria including extremophiles – organisms that can live in extreme conditions, [1] one kingdom – archaebacteria [1]; bacteria: true bacteria and cyanobacteria – bacteria-like organisms that can photosynthesise, [1] one kingdom – eubacteria; [1] eukaryota: organisms with cells containing a nucleus enclosing genetic material, [1] four kingdoms – protista, fungi, plants, animals [1]

c Domains are higher level of organisation than kingdoms – organisms they contain have fewer things in common. [1] Domains based on biochemistry of ribosomes and method of cell division. [1] Domain may contain several kingdoms. [1]

d Woese decided that there were too many differences between different types of bacteria for them all to be in the same group. [1] His ideas have been accepted because they have been backed up by evidence (e.g., DNA analysis), [1] and the new model works well in practice. [1]

2a Identify similarities and differences. [1] Traditionally these were in physical appearance, including internal structures such as the skeleton, but biochemistry and cell function is now considered. [1] Modern technology has made big changes, with use of microscopes to examine cells [1] and DNA analysis to identify precise relationships between organisms. [1]

b Classifying organisms and seeing how closely they are related to other organisms allows us to build up evolutionary trees. [1] DNA technology makes it easier to recognise relationships between organisms that look very different but have evolved into separate species only relatively recently, [1] or between organisms that look similar but are not closely related. [1]

3 Evolutionary trees model evolutionary relationships between organisms, [1] determining how long ago they divided away from a common ancestor. [1] They promote understanding of evolutionary pathways and relationships between species. [1]

B16.1

1a all populations of interdependent different species [1] living in a habitat [1]

b ecosystem made up of communities [1] of organisms in a habitat [1] and their interactions with abiotic elements of habitat [1]

2 Any five from food production, feeding, pollination, predation, building nests and shelters, nutrient recycling. [5] Accept any other valid example.

3 Look for evidence of good research, stable community chosen, example of plant and animal and their role in community, understanding of stability, ability of stable community to absorb change and act as reservoir of many different species. [6]

B16.2

1 light intensity, [1] temperature, [1] moisture levels, [1] soil pH and mineral content, [1] wind intensity and direction, [1] availability of oxygen and carbon dioxide [1]

2 capture and digest animals [1] and use the nitrate ions produced as animal proteins broken down [1]

3a Accept any valid factor. [1]

b Light intensity limits photosynthesis, [1] which affects distribution of plants and any animals dependent on plants for food. [1] Accept any valid explanation of factor outlined in **a**. [2]

4 New predator will compete with existing predators in community for prey, [1] reducing number of prey animals available to existing predators. [1] If new predator very competitive or if prey have no defences against new predator, [1] number of prey animals will be significantly reduced, causing big fall in existing predator numbers or even local extinction of existing predators. [1] If new predator not very competitive, number of prey animals and existing predators will be reduced only slightly. [1]

B16.3

1 simple mechanism for determining sample area [1]

2a Position quadrat (same size quadrat each time) [1] either using random number generator [1] or by having person hold quadrat, close eyes, spin round, open eyes, and walk 10 paces before dropping quadrat to frame sample area. [1] Sample as many areas as possible. [1]

b to give representative and unbiased sample [1] of organism number and distribution [1]

c mean: 6 (6.3), median: 6.5, mode: 6, 7, 8 [4]

3 Quadrats often used along transect, combining techniques. [1] Quadrats used for random measurements [1] to determine overall picture of population or distribution of organism/variety of organisms. [1] Transects used for specific study of particular section of habitat, [1] measuring zonal changes. [1]

B16.4

1 if anything happens to sole food source, [1] animal will starve [1]

2a fighting, [1] display [1]

b fighting: animal could be hurt or killed, needs lots of body resources [2]; display: needs lots of body resources, vulnerable to predation during display [2]. Accept any other valid point.

3a Any two from very good eyesight – see prey, good hearing – hear prey, good sense of smell – track prey, binocular vision – pounce on prey [4]

b Any two from special teeth – grind grass and break open cells, speed – avoid/escape from predators, good eyesight/peripheral vision – detect predator approach, good hearing – detect predator approach [4]

c Any two from good camouflage – escape predator notice, good eyesight/peripheral vision – detect predator approach, good hearing – detect predator approach [4]

d Any two from teeth and gut adapted to eating plants – grind leaves and break open cells, ability to reach top of trees (long neck or good at climbing) – reach food source, ability to grip branches – reach food source and remove leaves from branches Any other valid point.

B16.5

1a Any three from grow and flower very early before other plant get leaves, grow tall very fast to reach light, grow larger leaves, make more chlorophyll to maximise energy from any light that arrives. [3] Accept any other valid point.

b flowers and seeds produced [1] before trees are in full leaf [1]

2a to avoid competition both between parent plants and seedlings [1] and between seedlings themselves [1]

b Any three from fluffy/winged seeds to float on air, seeds in berries/fruits to be eaten and distributed by animals, explosive seeds to fire seeds away from parent plant, sticky/hooked seeds to be carried on animals, floating seeds to be distributed in currents. [3] Any other valid suggestion.

3 Points may include: deep taproot – difficult to remove, can regenerate if severed, low rosette of leaves – avoids lawnmower blades and grazing animals, long flowering period – produces large number of seeds, light seeds – very effective wind dispersal of seed over large area. [6] Any other valid point.

B16.6

1a organism that can survive and reproduce [1] in extremely difficult conditions [1] such as high/low temperature, high pressure, high salinity [1]

b Any two from enzymes that function in very high temperatures, enzymes that function at very low temperatures, ability to get rid of excess salt, ability to respire without oxygen. [4] Any other valid example.

2a light, [1] carbon dioxide, [1] water, [1] oxygen, [1] mineral ions [1]

b food from other living organisms, [1] water, [1] oxygen [1]

3a feature that makes it possible for organism to survive in particular habitat, [1] even in extreme conditions [1]

b Award marks for any three valid examples. [3]

c Award marks for a sensible and explanation of the adaptations given in part b. Two marks per adaptation. [6]

B16.7

1a extreme cold makes keeping warm difficult, [1] limited plant growth makes finding enough food difficult [1]

b extreme temperatures make maintaining body temperature difficult, [1] limited water makes finding enough water difficult [1]

2 Any three from small ears – reducing surface area of thin-skinned tissue to reduce cooling, thick fur – trapping insulating layer of warm air close to skin to reduce cooling, layer of fat/blubber – providing insulation to reduce cooling, furry feet – insulating against contact with ice to reduce cooling, large size – reducing surface area to volume ratio to reduce cooling. [6] Any other valid point.

3a Any three from large, thin ears for cooling over large surface area; loose, wrinkled skin to increase surface area to volume ratio and aid cooling; little or no fur to minimise insulation; long trunk to allow application of water to body for cooling. [6] Any other valid adaptation.

b Any three from ability to keep cool without sweating, behavioural adaptations such as avoiding hottest part of day/wallowing in mud, large ears, baggy skin, little fur, large surface area to volume ratio, functional kidney adaptations. [3] Any other valid adaptation.

c At least two from blubber/internal fat to insulate against cold water, thick fur externally (seals), large size for small surface area to volume ratio, small extremities, ability to take deep breaths, ability to slow heart rate during dives, ability to migrate to follow food sources. [6] Any other valid point

B16.8

1a photosynthesis, [1] cell support, [1] tissue support, [1] transport of substances around plant

b from soil through roots [1]

2a evaporation from leaf cells into air spaces, [1] diffusion down concentration gradient through stomata into surrounding air [1]

b Dry places often hot, so photosynthesis and respiration occur at faster rate [1] and water vapour lost very quickly. [1]

3a Any three from curled leaves – reduced surface area, traps moist air to reduce evaporation, small leaves – reduced surface area, thick cuticle – reduced rate of evaporation, stem-like leaves – reduced number of stomata to minimise water loss by diffusion into air. [6] Any other valid adaptation.

b extensive root system covering wide area – maximising water uptake from soil, [2] long roots going very deep – maximising water uptake from soil, [2] water storage tissues – to store water in fleshy leaves/stems/roots after rain [2]

B17.1

1a organism that makes its own food [1]

b because they produce glucose by photosynthesis [1]

2a demonstrate relationships between producers [1] and primary, secondary, and tertiary consumers [1]

b food chains suggest that each type of consumer eats only one other type of organism, when most consumers eat a variety of different foods [1]

3a As prey numbers go up, there is more food for predators, so predator numbers increase after an interval. [1] As predator numbers increase, prey numbers start to fall as more are eaten. [1] After an interval, fall in prey animals means fewer predators survive and breed, so predator numbers fall too. [1] As predator numbers fall, fewer prey animals are eaten and prey numbers begin to increase again (cycle repeats).

b Prey numbers may be affected by factors other than predators: weather conditions, disease, or competition affecting food supply; disease affecting prey; population balance between different types of prey for a particular predator. Predator numbers may be affected by factors other than prey: disease affecting predator; competition balance between different types of prey. [5] Any other valid point.

Answers

B17.2

1. organism that breaks down dead and waste material [1]
2. a precipitation, [1] respiration [1] transpiration, [1] evaporation, [1] condensation [1]
   b precipitation: water falls to land as rain, snow, hail, or sleet; [1] respiration: water released from animals and plants during life and after death during decay; [1] transpiration: water released into atmosphere by plants; [1] evaporation: water turned from liquid to water vapour as Sun heats Earth's surface; [1] condensation: water vapour condensed back to liquid as moist air rises [1]
3. Living organisms remove materials from the environment constantly. [1] If mineral ions taken from the soil by plants were not replaced, Earth's resources would be depleted quickly. [1] Decomposers break down plant and animal waste and dead animals and plants and return mineral ions to soil to be taken up by plants again, [1] and carbon to the atmosphere as carbon dioxide to be used by producers in photosynthesis. [1]
4. water major constituent of all living cells, [1] chemical reactions of life (photosynthesis and respiration) [1] take place in solution in water, [1] water needed by plants for support [1]
5. Decomposers break down plant and animal waste and dead animals and plants [1], returning resources removed from the environment by plants to the environment. [1] Constant recycling of materials often leads to very stable ecosystems. [1]
6. Carbon needed as carbon dioxide [1] for use by producers in photosynthesis. [1] Nitrogen needed as nitrate ions [1] by plants to make proteins and other chemicals. [1] Carbon and nitrogen taken up by animals through feeding relationships. [1] Carbon and nitrogen removed from environment by plants need to be part of decay cycle so that they can be recycled and used again by living organisms. [1]

B17.3

1. a cycling of carbon between living organisms and the environment [1]
   b photosynthesis, [1] respiration, [1] combustion [1]
   c prevents Earth's fixed amount of carbon being depleted, [1] returns carbon dioxide to the atmosphere for photosynthesis [1]
2. a carbon dioxide in air, [1] carbon dioxide dissolved in water, [1] carbon dioxide produced as plants respire [1]
3. photosynthesis: process by which plants use carbon dioxide and water to make glucose and oxygen using light, removes carbon dioxide from environment. [2] respiration: process by which plants and animals break down glucose and oxygen to make carbon dioxide and water, returns carbon dioxide to environment. [2] combustion: process by which organic material is burned in oxygen to make carbon dioxide and water in uncontrolled reaction, returns carbon dioxide to environment. [2]

B17.4

1. a detritivores, [1] decomposers [1]
   b Plants remove minerals from the soil constantly. When animals eat plants these minerals are passed on through food chains and webs. [1] If minerals were never returned to soil, soil would soon be infertile. [1] Decay enables minerals that have become part of bodies of living organisms to be recycled and returned to environment. [1]

2. a Rate of chemical reactions in microorganisms acting as decomposers [1] speeds up with increase in temperature. [1] Average temperatures much warmer in summer than in winter, [1] so rate of decomposition increases. [1]
   b Moisture makes it easier for microorganisms to digest food and prevents them from drying out, [1] so they grow better in moist conditions. [1] Rate of decomposition slows down in dry conditions, even if temperature is high. [1]
   c Many microorganisms involved in decomposition need oxygen for aerobic respiration. [1] Turning over compost bin contents increases air in mixture. [1] Turning compost bin contents increases rate of decomposition as microorganisms have plenty of oxygen for aerobic respiration. [1]

B18.1

1. a Any three from ability to farm/fish, ability to cure or prevent diseases, no natural predators, ability to control environment by heating/lighting [3] Any other valid point.
   b buildings and roads, [1] farming, [1] quarrying, dumping waste [1]
2. a Any three from land, metal ores, fossil fuels, wood. [3] Any other valid point.
   b Any five from use of electricity for lighting/heating/entertainment, increased food production, improved medicines, use of fossil fuels for transport, development of plastics, improved waste disposal, improved sanitation [5] Any other valid point.
4. Points may include: increased waste – including bodily waste, industrial waste, packaging, uneaten food, and disposable goods; exhaust gases from transport; use of pesticides and fertilisers in farming. [6] Any other valid point.

B18.2

1. a human bodily waste and waste water [1]
   b toxic chemicals can spread from waste into soil, [1] toxic chemicals can be washed into waterways, [1] sewage can pollute soil with dangerous chemicals and gut parasites, [1] toxins build up in organisms along food chain (bioaccumulation), [1] largest predators die or are infertile due to toxic chemical build-up [1]
   c to monitor pollution levels in waterways [1]
2. a pesticides and herbicides spread from crops into soil, [1] plant material contaminated with toxins, [1] small levels of toxins taken in by animals eating affected plant material, [1] toxins build up along food chains (bioaccumulation) until dangerous levels are reached in top predators [1]
   b Points may include: DDT in pesticide contaminated soil and waterways, organisms contaminated with toxins, DDT builds up in organisms along food chain, DDT levels become dangerously high in top predators (birds of prey, herons), effects of DDT not noticeable until dangerous levels reached, route through food chain not obvious. [6] Any other valid point.

B18.3

1. a acidic gases released into atmosphere [1] and spread around by wind [1]
   b sulfur dioxide and nitrogen oxides dissolve into rain and snow, [1] contaminating lakes/rivers/streams [1]
   c dilute sulfuric acid and nitric acid fall as acid rain [1] and soak into soil [1]

2 a flow chart should include: cars/power stations burn fossil fuels → acidic gases (e.g., sulfur dioxide, nitrogen oxides) formed → gases carried in the winds in atmosphere → sulfur acidic gases dissolve in rainwater and react with oxygen to form dilute sulfuric acid and nitric acid → acid rain falls [5]

b Sulfur dioxide and nitrogen oxides can be carried high in air by winds. [1] Acidic gases can be blown from a country that does not control its sulfur emissions to a country that has strict emission controls [1] and fall as acid rain. [1]

3 a 25 000 − 5000 = 20 000, [1], $\frac{20\,000}{25\,000} \times 100 = 80$ [1], reduction of 80% [1]

b Any two from more efficient catalytic converters in cars, cleaner fuels, legislation to control emissions from factories. [2] Any other valid point.

c levels of acid rain should fall [1] as sulfur dioxide emissions fall, [1] unless prevailing winds carry acidic gases from non-European countries [1]

4 a i 1850: 0 million tonnes, 1975: 4 million tonnes, [1] 4 million tonne increase [1]

ii 1975: 14 million tonnes, 2000: 8 million tonnes, [1] 6 million tonne decrease [1]

b Figure 2b shows increasing global sulfur dioxide emissions, causing increasing acid rain. [1] Acid rain directly damages plant life by falling on plants [1] and by soaking into soil and being taken up by roots. [1] Acid rain contaminates soil and watercourses, making them more acidic and eventually unable to sustain life. [1] Increasing sulfur dioxide levels threaten to reduce global biodiversity [1] as whole ecosystems can be destroyed. [1]

B18.4

1 a removal of large areas of forest by felling/burning [1] without trees being replaced [1]

b Tropical rainforests contain more biodiversity than any other land environment. [1] Loss of these forests means biodiversity of plant and animal life is also lost [1] as habitats are destroyed and species become extinct. [1] Many species are being destroyed before being identified and studied, so potential new sources of medicine or food could be lost. [1]

2 carbon dioxide produced by burning of trees, [1] carbon dioxide produced by decomposition of dead vegetation, [1] less carbon dioxide removed from atmosphere by growing plants [1]

3 a use of peat as fuel [1] and by gardeners as compost [1]

b Carbon dioxide is released into atmosphere as peat is burnt or used as compost, [1] increasing atmospheric levels of carbon dioxide [1] and depleting the carbon store. [1] Destruction of peat bogs destroys habitats and reduces biodiversity. [1]

4 Points may include: cheap compost needed by gardeners and horticulturists to improve soil properties, promote seed germination, and increase food production; alternative, 'peat-free' composts are available but are less popular; peat bogs and peatlands vital to biodiversity as they form habitat for many organisms adapted to live in acidic conditions; peat forms very slowly and under very specific conditions – cannot be replaced as quickly as it is being used. [6] Any other valid point.

B18.5

1 a Correct y-axis label and scale [1], Correct x-axis label and scale [1], data plotted correctly [1]

b carbon dioxide levels rising steadily [1] over time, [1] partly as a result of human activities [1]

c Energy transferred from Sun to Earth. Much of this heat is reflected back into space, [1] but some is absorbed by greenhouse gases in the atmosphere and reradiated back to Earth. [1] Earth's surface and atmosphere are warmed (greenhouse effect), maintaining conditions ideal for life. [1]

2 a Atmospheric levels of greenhouse gases increasing [1] as a result of human activity, [1] increasing greenhouse effect [1] and causing global temperatures to rise [1].

b Any two from loss of habitat – reducing biodiversity, changes in distribution – some organisms may disappear from some areas as habitat changes, changes in migration patterns – caused by changes in climates and seasons, reduced biodiversity – some organisms will become extinct as climate changes. [3]

3 Accept any well-researched example and explanation. [6]

B18.6

1 a i natural changes [1] in environmental factors such as temperature, rainfall level, water availability, dissolved gases in water, and daylight hours [1] between different seasons [1] in temperate parts of the world [1]

ii natural changes [1] in environmental factors such as soil structure or pH, altitude, water salinity, and water availability [1] between different geographical areas of the world [1]

b Natural mutations cause features that enable some individuals within a population to cope better with a change to their environment. [1] These individuals are more likely to survive and breed (natural selection), [1] passing on the beneficial feature to offspring. [1]

2 a number of breeding pairs of Dartford warblers in UK increasing [1]

b Dartford warblers cannot survive very cold winters. Number of breeding pairs dropped sharply in 1963, [1] suggesting cold winter that reduced population. [1] Number increased sharply in 2010, perhaps as a result of temperature increase. [1]

c Temperature changes. [1] Changes in number of Dartford warblers indicate that numbers have increased as UK temperatures have increased but drop sharply after cold winters. [1] Drop in number of Dartford warblers in Spain indicates that too high a temperature also affects distribution. [1] Evidence suggests that change in mean UK temperature [1] and seasonal extremes of temperature [1] affect distribution of UK birds both within the country and between countries. [1]

B18.7

1 a important for environmental health, [1] offers potential source of new food crops, [1] offers potential source of new medicines [1] Any other valid point.

b breeding programmes for endangered species – restoring endangered species to sustainable populations, [1] protection and regeneration of rare habitats – protecting different animals and plants, [1] reintroduction of field margins and hedgerows – allowing biodiversity to be maintained in agricultural land, [1] reduction of deforestation – maintaining habitats, [1] recycling resources – reducing habitat loss and pollution [1]

Answers

c Any one from increased field margins limiting land available for food production, reduction of deforestation limiting land available for food production, taxes on landfill waste increasing costs to businesses [4]. Any other valid point.

2a levels have fallen steadily [1]

b Data suggests that Kyoto agreement drove UK government to take action to limit carbon dioxide emissions [1] and that government intervention via legislation [1] has been successful. [1]

c Points may include: reduce or prevent increase in greenhouse effect and global warming – maintaining biodiversity by preserving Arctic and Antarctic ice habitat, preventing rises in sea levels that will destroy biodiverse mangrove forests, preventing temperature increase that could dry out wetlands and cause bleaching/death of coral reefs. [6] Any other valid point.

3 Data shows that as landfill tax increased, amount of material going into landfill fell. [1] Taxes on waste and emissions [1] can be used as an effective incentive to change human habits [1] and promote research into less damaging alternatives (e.g., recycling rather than landfill). [1] Any other valid point.

B18.8

1a mass of biological material in living organisms [1]

b Dry biomass shows amount of biological material at each level more accurately [1] but necessitates killing and drying out organisms. [1] Wet biomass values much easier to obtain as does not involve killing organisms, [1] but is less useful as water content of living organisms varies constantly, making results less repeatable and reproducible. [1]

2a Award marks for accurate pyramid correctly labelled. [3]

b Amount of material contained in biomass of organisms at each stage of a food chain less than it was at the previous stage. [1] Not all of organism at one stage eaten by organism at next stage (only leaves of grass eaten by sheep, only blood of sheep eaten by ticks). [1] Some materials taken in passed out and lost as waste products. [1] Much of materials taken in used in cellular respiration to release energy for cell metabolism and some energy transferred to surroundings. [1] Relatively small amount of material taken in converted to new biomass. [1] Large percentage of biomass in grass cropped by sheep not converted to biomass in sheep and large percentage of biomass in sheep not converted into biomass in sheep ticks. [1]

3a $\frac{1000}{500\,000} \times 100$ [1] $= 0.02 = 2\%$ [1]

b $\frac{50}{5000} \times 100$ [1] $= 0.05 = 5\%$ [1]

B18.9

1a Some of the biomass ingested by an animal cannot be used. [1] Most herbivores cannot digest cellulose in plant material. [1] Most carnivores cannot break down and digest hooves, claws, bones, and teeth. [1] Indigestible materials are egested as faeces, meaning biomass is lost. [1]

b Biomass used in cellular respiration to provide energy for movement [1] and to supply energy and raw materials needed for building new biomass. [1] Active animals carry out lots of respiration as active, contracting muscles respire more. [1] More of the biomass eaten is broken down and used for movement in active animals [1] and more energy is transferred to surroundings as muscles warm up. [1]

2a flow chart should include: producers → primary consumer → secondary consumer → tertiary consumer → decomposers [4]

b Biomass lost by consumers in faeces [1] – cellulose cannot be digested by herbivores, animal parts such as hooves/claws/bones/teeth cannot be digested by carnivores. [1] Biomass lost by producers and consumers in waste [1] – excess protein and water lost in urine, carbon dioxide and water lost in respiration. [1] Biomass lost in consumers in maintaining a constant body temperature [1] – energy transferred to surroundings. [1]

3 Only about 1% of energy from Sun's light falling on Earth (incident energy) used by plants for photosynthesis [1] to create biomass. [1] Plant biomass eaten by animals cannot all be digested. [1] Some is broken down and used in respiration to provide energy for living processes such as movement and regulating body temperature. [1] Only small amount of biomass eaten by animals used for growth to produce new biomass. [1]

B18.10

1 having enough food to feed a population [1]

2 Any three reducing factors from increasing birth rate, new pests and pathogens, changing diets in developed countries, environmental changes, cost of agricultural inputs, conflicts. [3] Any three increasing factors from maintaining or improving soil quality, efficient ways to produce food (e.g., selective breeding or GM technology), managing fish stocks, educating populations [3] Any other valid point.

3 Quinoa staple food in Bolivia. [1] Production of quinoa in Bolivia has increased since 1997. [1] Quinoa has increased in popularity in other countries, leading to increased exports [1] as farmers can charge more to foreign buyers than to local consumers and make more money. [1] Local consumption of quinoa has fallen as exports have increased. [1] Food security in Bolivia reduced as population increasingly dependent on imported pasta. [1]

4 Accept any well-researched opinion and explanation. [6]

B18.11

1a so that animals do not have to use much biomass in cooling down, [1] leaving more biomass for growth [1]

b Biomass lost through faeces, [1] urea, [1] and respiration for movement [1] and regulation of body temperature. [1]

2 Earth has limited surface area for plant growth. [1] Biomass lost at each stage of food chain. [1] Shorter food chains more efficient. [1] If people all ate plants instead of feeding plants to animals and then eating animals, food chains would be shorter. [1] Efficiency of food production would be greatly increased [1] as plant biomass would be used to produce human biomass directly. [1]

3 advantages: indoor work, animals grow faster so ready for market sooner, control of movement and temperature maximises conversion of food to biomass, weather conditions don't matter, fish farming conserves wild stocks; disadvantages: initial cost of buildings, cost of light and heating, higher feed bills, animals may be stressed (gain biomass more slowly), ethical concerns [6] Any other valid point.

B18.12

1a development of large commercial fleets capable of catching huge quantities, [1] uncontrolled overfishing [1]

b control size of the holes in nets so only largest fish caught, [1] ban fishing during breeding season, [1] strict catch quotas [1]

c Points may include: people dependent on fishing for livelihood and wary of reduced income, difficult to obtain overall picture of global fish stocks, difficult to apply quotas across large oceans fished by multiple countries. [3] Any other valid point.

2a 1969 (accept between 1967 and 1969) [1] 1.8 million tonnes (accept 1.7 to 1.9 million tonnes) [1]

b 0.1 million tonnes [1]

c $1\,800\,000 - 100\,000 = 1\,700\,000$, [1] $\frac{1\,700\,000}{1\,800\,000} \times 100 = 94\%$, [1] (accept correct calculation based on answers given in parts a and b)

d i $\frac{0.4}{0.1} \times 100 = 400\%$ increase [1]

   ii $\frac{1.2}{0.25} \times 100 = 480\%$ increase [1]

   iii $\frac{3.6}{0.6} \times 100 = 600\%$ increase [1]

   (accept any answers based on appropriate readings from Figure 2)

e some fish species almost extinct, [1] fish caught over quota discarded dead so cannot increase populations, [1] quotas difficult to enforce internationally [1] Any other valid point.

3 similarities: fermenter equivalent to enclosed shed or barn, fermenter temperature regulated and food supply maintained to give the optimum conditions, designed to achieve maximum growth over minimum time, cost of maintaining conditions outweighed by increased production; differences: fungus not an animal so controlled conditions cause no stress, no ethical issues, pH not monitored and maintained in farming, no free-range alternative in mycoprotein production. [6] Any other valid point.

Index

abiotic factors 258, 260–261, 279
abundance 262–263
accommodation 156
acid rain 290–291, 296–297
active sites 42
active transport 20–21
ADH 160, 187
adrenaline 160–161, 167
adult stem cells 28, 30–33, 228–229
aerobic respiration 134–137
AIDS/HIV 84–85
air pollution 290–291
alcohol 120–121, 139
algae 7, 125
alleles 199, 208–213, 234–235
alveoli 23, 55, 61
amino acids 41, 141, 204–205
ammonia 141
amniocentesis 214
amylase 46–47
anaerobic respiration 138–139
animal cells 6, 10–11, 15, 23, 28, 30–33
antibiotics 81, 94, 100–103, 248–249
antibodies 93, 106–109
antigens 190
archaea 252
arteries 54–55, 141
asexual reproduction 196, 200–201, 226–229
auxin 176–179
averages 262–263

bacteria 8–9, 76–83, 86–87, 100–103, 224, 230, 248–249, 252, 266, 269, 278, 282–283
bases 204
bioaccumulation 288–289
biodiversity 286–311
bioenergetics 124–143
    aerobic respiration 134–137
    anaerobic respiration 138–139
    photosynthesis 124–133
bioindicators 289
biological responses 144–193
    homeostasis 146–147, 182–193
    hormones 148, 152, 160–181
    negative feedback 166–167
    nervous system 146–159
    reflexes 150–151
    sight 154–157
biomass 276–279, 300–303
biotechnology 308–309
biotic factors 258–259, 261, 278, 282–283

birth rates 304
blind spot 154–155
blood 52–53, 91, 162–165
blood vessels 54–55
body temperature 135, 182–183, 303
brain 152–153, 160–161, 166–167, 170–171, 182–183, 187
breathing 23, 60–61, 136–137
breeding programs 298

cancer 108–109, 114–115
capillaries 54–55, 61, 182–183
carbohydrates 40, 46, 128–129, 136
carbon cycle 280–283
carbon dioxide 61, 124–127, 131, 134, 184, 294, 299
carbon monoxide 116
carcinogens 112, 114, 117, 121
cardiovascular disease 117
carnivores 268, 300–302
carriers 213
catalysts 42–49
cell cycle 26–27
cell division 26–35, 196, 198–199, 201
cell membranes 6–7, 20–21
cells
    animal 6, 10–11, 28, 30–33
    differentiation 28–29
    exchanging materials 22–23
    plant 6–7, 12–13, 28–29, 31
    structure 4–13
    transport 14–23
cellulose 7, 128
cell walls 7–8, 94
central nervous system (CNS) 148–153, 160–161, 166–167, 170–171, 182–183
cerebellum 152–153
cerebral cortex 152–153
chemotherapy 115
chlorophyll 7, 125–127
chloroplasts 7
cholesterol 57
chromosomes 6, 8, 26–27, 198–199, 211
cigarettes 113
classification 250–253
climate change 294–297
clinical trials 104–105
cloning 29, 31, 33, 179, 196, 226–229
combustion 280–281, 290–291
communicable (infectious) diseases 74–97
communities 258–261

competition 264–267
components of blood 52–53, 61
concentration gradients 14–16, 188–189
contraception 172–173
control of transpiration 68
coordination
    centres 147
    homeostasis 146–147, 182–193
    hormones 148, 152, 160–181
    negative feedback 166–167
    nervous system 146–159
corneas 154–155
coronary arteries 56–57
coronary heart disease 56–57
correlation 113
crops 222–223, 225, 230–231, 304, 306–307
cuticle 94
cystic fibrosis 212–213
cytoplasm 6–7, 17–19

deamination 141
decay cycle 278, 282–283
decomposers 278, 288–289, 303
decomposition 43, 46–49, 141, 282–283
defences to disease 90–91, 94–95
deforestation 292–293, 296–297, 299
dendrites 10
depression 74
development of medicines 104–105
diabetes 119, 163–165
dialysis 188–191
diet 74–75, 118–119, 304
differentiation 28–33, 36
diffusion 14–15, 61, 188–189
digestive system 38–51
dilute 16
dinosaurs 246–247
direct proportion 210
diseases 72–123, 248–249
    bacterial 86–87
    communicable 74–97
    human defences 90–91
    inherited 212–215
    non-communicable 74–75, 112–123
    plants 87, 92–95
    prevention 80–83, 89–91, 94, 98–99
disinfectants 80–81
distribution 262–263
division of cells 26–35
DNA (deoxyribonucleic acid) 202–205, 235
dominant alleles/phenotypes 208–212

Index

double blind trials 105
double circulatory system 55
double helix 202, 204
drawing graphs 45
drug development 102–105
duodenum 38, 49

ecology 256–311
    adaptations, interdependence and competition 258–275
    biodiversity 286–311
    ecosystem organisation 276–285
ecosystems
    biodiversity 286–311
    communities 258–261
    organisation 276–285
effectors 147–151
electron microscopes 4–5
elongation of roots 28–29, 176–177
embryonic stem cells 30–33
embryos 30–33, 214–215, 226–227
emulsification 49
endangered species 298
endocrine system 160–175
endothermic reactions 124
energy balance 294–295, 300–303
environmental factors 68, 74–75, 241, 246–247
environments
    biomass 300–303
    global warming 294–297, 305
    organisms 260–261
    resources 287
enzymes 38–39, 42–49
epidermal tissues of plants 62
estimation 67
ethene 179
ethics 32–33, 230–231
eukaryotes 6–8, 252
eutrophication 289
evaporation 66–69, 272–273, 279
evolution 200, 220–221, 234–255
evolutionary trees 252–253
exchanging materials 22–23
exercise 118–119, 136–139, 141
exothermic reactions 134
expression of genes 206
extinction 244–247
extremophiles 269
eyes 154–157

faeces 302
fallopian tubes 168, 170, 173
family trees 211
fatigue, muscles 138
fats/fatty acids 40–41, 46–47, 49

feedback 166–167
feeding relationships 276–279
female fertility 169, 174
fermentation 139
fertilisation 170, 198–199
fertilisers 287–289, 305
fertility 169, 172–175
fibrinogen 53
fish 307–308
fitness testing 139
focusing light 155–157
follicles 170–171
follicle stimulating hormone 160, 170–171, 174
food 40–42, 46–49, 222–225, 230–231, 264, 304–309
food chains 276–277, 288–289, 306
fossil record 242–245
fungi 88, 200, 230, 309
fusion 199, 228–229

gall bladder 38, 49
gametes 196, 198–201
gas exchange 15, 23, 55, 60–61, 125
genes 6, 8, 26–27, 199, 206–213, 224–225, 227, 230–231, 234–235
genetically modified crops 225, 230–231
genetic crosses 209
genetic engineering 213, 224–225, 227, 230–231
genetics 194–255
    classification 250–253
    cloning 226–231
    ethics 230–231
    evolution 200, 220–221, 234–255
    history 234–235
    inheritance 208–215
    reproduction 196–217
    sex determination 211
    speciation 240–241
    terms 208–209
    theories of evolution 220–221, 236–241
    variation 199, 218–234
genomes 202–203, 214–215, 224–225, 227
genotypes 208–213, 234–235
geographical changes 296
geographical isolation 241
geological time 246
germination 176–177, 179
gibberellins 179
global dimming 291
global warming 294–297, 305
glucagon 162–163

glucose 20–21, 124, 128–129, 134–136, 138–139, 162–165
glycerol 40–41, 46–47
glycogen 136, 162–163
GM crops 225, 230–231
golden rice 230
graphs 45
gravitropism 176–177
greenhouse effect/gases 294
greenhouses 130–131
growth 28–29, 78–81, 286–288
guard cells 66
gut 15, 20–21, 23, 37, 39

haemoglobin 52, 61
hair cells 12, 20–21
health 74–75, 118–121
heart 56–59, 111, 136–137
hepatic veins/arteries 141
herbicides 178–179, 288, 305
herbivores 94–95, 268, 300–303
herd immunity 99
heterozygous 208–213
homeostasis 146–147, 182–193, 303
homozygous 208–213
hormones 148, 152, 160–181
human chorionic gonadotropin (HCG) 107
human cloning/engineering 229–231
human defences to disease 90–91
human genome 202–203
human nervous system 146–159
human papilloma virus (HPV) 114
human population growth 286–288, 304
human reproduction 168–175
hybridomas 106–109
hydrochloric acid 46, 48
hydrogen peroxide 43
hygiene 82–83
hyperopia 156–157
hypertonic 17
hyphae 200
hypothalamus 182–183
hypotonic 17

identical twins 219
illness 74–75
immune responses 91, 190
immunity 82–83, 91, 98–99
immunosuppressant drugs 190–191
impulses 149
incident energy 302–303
industrial waste 287–288
infections 76–77, 82–83, 100–103
infectious diseases *see* communicable diseases

341

Index

infertility treatments 174–175
inheritance 208–215, 234–236
inherited disorders 212–215
insulin 160, 162–165, 224
intensity of light 126–127, 131, 154
intensive farming 307
interacting health problems 75
intrauterine devices 173
inverse square law 127
in vitro fertilization 174–175
iodine test for starch 128–129
ionising radiation 112, 114, 121
isolation 83, 241
isotonic 17

karyotypes 26
kidneys 186–191
kingdoms 250–251

lactic acid 138–139, 141
land pollution 288
large scale extinctions 246–247
leaky valves 58
leaves 23, 63, 66–68, 125, 266, 272–273
lenses 154–157
light 124, 126–127, 131, 154–157, 176–177
light microscopes 4–5
limiting factors 126–127
lipase 46–47, 49
lipids 40–41, 129, 162–163
liver 38, 49, 120, 140–141, 162–163
long sightedness 156–157
lung cancer 113
lungs 23
luteinising hormone (LH) 170–171, 174
lymphocytes 53

magnesium 127
magnification 4–5
malaria 88–89, 201
male fertility 174
malignant tumours 114
materials cycling 278–279
maximising photosynthesis 130–131
mean 67, 262–263
measles 84
measurement
    reaction times 149
    transpiration rates 69
median 262–263
medicines 98–99, 102–109, 249
medulla 152–153
meiosis 196, 198–199, 201
Mendelian inheritance 234–235
menstrual cycle 168–171
metabolism 42–49, 134–141

methane 283, 294
microorganisms 278, 308–309
microscopes 4–5
microvilli 15, 23, 39
mineral deficiency 92
mineral ions 20–21, 64–65, 92, 129, 184–187
mitochondria 6–7, 134–136
mitosis 26–35
mode 262–263
monoclonal antibodies 93, 106–109
monohybrid inheritance 234
MRI scans 153
MRSA 248–249
muscles 10–11, 134, 136–138
mutations 78, 114, 206–207, 220–221
mycoproteins 309
myelin 10
myopia 156–157

natural selection 200, 220–221, 236–241, 244–247
negative feedback 166–167
nerves 10, 148–151
nervous system 146–159
neurones 10, 148–151
nicotine 116
nitrate ions 129
nitrogen oxides 290–291
non-communicable diseases 74, 112–123
nuclear power 121
nucleotides 204
nucleus 6–7
nutrient broth solutions 78–79

obesity 118–119, 162, 165
oestrogen 160, 168–173
oils 40–41
orders of magnitude 9
organisms 245, 250–253, 260–263
organs 36–39, 62–63, 140–141, 148, 151, 154–157, 168–171
organ systems 37–39, 49, 63
osmosis 16–19
ovaries 160–161, 168–169
overweight 165
oviducts 168, 173
ovulation 168–171, 174
oxygen 52, 61, 124, 282, 288–289
oxygen debt 138–139, 141

pacemakers 58–59
painkillers 100–101
palisade mesophyll 62
pancreas 36, 38, 49, 161–165

partially permeable membranes 16–19
pathogens 74–103, 248–249, 304
pathways, reflexes 150–151
penicillin 100–103
penis 168
pepsin 46, 48
permanent contraception 173
permanent vacuoles 7
pH 45–48
phagocytes 53
phenotypes 208–213, 234–235
phloem 13, 62–65
photosynthesis 12, 124–133, 280
phototropism 176–177
pituitary gland 152–153, 160–161, 166–167, 170–171, 187
placebos 105
plant cells 6–7, 12–13, 15, 18–19, 23, 28–29, 31
plants
    adaptations 268, 272–273
    cloning 29, 31, 179, 226
    defences 94–95
    diseases 87, 92–95
    genetic engineering 224–225, 230–231
    hormones 176–179
    organs 62–63
    reproduction 200–201
    selective breeding 222–223
    transpiration 66–69
    transport 12–13, 18–21, 23, 62–65
plasma 52
plasmids 8, 224
plasmolysis 17–19
platelets 53
pollen 200–201
pollution 288–291, 296–297
polydactyly 212
populations 80, 240–241, 258–261, 263, 286–288, 304, 308
potometers 69
preclinical testing 104–105
predators 264–265, 271, 276–277
pregnancy 107, 116, 121, 174–175
prevention of diseases 80–83, 89–91, 94, 98–99
primary consumers 276, 300–303
producers 276, 300–301
progesterone 170–173
prokaryotic cells 8–9
prostate gland 168
proteases 46, 48
protecting habitats 298
proteins 41, 46, 48, 129, 141, 204–205, 207, 309

Index

protists 88–89
puberty 168–169
pulmonary artery/vein 56
pupils 154–156
pyramid of biomass 300–303

quadrats 262–263
quantitative sampling 262–263

radiation 112, 114, 121
range 262–263
rate of diffusion 14
rate of photosynthesis 126–127, 130–131
reaction times 149
receptors 147, 149, 151, 154–155, 187
recessive alleles/phenotypes 209–213
recycling 282–283, 299
red blood cells 52, 61
reflex arcs 150–151
reflexes 150–151
refraction, eyes 155
regeneration of habitats 298
regulation of glucose 162–165
replication, cell cycle 26–27
reproduction 196–217, 237–239
    asexual 196, 200–201, 226–229
    cloning 226–229
    fertility 169, 172–175
    fungi 200
    human 168–175
    inherited disorders 212–215
    plants 200–201
    sexual 196–201, 240–241, 265
resolving power 5
resources 287, 299
respiration 128, 134–143, 280, 303
    aerobic 134–137
    anaerobic 138–139
    mitochondria 134–136
respiratory system 90
retinas 154–155
ribosomes 6–7, 204–205
risk factors 112
role of hormones 161
rooting powder 178–179
roots 12, 20–21, 28–29, 176–177, 266, 273

sample sizes 262–263
sampling 67, 262–263
screening, genetic 214–215
secondary consumers 276, 300–303
seeds 129, 267
selective breeding 200, 222–223

selective herbicides 178–179
selective reabsorption 186–187
sense organs 148, 151, 154–157
sensory neurones 148–151
sewage 287–289
sex determination 211
sexually transmitted diseases 84–87
sexual reproduction 196–201, 240–241, 265
shoots 176–177
short sightedness 156–157
sieve plates 13
sight 154–157
simple sugars 40
sizes 5, 9, 22–23, 263
skin 90
slime capsules 8
smog 291
smoking 116–117
specialisation 10–13, 15, 23, 28–33
species 240–241, 244–247, 251
sperm cells 11
sperm ducts 168
spongy mesophyll 62
spores 200
stable communities 259
starch 46, 128–129
statins 57
stem cells 28, 30–33, 228–229
stents 57
stomach 37–39, 48
stomata 23, 66–68
storage 128–129, 136, 162–163, 272–273
stress 74
sugars 40, 64
sulfur dioxide 290–291
surface area 15, 22–23, 48–49, 272–273
survival of the fittest 220–221
suspensory ligaments 154
sustainability 304–309
sweating 182
symptoms of diseases 76, 84–89, 93
synapses 10, 150–151
synthesis of proteins 204–205

temperature 44–45, 68, 79, 126, 135, 182–183, 282, 294–297, 303, 305
tertiary consumers 300–303
testosterone 169
thermoregulatory centre 182–183
three domain system 252
thyroid 161, 166–167
thyroxine 166–167

tissue culture 226
tissues 36, 62, 136–138, 160–161, 190
tissue types 190
tobacco 116–117
tobacco mosaic virus (TMV) 85
transects 263
transfers of biomass 302–303
translocation 64
transpiration 66–69, 272–273, 279
transplants 164–165, 188, 190–191
trophic levels 300–303
tropisms 176–177
tumours 114
turgor 18–19
twins 219
type 1 diabetes 163–165
type 2 diabetes 119, 163, 165

ultraviolet light 121
units 4–5, 9
urea 52, 141, 184–187
urine 52, 184–187
uterus 168–171, 173

vaccines 82–83, 98–99
vacuoles 7
vagina 168
valves 54–58
variation 199, 208–213, 218–234, 236–241
vasoconstriction 183
vasodilation 182
vectors 83, 224–225
veins 54–55, 141
vena cava 56
ventilation 23, 60–61, 136–137
ventricles 56, 58
villi 15, 23, 39
viruses 76–77, 84–85, 115

waste 184–191, 287
water
    pathogens 77
    plants 64–69, 272–273
water balance 184–187
water cycle 279
water pollution 288–289, 305
white blood cells 53, 91

xylem 12–13, 62–65

yeast 139

zygotes 30

343

AQA Biology
Third Edition

- **Making assessment and progress tracking easy** – *AQA GCSE Sciences Third Edition* has built-in assessment and progress tracking based on the widely adopted structure used in *Activate* for KS3, to support effective assessment throughout the new linear courses. It also includes a unique checkpoint system for intervention

- **Supporting students of all abilities** – Supporting students of all abilities through the new, more demanding GCSE, with ramped questions and differentiated outcomes for every topic in the course, and additional differentiated support on Kerboodle

- **Building maths skills** MyMaths – The only AQA science resources with exclusive, direct, specification-matched links to MyMaths, via Kerboodle, as well as worked examples, practice questions throughout the Student Books, calculation sheets, and interactive maths activities

- **Prepare for the new practicals** – Developing practical skills throughout the Student Books, with specific practice for the new practical questions and a bank of practical activities on Kerboodle

- **Plenty of practice questions** – Multiple-choice, maths, practical, and synoptic practice questions are included throughout

- **Accompanied by** kerboodle

AQA GCSE Sciences Third Edition is accompanied by Kerboodle, the most popular digital solution for science teaching in the UK

kerboodle

Kerboodle provides digital Lessons, Resources and Assessment for use in the classroom and at home, plus Kerboodle Online Student Book access for teachers and students included in the package.

What's on the cover?
Foliose coral colony growing on a reef. Colonies are often more than 5 metres in length.

AQA GCSE Chemistry Third edition Teacher Handbook	AQA GCSE Physics Third edition Teacher Handbook	AQA GCSE Biology for Combined Science: Trilogy Third edition Teacher Handbook	AQA GCSE Chemistry for Combined Science: Trilogy Third edition Teacher Handbook	AQA GCSE Physics for Combined Science: Trilogy Third edition Teacher Handbook	AQA GCSE Sciences Kerboodle
978 0 19 835944 9	978 0 19 835945 6	978 0 19 839587 4	978 0 19 839588 1	978 0 19 839589 8	978 0 19 830885 0

OXFORD UNIVERSITY PRESS

How to get in touch:
web   www.oxfordsecondary.co.uk
email   schools.enquiries.uk@oup.com
tel   01536 452620
fax   01865 313472

ISBN 978-0-19-835943-2